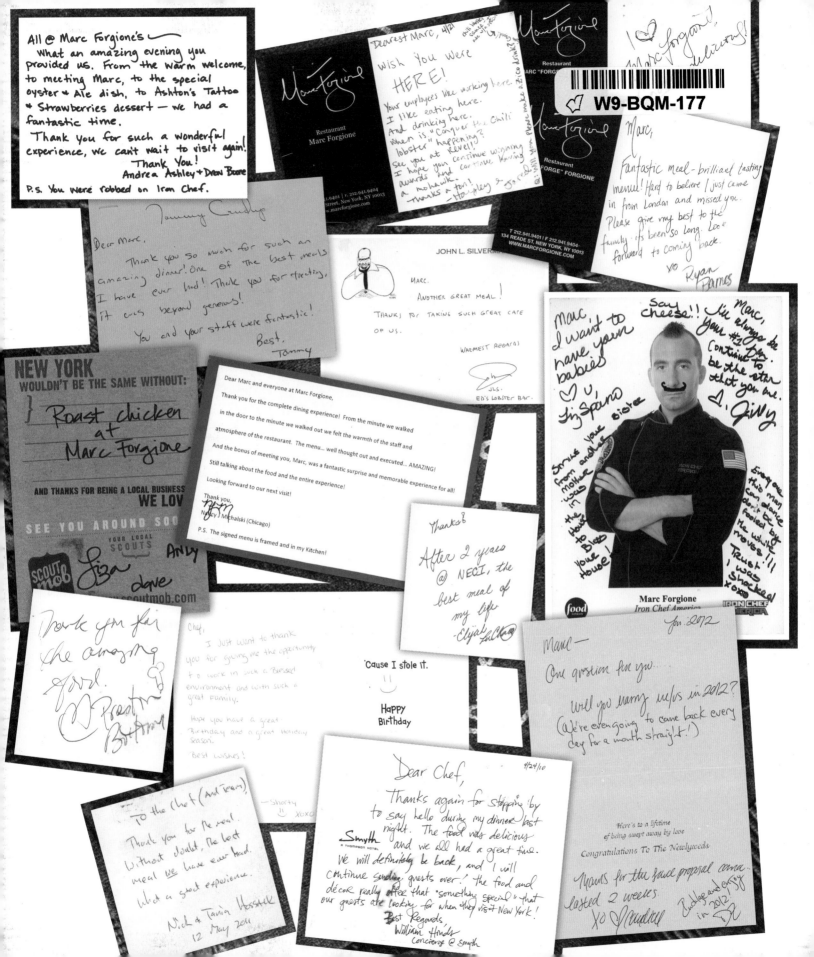

All @ Marc Forgione's—
    What an amazing evening you provided us. From the warm welcome, to meeting Marc, to the special oyster & Ale dish, to Ashton's Tattoo & Strawberries dessert — we had a fantastic time.
    Thank you for such a wonderful experience, we can't wait to visit again!
        Thank You!
        Andrea Ashley + Drew Boone
P.S. You were robbed on Iron Chef.

Dearest Marc, 4/21
Wish You were HERE!
Your employees like working here. I like eating here. And drinking here. When is "Conquer the Chili lobster" happening? See you at REVEL! I hope you continue winning awards and continue having a mohawk.
— Thanks a ton!
    —Hartley & Jared

Marc,
Fantastic meal - brilliant tasting menu! Hard to believe I just came in from London and missed you. Please give my best to the family - it's been so long. Look forward to coming back.
        xo Ryan Barnes

Dear Marc,
    Thank you so much for such an amazing dinner! One of the best meals I have ever had! Thank you for treating, it was beyond generous!
    You and your staff were fantastic!
            Best,
            Tammy

JOHN L. SILVERM
MARC,
ANOTHER GREAT MEAL!
THANKS FOR TAKING SUCH GREAT CARE OF US.
    WARMEST REGARDS,
    John
    JLS.
    ED'S LOBSTER BAR.

NEW YORK
WOULDN'T BE THE SAME WITHOUT:
Roast chicken at Marc Forgione
AND THANKS FOR BEING A LOCAL BUSINESS WE LOV
SEE YOU AROUND SOO
    YOUR LOCAL SCOUTS
    SCOUT mob
    Liza
    Andy
    dave
    scoutmob.com

Dear Marc and everyone at Marc Forgione,
Thank you for the complete dining experience! From the minute we walked in the door to the minute we walked out we felt the warmth of the staff and atmosphere of the restaurant. The menu... well thought out and executed... AMAZING!
And the bonus of meeting you, Marc, was a fantastic surprise and memorable experience for all!
Still talking about the food and the entire experience!
Looking forward to our next visit!
    Thank you,
    Nancy J Michalski (Chicago)
P.S. The signed menu is framed and in my Kitchen!

Thanks8
After 2 years @ NECI, the best meal of my life
—Eliyal LaCle

Marc, I want to have your babies ♡ u, Liz Spano
Smile your siote from mother anothers in the House to Bless your House!

say cheese!! I'll always be your #1 fan. Continue to be the star that you are. L. Gilly
Everyone this man can dance don't be fooled by the white moves!!! Trust I was shocked xoxo

Marc Forgione
Iron Chef America

Thank you for the amazing food.
♡ Preston Bottom?

Chef,
    I just want to thank you for giving me the opportunity to work in such a Blessed environment and with such a great Family.
    Hope you have a great Birthday and a great Holiday Season.
    Best Wishes!
        —Shorty
        !! xoxo

'Cause I stole it.
!!
Happy Birthday

Jan. 2012
Marc—
    One question for you....
    Will you marry me/us in 2012? (We're even going to come back every day for a month straight!)

To the Chef (And Team),
    Thank you for the meal. Without doubt, the best meal we have ever had! What a great experience.
        Nick & Tania Hostick
        12 May 2011

4/24/10
Dear Chef,
    Thanks again for stopping by to say hello during my dinner last night. The food was delicious and we all had a great time. We will definitely be back, and I will continue sending guests over! the food and décor really offer that "something special" that our guests are looking for when they visit New York!
        Best Regards,
        William Hinds
        Concierge @ Smyth
    Smyth
    A THOMPSON HOTEL

Here's to a lifetime of being swept away by love
Congratulations To The Newlyweds
Thanks for the food proposal coma. lasted 2 weeks.
xo Mandrell
Buddo and ? in 2012? in DR

Restaurant Marc Forgione
1.9401 F: 212.941.9404 Street, New York, NY 10013 www.marcforgione.com

Restaurant MARC "FORGE" FORGIONE
T 212.941.9401 | F 212.941.9404 134 READE ST. NEW YORK, NY 10013 WWW.MARCFORGIONE.COM

MARC FORGIONE

WITH OLGA MASSOV

PHOTOGRAPHY BY EVAN SUNG

HOUGHTON MIFFLIN HARCOURT
BOSTON   NEW YORK   2014

For information about permission to reproduce selections from this book, write to Permissions, Houghton
Mifflin Harcourt Publishing Company, 215 Park Avenue South, New York, New York 10003.

www.hmhco.com

LIBRARY OF CONGRESS CATALOGING-IN-PUBLICATION DATA
ISBN 978-1-118-30278-1 (cloth); ISBN 978-0-544-18728-3 (ebook)
Forgione, Marc, 1978–
Marc Forgione : recipes and stories from the acclaimed chef and restaurant /
Marc Forgione with Olga Massov ; photography by Evan Sung.
pages cm
Includes index.
1. Cooking, American. I. Massov, Olga. II. Title.
TX715.F6994 2014
641.5973—dc23
2013034986

Printed in China
TOP 10 9 8 7 6 5 4 3 2 1

I DEDICATE THIS BOOK TO MY FAMILY AND LOVED ONES WHO SUPPORT THIS LIFE I HAVE CHOSEN TO LIVE.

TO ALL THE EMPLOYEES, INVESTORS, AND SUPPORTERS OF ALL THINGS FORGE!

IT'S BEEN A WILD RIDE — THANK YOU ALL!

THE FLAT TOP

To some the flat top may be just a piece of equipment: something you use to heat a pan, or something you have to scrub at the end
of the night. Most cooks don't see this as the heart of the restaurant, but to me,
that's exactly what it is.

To me, the flat top symbolizes many things that are absolutely necessary in a functioning restaurant: stability, consistency, perseverance, reliability, order, and above all, getting the job done.
The flat top is never tired, never in a bad mood, never has a bad day. It is, in every sense of the word, the
beating heart of our restaurant.

The day the gas was turned on at Forge in June 2008, we turned the knobs to the left, heard that first flow of
flames from underneath, and cooking at the restaurant had begun. And that flat top has been on ever since.

Over the years we have had many, many pieces of our equipment repaired, reworked, and replaced. But not that flat
top—it has been a relentless and reliable workhorse—always there when you need it.

Every day starts exactly the same: The flat top gets turned on and the cooking begins. Placed in the center of the kitchen, the
flat top is used by all the stations throughout the day for prepping sauces, blanching vegetables, searing meat, making soufflé
base, and then once service begins, it sets the pulse for the evening: apps out on one side, and entrées out on the other.

Until I saw its beauty in this picture, I don't know if I ever realized just how important this graduated-heat flat top is to
me. When I look at its stains and scratches, I see the scars of a warrior who's been through many tough battles and is
still fighting hard. The stains from years of brown butter spills as the meat cook bastes the steak to perfection; the hot
spots that almost glow by the end of the night; the scratches from the early morning scrubbing where you can almost
see the faces of the morning porters, covered in sweat, working to make it look beautiful before the day begins—all
these "blemishes" make the flat top more beautiful to me. For the last four years the flat top has been the first
thing I see when I walk in the kitchen, and the last thing I check when I shut the kitchen down.

If the flat top could talk, it would tell tales of all the different nights we've had at the restaurant.
It would make for a great night to pull up to a bar, pour a glass of good bourbon, and just listen to its
stories: the ones who could handle it, and the others who, no matter how hard they tried, just
could not work its magic.

And if I could say anything to the flat top, it would be a resounding "Thank you."
I look forward to spending many more days and many more nights in
our restaurant's heart—there's nowhere else I'd rather be.

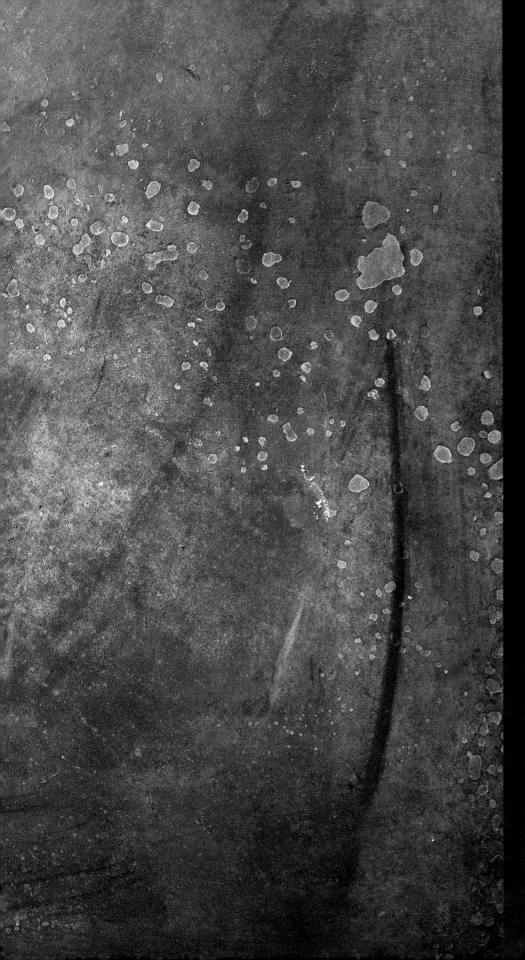

"See the path cut by the moon for you to walk on."
—Pearl Jam

ACKNOWLEDGMENTS

Where do I start? Marc Forgione—the restaurant, the book, and the person—are all results of the very hard work of many, many people that need to be thanked.

As far as the restaurant goes, I would like to thank every single employee who has ever walked through the door. Whether it was an hour of work or five years, I thank you for your time and effort.

In particular to Chris Blumlo, my business partner, without your drive to get this place open and keep it open, I wouldn't be where I am today. To Matt, Cary, Brielle, Mariette, Michael, even though you don't really "work," I do thank you.

To all my chefs and cooks who have had to endure the many hot nights in our "charming" little kitchen—THANK YOU!! Chris Lim, Phet, Steve, Ian, Barry, Chris, Greg P. To the ladies of pastry: Jenny, Tina, Ashton, Alexandra, you are the sugar in my coffee.

All the chefs who have trained me along the way: Rich D'Orazzi, Vicky and Kazuto, Gavin Portsmouth, Patricia Yeo, Pino Maffeo, Laurent Tourondel, Michel Guérard—without each of your influences there would be no restaurant.

To all the purveyors, farmers, fishermen, foragers, and butchers who you will read about throughout the book—thank you. I'm humbled by you every day.

To my investors, thank you a million times for believing in me; I can never explain my gratitude in words.

As far as the book goes, big thanks to Justin for believing in the story and giving me an opportunity to write the book I wanted to write.

To Evan and Kira and all their staff, for understanding how important each little detail was in the photographs on the following pages. Thank you for sharing a vision and having the patience to deal with the process.

Olga!!! I know it was a long, hard road. Thank you for all your hard work, and it was so nice getting to know you along the way.

To Alison Lew—thank you for your meticulous and skillful eye—without your expert design skills, the book wouldn't be half as beautiful.

Boundless thanks to the best recipe tester a chef could ask for—my angel of a mother.

On the personal front (you are all so influential in who and what I am today)—I would like to thank all my Forgione and Davieau family. To my brothers Bryan and Sean—aho! Thank you to my beautiful sister Cara; even though you don't eat meat, it's cool. My grandparents: Pop Pop and Granny, Pepe and Gram—thank you for the unconditional love and support. My parents: Paps and Jule—it's not easy to say thank you for everything because there is so much; not a day goes by when I am not learning about humility, love, passion, creativity, and hard work from the both of you.

To my muse and rock, Kristen, thank you for your strength, love, patience and support. You deserve to be canonized. To the Angelilli family, for the countless words of advice and opinions, thank you.

To Lonny and Cassie, thank you for being a part of our functioning dysfunctional family.

To my friends from Pine Avenue, Floral Park, high school, college, and beyond—thank you!

To Old Boy, your teachings have led me to a path with a purpose—thank you.

Last but not least, to everyone and anyone not mentioned in here who should be.

Thank you to everyone for dealing with me and my insanity!!! I know it's not easy.

FOREWORD

THE MOMENT YOU TASTE MARC FORGIONE'S FOOD, you know he is an exceptional chef. From his menu descriptions, to ingredient pairings, to how his cooking always manages to surprise you, Marc's food is a marvel. It doesn't hurt that at the end of the day, Marc is as humble and as hardworking as they get—and happens to be a nice guy to boot.

When Marc asked me to write this, I couldn't have been more honored and delighted. I had the pleasure of working with Marc and watching him grow as a chef while he helped me build the BLT Steak franchise. I'm so proud to see all that he has accomplished.

Marc is a chef with a rare combination of a relentless work ethic, insatiable curiosity, a highly developed palate, and strong leadership skills. A deeply inquisitive and inventive chef, Marc never rests on his laurels; he will never feel that he's accomplished enough and will always be reaching for the next highest peak. While his food and cooking are of the utmost serious level, deeply rooted in French technique, a key quality of his food is a word that might come as a surprise in how an "Iron Chef" is described—whimsical. You can't help but notice while eating his food that this is a chef who loves to experiment and who has a lot of fun in the kitchen.

Marc became one of my sous chefs while I was opening BLT Steak. At the time, he was one of the chefs working at Pazo, the famed Patricia Yeo's restaurant, in the space that BLT Steak took over. From the moment we met, Marc struck me as incredibly professional, focused, serious, humble, and dedicated. In opening and running BLT Steak, we learned a lot about how to run a steakhouse and about each other. Back then we knew that a steakhouse had a certain look and feel, and that it served steak. But that's it. Outside of those two things, we learned everything through a lot of trial and error. For example, after we discovered moldy steaks in our aging room, we learned how to keep them bone dry. After experimenting with cooking meat in the wood-fired oven—which is great in theory—we went with Marc's idea of using the broiler instead. Marc's instincts with this (as well as other things) were spot on: Using a broiler allowed us to cook and serve our food with far less delay and satisfy a larger volume of orders.

Through learning together and observing what a dedicated and talented chef Marc is, I came to trust him with important kitchen and business decisions. Marc was, in fact, so dedicated that he felt he needed to earn his stripes working abroad. I was impressed that he was willing to travel somewhere where he didn't speak the language; I knew that despite being an excellent chef, Marc was going to struggle—the road ahead was not going to be easy. I was even more impressed that Marc was able to secure a series of positions with Michel Guérard's restaurants in Eugénie-les-Bains, France, where he wound up working for well over a year, and where he forged an even more meaningful connection to ingredients, sourcing, and techniques.

Marc came back from France a changed man: more serious, more mature, and even more focused on food. His time in France transformed him into a more intellectual and thoughtful chef; it took him to another level of composing his dishes. It was as if he had gained a deeper understanding of himself and it was fueling his execution in the kitchen. He was more passionate about cooking than ever, and he worked even harder to get everything right. In some ways, he reminded me a little of myself when I was younger.

So, when I set out to open BLT Prime, I asked Marc to be my chef de cuisine. There was no one else I could trust with that job. He combined some of my (French) ideas with his (American) ones, and the results were excellent. In addition to being a very creative guy, Marc had all the makings of a leader: people liked working with him, and he was an excellent manager and a good mentor for the young line cooks. And he led by example—always the hardest working chef on the line. Shortly thereafter, I asked him to become my corporate chef, helping me to open restaurants all over the country.

Perhaps the best precursor to the successes that were to come his way was the time he acted as my sous chef, helping me to compete on an Iron Chef episode against Bobby Flay. I took that competition very seriously—I was not going to lose. Our secret ingredient was goat cheese, and one of the dishes that Marc created for the completion was the goat cheese ravioli, which scored very well with the judges and made it into this book. Throughout the competition, Marc was incredibly focused and dedicated. We trained very hard—and we won. Having Marc on the team was critical to the win.

This is, without a doubt, a cookbook for the passionate cook; one who will seek out challenges and relish them. And while the book may *look* complicated—its food is, without a doubt, sophisticated—most of these recipes are all meant to be, and are able to be, cooked at home. They will make you more courageous in the kitchen, and they will meaningfully improve your cooking skills.

I have many happy memories of working and cooking with Marc, teasing him about his mohawk, and traveling with him all over the country opening restaurants, but perhaps my favorite memory is of us cooking together for his father, the celebrated chef Larry Forgione, who was in the dining room one night. Marc was brimming with excitement and pride to have his father there honoring his craft. Watching a son cook for his father, displaying as much of his craft as he could, was a beautiful memory, one that will stay with me forever.

By the time you will hold this book in your hands, Marc will have opened three more restaurants: Khe-Yo, a Laotian kitchen, and two steakhouses, American Cut, one in Atlantic City and one in New York—all excellent, and all bearing his meticulous attention to detail and bold flavors. I'm excited to see what's in store for this talented chef. No doubt, he'll keep reaching for even higher peaks, one delicious dish at a time.

—Laurent Tourondel

HOW TO USE THIS BOOK

DO NOT BE PUT OFF BY THE SEEMINGLY COMPLICATED OR LONG RECIPES. This book is meant to be cooked from. While there will be some recipes that might sound intimidating, and a few that will require special equipment, most of these recipes can be made at home.

If you never cook, this book might look very intimidating, but I don't want it to be. All the recipes are written to provide as much information as possible, so if you are new to making something, the descriptions in the recipes will guide you. If you're a beginner cook, I'd like you to focus on a single component of a dish, take things easy, and get used to the process. If you are an advanced home cook, these recipes will help you hone your techniques, stretch your cooking muscle, and challenge how you compose a dish. You might not want to make the entire dish—but then again, you might.

Once you start cooking from this book and start getting the techniques, it'll get a lot easier—you just have to get over the hump. My mother, who was one of the testers, was very intimidated by the first three recipes—she called me and told me they were impossible. By the end of us testing the book, she would call me and ask me for something more difficult . . . she was finding the recipes too easy.

Don't focus on making your dish look just like it looks in the picture—focus on making it so that it tastes good to you. The recipes are foundational: If you learn how to sear a fish from this book, you will know how to sear a fish for the rest of your life. Think of this book not so much as a collection of recipes and dishes but as techniques you can apply to other recipes and dishes you will go on to create.

And if you are a chef (or would like to become one), cook these recipes in their entirety (all the components)—or focus on techniques unknown to you.

Here are a few notes that I hope are helpful:

+ The sous-vide technique has become very popular in fine dining restaurants in the last thirty years. *Sous-vide* literally means "under vacuum" and requires two pieces of rather pricey equipment: a Cryovac machine (which removes air from the bag holding the food) and an immersion circulator (see Tools, page 400), which is a tool that is put into a tub of water and regulates the water temperature, gently (and evenly!) cooking the food. Wherever possible, we have included alternative cooking instructions when sous-vide is called for. Where the alternative cooking instructions are not listed, the sous-vide technique is essential to the dish.

+ Sometimes, when making reductions, the book will tell you to make two or three times as much sauce as you will need for the recipe. This is because you need a certain amount of liquid in order for the flavors to concentrate and reduce. It's hard to make a reduction with a small amount of liquid. You can save any leftover sauce and use it in other dishes.

+ Many of the recipes are finished with micro herbs (see Sources, page 403). When the dish arrives at your table, the micro herbs make for a dramatic presentation. However, the company whose micro herbs we buy, Koppert Cress (see page 301), grows micro herbs that contribute as much to the flavor of the dish as they do to the look of the dish. If you do not want to bother with micro herbs, that's perfectly fine, too.

+ Throughout the book I use spice blends that I order from an amazing company, La Boîte à Épice (see page 125). I implore you to give these spices a try. Once you do, you will be tempted to use them in everything. Not only are these some of the best quality spices you can get your hands on, but they will also transform your food in noticeable and positive ways.

+ Throughout the book you will see stories about some of the purveyors that we work with at the restaurant. These are the people who have been good to me, and I've come to love certain products. I wanted to tell their story as well, because they, too, are part of the Restaurant Marc Forgione story and are part of the reason that the food at the restaurant tastes the way that it does.

+ Most important, remember this as you cook: While cooking from this book will enhance your technique, make you a better cook, and make you more fearless in the kitchen, cooking, above all, is supposed to be a *fun* and creative process. Take your time. Pace yourself. Enjoy it.

Here are some general guidelines that might be helpful to keep in mind throughout the book:

1. All pepper is ground fresh.

2. All herbs are fresh unless dried is specified.

3. All butter is unsalted.

4. All salt is kosher unless otherwise indicated. At the restaurant we use the Diamond Crystal brand. The finishing flaky sea salt that we use at the restaurant is Maldon.

5. If it doesn't already specify to do it in the recipe, it's always better to briefly toast the spices in a clean, dry skillet over a low flame. It awakens their flavors, making your final dish that much more incredible. Spices, for the most part, start out whole, and are ground only after they are toasted.

6. All eggs are large and farm-fresh. If you can get farm-fresh eggs, make every effort to do so—it will make an amazing difference in your food.

7. Milk is whole and preferably nonhomogenized so the cream rises to the top. Cream is always heavy cream.

8. Keep some blended oil on hand as it's used in many of the recipes here. To make it, combine 3 parts canola oil with 1 part olive oil.

9. Foie gras is grade-A duck (about 2-pound lobes).

10. All sugar is granulated unless otherwise indicated.

11. Flour is all-purpose unless otherwise indicated.

12. Some recipes require the minutest precision—cup and spoon measures just won't do. For those recipes, we've indicated the measurements in grams.

INTRODUCTION

A BUSINESS MIRACLE. This is a story of an improbable restaurant miracle. It's also a cookbook that, if you don't get intimidated by a handful of sous-vide recipes and odd spice blends, will make you a better cook. It'll make you feel less daunted by any kind of recipe. It'll allow you to stay in your comfort zone but also, if you let it, push you further. It'll make you fearless, if not in life, then definitely in the kitchen. At least that's my goal.

But as important as the recipes are, the story of how my restaurant survived is a great story—a story I want to tell. I think that no matter how seasoned, how experienced you are in the kitchen, you're never prepared for opening a restaurant (especially your first), much as you're never fully prepared to become a parent. Inevitably, things will go wrong; there will be plenty of curveballs, and you just need to be prepared for it all to happen.

But if, before I opened the restaurant, someone had sat me down and told me how it was all going to happen and the events that would take place, I wouldn't have believed them. Either that or I would have chickened out of opening my own place.

When I tell people about the first few years of the restaurant's life, they are surprised to hear that I really struggled, that there were some dark, sad times when I questioned myself. I think that because Larry Forgione is my old man, people think that I just woke up one day, and the restaurant appeared before me, fully formed and functional. That it was all just a product of being born into a chef family. That, because of my dad, I sprouted from the kitchen gods and was gently placed in a kitchen where I've reigned supreme ever since.

Nothing could be further from the truth.

If you look at the story of our restaurant, Hollywood couldn't have written a better script. Deep in the red, we were on the brink of selling the business. So many things that could have gone wrong did go wrong. There were no guarantees. When the turnaround came, it was fast and incredible—we were all pinching ourselves. The fact that this restaurant survived and is still around is a miracle. A business miracle. But when the going was tough, it was painful.

There were more times than I can count when I didn't know if we were going to make it. We opened with no money, were short-staffed, and got caught in the mother of recessions. We made it through, but now that we're in the fifth year of the restaurant's life and finally making money, we're still paying off debt. It's been a long journey to get to where we are now.

When times were tough, we could've changed our menu; we could've changed our way of cooking; we could've served different food—burgers, maybe—but we didn't. We kept our heads down, held our breath, and continued to cook the way we felt was right. We listened to our gut and just hung on, hoping for a miracle. And somewhere along the way, people started to notice, and gradually, little by little, our luck began to turn.

I was approached to write this book in 2011, and I immediately knew that in addition to the recipes from the restaurant, I wanted to share our story with you. Without these recipes, we wouldn't have a cookbook;

and without our story, we wouldn't be where we are today and we wouldn't have these recipes.

I wanted to tell you our story not because I want to be self-indulgent and wax poetic for pages and pages, but because I think our story is a good one to know. Whether you plan on working in a restaurant, running one, or eating in one, the stories of how we get to the place where we are, are important. They provide context; they help to establish an identity. When you read our story, you will know what drives us and what makes us tick.

Some of what you're about to read might come across as the sob story of a chef building a restaurant. I get it—I am not a war veteran, I didn't go through combat. But at the same time, we all go through trying experiences. And this is *my* story; this is *kitchen combat*. I wanted to share this story with anyone who has ever thought of running their own place: budding chefs, young people dreaming of cooking for a living. Everyone can write a business plan, but to hear real stories about the trials and tribulations of a real restaurant might be helpful and comforting should anyone meet the challenges along the way. The story of my restaurant is an amazing, hard-to-believe, great story. And to tell you the story of my food is to tell you the story of the restaurant and how we got here.

I THOUGHT I WANTED TO BE A FOREST RANGER AND SMOKE POT

I didn't always know I was going to be a chef. As a kid, I liked being in the kitchen, but as a teenager, not so much. Some of that was because of what my dad did for a living, and back then there weren't too many rebellious teenagers who wanted to follow in their fathers' footsteps. And I was a pretty regular kid who was into everything a typical teenager would be into: I hung out, played sports, and got in trouble—just like most other kids.

I was fourteen when I got my first job in the hospitality industry, so to speak. Two buddies and I signed

Marc + his Dad

up to be dishwashers in catering halls in Long Island. Within a month, for reasons I can't still figure out, I was promoted to be a bartender. I couldn't even drink, but I was mixing drinks for others!

I got my first real restaurant job at my father's restaurant, An American Place, when I was about sixteen. At the time, I didn't even realize what an amazing restaurant it was and how lucky I was to work there. The ingredients were perfect; the chef, Richie, was amazing; there were three or four specials every day. It was a serious, no-bullshit kitchen, and I was just a kid running around in there. It was really, really cool.

On my first day at An American Place, about ten seconds in, one of the cooks gave me a cleaver to chop chives, and, immediately, I chopped the tip of my thumb off. Ten seconds in. Suddenly there was blood everywhere, and I thought I'd be sent home for sure. But the other cooks bandaged me up and ten minutes later I went back on the line. The chef laughed, "If it doesn't fall off, you don't go home,"—a line I still use at the restaurant to this day. It felt good to be treated like everyone else, and not get special treatment just because I was the owner's son. You don't go home just because you're hurt—you push through it. Also: Don't chop chives with a cleaver.

My job was humble—I started out prepping ingredients. Then I moved my way up to salads and to different stations from there. And even though I didn't know I wanted to be a chef, right from the get-go I was always drawn to the chef lifestyle. While most teenagers don't look forward to waking up early and working fourteen-hour days, to me it felt exhilarating. I liked being around food, and I felt at home with cooks, listening to their stories and grabbing a drink with them after work. I enjoyed working hard and getting my ass kicked. It was humbling, motivating, and grueling—a culinary boot camp. And I loved every minute.

When I got to college, I wasn't focused. College didn't really interest me; I wasn't motivated. Over the first few years, I switched my major several times. My freshman year, I was a psych major. The following year, I was a forestry major—I thought I wanted to be a forest ranger, smoke pot, and wear tie-dye. Then, I switched to business management because I didn't know what I wanted to do, and business management sounded like something useful. By junior year, I had to pick, and stick with, a major in order to graduate. So I picked hotel and restaurant management. But up to that point, and even afterward, I didn't seriously think about becoming a chef. It was more of a well-I-don't-know-nothing-else-interests-me type of a decision. And it turned out that UMass Amherst, where I was enrolled, had one of the best hotel management schools in the country! I took the restaurant management track (at that point, I had about four years of cooking experience under my belt) and wound up doing pretty well. After graduation, I went backpacking through Europe for two months with five of my good buddies.

Europe was an eye-opening experience and gave me a sense of recognition of something inside of me. There was this force that kept guiding me toward food, and I was beginning to feel as if this was what I was supposed to do. And so, partly because I needed the money and partly because my dad needed the help, the day after I got off the plane, I started cooking at An American Place. I haven't stopped cooking since that day.

For a while, I was going back and forth between working for my dad and for Patricia Yeo at her famed restaurant AZ. At some point, Patricia felt that I was good

Photo of Marc Forgione with Michelle Obama on the restaurant shelves

3

enough to be promoted to sous-chef. While the promotion meant a huge honor, I thought I was way too young and too inexperienced to be given that job just yet. Once you become a sous-chef, you're a sous-chef until you're an executive chef. And I felt that I had a lot more to learn before I could comfortably wear that title. I might have deserved the promotion because I was the best cook at *that* kitchen at *that* time, but that didn't mean I deserved it overall *or* should have taken it. I've always been competitive (chefs are competitive by nature), but the person I competed with the most—was myself.

I decided that what I really needed was a kick in the ass. I knew I needed to grow up, and I wanted to get away from being "Larry Forgione's son." I had incredible respect for my dad's accomplishments, but I needed to be viewed as a chef in my own right, not as a famous chef's kid. So I decided to go where no one knew who I was (or gave a shit)—Europe.

I compiled a list of chefs I wanted to apprentice under. I felt like it had to be go-big-or-go-home, so I shot for the A-listers: Michel Bras, Paul Bocuse, Pierre Gagnaire, and Michel Guérard, who was my number-one pick. Sometime before, I had found a magazine spread on Chef Guérard and his three-Michelin-star restaurant: There was this beautiful garden where you picked your herbs, in this small, charming village in the middle of nowhere in the southwest of France. Something about that place just called to me. When I showed the list to my dad, he laughed—he thought I put Michel Guérard at the top of my list as a joke. I had no idea that years ago, my father had worked with Chef Guérard and they were friendly. So my dad wrote a letter to Michel, and Michel wrote back. Normally, he wrote, they wouldn't consider it, but if I came as a *stage* (an unpaid apprentice or intern), just to learn, it would be acceptable.

GUM FOR DINNER

And so, in the summer of 2004, armed with a small bag and little else, I flew to Paris. From there, I took the train down to Eugénie-les-Bains, one of those beautiful places you see in the promotional tourist flyers—except it's actually that beautiful in real life. But it's so remote, and so small, that no one there speaks any English. As in zero. *Rien*. Not even "hello." I got off the train, and

4

this guy walked up to me and introduced himself, in French, of course. His name was Monsieur Mootz, and he was there to pick me up and take me to the kitchen to meet the chef. Chef Stéphane Mack, who ran the restaurant kitchen where I was going to be apprenticing, shook my hand and immediately launched into fast-paced, full-on French. I didn't understand a single word, but I just kept nodding. *Oui, chef. Merci. Merci. Au revoir*. That was the extent of my French.

Once the introductions were over and done with, M. Mootz took me to the house where I was going to live. The drive from the restaurant to the house, which was on the edge of the town, took exactly one minute. "*Bonne soirée*," said M. Mootz, and drove away before I could bid him the same.

In the house, my room was straight out of that famous Van Gogh painting: a tiny cot, a wooden table with a chair, and a stand-up shower without a shower curtain (though I don't think Van Gogh had the shower). I put my bag down and looked around me: no phone, no television, no Internet—the room was very spartan and very isolated. At that moment, I felt a tinge of panic: I was by myself in this weird, obscure place, and I didn't speak the language. What was I doing there?

I looked out the window: It was getting late and the sun was just starting to set. Famished, I set out to get something to eat. I left the house and started to walk. I didn't see anyone on the streets—the whole village was so quiet, it was as if it had been deserted. It took me a few minutes to realize that everything in town had shut down for the night and not even a bakery was open. So I returned to my room, rummaged in my bags, and found a pack of gum. And that's how I spent my first night in Eugénie-les-Bains—alone, with gum for dinner. I was in France, about to start apprenticing in one of the best restaurants in the world, and I ate gum for dinner.

In the morning, before I had to report to work at eight a.m., I found an open *boulangerie*, bought a baguette with butter, and watched the sun rise while eating my breakfast. You don't get much more French than that: French countryside, sunrise, baguette, and butter. And gum for dinner the night before, because in a small town in France, everything shuts down on Sunday night. Lesson learned.

BEING BY YOURSELF

At first, being in France was terrible; I hated every minute of it and just wanted to go home. I didn't speak the language, and because I didn't speak the language, I couldn't understand what anyone was saying; and because I couldn't understand what anyone was saying, I screwed up a lot. And because I couldn't speak, I was quiet, which made everyone think I was arrogant. Everyone hated me because I made mistakes, and they thought I was stuck up.

But little by little, I picked up the language and made fewer and fewer mistakes until, finally, I stopped making them altogether. I stopped hating where I was; I was actually really starting to enjoy every aspect of my job. I got along with the other cooks, and ended up becoming really close with a lot of people at the restaurant. And instead of staying three months, I stayed a year and three months and was asked to return the following year. Eugénie-les-Bains wound up being a truly amazing experience.

It was during my apprenticeship in France that, for the first time in my life, I started to feel a visceral connection to food. A huge part of that feeling came from spending my mornings in the garden, trimming herbs and tending plants; plucking feathers from chickens; opening two hundred oysters and cleaning thirty lobsters every day. Whether it was from the ground, the air, or the sea, I dealt with food from start to finish. If it was a fish, I scaled, gutted, and filleted it. If it was a chicken, I plucked it and cut it into pieces. When you work with food where you get to see its life cycle from source to plate, your perception of that ingredient, your understanding and appreciation for it, change with time. And you begin to *feel* the food, if you will, not just in your head and your heart, but also in your gut. It becomes a visceral and indelible part of you.

In looking back on my time in France and what I took away from there, it was far more than just technique and skill—cooking was just 60 percent of what I learned there. I took away a deeper sense of self as well. And I think that it's critical for anyone who is serious about becoming a chef to go abroad to a country where they don't speak any English. It doesn't have to be Europe; it can be Asia, or South America, or Africa. But it needs to be a place where you are taken out of your element and are forced to be inside your head *a lot*. You really grow up and learn about yourself. And to learn *about* yourself you have to *be* by yourself. Spend *time* with yourself. I learned a lot about myself as a cook, as a brother, as a son, as a friend, as a person.

And it was during this experience in France that I really, truly, 100 percent realized that I was going to be a chef. And not only was I going to be a chef, I was going to be a *serious* chef. I remember thinking, about what my high school football coach used to tell me: "Men, we're gonna throw balls over our shoulders, and go in head first," as I began to feel this amazing passion for the craft. It was in France that I really decided that someday I was going to open my own restaurant.

I started to keep a notebook of ideas, writing thoughts for dishes and concepts, eventually spilling over into another notebook, and another. I've kept all those notebooks with me, and it's amazing to look through them and see how I've grown as a chef.

THE LAURENT TOURONDEL YEARS

Before I went off to my apprenticeship in France, I had helped Laurent Tourondel open BLT Steak. Good thing I had already committed to going to France by that time. Otherwise, France might not have happened, because I really liked working with Laurent. But we kept in touch while I was there, and when I came back, he asked me to open BLT Fish with him, and then made me executive chef at BLT Prime. I was about twenty-six years old. None of this made any sense—I should've been a sous-chef at most, but instead, he made me the chef de cuisine. Every time I wanted to get my butt kicked, someone was handing me the keys to the car. For whatever reason, there was a pattern of me getting jobs I didn't think I was ready to take on. But I trusted Laurent's judgment and took the position. Everyone was loving BLT Prime, the reviews were great, and it was fun to cook there.

After a while, Laurent made me his corporate chef, which meant I was responsible for opening up and managing BLT restaurants across the country. I loved doing it, but I began to miss coming into one kitchen and cooking there day in and day out. I was ready to finally have a kitchen of my own.

But internally, I struggled with that decision. Even though I was ready to spread my wings, I didn't want to leave. Laurent's influence had been incredibly important. If you ask a lot of successful chefs who they look up to, they can usually name one chef who really, truly mentored them, took them under their wing and looked after them. And for me, that was Laurent. In looking back, he was grooming me precisely for the moment when I felt ready to strike out on my own. He showed me what it was like to open a restaurant, bringing me into business meetings just to listen and absorb. Without my time spent with him in that capacity, I don't think I would have ever been able to attempt to open my own place. Laurent showed me the business side of opening your own place: His incredible attention to detail and care went into every decision, no matter how small. Before Laurent, I never got to see a chef sit down at the table and pick out a napkin or a table setting for the dining room of his new restaurant. Everything mattered to him: menu covers, menu typeface, even the line spacing of the dishes. Watching him pay so much attention to each aspect of running a restaurant carried over to how I work now.

2008

Baptism by Fire

These days, when I read over our original business plans, it strikes me as funny that my vision for my restaurant was as crystallized as it was from the very beginning. About a year prior to opening the restaurant, as I started to think about a place of my own, I began to keep a journal filled with general thoughts and visions for my future place. One entry read, "Each table should have its own lighting from above, just enough to see the table, but at the same time feel intimate as well as feel part of a busy dining room." If you walk into the restaurant today, that's exactly how it looks.

Opening your own place is a multifaceted affair. I had the kitchen know-how, but I needed a business partner, someone who understood the financial side of it and who was practical. So my college friend Lou introduced me to his college buddy Chris Blumlo. Blumlo and I went to UMass Amherst at the same time and ran in the same circles, but oddly enough, we didn't hang out in college. We hit it off right away, meeting several times a week to flesh out our vision for the restaurant. After some time, we put together a business plan and then started to look for a space.

The space where we wound up opening the restaurant was the first place I looked at. A friend of a friend

Business partner Christopher Blumlo

had called me and said, "I know this guy in Tribeca who wants to get out of his restaurant. You should come and check out the space."

Tribeca. Strange as it sounds for a guy who grew up in New York, at that time I'd only been to Tribeca twice in my life. It wasn't a place where a young guy would go to hang out; it was more for families, quiet.

So I went down to Tribeca one crisp September night to check it out. I remember everything about that evening; the leaves had just started to change color. As I was turning off Hudson Street onto Reade, I saw this cozy tree-lined street, a beautiful deck with wide open doors, and marble tables with bistro chairs. Everything was quiet and still, and I felt like I had just been transported out of New York into a small town. It's so rare to see a restaurant with doors that open from floor to ceiling—and it was exactly what I wanted. I remember walking up to the restaurant and thinking, "Please, God, let this be the restaurant that I am coming to look at!" And then I got close enough to see the building's address—and my heart skipped a beat.

I knew I wanted the space as soon as I started to talk to the owner. Even without properly seeing the

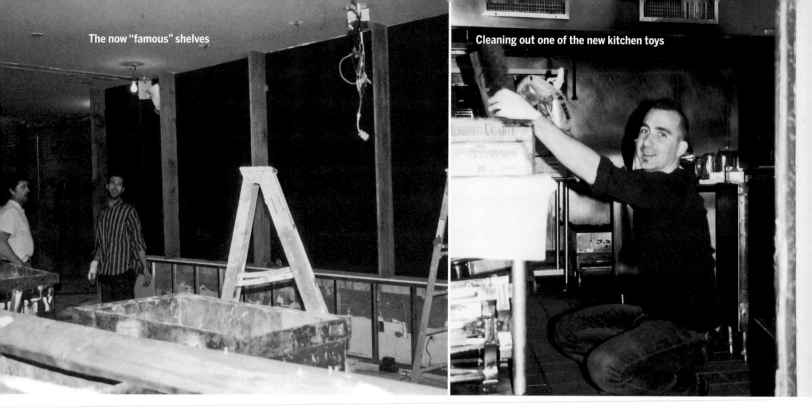

inside, I knew it—suddenly I just had this feeling that this *had* to be the place. If you read our original business plans, it says something like "exposed wood, candlelight, natural brick." When I walked in, the inside was covered in white subway tile. There were these huge mirrors hanging, too. The back room, where there was a giant movie screen, had a big black curtain. I had no idea that behind all that were beautiful wood beams and red brick, but in my gut I felt it was the right place. I asked the guy what was behind the tile and he just rolled his eyes. "Some ugly old red brick."

That feeling in my gut before I even stepped in—just felt right. And all that other stuff, the brick and the iron details that I wanted so much, just happened by chance. Even before I saw the inside, before I knew that the details I wanted even existed, just *walking up* to this place gave me goose bumps. I just *knew* this was the perfect place.

Later, I learned that in its previous life, before it became a restaurant, the space had been a butter and cream holding facility. Butter and cream were stored in the basement, which was a giant refrigerator, and when they needed to be shipped somewhere, they were

raised to the ground level via an elevator (where the bar is now) and carried out of the big front doors.

So I told the owner I wanted the space. And as a gesture of good faith, I promised him a rather big chunk of money within two weeks. *Two weeks!* At the time, Blumlo and I had zero in the bank. We just signed this piece of paper and then immediately thought, *Shit, how are we gonna raise that much money?*

We started cooking private fund-raising dinners at apartments all over the city. I'd arrange to come over to someone's home, cook him and his guests a multicourse meal, talk about the food, and so on, and then say to the diners, "I'm going to build one of the best restaurants in New York—trust me." And people did—within a couple of weeks, we had raised enough money for our good-faith deposit and to open the restaurant, but *just* enough to scrape by on, no more, no less. Looking back on all this: promising someone a crazy amount of money with nothing in the bank, was utterly, stupidly insane. Maybe that was the kind of insanity we had to have at the time, but in retrospect it was a risky move. The next stage, putting everything together, was rather sobering—we had to budget for everything, and Blumlo, being the numbers guy, had me on a tight leash.

Back in the day, my vision for opening a proper restaurant included an unlimited budget where you go and pick out whatever equipment you want. The way I saw it, we were building my dream, and you don't put a price tag on your dreams. But in the real world, dreams have prices, and often steep ones.

We went to the Bowery to pick out equipment. And no matter what I pointed to—a Viking stove, an island pass, a sink—I was told it was too expensive and I had to pick out something cheaper. I wanted to cut a hole in the wall of the restaurant so you could look into the kitchen when you walked through the dining room. I wanted a little window in the bathroom that had a one-way mirror letting you see into the kitchen. I wanted all these cool, fun nuances that would make the restaurant a unique place, like a wood-burning oven, for example. And none of it was happening—it was all just too expensive.

After that fruitless trip, we went to Madison Avenue to these fancy showrooms to pick out china. The same thing happened—we couldn't afford anything.

Everything I picked out, and I mean *everything*, was too expensive; from plates to stoves to you-name-it, I was told I couldn't have it. So finally, frustrated, I threw my hands up and walked away.

A few days later, we returned to the Bowery; I took some time to review my options and think about our finances. We scrapped the idea of the hood for the wood-burning oven—it was just too expensive—and found an antique oven that now stands in the dining room; we use it to warm our bread. I was determined to have my dream restaurant, but I also had to be flexible and adjust to our financial situation.

Shopping eBay for Dishes

So I compromised: I bought everything used—refrigerators, stove, hotel pans—because that was what we could afford. I couldn't buy fancy china over on Madison Avenue, so I spent several weeks hanging out on eBay trying to find the right plates, glasses, and creamers. Bit by bit, things were coming together.

Surprisingly, the hardest things to find were the chairs. We were about two weeks from opening and by then had gone everywhere to look for them: western Massachusetts, upstate New York, every antique shop we could find. Nothing looked right to us. The opening date was looming, and we had no chairs.

We wound up finding our chairs at Crate & Barrel, just a few blocks away! We had spent all this time looking far and wide, and the chairs were right under our noses. They weren't cheap, but they were right.

The last piece of the puzzle was the lighting, and it was the one thing I wound up not having to compromise on. We installed the custom lamps I originally envisioned, and they still hang in the restaurant now. Having the right lighting was critical for me.

The lack of money was frustrating, but it wasn't anybody's fault. And I learned a valuable lesson: Sometimes you have to just figure it out and play the hand you're dealt. I just wasn't used to that. I came from An American Place, BLT, Michel Guérard, and I didn't know how much things really cost. At those restaurants, you got the plates you wanted, and the price didn't matter; you just got what you wanted.

It was a valuable lesson, and something that I want anyone reading this book to understand—sometimes, to make your dream come true, you have to sacrifice a little bit, or even a lot. If we had borrowed another two hundred thousand dollars from somebody to buy all the things that I wanted, who knows—I might not be sitting here today writing this book because we would've crapped out. Because we *really* didn't have enough money. We *just* squeaked by with what we had. So I want the young people who might be considering having their own restaurant one day, or young chefs who are thinking about it, to know the story of how we got to where we are. Everybody's story is different, but if you read about one restaurant's journey, you get a better idea of what it might take. We didn't just wake up one day to overnight success, collecting accolades. Each good thing was a result of struggle, persistence, and a strong gut feeling that if we stuck to what we did, we'd eventually get there.

We had three months to renovate the space and hire kitchen and wait staff. Our first day of training was going to be May 6, 2008. And that's when I met Matthew Conway, who became our general manager and sommelier. Our meeting was like something out of a gangster movie. He was supposed to meet me in the restaurant, which, at the time, was a preconstruction, closed building. I was sitting in the corner with my leather jacket and fingerless gloves on, and in walked this young, impressionable man, looking a little skittish, like he might be in the wrong place. When he saw me, I motioned over to him, *Godfather* style—"Over here, kid"—and we sat there for the next hour talking about everything: food, wine, cocktails, the restaurant business in general, and what he wanted to do. To be 100 percent honest, I wasn't so sure about him at the beginning of our conversation, but by the end, there was something in his demeanor that struck me the right way, and I knew he was the right guy for the job. At the time, Matthew was working at Café Gray, and

Craig Bero

a good friend of mine, Jimmy Bradley, who owns The Harrison and The Red Cat in New York, recommended that we talk to him. Believe it or not, Matthew is still with us to this day—one of the few employees who's been with the restaurant since day one.

Hiring the kitchen crew was the easy part. I locked that down early on. At the opening, we had about twenty-five people between the front and back of the house. Everything else took time and a lot of hard work.

Before any construction started, we had to get the raw materials for the interior. All the wood that we're famous for now, every single piece, Blumlo and I hauled with our bare hands.

Blumlo's family owned a sawmill, so one morning, we woke up at 4:30 a.m. and drove to his family's sawmill in New Bedford, Massachusetts. There was all this wood in the backyard that had been sitting out for more than fifty years. Many pieces had grown gray over time, and remain so to this day. So Blumlo and I packed the wood into our truck, had lunch at his aunt and uncle's house, and drove back to New York. Then we laid out the wood all over the floor of the restaurant and let it dry for a few days. Only after that could we start construction.

We went in with sledgehammers and gutted the basement, the kitchen, and pretty much everything in between. I, myself, knocked off a few pieces of the subway tile, and it felt satisfying.

But as the restaurant was coming together, Chris and I were ready to kill each other. A pragmatist who never forgot about the bottom line, Blumlo kept reminding me what we could, and more important, *couldn't* afford. I was the creative one, saying, "But we *need* to have this; we *need* to have that." But Blumlo wasn't having any of it—he was unemotional about our needs and his job was to make sure we didn't spend ourselves into oblivion. It wasn't personal, but we were butting heads. The money was tight and tensions were high. We both wanted to make something amazing; we were just looking at it from different vantage points. In any partnership, be it business or personal, it's

Full gut job

100-year old wood drying out in the restaurant

most beneficial to have both: the head and the heart. Too much of one and not enough of the other could spell trouble for whatever you want to build. In looking back, thank God I had the voice of reason in Blumlo. Without his pragmatic approach, who knows where we'd all be today?

And while the restaurant was taking shape, amidst the rubble, there was Craig Bero. Blumlo and I would be sitting in our unheated, dilapidated space going over blueprints, wearing hats and gloves for warmth, and Craig would come over with hot coffee and fresh pastries just to say hello. Often he'd come over with neighborhood people, "Meet Marc and Chris," he'd say, "they're going to open a great restaurant here!" In a thoughtful, gentle, neighborly, almost small-town manner, Craig was our introduction to the area and its residents.

Blumlo and I met Craig by happenstance—stopping for coffee at the Cosmopolitan Café in Tribeca, which he owns. Later on we learned that Craig happened to have been a server at the River Café in Brooklyn while my father was a chef there years ago. The three of us got to know one another, and while we were going through construction, Craig would just come over to make sure we didn't freeze. In addition to introducing us to the Tribeca community, he was instrumental in connecting us to different vendors and artisans. As if hot coffee and pastries weren't generous enough, Craig helped us in ways that went above and beyond: The iron shutter in the back of the restaurant was from Craig. He had also introduced us to the welder to make the original "Forge" sign. From feeding us and literally keeping us warm, to introducing us to the community board, Craig became a huge emotional part of the restaurant's beginnings.

Hospitalized on Opening Day

The morning of the day the restaurant was supposed to open, I landed in the hospital—and stayed there for a week. I woke up so early that it was still dark out. I got out of bed to get some water, but on my way to the kitchen, I suddenly felt sharp abdominal pain so intense that I fell to the floor. It felt as if someone was stabbing me in the stomach.

Back then I was living in Chelsea and the nearest hospital was the now-shuttered St. Vincent's. I wound up, literally, crawling there at six in the morning.

I checked myself into the hospital, and was told they planned to keep me overnight. While the nurse was giving me painkillers, I grabbed her hands and told her I needed to be at work before five p.m. She looked at me and just laughed—and then told the doctor I was delirious. I was stubborn: I tried to get up and leave, but the hospital personnel held me down. I kept saying, "I have to leave, I have to go!" But they were adamant: "You can't. We have to run tests on you. You could be very sick." I just kept repeating, "No, you don't understand. My restaurant is opening *today*, and I have to be the one to open it!"

I wound up being admitted with a severe intestinal infection, and I stayed there for the *whole first week* of the restaurant's life! Can you imagine, opening a restaurant and being too sick to be there in person? Or coming into a newly opened restaurant and discovering the chef is nowhere to be seen? Scrambling, I managed to arrange for my father and a few friends to cook that week. But I remember lying in the hospital bed and looking up thinking, "Okay, I get it, it's *not* going to be easy. But give me a fucking break! Throw me a bone here!"

A week later when I was getting out of the hospital, I got news that one of my best friends from college suddenly, and unexpectedly, passed away. It was a complete shock; I couldn't wrap my head around it.

That same week, my grandfather passed away as well. As if the hospital wasn't enough, losing my grandfather and my friend all in the same week felt like being sucker-punched.

But I had no time to emotionally fall apart. I had to plunge headfirst into work. And there was a lot of it. I had no butcher or prep cooks because we didn't have the funds for it yet, so we had to make do with what we had. I saw the payroll that Blumlo put together and said, "Okay, I'll make it happen." We were doing 110 to 120 covers and I had to get to the restaurant at seven a.m. to prep everything for the day, do all the butchering, and do all the cooking.

The second week we were open, our air conditioning broke. I remember looking into the dining room and seeing Gael Greene, formerly of *New York* magazine, wiping her forehead with a napkin. My girlfriend's entire family came in and her mother was fanning herself with a menu—you could see the beads of sweat on her face. I almost died.

When the restaurant opened, our bank account had a big, fat zero in it, and every single penny made a difference. We raised twenty thousand dollars the first week, and another twenty thousand dollars a week later.

The only people left from the original staff

And we were using the first twenty thousand to pay the staff. Blumlo and I were living hand to mouth; we didn't pay ourselves for I can't even remember how long. Sometimes, I'd take out some money to buy myself some milk, bread, and water for my house. But that was about it—there was no paycheck coming through. And we didn't know how long that was going to last.

Our opening staff displayed amazing grace under pressure. In that uncertain, stressful time, they were asked to do things that I'd never wish upon my worst enemy and I will always be grateful to them for their incredibly hard work. But when you have seven people trying to do a menu that requires twelve people—you can imagine what transpires. On paper, our food was exactly what I wanted, but on the plate, the execution was not close to the concept—it wasn't consistent. If I took a day off, I was sure to have a mental breakdown—I didn't feel confident not being in the kitchen. My days off were a blur of sleeping, fighting a hangover, and having a meltdown.

I remember coming in to work and just trying to get through the day. On any given day the responsibilities I had ran the gamut: I had to order six steaks knowing I'd need to order twenty more for the weekend. But since we didn't have any money, and we owed the meat guy two months of balances, how the fuck was I supposed to get that done? Charm him into selling me meat? We were handing out paychecks, but knew that half of them were going to bounce.

And the early reviews showed where we were lacking—they weren't kind to us, and some of it was deserved. We weren't running the restaurant I had originally envisioned. Don't get me wrong—we were making great food and I was proud of it. But I wanted us to do even better, and with so few cooks on the line and me being the butcher, the meat cook, and everything in between, we were a few hands short to be truly outstanding. Maybe I should've just sucked it up budgetwise and hired another prep cook—that probably would have helped us out a great deal. But hindsight is twenty-twenty.

What we lacked was consistency, and in an excellent restaurant, every dish has to be made as if a *New York Times* dining critic is asking for it. When I cooked food for the staff, they loved it—it was amazing. But it's easy to make a dish once. An executive chef is expected to make a dish once, give it to his staff, and have them replicate it over and over and over and over, and execute it perfectly each and every time. And that just wasn't happening.

So 2008 was baptism by fire. We got some loyal clientele, and I learned a lot during those few months, but it was a humbling, grounding experience. And as we were on our way to doing better, the recession hit everyone fast and furious, turning 2009 into another year of uphill battles. It was the year we really had to hang on for dear life.

2009

Things Fall Apart

I turned thirty right before the New Year—it was a raucous night. The coming year wasn't anywhere on my mind, but it probably should've been. The weight of the impending recession loomed even in late 2008, but we just weren't paying as close attention as we should have been.

When 2009 rolled in, talk of recession increased, and the markets were tanking, but we didn't understand just how bad it was about to get. Things really fell apart around February. Many of our patrons lost their jobs, and suddenly, people were staying at home instead of going out to eat. The restaurant attendance dried out almost overnight. Empty tables and chairs made things more dire for us, financially, and we had to take out more loans.

To throw another wrench in the works, in February, we had to change the restaurant's name. Our name used to be Forge, my nickname, and we thought it fit us perfectly. A few months prior, a restaurant based in Miami by the same name, Forge, threatened us with a lawsuit if we didn't change our name, claiming it was causing brand confusion and affecting their clientele. I have no idea how you could wind up dining at Forge in New York while trying to dine at Forge in Miami, but we decided not to fight them on it and changed our name to Marc Forgione. We had a "funeral" party for the old name and invited some media for the renaming.

Then in March, I got invited to the Maldives on a cooking trip. I remember, about a week into being there, I got the numbers from Blumlo—and I thought they were missing a zero. We were averaging fifteen to twenty covers a night and I thought I was going to come back to a shut down restaurant. Immediately after that email, I gave an interview where I was asked what it was like to be a successful restaurateur in New York, and all I could do was think, "I might be going back to an empty dining room. I might be done. This could be it." It wasn't what I thought success would feel like.

When I came back, the restaurant was continuing to do fifteen to twenty covers a night – barely slogging along. My sous-chef wound up leaving—it just wasn't a good place to be. I understood that it was time for him to go, but I knew that things were going to get harder with even fewer hands on deck. By then, it was just me and three cooks in the kitchen.

Necessity Is the Mother of Invention

As a result of having so few hands in the kitchen, some of our best dishes that year were products of sheer necessity. I was working fourteen-hour days, six days a week; and when you're constantly short-staffed, in order to survive, you have to become more inventive. If we hadn't managed to adjust, we wouldn't have made it. If I had just thrown up my arms and said, "I can't cook like that," we would've died. I had to put my ego aside and say, "Okay, *this* is how we're going to make this work."

Our Chicken Under a Brick (see page 213) was a happy accident. Because I didn't have time to season

the chickens when the orders were coming in, I started to season the skin in the mornings and would let the salt penetrate the chicken over the course of the day. This move turned out to be the secret to making the crispiest, most delicious chicken skin ever. At the celebrated Zuni Café in San Francisco, they do an even longer cure, and their chicken is one of my favorites.

Another hit that came out of that short-staffed year was a breaded, deep-fried pork chop. With so few hands in the kitchen, deep-frying was easier than pan-frying. But if you had told me a few months earlier that I was going to be deep-frying a pork chop, I would've said that you were crazy—who deep-fries a pork chop? Well, we did.

Cooking meat was another example of stretching our dollars: I couldn't get the twenty-eight-day dry aged steaks; instead I was getting flatirons. And we were making those steaks taste like a million bucks.

Lobster ravioli (see page 179) was another example of kitchen ingenuity, though this was a display of stretching our already-empty wallet. A pricey appetizer, it allowed us to be creative with our ingredients and make them go a long way. People loved it—in the middle of recession, ordering lobster, even if it was a few pieces tucked into a few ravioli, felt luxurious and comforting. We added some white asparagus and a mix of morels and white button mushrooms, and, since lobster and corn were a natural fit, plated it over a corn-polenta puree. The liquid we cooked the lobster in was saved and would become lobster stock for other dishes (see page 385).

In the end, patrons were coming in and leaving very happy with their food. But I wanted to do even more; I just had to ride it out through this recession—I had to hang on.

It's Not Personal—It's Business

We took out more loans, constantly trying to figure out how to pay people, how to order food while having to explain to purveyors that we didn't have the money to pay them back, but that we would—in the future.

Some purveyors, like Dairyland (see page 403), LaFrieda (see page 249), and a guy named Andrea from this place called Litchfield Farms (now Community Catch; see page 82), trusted me and didn't pull their business even though, for a while, I owed them a *lot* of money. Others weren't as understanding or had less flexible balance sheets and pulled their business. A few even tried to sue me.

The purveyors who stuck with me said, "Look, even though you owe me money, I am still going to deliver you meat." "I know you owe us, but we'll still drop the fish off for you." Those who trusted me and didn't pull their business are still the purveyors I use to this day, and I plan to be with them until the very end. I don't hold a grudge against those vendors that had to stop dealing with us: It's not personal—it's business. But at the same time, I am particularly grateful to those who stayed and trusted us. At the end of the day, it's people dealing with other people, and it's really all about relationships. The purveyors who stuck by me treated me like a human being first and a client second. They showed a great deal of grace and humanity and I will forever be grateful to them. I can't ever properly tell them just how much their actions meant to me.

A Turning Tide

We got to the summer of 2009 and things were just dead; the restaurant was practically empty in August. It was costing us more to open the doors for a dishwasher, a waiter, and myself than to keep them closed. My cooks were in a tight spot: They needed the money but couldn't get another job because no one was hiring in the wake of the recession. At the same time, they were pulling *some* kind of a salary, while I was not paying myself anything. When you're running a business, *especially* if you're losing money, you're the last person to get paid.

Finally, in September, Blumlo and I sat down to have a tough conversation. We were looking at our numbers, and they were horrible—we owed a lot of money, and that amount was getting bigger and bigger. With tears in our eyes, we both came to the conclusion that it was probably best to sell the restaurant. I felt like I had failed—my dream was dying.

Around the same time, Danny Abrams had started coming in for dinner and finally approached me with an offer to do a restaurant swap. I was to take one of his restaurants in the West Village and he was going to take my space on Reade Street. We met up to discuss this several times, and everyone, including Blumlo, agreed that it was the best possible outcome. On the night of October 4, 2009, I sat down at home, wrote an informal offer letter, and went to bed.

I woke up the next day to find a voicemail on my cell phone. A man speaking in heavily French-accented English said, "Bonjour, Monsieur Forgione! I wanted to personally congratulate you and welcome you to the Michelin club. Your restaurant was awarded a star. Congratulations! We'd love for you to join us tonight for a celebratory glass of Champagne."

I replayed that voicemail several times—I simply couldn't believe it. I thought it was a prank and even called my old boss Laurent to make sure it wasn't him. "Hey man, was that you on the voicemail?" Laurent laughed, "No way! Congratulations! Go check the list—but that wasn't me!"

As soon as I realized that the voicemail, and therefore the Michelin star, was real, I knew my luck was changing. The tide was turning. Someone had noticed what we were doing and liked it enough to give us a star. I was on cloud nine.

As soon as I came to my senses, I immediately ripped up the offer I had typed the night before. I didn't want to go down in history as the only chef who got a Michelin star and sold his restaurant on the same day. I called Danny right away and explained the situation. And though he was disappointed that the swap wasn't happening but was happy for me. We ended our conversation on good terms; he understood where I was coming from and said he would've done the same thing had he been in my shoes.

That Michelin star was more than just a reward or a lifeline for me. It carried an important lesson: Stick to doing what you do best, don't deviate from the plan, and someone will notice. The Michelin critics did.

Right off the bat, we started doing ten more covers a day and there was more interest in the restaurant. And while we were still losing money, we were losing less of it.

It also felt a little gratifying to have the star: While everyone was telling me to change my menu, to "give

the people what they want," to adapt the food to the difficult times, I stood my ground and didn't change my approach to cooking. Offering hamburgers, everyone argued, would attract a wider clientele. The restaurant would be filled with people. And while on paper, their advice made sense, something about it felt off. Making hamburgers might have attracted more people, but I wasn't a hamburgers person. There's nothing wrong with a good burger, but that's just not who I was. I remember arguing with Blumlo, "Just because you put steak frites on the menu doesn't mean doors are gonna fly open." So I kept pushing back because I felt that serving burgers wouldn't change our bottom line— we'd be serving more people, but our profit margin would remain the same.

Bistro fare was not the answer, either. The answer was, all along, under our noses: Stick with what we were doing best. And pray. And if we were going to go down, at least we would go down fighting. The way I saw it was, "If you're going to kill me, do it, but I'm going to die trying."

I'm not patting myself on the back for having a "vision"—it just worked out the way that it did. But I'm glad that I listened to my gut and didn't change the menu; I'm glad that I stuck to cooking the food that I thought I was *meant* to be cooking. The same gut feeling I had when I first saw the restaurant space was what said to me, "Don't change a thing. Just keep doing what you're doing. Just keep doing it, and if it doesn't work, it just wasn't meant to be."

If I had wavered and changed the menu, I don't think we would've gotten that star. Someone noticed what we were doing and liked it; and I'm pretty sure that one of the things they noticed was that instead of buying twenty pounds of chopped meat and making twenty burgers, we were buying four lobsters and making twenty lobster dishes out of them. And instead of being stymied by our tight budget and growing debt, we tried to be creative and, for the most part, succeeded.

In retrospect, being put in this position, after having worked at Michelin- and *New York Times*–rated restaurants where creativity was not constrained by budgets, was one of the best professional challenges. Being creative with all the available resources is a lot easier than being creative on a tight budget.

Around the time when we got the star, Barry Frisch, one of my sous-chefs, joined our team. He was supposed to be with us only for a couple of months, but circumstances changed and he stayed with us indefinitely, which was a huge gain for us. The sous-chef before him had a drinking problem, so eventually I had to let the guy go. With Barry, and more hands in the kitchen, the food started to get a bit more intricate. But I still had only one day off, which, for me, was a day for sleeping and stressing out. And most likely nursing a hangover.

Looking within Myself

I was in a curious place in my life. I was thirty years old, a business owner, and I had just moved in with my girlfriend. All of a sudden, life got very serious, and I was finding it all a bit overwhelming. My friend Robbie suggested that I join him in taking part in some Native American rituals, and it sounded like a good idea. When I was growing up, my father was always very involved in Native American tradition and rituals, so in a way, it was always part of my life. I decided to go, thinking maybe it would help me figure things out.

We left the city and went to my friend Barnaby's house, where a teepee had been erected in the backyard. There were about twenty or thirty people as well as a shaman, who gave us some Native American medicine and began to pray—either to the grandmother or the grandfather spirits. As I listened to him, all these questions were swirling in my head. I was desperately searching for answers, feeling like I had arrived at a crossroads. *Can you handle all that's coming up? Can you step up to the plate? Or are you going to crumble?*

Every time I asked the grandfather or the grandmother what I was supposed to be doing, the answer was always the same: *Quit your whining. You got yourself this far. Wake up and keep on pushing through. You can do this.*

And I don't know what, specifically, worked, but these ceremonies, as I got more involved in them, really helped me emotionally and spiritually. In 2008 and a good part of 2009, I spent a lot of time beating myself up. I was at the point in my life where I needed deeper, more purposeful meaning. I questioned things so much that I started to doubt myself.

But these sessions propelled me forward and helped me draw strength from within. Instead of focusing on the external and the ephemeral, I was able to find strength inside myself. The answer in that teepee, as always, was just to look within myself. It was a powerful realization.

When I opened my restaurant, I was young and a bit ignorant of the realities of the world. Everything that happened during those two years had forced me to grow up really quickly. I had the biggest expectations of myself and the restaurant—and with the economy being what it was, what I was experiencing, while good, wasn't what I had envisioned. As 2009 drew to a close, we were finally becoming the restaurant I had imagined from day one. When we were raising money for the restaurant, I had no doubt in my mind that this is what it was going to be on opening day. But life has a funny way of humbling you and making you grow up really quickly!

2010

A Flurry of Activity

Of all the cooking shows out there, *The Next Iron Chef* was the one I wanted to be on. Ever since I saw the first season, which Chef Michael Symon won, I thought, *Wow, I'd love to get the opportunity to do that.* At the time the first season ended, I didn't think I was ready to do it, but as time went on I thought it would be a good challenge for me and would teach me a lot as a chef.

The spiritual work I had been doing for the past six months started to pay off sometime in March; I was beginning to understand myself a little better. The restaurant was moderately busy, especially given that it was winter; and I felt like I was finally getting a handle on my personal life.

In the spring, our pastry chef left and I was trying to do the pastries on my own, adding another responsibility to my plate. It was proving to be too much. At that time, one of our hostesses, whose nickname is Lady Ashton, asked me if she could bake me a chocolate cake (the recipe is on page 325). And with that chocolate cake—which was amazing by the way—she went from the front of the house as a hostess to the back of the house as a pastry chef. Which was great, because the restaurant was starting to get busier.

And then it happened: In early April, a Food Network talent scout called me for a phone interview—she said my name had come up for the third season of *The Next Iron Chef*. The scout asked me everything about my life: where I came from, with whom I've worked, why I loved food. It felt like a therapy session; it was actually kind of fun. I guess it went very well, because Food Network called me back and said that I had made it through the first round of auditions.

Round two was in the Food Network's offices in Chelsea. I walked into this dark room where they shone a light in my face. I couldn't really make out the faces behind the light, and questions were coming at me from every direction. When it was over, they just said to me, in a typical showbiz sort of way, "Thanks for coming in. We'll call you."

On my way out, I happened to glance at a piece of paper on the table that listed the names of the other chefs coming in to interview, and there were some big ones: Tourondel, Gütenbrunner, White—I was up against serious talent. I thought maybe I'd been brought in to be typecast as an upstart young kid.

I was told that casting decisions would be made by the time taping began on the Monday following Memorial Day, but by the third week of May, I still hadn't heard anything decisive. They kept saying, "Sorry to string you along, but we still don't know." I wasn't told no, but I wasn't told yes, either. It was a waiting game.

Sir, It Is Time for You to Leave My Restaurant

Meanwhile, the month of May was keeping us sufficiently busy. We weren't completely full, but we weren't empty either. The thing about 2010 was that no matter how bad of a night we had, it was still much better than any night we had in 2009. And then Ron Lieber came in, got kicked out of the restaurant, and wrote that infamous piece in the *New York Times*.

It was a Saturday night, still early. We had about six tables come in and we had put them in the back by the kitchen door. About ten amuse orders had come in, and the completed dishes took a really long time getting out of the kitchen. Meanwhile, I was showing the cook how to do one of the evening's appetizers, so I wasn't staying on top of the amuses. I came back around and saw the amuses still sitting there.

I was annoyed. "How the fuck did the amuses not leave already when the appetizers are ready to go?"

And one of my runners, who still works at the restaurant, bless his heart, responded, "You know, if *you* hadn't made the amuses so complicated, they *would* have gone out already."

I don't know, maybe he was having a bad day or something, but the response was so out of character for him. My entire kitchen staff was there—everyone suddenly grew quiet. That manner of addressing the chef, *especially* in front of the entire kitchen staff, was completely out of line.

So I started to yell and wave my arms—and in the process, slammed my hand on a table. And when I did that, the ticket rail that was filled with glass marbles fell. Suddenly, all you heard was this thundering sound of marbles falling everywhere. And in the midst of it all, some guy peeked his head into the kitchen and said, "Look, whatever you're yelling about in here, try to keep it down. We're not interested out there." And then he disappeared.

The kitchen grew even quieter. For a patron to come into a restaurant kitchen and discipline the chef is in and of itself pretty ballsy. But I kind of understood—what was going on in the kitchen was, admittedly, very loud.

I took a deep breath and calmed down a bit. The next few minutes are ones I'll never forget—they play in my mind like a movie reel. I remember thinking, *You could just stay here and cook the food, or you could go out there and say something.* It was as if I had a vision: I saw a road with two paths, stay or go out there. Something in my body, for whatever reason, said, *Go out there.*

I walked out into the dining room and headed for the table where the man was sitting—I wanted to offer an explanation and an apology to him and the other patrons in the dining room.

I hadn't planned on asking anyone to leave. But as I started to head in the direction of the man's table, I saw a woman, presumably his wife, start to gather her things. At the time I found it odd. "Sir," I said (I remember calling him "sir"), "just so you know, the

only reason I was getting upset in there is because I want to make sure that all your food is perfect."

He was facing away from me as I addressed him. He cut me off midsentence. Without even looking at me, he raised his hand inches away from my face as if to hush me. "Yeah, yeah, we're not interested." He still hadn't turned around to face me.

I clenched my fists as hard as I could, and took a deep breath. At this point I was staring hard at a spot on the wall.

"Okay, ladies and gentlemen," I finally managed to say, "you are all welcome to stay, but I'm not going to serve any food at this table while this gentleman is sitting here. *Sir*, it is time for you to leave my restaurant."

The man finally turned to look at me. "So *I* have to leave?"

"Yes. *You* have to leave."

He started to get up. Later on, in his article, he would write that my yelling, the scene that I caused, made the diners exchange uncomfortable glances,

Chef Stephen Wambach and Ian Rusnak finishing a dish

suggesting that his major concern was to keep the peace and ensure a pleasant dining experience. He was there, as he reminded me, paying money to eat, not to listen to me admonish my staff. But as he started to get up, he began, very loudly, to address the other patrons. "Oh, it looks like *I'm* the bad guy and *I* have to leave!" The dining room grew so quiet you could hear a pin drop.

We walked him out, and I went back to the kitchen; the rest of his table had also departed. I made midcourse dishes and special appetizers for the other five tables sitting in that section. I went around, sat at each table, and apologized for the scene that had unfolded. One table agreed with Ron Lieber: My yelling was ill-advised. Another table sided with me: I had a right to run my kitchen the way I saw fit. But we all talked about it, and there was a healthy, respectful discourse. By the end of the night it had sort of turned into a joke—"At least there was a good show while you were dining!"

After service ended that night, I bought a drink for the runner who had commented on the amuses, and we hugged it out.

The weekend came and went, but on Monday, I got a call at the restaurant from the *New York Times*. I got on the phone, and the voice on the other end said to me, "Hey, my name is Ron Lieber. You might not remember me, but I'm the guy you kicked out on Saturday night."

He paused, as if to give me a chance to apologize. Instead, I just said, "What's up, dude?"

"I'm writing an article on this incident . . . "

Right away I said to him, "I'm telling you, this is *not* a good idea to write that article. For either one of us. It's not going to come out right and *neither* one of us will look good at the end of this. It's just going to cause something stupid."

But we talked anyway—it was obvious he wanted to do the piece. I made it very clear to him that he got kicked out for one reason and one reason only: He was rude, out of line, and above all disrespectful to me in my kitchen. And where I come from, you never show disrespect to anyone in his own house.

At the end of our conversation, he asked me, if I could do it all over again, would I still do the same thing?

I didn't even pause. "Absolutely."

A few days later, Lieber's piece came out and went viral. It turned into a national debate. Within a few hours of being published, the piece garnered dozens if not hundreds of comments from all over the country—Wisconsin, California, Texas—it was a coast-to-coast discussion piece, and it happened instantly. Everyone threw their hat in: Some people were firmly in my camp, and others sided with Lieber, pledging never to set foot in my restaurant.

The piece, for the most part, didn't bother me, but what frustrated me was that I never got to tell my side of it, not on the same platform anyway. As a *New York Times* writer, Ron Lieber had a large, captive audience, and it didn't feel fair that while he had the opportunity to tell his side of the story, I never got the same opportunity to tell mine. What *would've* been fair is for the paper to have had us do point-counterpoint pieces side by side. But that didn't happen. Instead, it was a very personal piece, and it felt somewhat demeaning—Lieber wrote that he felt he was kicked out because my manhood suffered at his bravery. Instead, the piece clearly read as if he, himself, felt slighted and "smacked around," and because he is a writer for the behemoth *New York Times*, it was his duty to rein in the big bad chef who abuses his staff.

But that incident signaled a turning point for us at the restaurant. Everybody, at some point in their life, reaches a point (or several) when they make a decision that affects the rest of their life. Ninety-five percent of the people don't even realize what that point is. It just happens; they don't think about it.

I'm very lucky to know exactly when that instant occurred for me—it occurred at that very point in time, and I got to see it. It was simply a choice of staying in the kitchen or going out and clearing the air with Mr. Lieber. And I chose to go out there. But in looking back on the whole incident, that was the moment that changed so many things for me. In looking back, I *know* that was a defining moment for me. Maybe if I hadn't gone out there, he would have eaten his dinner, left, and never wrote about us in the *Times*. And then I wouldn't have gotten on the *The Next Iron Chef*, and maybe I wouldn't have written the book you are now holding in your hands. I feel lucky to be able to pinpoint that moment in my life.

For the record: Since we opened the restaurant, I've kicked out only four people. And all four times, Ron Lieber included, it was because the patrons were being disrespectful. One patron called my female manager a "cunt" and was asked to leave. Another time, a customer ordered a steak and sent it back because he said it was overcooked. We cooked him a new steak and sent it out. He sent it back again, citing the same issue, and as the waitress was heading back into the kitchen, said, "What, you're *so* stupid that you can't order a fucking steak? I don't know how you make it to work being as dumb as you are." He, too, was asked to leave. You get the idea.

The point I am trying to make here is I'm *not* Gordon Ramsay, and I didn't take cues from his show on how to treat my team. But at some point or another, each and every chef, from time to time, has to address his staff in a manner that might come across as stern. No matter how nice and calm you are, it just happens. The kitchen is a high-pressure area; everything moves quickly, and there's a lot happening. Sometimes tempers flare and people yell, but conflicts get resolved and life moves on.

I'm sure that as a result of the Lieber piece, we lost a few customers forever. That is unfortunate, but it is what it is. But immediately after the article came out, the restaurant started doing twenty to twenty-five more covers a night! At first we were worried that people might be coming in to try and get kicked out, but nobody acted up, and Lieber's article, ironically, wound up helping, instead of hurting, us. The month wound up flying by—and we were busy!

The Next Iron Chef

I finally found out that I was cast in *The Next Iron Chef* right before Memorial Day weekend. It felt very last minute, but I thought that was how it was supposed to happen. Later, I found out that the other chefs had known for months that they'd been cast. I still don't know if it was the Lieber incident that made me look like a more interesting contestant, but I got on the show, and the rest, as they say, is history.

So that Memorial Day Monday, I flew to Los Angeles to film the show. I told Barry, my sous-chef, that he couldn't take any days off until I came back. It could have been a week into filming or four weeks, depending on how long I lasted. The rule of *Next Iron Chef* was: You lost, you went home. Barry wound up working four weeks straight without a single day off.

Before I went to Los Angeles, my mom gave me some good advice. "Whatever the first thought is that comes to mind when you see the ingredients," she said, "go with that first thought. Go with your gut. You got to where you are by being you and listening to your gut. Don't stop being you." And I followed her advice. Every time I saw an ingredient, I'd close my eyes, and the first thing I saw, that's what I went with.

Being on the show was an incredibly intimidating, humbling experience. All of a sudden I was thrown into a competition with some of the country's top chefs. The first person I saw when I got there was Ming Tsai, and shortly thereafter I met everyone else. There were James Beard award winners, Michelin star recipients, and awards all over the place—a star-studded cast. From the very first battle, I felt like the dark horse. I won the second battle overall, and while it boosted my confidence, I didn't think I could win the whole thing. At the end of the show, people were telling me that they knew early on I would be there until almost the very end, if not *the* very end, but at the time, I just couldn't see it. I was just hoping that some exposure would help the restaurant. The lack of pressure to win might have been the best thing for me. It allowed me to take chances and shoot from the hip. Some of that helped me in the process, and some of it hurt me. But overall, it wound up working well for me. While others might have been agonizing that a certain decision might make or break their battle, and made safer choices in the end, I just went with my gut feeling. I wasn't playing not to lose; I was playing just to play.

At the semifinals, four chefs were left: Ming Tsai, Celina Tio, Marco Canora, and me. *This just might be possible,* I thought to myself. The theme of the battle was Las Vegas, where everyone received a luxury ingredient. The judges announced Marco Canora as the winner of that battle, so he moved up. Celina Tio didn't win, and immediately had to leave the room. So it was just Ming Tsai and me left with the judges. Up until that point, we all kind of thought that the show was set up to get Ming to win that season. It kind of made sense: Ming has all the accolades, a show, and was already a celebrity. So in my head I started to get ready to go, thinking, *I made it all the way to the semifinals—great showing anyway. This should really help the restaurant.*

And as Alton Brown started to announce the winner, I started to leave—I was convinced that I was the one who was going home. It took a few seconds to register that I had won the semifinals and was staying for the final round. It was only at that point that it occurred to me, for the first time, that I could actually win this whole thing.

The theme of the final battle was "Honor," specifically Thanksgiving. All ten battles on the show had theme words associated with them. When I heard the word "honor," I immediately interpreted it as, literally, "honoring the Pilgrims and the Native Americans" who came together for the very first Thanksgiving meal. When they announced it, I felt as if I had found the golden ticket. As cheesy as it might sound, the year leading up to this competition had been the toughest of my life, and what had helped me through it all was attending the Native American rituals. Without a second thought, I decided that this battle was my

Just found out I won

opportunity to do something to honor the Native Americans who have given me so much comfort during a tough time. Instead of what we now consider a traditional Pilgrim-influenced Thanksgiving meal, I wanted to do something that reflected the people who were here before the Europeans arrived.

I did some research about the very first Thanksgiving. Surprisingly, we know quite a bit about it because a gentleman by the name of Edward Winslow meticulously documented it in a letter he wrote to England describing the dinner.

I decided to take all the ingredients present at that meal: huckleberries, cornmeal, duck, venison, squash, and such, and get rid of what we think of as traditional Thanksgiving dishes. There was no cranberry sauce, turkey, or mashed potatoes—none of those were present at the first Thanksgiving. The year 1621, was, in fact, the year potatoes arrived on the shores of what is now the United States, but they weren't at the feast. Instead, the Pilgrims and the Native Americans shared sweet potatoes. The original Thanksgiving meal would feel untraditional to the modern palate. It was a big risk—but one I was willing to take.

To put it in baseball terms, this is how I saw it: You're a baseball player, it's the bottom of the ninth, and the pitches are coming down the middle. You could probably win with a bunt, if you wanted to, but you feel like you could hit that home run, so you just swing for it. If you miss it, everybody hates you and blames you for taking that risk. But if you hit the ball out of the ballpark—well, then you're a legend!

After we presented our dishes before the judges, they locked themselves away for three hours to deliberate. Those were the slowest three hours of my life; the suspense was killing me and Marco. Finally, after what seemed like an eternity, they brought us back to announce the winner. When they pulled down the curtain, and the picture behind it was of my face—my knees buckled and I would have fallen had my chefs not caught me. Tears were coming out of my eyes, and I was grinning from ear to ear like a five year old. I couldn't believe I had won. After two of the hardest years of my life, to win this competition and to feel such euphoria and joy was overwhelming.

My family had the opportunity to watch the finale as it was taping, but were not allowed to hear the results. The evening after the finale was taped, I had to stay behind to hear the judges' decision, and once it was done I headed to the Gansevoort Hotel where my family was waiting for me.

I walked into the Gansevoort and found my entire family completely and over-the-top drunk. My mother was reading tarot cards in the bathroom; my sister was drunk and crying. They couldn't take the stress of waiting, so they just went on a bender. When I walked in, I had my shoulders shrugged, the kind of body language that suggested I had just lost. And then they all rushed over to hug me and everybody just started crying. And I said quietly to the group, as we were all holding one another, "You know, I don't understand why everybody's

COAST to COAST
WINE & DINE DINNER
NOVEMBER 15, 2011

BRAD FARMERIE
SEA URCHIN CUSTARD, LOBSTER, LIME, CAVIAR

RAJAT PARR
2009 SANDHI "SANFORD AND BENEDICT" CHARDONNAY, SANTA RITA HILLS

· · · · · · · · · ·

JOHN FRASER
GLAZED SWEETBREADS, CRISPY TÊTE DE VEAU, BURGUNDY TRUFFLES, BRUSSELS SPROUTS, CREAM OF WHEAT

ANDY ERICKSON
2007 ERICKSON WINES "CERRO SUR" CABERNET FRANC EN MAGNUM, NAPA VALLEY

· · · · · · · · · ·

MISSY ROBBINS
CAPRINO AND RICOTTA GNOCCHI, GOAT BUTTER, WHITE TRUFFLES

JAMEY WHETSTONE
2008 WHETSTONE WINE CELLARS "BELLA VIGNE" PINOT NOIR, SONOMA COAST

· · · · · · · · · ·

JUSTIN BOGLE
HAWAIIAN ESCOLAR, MATSUTAKE, PERSIMMON, FOIE GRAS CONSOMMÉ

EHREN JORDAN
2007 FAILLA WINES "MONUMENT TREE" CHARDONNAY EN MAGNUM, ANDERSON VALLEY

· · · · · · · · · ·

MARC FORGIONE
VENISON, BOUDIN NOIR, CHESTNUTS, GOLDEN RAISIN GASTRIQUE

HELEN KEPLINGER
2007 KEPLINGER WINES "RED SLOPE" GRENACHE EN MAGNUM, KNIGHTS VALLEY

· · · · · · · · · ·

ASHTON WARREN
BANANA BREAD PUDDING HOUSE-INFUSED BANANA JAMO

· · · · · · · · · ·

RICHARD BETTS
SOMBRA MEZCAL, CLEMENTINE, MINT

FEEDING AMERICA

crying. Winning isn't that sad of a thing." As soon as they heard that, my mom started howling like a coyote and security had to actually escort her out of the hotel. My brother ordered more shots. And that is when my dad grabbed me and we went outside.

Now, it's fair to say that my father isn't the most communicative or emotionally open guy—with me or anyone else—but he was clearly moved by what he saw me do in the kitchen stadium. Plus, he was a little drunk. At some point, he pulled me close and said, "While I was watching you present your food, for the first time in my life I felt like I was watching a man, and not just my son. I'm so proud of you." And then my father started to cry. So, in turn, I started to cry. There we were, grabbing one another by the back of the head, our foreheads together, sobbing and hugging. At some point, a homeless guy wandered over to us. He stared at us crying and hugging and finally said, "I just want to tell you guys both, I've been homeless for seventeen years, and I haven't seen my son or daughter in twenty. And after seeing what I just saw, I think I'm going to go and find them. God bless you both." And he walked away.

The next morning, I woke up with an unfamiliar feeling of lightness and calm. It was the first time in my professional life as a chef running my own restaurant, that I woke up without a knot in my stomach.

Instead, I realized I was smiling. Though slightly hungover and achy from celebratory drinks with my family, I felt this unfamiliar-to-me sense of calm. I felt weightless, as if, for the past two years I had been walking around with an eight-ton elephant on my back, and, suddenly, it was gone. I found myself pacing back and forth in my apartment, swinging my arms around, feeling light and free. It was the first day that I knew the restaurant was going to be alright.

I went out for coffee, skipping down the street and whistling. That day I walked all over the city, just smiling to myself and saying hello to people on the street. Feeling spontaneous, I decided to get tattoos to commemorate my win and added the number *1621*, the year of the first Thanksgiving, to both of my arms.

While I wanted to share my exciting news with others, under contract rules I couldn't tell anyone I had won until the season finale aired. So for months, I had to walk around with this huge secret. I returned to the restaurant, and life was back to the usual grind. We still had bills to pay, and I had a restaurant to run. When you win the *Next Iron Chef* battles, you get some money as a reward. Each and every one of those checks went straight into the restaurant—every single penny. As soon as it would reach me, I'd give it to Blumlo, who would deposit it in our bank and pay some bills. It wasn't glamorous but it felt great to know

Something to remember the victory with

the restaurant, and our restaurant family, were going to be okay. When the show aired in the fall, we set up Sunday night *Next Iron Chef* viewing parties at the restaurant, with a big-screen television and everything—it was fun to watch it all together with our patrons.

In looking back, *The Next Iron Chef* was, *by far*, the hardest, most intense cooking challenge I've ever had. I met some immensely talented people and made some lasting friendships. But it was a grueling four weeks: You lived, breathed, and exhaled food and nothing but food without a break. It was physically *and* mentally draining; you were always thinking about what you were cooking next. While I was there, I couldn't really call my restaurant or my girlfriend. I was allowed to, but I was having a hard time talking to people not involved in the competition. It was four weeks of being totally consumed by everything having to do with the show—everything was *Iron Chef*. I had to pretty much shut myself off from the rest of the world.

And without a doubt, competing on the show, against such immensely talented chefs, made me a much better, more resourceful, and more inventive cook. It made me even more fearless in the kitchen, and the dishes that followed after the competition ended and I got back to New York, showed that fearlessness. Something happened to my brain during the competition; something opened up creativity-wise, and it hasn't shut down since.

When you are forced out of your comfort zone, when you are required to think fast, you either rise to the occasion or crash and burn. For me, it was akin to a spiritual awakening and by far the best thing that has ever happened to me as a chef. It gave me the courage to say, "Fuck it! I can try *anything* I want to."

So much of cooking is about confidence, and when I was starting out on my own as a chef and tried to take risks with my food during the recession, people were pushing back. Just as no one wanted to take risks with their finances at the time, no one wanted to take risks with food. Everyone wanted to eat the old standbys, the well-known comfort dishes: steak, mashed potatoes, roasted chicken. In winning the *Iron Chef* title, the confidence, and morale, of everyone at the restaurant, especially myself, was growing again. The restaurant started to fill up, we started to take more risks with our food—and our patrons were loving it.

Sam Sifton, the Everyman

Fall snuck up on us after a fairly busy summer. I was at home getting ready for a business trip to Orlando one evening, about to sit down to dinner—solo—when my phone rang. It was Blumlo: "Sam Sifton just sat down."

Sam Sifton was then the dining critic for the *New York Times*. And he was sitting down to eat at the restaurant—I had to be there! I grabbed my keys and rushed over to the restaurant. At the end of the night, I felt as if the evening had gone very well. *Thank God we didn't miss him*, I thought. We made him some great food and noted what he ate.

The following day I was already in Orlando, and Sifton called me on my cell. "I'm publishing a review of the restaurant next week and just wanted to fact-check a few things."

And then he proceeded to ask me detailed questions about food I couldn't remember him eating the night before, until I finally said, "*When* did you have time to eat all that stuff?" And that's when he laughed. "You'd be very surprised to learn how long I've been coming to your restaurant and enjoying it." There was a pause before he continued, "Don't worry about not recognizing me—most people don't catch me."

How the fuck did we miss him?

One of the things that made Sam Sifton a perfect restaurant critic is that he has that everyman look about him and blends in easily with the crowd. He had probably been coming in for four or five months before anyone caught on. But in retrospect, I'm glad we didn't know he was there. We served him the same way we served everyone else, and he wrote a great review of the restaurant.

At the restaurant, I preach excellence with every single dish. Every single dish has to go out and be perfect. Not just the dish for the Sam Siftons of the world, or your mom, or your girlfriend. *Every. Single. Dish.* When Ruth Reichl donned her disguises and went around reviewing restaurants as an everyday person, she uncovered a systemic problem that restaurants, particularly fine dining establishments, had: If you were somebody with power, the red carpet was rolled out for you; but if you were a nobody, your meal could've been good, or average, or maybe even subpar. Because there was no reason, no incentive for the restaurant to impress you, or maybe because some of those restaurants thought that the average person couldn't tell the difference between great food and mediocre food. I wanted everyone, each paying customer, to have an amazing experience at my restaurant—every patron deserved that.

And for that very reason, we didn't then, and still don't, have special food that we set aside for our "special" diners. Because we believe that every person paying money for their meal, wanting a good dinner, is special. We don't have VIP steaks or fish—everything is the same for everybody. We want someone like Sam Sifton, who has a great deal of influence, to be treated in the same manner as any regular person with no influence at all coming in to eat at the restaurant. The review was a testament to the way we work. He could have been waited on by any server, any cook, any manager. We don't have a special busboy or waiter. We don't have a general manager managing the wine for VIPs. Everyone gets the same treatment.

So the fact that we got such a great review and had no idea that Sifton was coming in all along stood as a testament to the religion I preached and continue to preach in my kitchen: Cook every dish as if you're cooking your last. You can ask any of my line cooks—the food does not go out unless it's done the way it's *supposed* to be done.

Most new restaurants in New York get reviewed within three months of opening. Here's what happens: A famous chef opens a new restaurant, and spends three months there with his corporate manager, corporate chef, corporate sommelier—the works. Everyone from the *Village Voice* to the *New York Times* reviews them in that three-month time frame, and then the whole corporate team ships out for a new venture. We got reviewed several years after opening—that's a bit unusual.

Lonny Sweet + Cassie Pallas

Marc + Little Hawk

The week the *New York Times* review came out was dubbed the Magic Week. From Sunday through Friday of that week, something amazing and positive happened every single day for the restaurant. On Sunday *The Next Iron Chef* premiered, and I had been introduced to the world as Chef Marc Forgione. On Monday, we learned that we had retained our Michelin star for a second year. On Tuesday, *Zagat* raised us two points in food. On Wednesday, the *New York Times* review came out. On Thursday, I was named a Rising Star for Star Chefs. And on Friday, we were at Taste of the Greenmarket and everyone was coming over to say hello and congratulations on the *New York Times* review. And since that week (knock on wood), the restaurant has never been slow.

A few nights before we did the *Next Iron Chef* finale party, I had asked my good friend Little Hawk, a powerful medicine man of the Cherokee tribe, to come and bless the entire restaurant and, specifically, this one corner of the room, where we were having some trouble. The corner of the room in question, for whatever reason, Table 34 in particular, was just a magnet for hostility: that's where Ron Lieber sat; it's where people would frequently get into disagreements. And I knew that once the word got out that I had won *The*

Next Iron Chef, the restaurant was going to get busy and I didn't want any additional problems. So I invited Little Hawk to bless the entire space, and in particular that corner. He blessed the restaurant that day; it was a beautiful and moving ceremony. And since that day, that corner of the room has been problem-free. Call it what you will, but there's been no negativity there since.

For the actual party, Little Hawk brought a freshly killed deer, which I thought was a funny coincidence because for battle Thanksgiving on *The Next Iron Chef* I made a venison loin (see page 264) as part of the meal.

"Look," he said to me, "your life is about to change, and for the better, too." I never uttered a word of my win to him, but he just knew. "But before we do all that, before the party starts, I want to teach you how to skin a deer." And in the kitchen he went. It was a humbling moment for me. *Remember where you come from,* Little Hawk was saying. *Don't lose sight of who you are.*

We skinned the deer together and made a venison chili out of the meat. Every bit of the animal went to use; not a scrap was wasted. Even the skull was saved and now graces the restaurant as a memento. Right before the party began, Little Hawk gave me a necklace, which I haven't taken off since. The necklace's symbol reminds me to reach for the stars but also to stay grounded.

In mid-November we hired another sous-chef, Chris Zabita, and a few more cooks, and I became more involved in running the restaurant and not just being in the kitchen. We started to pay purveyors on time, buy the china that we needed, and finally purchase chef coats. We were fixing stuff that needed to be fixed. On Sunday nights, we threw *The Next Iron Chef* viewing parties, which doubled our covers. And in 2010, thanks to an amazing fourth quarter, the restaurant actually showed a profit. It wasn't a huge profit, but it was enough for us to cheer when we saw it on the balance sheet. When you go from losing money for a year and a half to having a gain, even a small one is cause for celebration! We had come a long way.

Around that time I also met Lonny Sweet, who became my agent. Who would've thought that a line cook from Long Island would eventually have an agent? Certainly not me. Without him, many things would not have happened. Without Lonny, you would not be reading this book right now.

2011

A Well-Oiled Machine

2011 was the year when we finally became the restaurant we had always wanted to become. We had enough hands on deck that people could take time off. We were paying back our investors, paying our purveyors on time, and paying our staff without worrying that our checks might bounce. The restaurant was finally running like a well-oiled machine; it had a rhythm all its own. We hired a meat cook, which means I was finally off the line and was able to focus on expediting and managing the process of getting the food ready and out the door. Finally, we had time to finish the food at the pass; we set up a whole station with finishing oils, salts, and micro greens, and it made a huge difference.

We were busy every single day of the week. On any given night I'd walk around the dining room and meet diners from all across the country: Texas, California, Wisconsin, Pennsylvania. They weren't just visiting New York; they were especially coming to New York to eat at one or two restaurants, and we were *one of the two*! We had become a destination.

We finally got around to putting together our Classics Tasting Menu. The first day we unrolled the menu, we got about twenty-five orders of the tasting menu in one night. I remember that number because it hasn't been that high since, and anyone who has ever cooked at, or run, a restaurant, will know how difficult it is to coordinate twenty-five tasting menus while also serving people who are ordering à la carte. It was a crazy night in the kitchen.

As we grew in popularity, people started to trust me more with cooking unusual things. I don't know if it was because I had won the *Iron Chef* title, but dishes that weren't selling before I won started to appeal to our patrons. We added snails, sweetbreads, and tongue to the menu, and we got to be more playful with dishes like Foie Gras Elvis Presley (see page 284) and Buffalo Tartare with Hottish Sauce (see page 226). We started to experiment with the sous-vide technique: Veal Tenderloin wrapped in blood sausage (see page 255) was one of the dishes that resulted.

One of our most popular dishes, Tortellini d'Avanzi (see page 182) was created that year. The tortellini was a combination of a little kitchen ingenuity and a strong desire to treat all our ingredients with respect. One night, we wound up with some leftover veal breast confit. The following morning when I came in, there was a note from one of my sous-chefs, Barry: "Hey, I made these tortellini. No idea what to do with them, but they taste good, so let me know what you think." Apparently, that morning, Barry took a look at the leftover veal and thought it might make a decent ravioli filling. Drizzled with truffle-infused balsamic vinegar, it was, in fact, very, *very* good. So good, in fact, that we put it on the menu that same night. One of our investors happened to be in for dinner that evening, and

after tasting the tortellini, he declared them to be the best piece of pasta he'd ever put in his mouth. It was his idea to tell everybody to eat the tortellini in one bite with the mushroom and the Parmesan.

That year we were also able to give something back to the community. One night we organized a benefit at the restaurant called Coast to Coast to raise money for Feeding America, a leading domestic hunger-relief charity. We got five winemakers from California together with five New York Michelin-starred chefs: Justin Bogle (Gilt), Brad Farmerie (Public), Missy Robbins (A Voce), John Fraser (Dovetail), and me. Each chef made a dinner course at the restaurant and paired it with one of the California wines. The dinner was wildly successful, and we raised over forty thousand dollars.

We grew our network of purveyors and started working with folks like Foraged and Found Edibles (see page 298), who supply us with foraged (and found) wood sorrel, stinging nettles, fiddlehead ferns, ramps, chanterelles, porcini, and the like; and Møsefund, who raise amazing Mangalitsa pork (see page 287). I was introduced to the Mangalitsa breed after *The Next Iron*

Chef, and I just fell in love with the fat, which tastes incredible even when raw. I met Joe Jurgielewicz (see page 209) and was introduced to his amazing white Pekin duck—the best duck I've ever had, and what we now serve at the restaurant.

That summer, Barry went away to France to do an apprenticeship. When he first sat down with me to discuss it, he was very nervous; he didn't want to come across as not committed to working at the restaurant. When I realized what he was asking, I cut him off. "If you don't go, you're fired," I said. Instead of hiring someone else to fill in for him, I picked up his shift and was "back in the shit," as they say, doing all the ordering and closing just like in the early days of the restaurant. While Barry was in Europe, Chris Zabita got to step up and take on more responsibility, which was great for him, because now he and Barry are co-sous-chefs and help each other out.

It was important to me that Barry was learning and growing in his career, and an apprenticeship in another country was a sure way to accomplish that. Not so long ago, it used to be common practice for chefs to apprentice abroad, but for some reason, unfortunately, it doesn't happen all that often anymore. I tell people all the time that if they want to be serious chefs, they need to go and apprentice in another country—France, Italy, wherever. Not because they cook better than we do here, but because when you're by yourself in an environment like that, you grow up really fast. When you're in your head for an extended period, when you put yourself in an alien environment where they don't speak English and you're struggling with their language, when you stay quiet for three-plus months—*you learn a lot about yourself.*

Cook Your Food. Stay in Your Kitchen.

I suddenly found out that once you get on television, you get pulled in a lot of different directions. Consult here; open this there; do this with us; come see this. There's nothing wrong with consulting and nothing wrong with putting your name on something. It's natural to want to create your own brand and put your mark on the world. If you're ambitious, you are always reaching higher and higher. But when you are asked to consult on something in Tucson, Arizona, what does it *really* have to do with you? You are here, they are there. What business do you have with them?

I had to say no to a dozen things before I said yes to one. In the fall of 2011, I started working on a steakhouse in Atlantic City, called American Cut. The name was a partial nod to my father and An American Place. The steakhouse seemed like a natural extension of what I was already doing. I knew that eventually I'd want to open up my own steakhouse. I had opened a few while working with BLT, so I knew how a steakhouse was run, and I had what I thought were cool ideas about how to elevate it. It was just a matter of finding the right fit. When the Revel resort group came to me with their plans, it immediately felt right. Everything about that idea sounded great. Taking part in something as monumental and exciting as the Revel

Atlantic City project felt like the right move, and it helped that AC was close to home—not far away like Vegas or Miami. I didn't want to be far from the restaurant I worked so hard to keep.

I know that some chefs, from the get-go, dream of building an empire. And maybe it sounds dumb, but my whole professional life, the *only* thing I ever wanted to do is have my own restaurant. I wasn't averse to opening a few, but it wasn't the goal—the goal was just the one. And now that I *had* my restaurant, and finally had it *just* the way I wanted it, and it was finally working the way it *should* be working, everybody suddenly wanted to pull me *out* of it to do something else! I wanted to yell, "Look! I'm *finally* here, and now you want me to leave?" It felt like the most ironic thing in the world.

And the thing I heard the most in 2011 from patrons was, "I can't believe you're still *here*!" Where else was I supposed to be? I just wanted to keep working in my restaurant and continue to make it better.

So what I really want to say to the young people who are interested in becoming chefs is this: Once you finally get where you want to be success-wise, take a minute to just enjoy it. Be in your restaurant. Cook your food. Stay in your kitchen. Stay there for a while.

If you want to be famous, go be famous. But *stay in your kitchen.* If you do that, if you focus on cooking *your* food, I am pretty certain that good things will happen.

I'm not suggesting that you stay in your kitchen, on the line, indefinitely. There will be a time when you can step back a bit, manage the actual restaurant a little more, have time on your hands to think about where your business is going, think about it all strategically.

With the popularity of cooking television channels and shows, and America's renewed interest in food (all good things, by the way), the food industry has become glamorous and alluring. I think people may forget just how much work, sacrifice and dedication goes into this business. I often hear of people who want to skip the hard work part, get to the "celebrity" part so they do not have to be in the kitchen anymore. But that is not "making it." "Making it" in this business is being *in* the kitchen. The names that are known today—Keller, Jean-Georges, Wylie, Grant, Symon, Carmellini, Bloomfield, Kahan, Boulud—I don't have space to list everyone I can think of. These chefs are who they are because they *stayed* in their kitchens and *cooked* their food. They didn't chase the fame; they focused on the trade they chose because they loved the work, loved the precision, loved being the best in their field. They loved their trade and worked hard (and *still* do) every day to get better and better at it.

And here's the thing—if you want to do this for a living, if you want to pick this difficult (to put it mildly) life, be on your feet all day, work twelve- to fourteen-hour days, give up weekends and holidays, you need to ask yourself, "*Why* do I cook?" I'm already assuming that you love to cook, so skip that part. Ask yourself what motivates you, every day, to cook. What drives you, what challenges you, what inspires you?

Don't cook like you're afraid to get in trouble. It'll show. Don't play it safe in an attempt not to fail—that, also, will show. If you are cooking "to get by" or you're playing it safe, go do something else.

One night a while back, I was showing one of my cooks how to cook a fish. I said, "This is how I want the final result to look. See that crispy skin? *That's* how I want it. But don't do it for *me*—do it because *you* want to figure out how to get that skin crispy. I can show you how I do it, but then it's up to *you* to make sure that every single piece of fish after this one ends up like this. Don't do it my way only because you're afraid to get in trouble. Do it because *you* want to make the *best* piece of fish with the crispiest skin."

The young kids who will be successful . . . you can recognize those kids right off the bat. And I don't think that's just in cooking—the same goes for anything in life. If you were to ask Jean-Georges Vongerichten, I guarantee you that when he was sixteen years old, he looked around the kitchen and said, "I'm going to be the best one in this kitchen today. And tomorrow. And the day after tomorrow." I *guarantee* it. I've been cooking professionally since I was seventeen years old, and it's *always been* a competition—with nobody else but myself.

Cook to show the world that you know how and that you're not afraid of taking risks. Show the world that you can do it. Don't ask for approval—just cook. Cook every night like you are the best on the line. Cook every single dish like it's your last. And be grateful for each and every blessing.

And remember to never stop challenging yourself and those you work with. Complacency, especially in this business, is dangerous, and brings about the death of many restaurants, particularly those in food-focused cities like New York. Even though we are now busy and popular, we still push and challenge ourselves every single day. By the time you hold this book in your hands, we will have created dozens of new recipes and explored new techniques. The second you stop trying to accomplish something, you might as well close the doors, because you're not going anywhere. The second you become stagnant, you're done. There are a thousand other chefs who want to take your place. A restaurant is a constantly evolving, growing, living, breathing thing—treat it as such. And stay hungry for knowledge. Never stop learning, ever. But also be grateful for what you have.

Every day, I meditate; I burn sage and I give thanks. I thank the universe for my great fortunes. When I come into my kitchen and look at my cooks—I have twenty now—I think about how far we've come. I walk around the dining room and say thank you to people. I thank them for coming in, say hello, shake their hand, give them a hug. Because in a city where you can go *anywhere* for dinner, they chose to come *here* and eat my food. And for that, I am genuinely grateful.

JULIE FORGIONE, MARC'S MOTHER

Marc's mother, Julie, tested a lot of the recipes in this book. Here are her thoughts.

At the beginning, when I started testing Marc's recipes, I often found myself stressed out and overwhelmed. Making the dishes required a thorough reading of the recipes and some thinking about them ahead of the cooking. I was stressing over finding the right ingredients and getting the techniques just right. When I got the first set of recipes to test, my first thought was, *Well, gosh, if he'd just made them easier, less laborious, or offered more substitutes—life would be so much easier.* But then I realized something: What would that be accomplishing?

Once I got past a handful of recipes, I started to get more comfortable with what was coming next for testing. I even commented to Marc, "You know, I'm starting to get to know you in a whole different way, as a chef and with what you're trying to do with these recipes!"

Once you get to know the recipes, you realize that you can make changes if you need to and not be so stressed out by it, which is what Marc is trying to accomplish. He's giving you recipes that show you the way he thinks, and once you get that, they are easy to adapt—if you wish to leave a few things out, you can do so.

Some recipes are just fun. Everyone, even a beginner, should be able to make them. Pasta, for example, is something that everyone can make. I had so much fun testing the pasta

recipes. I hadn't made pasta in years, because living in New York, there is always a lot of good fresh pasta around. But I wanted the recipes to work for people like me, home cooks who might be intimidated by the recipes, so I tested the pasta recipes over and over until I got them just right.

Marc's cooking is definitely technique driven, and now that I have these techniques down, there are recipes I keep going back to. Now that I have a larder of these wonderful oils and spices, as well as the techniques I've learned, cooking is so much more fun and rewarding. I love making risotto (see page 147) and caponata (see

page 89), to name just a few. I also regularly make chimichurri (see page 242) and tomato consommé (see page 170). While before I'd never think of draining tomato water, people loved the results so much that I love making it now.

The feeling of accomplishment when you get a dish done is just amazing. And it was fun to get the family involved and bring everyone together in the kitchen. Once you master a few dishes, you, too, will feel empowered, like you can do the next dish, and the next dish, and the next. You will be fearless in the kitchen—which is a pretty good way to be, I think.

TO AMUSE

"A small plate is to an entrée as a poem is to a novel: more deliberately composed, more specific in tone and focus, void of any unnecessary components, and crafted with care to reflect one complete idea—or taste. When done right, an artful bite can tell a more vivid story than an entire plate. As a chef, that's a tantalizing challenge."

—JOSE GARCES

POTATO ROLLS

MAKES ABOUT 22 ROLLS The bread at the restaurant was something we put a lot of thought into. I feel that the bread "course" at a good restaurant really sets the stage for your meal. It can't be an afterthought—it has to be at the same level as the rest of your food. The final three ideas for the bread were: soft pretzel rods with three mustards, black pepper brioche muffins with caramelized onion butter, and potato rolls with sea salt and butter. We found that the combination of the potato rolls with the caramelized onion butter was the best. So thank you, Jenny McCoy, for the amazing recipe.

FOR THE CARAMELIZED ONION BUTTER

Canola oil

1 Vidalia onion, thinly sliced

1 pound unsalted butter, room temperature

3 tablespoons chopped fresh chives

3 tablespoons chopped fresh curly parsley

Flaky sea salt, such as Maldon

FOR THE POTATO ROLLS

6¾ ounces Yukon Gold potatoes, peeled

1 large egg, room temperature

1 tablespoon powdered yeast

1 tablespoon whole milk

2 cups all-purpose flour, plus more as needed

1½ tablespoons granulated sugar

1¼ teaspoons kosher salt

1½ ounces (3 tablespoons) unsalted butter, cut into several pieces, plus additional melted butter for brushing rolls

Flaky sea salt, such as Maldon

MAKE THE CARAMELIZED ONION BUTTER

1. Place just enough oil in a 3-quart saucepot to cover the bottom of the pan and set the skillet over high heat. Just before the oil starts to smoke, add the onion to the pot. Reduce the heat to medium and cook until the natural sugars in the onion have caramelized (add a little water from time to time if the onion begins to stick). Transfer the onion to a food processor and process until smooth. Transfer the onion puree to a fine-mesh strainer set over a bowl and set a light weight, such as a can, on top of the onion to press out any excess liquid. Let the puree cool.

2. Place the puree in a bowl of a stand mixer fitted with the paddle attachment and add the butter, chives, and parsley. Mix on high speed until completely combined. Transfer the Caramelized Onion Butter to a pastry bag or a resealable bag with one corner snipped off, and pipe the butter into small butter dishes. Top with a sprinkle of flaky sea salt. Cover and refrigerate until needed. The butter can be made up to 1 week ahead of time.

MAKE THE POTATO ROLLS

3. Place the potatoes in a large pot and add enough water to generously cover them. Bring the water to a boil over high heat and cook the potatoes until fork-tender, 15 to 20 minutes. Drain the potatoes, and while they are still warm, peel them and pass them through a ricer. Allow the potatoes to cool completely.

4. In the bowl of a stand mixer fitted with the paddle attachment, combine the cooled potatoes, egg, yeast, and milk. Mix on medium-low speed until well combined.

5. In a medium bowl, whisk together the flour, sugar, and kosher salt, and add the dry ingredients to the potato mixture. Replace the paddle attachment on the mixer with the dough hook, and knead on medium-low speed for 5 to 7 minutes or until the dough is pliable and elastic (when you try to rip a piece off, it will stretch before it tears). Add the butter, and continue to mix with the dough hook until the butter is fully incorporated. If the dough is still sticky, add additional flour as needed, a little bit at a time, just until the dough is smooth.

6. Preheat the oven to 350°F; position the rack in the middle. Line 2 baking sheets with a Silpat or parchment paper.

7. Form the dough into balls slightly larger than a golf ball, about 1½ ounces, and place them 3 inches apart on the lined baking sheets. Allow the dough to proof until the rolls have doubled in size, 45 minutes to 1 hour.

8. Bake the rolls for 7 minutes, rotate the trays front to back, and continue baking for 3 minutes more or until the rolls are golden brown. Brush the rolls with some melted butter and sprinkle with flaky sea salt. Serve immediately (see Note) with the Caramelized Onion Butter on the side.

Note *These rolls are best right out of the oven, brushed with some melted butter and sprinkled with sea salt. If you need to reheat the rolls, place them in a 375°F oven for 3 to 4 minutes or until warm, then brush them with melted butter and sprinkle with sea salt.*

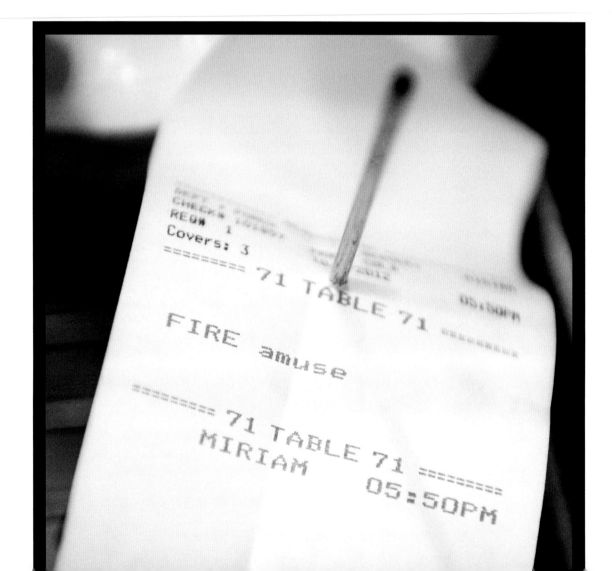

"EVERYTHING BAGELS"

MAKES 40 GOUGÈRES A few years ago, Barry Frish, one of my sous-chefs, did a *stage* at Le Chateaubriand, in France. There he mastered the art of making the perfect *gougère* (a savory pastry with cheese). I doubt that in France they would turn a *gougère* into a play on an everything bagel, but hey, we're not in France.

FOR THE EVERYTHING SPICE MIX

2 tablespoons onion flakes

2 tablespoons garlic flakes

¼ cup sesame seeds

¼ cup poppy seeds

2 tablespoons flaky sea salt, such as Maldon

FOR THE VEGETABLE CREAM CHEESE

8 ounces cream cheese, softened

2 tablespoons minced red onion

3 tablespoons coarsely grated carrots

2 tablespoons chopped fresh chives

FOR THE GOUGÈRES

128 grams (9 tablespoons) unsalted butter, cut into pieces

160 grams all-purpose flour

7 grams kosher salt

5 large eggs, room temperature

267 grams whole milk

100 grams finely grated Parmigiano-Reggiano

20 grams granulated sugar

MAKE THE EVERYTHING SPICE MIX

1. Place the onion and garlic flakes into a food processor fitted with a metal blade. Pulse until the mixture is finely ground and resembles the topping on everything bagels. Transfer to a large bowl and combine with the sesame seeds, poppy seeds, and flaky sea salt.

MAKE THE VEGETABLE CREAM CHEESE

2. Place the cream cheese and onion in a food processor fitted with a metal blade. Pulse until the mixture is well combined and the cream cheese is smooth. Transfer the mixture to a bowl and fold in the carrots and chives. Transfer the mixture to a pastry bag fitted with a metal tip large enough to pipe the filling through. Set aside or refrigerate until needed. If refrigerating, allow the pastry bag to sit at room temperature for 10 to 15 minutes to warm up a bit before using.

MAKE THE GOUGÈRES

3. Preheat the oven to 350°F; position a rack in the middle. Line 2 baking sheets with parchment paper.

4. In a medium saucepan set over medium-high heat, combine the butter and 1 cup of water and bring to a boil. Reduce the heat to low and add the flour and salt. Cook the batter for 3 to 5 minutes, stirring constantly, until it turns into a thick paste and no longer sticks to the sides of the pan.

5. Transfer the batter to the bowl of a stand mixer fitted with the paddle attachment. Mix on low speed, incorporating the eggs one at a time; do not add the next egg until the previous one is completely incorporated. In a slow, gradual stream, add the milk to the batter with the mixer running. Fold in the cheese and sugar.

6. Transfer the batter to a pastry bag fitted with a #5 or ½-inch tip. Pipe 1-inch rounds of batter onto the prepared baking sheets, spaced 1½ inches apart. Wet your finger and smooth out the top of the *gougères*. Sprinkle them evenly with the Everything Spice Mix. Bake for 10 to 15 minutes or until the *gougères* are puffed up and golden brown; do not open the oven during baking. Remove the pan and set it on a rack to cool. Leave the oven on.

ASSEMBLE THE DISH

7. Take the cooled *gougères* and pipe ½ teaspoon of the Vegetable Cream Cheese into the center of each puff. Place the *gougères* in a shallow baking pan and warm them in the oven for 3 minutes. Plate and serve immediately.

"ICED TEA"

MAKES 60 (½-INCH-SQUARE) PÂTES DE FRUITS My sous-chef, Chris Zabita, came to me one day with the idea of doing savory *pâtes de fruits* (jellied squares rolled in sugar). At first I turned my nose up at the idea, thinking it too precious, but Zabita kept giving me lots of different flavors to try, and when I tasted the iced tea version, I knew we had something cool on our hands. This amuse uses a device called a refractometer, which is used to measure the percentage of sugar in substances. The concentration that the refractometer records is referred to as Brix.

SPECIAL EQUIPMENT

Refractometer

FOR THE BLACK TEA SUGAR

3 tablespoons black
tea leaves

1 cup granulated sugar

FOR THE PÂTES DE FRUITS

15 grams loose
black tea leaves

330 grams boiling water

150 grams sugar

100 grams Isomalt (see
Sources, page 403)

10 grams NH pectin (see
Sources, page 403)

50 grams corn syrup

10 grams fresh lemon juice

MAKE THE BLACK TEA SUGAR

1. Finely grind the tea in a spice grinder. Measure out 2 tablespoons of ground tea and toss it with the sugar. Set aside.

MAKE THE PÂTES DE FRUITS

2. In a teapot, combine the tea leaves with the boiling water. Let steep for 3 minutes, then strain the tea and measure out 300 grams of the liquid and set aside.

3. In a bowl, combine the sugar, Isomalt, and pectin.

4. In a saucepot, combine the reserved tea, corn syrup, and the lemon juice and bring to a boil over high heat. Whisk in the sugar mixture and cook for 16 to 20 minutes or until the liquid registers 75 Brix on a refractometer.

5. Pour the liquid into four 7½ x ½ x 1-inch *pâte de fruits* molds (see Sources, page 403) and let set at room temperature for approximately 5 hours.

6. Cut the *pâtes de fruits* into ½-inch-square pieces and toss them in the Black Tea Sugar to coat.

"DORITOS"

MAKES 60 CHICHARRONES Even though I don't eat them anymore, Doritos will always have a special place in my heart. We were trying to come up with a way to make *chicharrones* (deep-fried pork rinds) a little different, and after some research on what goes into making the Doritos spice, it was only a matter of throwing the stuff in the dehydrator and seeing what came out. These are dangerously good. A dehydrator isn't very expensive and is a good investment for any home cook—I think once you have one, you might become addicted to it.

SPECIAL EQUIPMENT

Food dehydrator

FOR THE NACHO SPICE MIX

3 bell peppers, mixed colors, seeded and sliced into 2-inch-wide strips

1 cup shredded cheddar cheese

1 cup shredded pepper Jack cheese

2 tablespoons onion powder

Kosher salt

FOR THE CHICHARRONES

8 ounces pork skin (ask your butcher)

2 cups canola oil

MAKE THE NACHO SPICE MIX

1. Place the peppers and cheese in a dehydrator (see Note). Keep the peppers in the dehydrator for 3 days and the cheese for 5 days.

2. Transfer the peppers and cheese to a spice grinder, working in batches if needed, and process until smooth. The cheese will be very greasy and stick to the sides, so make sure to scrape down the sides periodically. Place the mixture in a warm place on a paper towel–lined plate to absorb the extra grease. Let sit 15 minutes. Repeat the process 3 or 4 times until all the excess grease is absorbed and the cheese and peppers have been ground to a fine powder. Let the mixture dry and grind it once more in the spice grinder. Transfer the mixture to a bowl and combine it with the onion powder. Season to taste with salt.

MAKE THE CHICHARRONES

3. Bring a large pot of heavily salted water to a boil. Add the pork skin and reduce the heat to low. Simmer, covered, for 1 hour or until the skin is fork-tender. Transfer the skin to a tray or a rack and let cool to room temperature.

4. Using a paring knife, carefully trim away all of the fat that is on one side of the skin—essentially, you are skinning the skin. Cut the skin into postage stamp–size pieces. If using a dehydrator, place the skin pieces in the dehydrator for 1½ to 2 hours. Alternatively, preheat the oven to 200°F; position a rack in the middle. Place the skin pieces on a shallow baking pan and place it in the oven. Turn the oven off and leave the skin in the oven overnight. When the pork skin pieces are properly dried, they should resemble glass.

5. Place the oil in a large skillet and heat the oil until it registers 350°F on a deep-frying thermometer. Add the pork skin pieces to the pan and fry until they are crispy, about 1 minute. Transfer the *chicharrones* to a paper towel–lined tray, and season with the Nacho Spice Mix.

Note *If you don't own a dehydrator or do not want to bother with the spice mix, which does take a lot of time to make, toss the* chicharrones *with some Amber spice mix (see Sources, page 403).*

"CAESAR SALAD"

SERVES 4 One day my sous-chef, Chris, came in with some Parmesan spheres he had made from a low-grade cheese. Given that he used a poor-quality cheese, they were pretty gross. But I saw the potential in Parmesan spherification, and after some thought, we came up with the idea of serving all the flavors of a Caesar salad in one bite on a spoon. It's a really cool amuse-bouche and has stuck it out here at the restaurant. It uses a sodium alginate spherification technique, and though it might sound complicated and intimidating, it's really fun, especially if you want to get in touch with your inner chemist, or want to show your kids a fun trick. Sodium alginate sounds like something produced in a lab, but it's actually extracted from seaweed and can be used as a thickener due to its absorptive properties. This technique became popular after Ferran Adrià used it to turn olive juice into an olive. We get our sodium alginate from a company called Willpowder (see Sources, page 403).

FOR THE PARMIGIANO-REGGIANO SPHERES

7 grams sodium alginate

45 grams (¾ cup) shredded Parmigiano-Reggiano

¼ teaspoon freshly ground black pepper

Kosher salt

3 grams calcium lactate gluconate (see Sources, page 403)

2 grams xanthan gum

Extra-virgin olive oil

FOR THE CAESAR SALAD SPOONS

¼ cup oil-cured pitted black olives

1 tablespoon walnuts

1 slice bread (such as Pullman loaf)

1 marinated anchovy fillet

1 cup chiffonade of romaine lettuce

2 tablespoons extra-virgin olive oil

1 tablespoon flaky sea salt, such as Maldon

1 tablespoon Pierre Poivre spice mix (see Sources, page 403) or smoked paprika

1 lemon, cut into wedges

4 sprigs Tahoon cress (see Sources, page 403) or a few slivers of watercress (optional)

MAKE THE PARMIGIANO-REGGIANO SPHERES

1. In a nonreactive bowl, make a sodium alginate solution by combining the sodium alginate with 1,500 grams water. Set the solution over an ice bath while you prepare the Parmigiano-Reggiano cream.

2. In a medium saucepot, combine the cheese, pepper, and salt to taste with 240 grams water. Bring the mixture to a simmer over medium heat, then reduce the heat to low and simmer for 5 to 10 minutes or until the mixture begins to thicken. Using an immersion blender, blend the Parmigiano-Reggiano cream until smooth. Taste for seasoning and adjust if necessary. Pass the mixture through a chinois into a container, cover, and refrigerate until cold.

3. Combine the cold Parmigiano-Reggiano cream with the calcium lactate gluconate and xanthan gum. Using an immersion blender, puree the mixture until smooth and uniform; it should be thick. Do not over-add the xanthan gum, as it will make your mixture gummy and uncooperative.

4. Pour the sodium alginate solution into a shallow pan; the solution should be at least 1½ inches deep for the spherification to work. You don't need to use

all of the solution, so long as the depth is at least 1½ inches. Discard the extra solution if there is any left over. Using a ½ teaspoon measure, scoop spoonfuls of the Parmigiano-Reggiano cream and let them gently slide into the sodium alginate solution, as if you were poaching a tiny egg. The Parmigiano-Reggiano cream will almost immediately form a small sphere that resembles a tiny "yolk." Allow the sphere to soak for approximately 2 minutes. The longer the sphere is in the solution, the thicker its shell will be. Using a slotted spoon, gently transfer the sphere to a bowl of clean water to rinse off the soaking solution. Using the slotted spoon, transfer the sphere to a clean shallow container and gently slide it off the spoon. Drizzle the sphere with some extra-virgin olive oil, just enough to coat the outer skin. Repeat with the remaining Parmigiano-Reggiano Cream; you will need to make a total of 12 spheres. As you complete them, slide the spheres near the ones you've already made; make sure you do not stack them on top of one another and allow for a bit of space between them.

MAKE THE CAESAR SALAD SPOONS

5. Preheat the oven to 200°F; position a rack in the middle. Place the olives on a shallow baking pan and bake for about 6 hours or until the olives are dehydrated and leathery looking. Transfer the tray to a cooling rack and set aside. Raise the oven temperature to 300°F.

6. In a small dry pan, toast the walnuts over low heat for about 5 minutes, or until fragrant. Transfer the nuts to a bowl and let cool.

7. Place the bread on a shallow baking pan and toast it in the oven until well dehydrated, 5 to 10 minutes. Transfer the toast to a cooling rack and let cool completely.

8. Halve the anchovy lengthwise and cut the halves crosswise into 6 pieces each; you should have a total of 12 (⅛- to ¼-inch) anchovy pieces.

9. In a food processor fitted with a metal blade, process the toast until it resembles a coarse powder. Transfer the toast powder to a bowl and set aside.

10. In a mini food processor, combine 1 teaspoon of the dehydrated olives with the toasted walnuts and pulse until they form a coarse powder. Reserve the remaining olives for another use (see Note).

11. Drape a few strands of the lettuce over 4 large Asian-style soup spoons. Divide the Parmigiano-Reggiano Spheres among the spoons; you should have 3 spheres per spoon. Divide the anchovy pieces, walnut-olive mixture, and powdered toast equally among the spoons. Top with a drizzle of the olive oil, some flaky sea salt, a sprinkle of the Pierre Poivre, and a squeeze of lemon juice. Garnish with the cress and serve.

Note *Grind the remaining dehydrated olives in a spice grinder or a mini food processor and use them the same way you use salt; sprinkle them over eggs, pasta, or salads.*

SERVES 4 This is our version of the classic combination of fried chicken and honey. I believe my good friend Ben Burakoff, a former line cook, came up with the idea.

20 duck tongues (about ½ pound), rinsed in cold water

2 cups Veal Stock (see page 382) or store-bought

2 cups Chicken Stock (see page 382) or store-bought

½ Vidalia onion

1 Bouquet Garni
(see page 387)

2 quarts buttermilk, divided

Canola oil

2 cups all-purpose flour

1 tablespoon Ararat spice mix (see Sources, page 403)

1 teaspoon kosher salt, plus more as needed

1 recipe Duck Glaze
(see page 391)

1. In a medium pot, bring 2 quarts of salted water to a boil over high heat. Add the duck tongues, reduce the heat to low, and gently simmer the tongues for about 10 minutes, periodically skimming any impurities that rise to the surface. Drain the tongues and transfer them to a medium Dutch oven.

2. Preheat the oven to 300°F; position the rack in the middle. In a saucepan, combine the veal and chicken stocks, onion, bouquet garni, and 1 quart of the buttermilk, and bring to a boil over medium-high heat. Pour the hot buttermilk mixture over the duck tongues in the Dutch oven, cover, and braise for 1 hour in the oven.

3. Remove the tongues from the liquid and let cool for 15 minutes. Using your fingertips or a pair of tweezers, pull out the cartilage in one piece from the fatter end of each tongue. Strain the braising liquid through a fine-mesh strainer into a bowl, return the tongues to the liquid, cover, and refrigerate overnight.

5. Remove the tongues from the braising liquid and place them in a container with the remaining 1 quart buttermilk. Let sit at room temperature for at least 1 hour.

6. Add 1 inch of oil to a large skillet and warm the oil over medium-high heat until the temperature registers 350°F on a deep-frying thermometer. Meanwhile, in a medium bowl, combine the flour, Ararat, and salt. Remove the tongues from the buttermilk and dredge them in the seasoned flour. Gently add the tongues to the skillet (be careful, as the oil may spatter) and fry for 2 minutes or until the tongues are crispy. Transfer the tongues to a paper towel–lined tray. Season with salt and serve with warmed Duck Glaze on the side.

FISH

"One of the reasons I love fishing and cooking fish: There's always something new to learn. Someone's always calling me about some fish I've never heard of. There are too many fish in the sea, so I'll never run out of new stuff to cook with and fish for."

—DAVID PASTERNACK

BIGEYE TUNA + PICKLED CORN SALAD + AMBER + CHILI OIL

SERVES 4 This dish came about in the summer of 2011 after I did *Next Iron Chef*. Chef Celina Tio made a chowchow for one of the battles when we were all competing, and it was incredible. Believe it or not, that was the first time I had ever eaten chowchow and I totally loved it. The combination of flavors got stuck in my head, and I knew that I'd be playing with the recipe when I got back to New York.

One Saturday when I went to the greenmarket, I saw corn and bell peppers, and was instantly reminded of Chef Tio's chowchow, and I knew it was what I was going to make that night.

It's important to have truly great corn when making this chowchow, as it takes center stage. We get our corn from the wonderful people at Lebak Farms who sell at the Tribeca greenmarket. Their summer corn is bursting with sweetness and is absolutely perfect for this recipe.

Keep in mind that it gets a bit smoky when you're blackening the tuna, so either do this indoors with a very strong fan or wide-open windows, or take that step outdoors and cook on the grill.

FOR THE PICKLED CORN SALAD

2 cups corn kernels (from about 4 ears corn)

½ cup white wine vinegar

1 tablespoon granulated sugar

1 teaspoon kosher salt, plus more as needed

1 teaspoon ground turmeric

½ cup extra-virgin olive oil

Juice of 2 limes

1 red bell pepper, brunoise (see Note)

1 yellow bell pepper, brunoise (see Note)

1 shallot, brunoise (see Note)

2 tablespoons chopped fresh tarragon

1 tablespoon chopped fresh curly parsley

1 tablespoon Amber spice mix (see Sources, page 403)

FOR THE CHILI OIL

1 cup Blended Oil (see page 395)

¼ cup chili powder

FOR THE BREAD CRACKERS

4 paper-thin slices Pullman loaf

Extra-virgin olive oil

Kosher salt

Freshly ground black pepper

FOR THE TUNA

¼ cup Amber spice mix (see Sources, page 403), plus more as needed

2 (4-ounce) tuna fillets, trimmed to rectangular blocks

Extra-virgin olive oil

Kosher salt

TO ASSEMBLE THE DISH

Micro sorrel (see Sources, page 403)

Flaky sea salt, such as Maldon

Amber spice mix (see Sources, page 403)

+ **Brunoise** is a term used for food that is diced smaller than "fine dice." Traditionally brunoise cut is between 1 to 3 millimeters (1/16 inch) on each side.

MAKE THE PICKLED CORN SALAD

1. Place the corn in a nonreactive container. In a small nonreactive saucepot, combine the vinegar, sugar, salt, and turmeric with ¼ cup of water and bring to a boil over high heat. Pour the marinade over the corn, cover, and refrigerate overnight.

MAKE THE CHILI OIL

2. In a small saucepot, warm the Blended Oil and chili powder over medium-high heat until the oil registers 200°F on a deep-frying thermometer. Stir, and transfer the pot to a cooling rack. Let stand at room temperature for 3 hours. Strain through a fine-mesh strainer lined with a coffee filter into a bowl and set aside.

MAKE THE BREAD CRACKERS

3. Preheat the oven to 300°F; position the rack in the middle. Lay the bread slices out on a baking sheet. Drizzle with olive oil and season with salt and pepper. Bake for 5 minutes or until crispy. Transfer to a cooling rack and set aside.

MAKE THE TUNA

4. Spread out the Amber in a shallow dish. Pat the fillets dry, drizzle them with olive oil, and season with salt. Press the fillets into the Amber to evenly coat them, shaking off any excess. Drizzle more olive oil over both sides of the fillets.

5. Heat a large cast-iron pan over high heat until a drop of water added to the pan instantly evaporates. Add the tuna and sear for about 10 seconds on each side. Transfer to a plate and allow the fish to stand at room temperature for 20 minutes before slicing it into ¼-inch-thick pieces. Drizzle with more olive oil and set aside.

ASSEMBLE THE DISH

6. Right before serving, strain the corn, discarding the marinade. Add the olive oil and lime juice to the corn. Let sit for 5 minutes, and then add the bell peppers, shallot, tarragon, parsley, and Amber.

7. Divide the Pickled Corn Salad among 4 plates. Top each serving with the tuna and add a Bread Cracker on the side. Scatter sorrel around and sprinkle flaky sea salt over the fish. Drizzle some Chili Oil over the top and add a pinch of Amber before serving.

stall every Saturday (during the fishing season), selling his catch with a smile on his face and a kind word for each customer. A blackboard announces what is sold on any given day—the selection varies, but rest assured, it is some of the freshest fish you'll ever get your hands on. If you're a regular, Alex will recognize you and chat for a few minutes. He has an uncanny ability to remember what fish you like, and will make suggestions based on what he has in stock that day.

Born in New York and raised in Chelsea, Alex was drawn to the docks from an early age and started fishing in 1972, which tells you he's seen a thing or

bought his own boat, *Duffy*, which he renamed *Blue Moon*. And thus, his company was born.

In 1988, Alex started coming to the New York greenmarket scene. Tribeca was his original spot, and he still has a fondness for the location, coming every Saturday, rain or shine. These days, Blue Moon Fish also sells at Grand Army Plaza (where Alex met his wife, Stephanie, who still mans the stand there), as well as at the Union Square greenmarket. When not selling fish to hungry Brooklynites, Stephanie keeps an ever-vigilant eye on the company's books—she's the brains of the operations, as Alex says.

I stop by the greenmarket to pick up fish, I find Alex always smiling—this is a man who clearly loves his trade.

Because Blue Moon Fish sells some of the freshest fish available, it has become an indelible institution on the New York greenmarket scene, supplying fish to top restaurants as well as hungry greenmarket goers. It's comforting to know that the fish you'll be serving your patrons or cooking for your dinner that night has never been frozen—that quality is what gets Blue Moon Fish the most loyal customers around.

ALEX VILLANI of Blue Moon Fish at Tribeca greenmarket

BLUE MOON LOCAL FLUKE + RAMP PESTO + MORELS + LEMON VINEGAR

SERVES 4 Fish, just like produce, has its seasons. In the spring, fluke is abundant on Long Island, and we get ours from Alex Villani, the man behind Blue Moon Fish. This dish always gets rave reviews from our patrons, and we wanted to share it with you. In the spring, we pair fluke with ramps and morels, celebrating another growing season that's about to start. It's a light, springtime dish that makes for a nice reprieve after the heavier winter fare. The bracing lemon vinegar offers a nice bright finishing note, leaving you wanting another bite.

FOR THE LEMON VINEGAR

2 cups white wine vinegar

1 teaspoon ground turmeric

Peels of 3 lemons, white pith removed

2 sprigs fresh lemon thyme

1 fresh or ½ dried bay leaf

FOR THE RAMP PESTO

¼ cup pine nuts

4 cups chopped ramp greens (reserve the bulbs for another use)

1 cup extra-virgin olive oil

½ cup finely grated Parmigiano-Reggiano

1 teaspoon red pepper flakes

Kosher salt

FOR THE ASPARAGUS

12 pencil-thin asparagus spears, trimmed

2 tablespoons extra-virgin olive oil

Kosher salt

Freshly ground black pepper

FOR THE MORELS

1 pound morel mushrooms, cleaned and stemmed

Canola oil

¼ cup sliced shallots

1½ ounces (3 tablespoons) unsalted butter

3 sprigs fresh thyme

3 fresh or 1½ dried bay leaves

1 cup dry white wine

FOR THE FLUKE

4 (5-ounce) fluke fillets

Kosher salt

Freshly ground white pepper

Extra-virgin olive oil

1 ounce (2 tablespoons) unsalted butter

TO ASSEMBLE THE DISH

Baby sorrel leaves (optional)

2 tablespoons chopped fresh curly parsley

Extra-virgin olive oil

Smoked salt (see Sources, page 403) or flaky sea salt, such as Maldon

MAKE THE LEMON VINEGAR

1. In a 2-quart nonreactive pot, combine the vinegar, turmeric, and lemon peels and bring to a boil over high heat. Reduce the heat to low, cover, and simmer for 1 hour. Add the thyme and bay leaf and transfer to a nonreactive container. Wrap the container tightly in plastic wrap and let the accumulated moisture gather on the inside so it looks like it is raining inside the container. This allows the herbs to infuse the vinegar. Let stand for 1 hour.

MAKE THE RAMP PESTO

2. In a small dry skillet, toast the pine nuts over low heat, shaking the pan frequently to prevent burning, until golden and fragrant, about 2 minutes. Transfer the pine nuts to a plate to cool.

3. Bring a 4-quart pot filled with salted water to a boil. Blanch the ramp greens in the boiling water for 1 minute and immediately transfer to an ice bath. Let cool, squeeze out all of the excess water, and then freeze the ramp greens for about 30 minutes. Place the toasted pine nuts, ramp greens, and olive oil in a blender and blend on high power for 30 seconds. Transfer the mixture to a bowl set over an ice bath and fold in the cheese, red pepper flakes, and some salt. Allow the mixture to cool, and refrigerate until ready to use.

4. In a large bowl, toss the asparagus with the olive oil and season with salt and pepper. Light a grill or preheat a grill pan. Grill the asparagus over medium-high heat for 2 minutes, or until well-marked and slightly charred, turning once. Alternatively, preheat a broiler, and place the asparagus on a baking sheet. Broil the asparagus for 1 minute or until slightly charred. Cut the asparagus into 6-inch pieces and set aside.

MAKE THE MORELS

5. Slice the mushrooms into ¼-inch rings. Add enough oil to a large sauté pan to coat the bottom of the pan and set it over high heat. Just before the oil starts to smoke, add one-third of the mushrooms to the pan in an even layer. Reduce the heat to medium and add one-third (about 1½ tablespoons) of the shallots. Once the mushrooms release their liquid and begin to brown, add 1 tablespoon of the butter, 1 sprig of the thyme, and 1 bay leaf, and cook until the butter and mushrooms are nicely browned, about 4 minutes. Add one-third of the wine and deglaze the pan, scraping the brown bits off the bottom of the pan with a wooden spoon, until the pan is dry. Transfer to a parchment paper–lined tray. Repeat with the remaining mushrooms, shallots, butter, thyme, bay leaves, and wine.

MAKE THE FLUKE

6. Pat the fish dry and season with salt and pepper. Add enough oil to a large sauté pan to coat the bottom of the pan and set it over high heat. Just before the oil starts to smoke, add 2 fluke fillets to the pan. It's important that you do not overcrowd the pan, so make sure you select a pan that's large enough for both fillets. Cook for 1 minute, add 1 tablespoon of the butter to the pan, and cook for 1 minute more. Flip the fish and baste with the butter in the pan for 1 minute. Remove the fillet from the pan and keep it warm on a parchment–lined plate. Repeat with the remaining fillets and butter. Wipe the pan between batches. (You can speed up the process by using 2 pans.)

ASSEMBLE THE DISH

7. Divide the Ramp Pesto among 4 plates. Divide the sorrel evenly among the plates, placing it on top of the pesto. Place a piece of fluke over the sorrel on each plate and spoon some of the morels around. Divide the asparagus among the plates. Stir the parsley into the Lemon Vinegar and drizzle it over the fish and around the plate, along with some extra-virgin olive oil. Sprinkle with some smoked salt before serving.

TUNA NIÇOISE + YELLOW WAX BEANS + SILVER DOLLAR POTATOES

SERVES 4 Niçoise salad, made famous in the United States by the late, great Julia Child, is a traditional French mixed vegetable salad topped with tuna and anchovies. In keeping with tradition, the salad components are arranged on a bed of lettuce set on a large plate. The tuna typically used in a niçoise salad is a quality tuna packed in oil. Obviously, the better the quality of your tuna, the tastier your salad will be. While the traditional version uses no cooked vegetables (such as potatoes), more and more restaurants will serve niçoise with boiled potatoes and blanched haricots verts. Our version features seared tuna steaks, Preserved Meyer Lemons (see page 391) and oil-cured white anchovies.

FOR THE OLIVE TAPENADE

1 cup pitted Moroccan oil-cured olives

1 oil-cured white anchovy fillet

Juice of ½ lemon

1 teaspoon chopped garlic

½ cup extra-virgin olive oil

FOR THE TUNA STEAKS

4 (5-ounce) tuna steaks (ask your fishmonger to cut you 2x2-inch center-cut fillets)

½ cup chopped fresh curly parsley

3 tablespoons chopped fresh chives

3 tablespoons chopped fresh tarragon

3 tablespoons chopped fresh chervil

Extra-virgin olive oil

Canola oil

FOR THE WAX BEAN SALAD

1 cup yellow wax beans

1 cup haricots verts or green beans

¼ cup Pickled Red Onions (see page 386)

3 tablespoons minced Preserved Meyer Lemons (see page 391)

1 tablespoon chopped fresh curly parsley

1 cup extra-virgin olive oil

⅓ cup fresh lemon juice

1 teaspoon piment d'espelette or hot paprika

Kosher salt

FOR THE SILVER DOLLAR POTATOES

3 large Yukon Gold potatoes (1½ pounds)

8 ounces (16 tablespoons) Clarified Butter (see page 390) or melted unsalted butter

TO ASSEMBLE THE DISH

4 oil-cured white anchovy fillets, halved lengthwise

Upland cress (see Sources, page 403; optional)

Flaky sea salt, such as Maldon

12 baby radishes (see Sources, page 403) or French breakfast radishes

1. In a food processor fitted with a metal blade, pulse the olives, anchovy, lemon juice, and garlic until finely chopped. With the motor running, slowly drizzle in the olive oil until incorporated. Set aside.

MAKE THE TUNA STEAKS

2. Rinse the fish and pat it dry. Make a 1-inch slit in the center of each tuna fillet and stuff about 1 tablespoon of the Olive Tapenade into each cavity. Set aside the remaining tapenade. In a medium bowl, mix together the parsley, chives, tarragon, and chervil. Brush the tuna with olive oil and coat it in the herb mixture on both sides. Set aside.

3. When ready to serve, add enough canola oil to a large sauté pan to cover the bottom of the pan and set it over high heat. Just before the oil starts to smoke, add the tuna and sear for 20 seconds on each side. Transfer to a parchment paper–lined tray.

MAKE THE WAX BEAN SALAD

4. Trim the wax beans and haricots verts, and bring a pot of salted water to a boil. Blanch the beans in the boiling water for 1 minute and immediately transfer to an ice bath. Let cool to room temperature.

5. Cut the beans in half lengthwise and toss with the Pickled Red Onions, Preserved Meyer Lemons, and parsley. In a small bowl, stir together the olive oil, lemon juice, and piment d'espelette. Drizzle the dressing over the vegetables and toss to combine. Season to taste with salt and set aside.

MAKE THE SILVER DOLLAR POTATOES

6. Preheat the oven to 400°F; position the rack in the middle. Cut the potatoes in half widthwise, and using a 2-inch ring mold, punch out uniform cylinders; you should wind up with 6 cylinders. Using an adjustable mandoline, slice the cylinders into ⅛-inch-thick slices. Bring a pot of salted water to a boil. Blanch the potato slices in the boiling water for 1 minute. Transfer the potatoes to a baking sheet and brush them generously with clarified butter. Line 6 (4-ounce) ramekins in foil and fill each ramekin with potato slices. Pour enough of the clarified butter to come to ¼ inch from the top of the ramekin. Bake the potatoes for about 1 hour or until the edges are crispy. Transfer the potatoes out of the ramekins and set aside. Reserve any remaining clarified butter for another use.

ASSEMBLE THE DISH

7. Divide the Wax Bean Salad among 4 plates, and scatter the Silver Dollar Potatoes around. Slice the Tuna Steaks and place them on top of the bean salad. Top with the halved anchovies. Drizzle some of the bean salad dressing from the bottom of the bowl around the plate, dot with bits of the Olive Tapenade, and finish with some Upland cress, if using, and flaky sea salt. Serve with the radishes.

Make It Faster *Instead of making the Silver Dollar Potatoes, go a bit more traditional route: Boil some fingerling potatoes in salted water and serve alongside the salad.*

COPPER RIVER SALMON + CREAM CHEESE CROQUETTES + EVERYTHING BRIOCHE

SERVES 4 Often, pretty commonplace things inspire me in the kitchen. One day, I was eating a Zucker's king salmon everything bagel with cream cheese, marveling at how good it tasted. Zucker's Bagels, lucky for me, is just a block away from the restaurant, and is one of the few places that actually offers different types of quality smoked and cured salmon. I find that flavor combination to be pretty inspirational.

These croquettes are something we came up with for Battle Cream Cheese in the kitchen stadium during one of the Iron Chef competitions. It was a play on my favorite kind of bagel, the "everything" bagel, with smoked salmon and cream cheese. I loved the result so much that we added it to our menu to share with our guests.

SPECIAL EQUIPMENT

Pasta Machine

FOR THE CURED SALMON

One (12-ounce) center cut salmon fillet

¼ cup absinthe

1 tablespoon fennel seeds

1 tablespoon coriander seeds

1 tablespoon cracked white peppercorns

2 cups kosher salt

1 cup packed dark brown sugar

2 tablespoons chopped fresh dill

FOR THE CROQUETTES

4 cups heavy cream

11 ounces cream cheese

2 tablespoons powdered gelatin

Kosher salt

1 teaspoon Pierre Poivre spice mix (see Sources, page 403) or smoked paprika

2 cups all-purpose flour

2 cups Bacon Bread Crumbs (see page 381) or regular bread crumbs

6 large eggs, lightly beaten

Canola oil

FOR THE EVERYTHING BRIOCHE CRACKERS

4 (¼-inch thick) slices brioche

2 large eggs, whisked

¼ cup Everything Bagel Spice Mix (see page 393)

FOR THE TOMATO SALAD

12 cherry tomatoes, halved

½ cup sliced cucumbers

¼ red onion, thinly sliced

1 tablespoon capers, rinsed

Kosher salt

Juice of 1 lemon

Extra-virgin olive oil

TO ASSEMBLE THE DISH

¼ cup micro borage (optional)

Extra-virgin olive oil

1 lemon, cut into wedges

Mustard oil (see Sources, page 403)

Chive oil (see page 395)

Smoked salt

4 caper berries

MAKE THE CURED SALMON

1. Pick the bones out of the salmon and rub it with the absinthe. Cover and refrigerate for 6 hours or overnight.

2. In a small dry skillet, toast the fennel, coriander, and peppercorns over low heat until fragrant, about 3 minutes. Transfer to a plate to cool. In a small bowl, combine the salt, sugar, dill, and the cooled toasted spices. Spoon some of the cure over a piece of plastic wrap set out on the counter. Place the salmon over the cure and pack more cure around and over the salmon. Wrap the fish tightly and transfer it to a dish deep enough to hold any juices that might leak out. Refrigerate for 7 to 10 hours. Rinse the fish under cold, running water, pat dry, and slice it into 12 paper-thin slices. Set aside.

MAKE THE CROQUETTES

3. In a 2-quart pot, bring the cream and cream cheese to a simmer over medium heat, stirring to dissolve the cream cheese. While the mixture warms, bloom the gelatin in ⅓ cup of water—let it stand for 5 minutes. Whisk the bloomed gelatin into the warm dairy mixture until dissolved, but do not let the liquid come to a boil or you will wind up with a grainy texture and will need to start over. Pass the liquid through a fine-mesh strainer, and season to taste with salt and Pierre Poivre. Cover and transfer the liquid to a freezer for 6 hours or overnight.

4. Let the custard thaw until it is soft enough to be scooped out. Meanwhile, set out a breading station by placing the flour, bread crumbs, and eggs in 3 separate shallow containers. Using a small cookie scoop, scoop out ½-ounce balls of custard and roll each in the flour, then the eggs, and finally the bread crumbs. Repeat process on each ball. Place the croquettes back in the freezer for 30 minutes. You will need 12 croquettes for this recipe—the rest can be frozen for later use.

5. When ready to serve, heat 2 inches of oil in a Dutch oven or a deep skillet set over medium-high heat, until it registers 350°F on a deep-frying thermometer. Gently add the croquettes, directly from the freezer, to the hot oil and fry for 30 seconds or until golden brown. Transfer the croquettes to a paper towel–lined tray and season with salt.

MAKE THE EVERYTHING BRIOCHE CRACKERS

6. Preheat the oven to 350°F; position the rack in the middle. Using a pasta machine, and moving from the highest setting to the lowest, carefully roll the bread slices through the machine without tearing the bread. Transfer the pressed bread to a shallow baking pan, drizzle with the eggs, and season with the Everything Bagel Spice. Bake for 3 minutes or until the bread is crispy. Transfer to a rack and set aside.

MAKE THE TOMATO SALAD

7. In a medium bowl, combine the tomatoes, cucumbers, onion, and capers. Right before serving, season the vegetables with salt, and drizzle with the lemon juice and olive oil.

ASSEMBLE THE DISH

8. Cover each plate with 3 pieces of the Cured Salmon. Divide the Croquettes among the plates, placing them over the salmon. Spoon some Tomato Salad around and top with the micro borage, if using. Drizzle some olive oil over the salmon and squeeze a few drops of the lemon juice. Drizzle the mustard and chive oils around the plate and finish with smoked salt and a caper berry. Serve with the Everything Brioche Crackers.

HOW TO
REMOVE SKIN FROM A
FILLET OF FISH

1. Using a chef's knife held at a 45-degree angle, slice into the tail until your reach the skin. Turn the knife flat so it's parallel to the surface and go forward an inch or two.

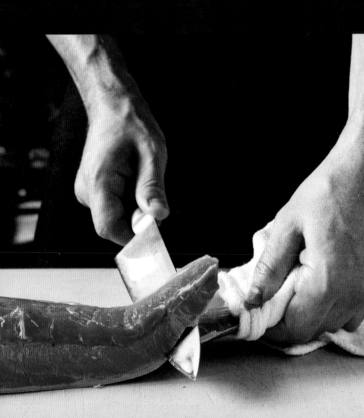

2. Using a kitchen towel, take firm hold of the skin on the end, and in one fluid motion, push the knife forward, separating the skin from the meat. The knife should be at a slight (15-degree) angle, the height of two stacked pennies, as if you're sharpening a knife.

3. The finished product.

SERVES 4 I've always been fascinated by Japanese cuisine. I love how clean and pure everything tastes, and the time and effort that goes into something that we take for granted, like *katsuobushi* (bonito) flakes, is mind-boggling.

FOR THE HIRAMASA TARTARE

One (½-pound) hiramasa, filleted (see page 92 or ask your fishmonger to do this)

Extra-virgin olive oil

1 jalapeño, brunoise (see page 48)

Finely grated zest of 2 limes

Kosher salt

Mustard oil (see Sources, page 403)

FOR THE MISO-DASHI

¼ ounce (7 grams) freshly shaved *katsuobushi* or dried bonito flakes

Canola oil

¼ Spanish onion, coarsely chopped

2 tablespoons coarsely chopped fresh ginger

¼ cup white miso paste

1 cup dry white wine

½ cups low-sodium soy sauce

½ cup fresh Kalamansi lime or fresh regular lime juice

1½ tablespoons mustard oil (see Sources, page 403)

Kosher salt

FOR THE FRIED GINGER

One (2-inch) piece fresh ginger, peeled

Canola oil

1 cup rice flour

TO ASSEMBLE THE DISH

Paper-thin slices of jalapeño, for serving

Micro red shiso (see Sources, page 403) or chiffonade of shiso (optional)

Katsuobushi

American caviar (optional)

MAKE THE HIRAMASA TARTARE

1. Slice 12 (⅛-inch-thick) slices off of the hiramasa fillet. Overlap 3 pieces on a large piece of parchment paper. Repeat with the remaining hiramasa slices. Drizzle a little olive oil on each piece. Place another piece of parchment on top and gently pound the fish to carpaccio-thin slices. Finely dice the remaining hiramasa. Mix the diced hiramasa with the jalapeño, lime zest, salt, and just enough mustard oil to coat the fish.

2. Lay out 4 pieces of plastic wrap and put the carpaccio slices in the middle, 3 slices per piece of plastic wrap. Place a small mound of tartare in the center of the slices and roll up tightly in the wrap into a ball a little bigger than a golf ball. You will have 4 balls each weighing 2 ounces. Refrigerate until ready to use.

MAKE THE MISO-DASHI

3. In a large stockpot, combine the *katsuobushi* with 4 cups of water and bring to a boil over high heat. Reduce the heat to low and simmer the broth until the flakes sink to the bottom of the pot, about 40 minutes. Turn off the heat and let sit.

4. Meanwhile, in a medium sauté pan set over high heat, add just enough oil to coat the bottom of the pan, and heat until just before it starts to smoke. Add the onion and ginger and reduce the heat to medium. Cook, stirring, until the onion is golden brown, 3 to 4 minutes. Stir in the miso paste and cook until it starts to brown on the bottom. Add the wine and deglaze the pan, scraping the brown bits off the bottom of the pan with a wooden spoon. Cook until the pan is nearly dry.

5. Stir the miso mixture into the warm broth and bring to a boil. Transfer the broth to a nonreactive container and wrap it tightly in plastic wrap. Let stand for at least 30 minutes or up to 1 hour. The moisture that will accumulate inside will look like it is raining.

6. Make the ponzu by combining the soy sauce with the lime juice. Set aside.

7. Strain the cooled miso broth through a fine-mesh strainer and return it to the container. Whisk in the ponzu and mustard oil. Season to taste with salt and refrigerate until needed.

MAKE THE FRIED GINGER

8. Using either a mandoline or a very sharp knife, slice the ginger as thinly as possible. Stack the slices and thinly julienne them. Transfer to a bowl filled with cold water and refrigerate for at least 1 hour.

9. In a small saucepot, heat 1 cup of oil over medium-high heat until the temperature registers 300°F on a deep-frying thermometer. Drain the ginger and thoroughly pat dry to remove as much water as possible. Place the flour in a medium bowl and toss the ginger in the flour to coat. Fry the ginger in the oil for 30 to 45 seconds or until crispy. Using a slotted spoon, transfer the ginger to a paper towel–lined tray and set aside.

ASSEMBLE THE DISH

10. Unwrap and divide the hiramasa among 4 chilled bowls. Add the sliced jalapeño and sprinkle the Fried Ginger on top. Add the shiso (if using), and shave some more *katsuobushi* over the fish. Ladle the Miso-Dashi broth around the fish at the table. Add some caviar, if using, and serve.

SERVES 4 This appetizer has been on our menu from the very beginning, and is one of our most popular dishes—it's on our tasting menu. Despite the long list of ingredients, it's actually very easy to make, and I guarantee that if you serve this at your next dinner party, it'll be the dish everyone will be talking about. It not only looks impressive—it tastes absolutely incredible, too. I remember playing around with different flavors and textures while I was creating this dish, and while I loved what I was getting as a result, but it still wasn't quite perfect on my palate. One day, while looking for something to finish the dish, I noticed a small mound of leftover toasted pine nuts lying around. And me being me, I just thought, *Why not?* I threw the nuts in and tried it—it tasted absolutely perfect. Exactly the missing piece I was looking for. The smokiness from the toasting, the sweetness that pine nuts are known for, and their fattiness were all perfect complements for the fish, avocado, and spicy lime sauce.

This fish began as Kona Kampachi, a type of yellowtail raised off the coasts of Hawaii. The company we work with has since moved to Mexico and the fish is now just plain kampachi.

We serve this dish with a spoon that contains a small bud called a Szechuan button, which at first might seem like theatrics. We tell you to place it on your tongue and move it around your mouth and wait for it to start to "pop," meaning that the button will create a tingling sensation in your mouth, making your palate more ready for all the flavors you're about to experience.

FOR THE SAUCE

¼ cup extra-virgin olive oil

¼ cup mild honey

¼ cup fresh lime juice

2 tablespoons teriyaki sauce

1 tablespoon mustard oil (see Sources, page 403)

Kosher salt

Freshly ground black pepper

FOR THE AVOCADO MOUSSE

1 avocado, halved and pitted

2 tablespoons fresh lime juice

2 tablespoons extra-virgin olive oil

4 to 6 dashes green Tabasco sauce

Kosher salt

FOR THE TARTARE

10 ounces (2 cups) large-dice kampachi (see headnote)

3 tablespoons extra-virgin olive oil

2 tablespoons brunoise cucumbers (see page 48)

Kosher salt

½ cup diced avocado

1 teaspoon fresh lime juice

1 tablespoon extra-virgin olive oil

TO ASSEMBLE THE DISH

¼ cup pine nuts

4 red radishes, julienned

Micro cilantro (optional)

4 (1x¼-inch) sashimi-style slices kampachi

Olive oil

Fresh lime juice

Potato chips

4 Szechuan buttons (see Sources, page 403)

1. Combine the olive oil, honey, lime juice, teriyaki sauce, and mustard oil in a small bowl. Season to taste with salt and pepper. Refrigerate until ready to serve.

MAKE THE AVOCADO MOUSSE

2. Place the avocados, lime juice, olive oil, Tabasco, and salt to taste into a blender and puree on the highest speed until smooth. You may need to use the bottom of a ladle to get everything started. Transfer to a non-reactive container, cover, and refrigerate until ready to serve.

MAKE THE TARTARE

3. In a medium bowl, combine the fish, olive oil, cucumber, and salt to taste. In another bowl, combine the diced avocado, lime juice (to keep it from oxidizing), and olive oil. Season to taste with salt and set aside.

4. Place a quarter of the diced avocado on the bottom of a 2-inch ring mold. Fill the mold three-quarters of the way with the fish, packing the fish tightly. Repeat with the remaining avocado and tartare—you should fill 4 molds. Transfer the ring molds to a tray and refrigerate until ready to use.

ASSEMBLE THE DISH

5. When ready to serve, in a small dry skillet, toast the pine nuts over low heat, periodically shaking the pan to prevent the nuts from burning, until golden and fragrant, about 3 minutes. Transfer to a small bowl and let the nuts cool completely.

6. Unmold the Tartare into chilled bowls by inverting the molds over the bowls. You will have the tartare on the bottom and diced avocado on top. Pour enough of the Sauce to come a quarter of the way up the molded tartare. Garnish with the julienned radish and micro cilantro, and scatter the toasted pine nuts around.

7. For each bowl of tartare, place a quenelle of the Avocado Mousse on a large soup spoon and top with a slice of the kampachi. Drizzle with olive oil and lime juice, and garnish with a sprig of micro cilantro. Place a few potato chips on the side of the bowl.

8. Divide the Szechuan buttons among 4 Asian soup spoons and serve with the bowls of tartare and avocado mousse. Before eating, place the Szechuan button bud under your tongue and wait until your mouth begins to "pop" before eating the dish.

WILD SOCKEYE SALMON + SMOKED POTATO GNOCCHI + BACON + SUGAR SNAP PEAS

SERVES 4 I've always liked smoked salmon, but wanted to experiment with the flavors of salt and smoke, and play a trick on those taste buds. So instead of smoking the salmon, I made a smoked potato puree. Tasting the smoke kind of gets your brain going in the direction of the familiar flavors embodied in combining smoke and salmon, but instead of the salmon, it's the potatoes that get the smoked flavor. It's a bit unexpected and a lot of fun.

FOR THE PEAS

1 sprig fresh mint plus
2 tablespoons chiffonade
of fresh mint

2 tablespoons granulated
sugar, plus more as needed

Kosher salt

1 cup shelled English peas

1 cup sugar snap
peas, trimmed

1 ounce (2 tablespoons)
unsalted butter

1 shallot, thinly sliced

1 teaspoon Chios spice mix
(see Sources, page 403)
or a mix of dried tarragon,
parsley, basil, and mint

FOR THE LARDONS

2 tablespoons canola oil

1 cup uncooked
bacon lardons (see
Technique, page 381)

FOR THE SMOKED POTATO GNOCCHI

3 russet potatoes
(2½ to 3 pounds)

100 grams Smoked
Onion (see page 390)

1 large egg yolk

Kosher salt

50 grams (about
6 tablespoons plus
2 teaspoons) all-purpose flour

FOR THE SALMON

4 (5-ounce) salmon fillets,
preferably wild sockeye, skin
removed (see page 59)

Kosher salt

Extra-virgin olive oil

4 sprigs fresh lemon thyme

Juice of 1 lemon

TO ASSEMBLE THE DISH

1 ounce (2 tablespoons)
unsalted butter

Smoked salt or other
finishing salt

Affilia or plain pea shoots
(see Sources, page 403)

Little mint leaves

Sherry vinegar

MAKE THE PEAS

1. In a medium pot, combine the mint sprig, a pinch of sugar, and a pinch of salt with 4 cups of water and bring to a boil. Blanch the English peas and mint sprig in the boiling water for 1 minute. Transfer to an ice bath and let the peas cool. Repeat the blanching and ice bath process with the sugar snap peas. Drain the sugar snap peas and cut them on the bias. Set aside.

2. In a medium skillet, melt the butter over medium heat until foamy. Add the shallot and cook, stirring, until soft, 2 minutes. Add the English and sugar snap peas, the remaining 2 tablespoons sugar, Chios spice mix, and salt to taste. Remove from the heat, and let the vegetables cool to room temperature. Mix in the mint chiffonade and set aside until ready to assemble the dish.

MAKE THE LARDONS

3. Heat the oil in a medium sauté pan over high heat. Just before it starts to smoke, add the bacon, immediately reduce the heat to medium, and render the lardons until crispy, 6 to 8 minutes. Strain the lardons, reserving the fat, and keep both warm.

MAKE THE SMOKED POTATO GNOCCHI

4. Preheat the oven to 350°F; position the rack in the middle. Place the potatoes on the oven rack and bake 40 minutes to 1 hour or until fork-tender.

5. While the potatoes are cooking, whisk together the Smoked Onion puree and egg yolk with a pinch of salt. Set aside.

6. As soon as the potatoes are cooked, remove from the oven, cut in half, and scoop out the flesh into a food mill or a potato ricer. Pass through the food mill into a large bowl. Weigh out 500 grams. Spread out the riced potato over a large cutting board. Sprinkle with the flour. Drizzle with the egg yolk–onion mixture and mix the ingredients together with your hands until the mixture starts to turn into dough. Once the dough is formed, cover with a kitchen towel and let rest for at least 30 minutes.

7. Roll the mixture into 1-inch-diameter logs. Cut into 1-inch gnocchi. For this recipe you will only need 20 gnocchi. The remaining gnocchi can be frozen for up to 3 months for later use.

MAKE THE SALMON

8. SOUS-VIDE COOKING INSTRUCTIONS (see step 9 for Alternative Instructions): Fill an immersion circulator with water and preheat the water to 110°F. Rinse and pat the salmon dry and season it with salt on both sides. Place each fillet in a vacuum-seal bag. Drizzle some oil over the fillets; place a sprig of thyme in each bag, and seal the bags. Poach the fillets in the immersion circulator for 18 minutes. Transfer the bags to a cooling rack and let stand for 3 minutes. Open the bags and strain the cooking liquid into a bowl. Stir the lemon juice into the cooking liquid. Set the salmon aside.

9. SOUS-VIDE ALTERNATIVE INSTRUCTIONS: If you don't own an immersion circulator, preheat the oven to 350°F; position the rack in the middle. Place the fillets on a Silpat- or parchment paper–lined baking sheet, season with salt, drizzle with oil, and top each piece with a sprig of thyme. Bake for 5 to 7 minutes or until medium-rare. Set aside while you assemble the dish.

ASSEMBLE THE DISH

10. Bring a pot of salted water to a boil. Place the gnocchi into the boiling water and once they float to the top, about 10 seconds, remove immediately. Heat up the butter in a medium sauté pan over medium heat. Just as it starts to brown, add the gnocchi to the pan and cook for 30 seconds. Add the peas and lardons, and toss to combine.

11. Divide the gnocchi among 4 plates. Top with a piece of salmon. If you roasted the salmon, drizzle it with lemon juice. Drizzle with the reserved salmon cooking liquid and reserved bacon fat, and finish with the smoked salt. Sprinkle with the pea shoots and mint leaves, and drizzle some sherry vinegar around the plate before serving.

HOW TO
DEBONE A WHOLE FISH

1. Whole fish. (Cut the fins and the gills off the fish—see How to Fillet a Fin Fish, page 92).

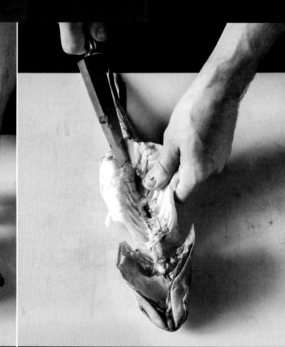

2. Remove the fish collars.

3. Place the fish on its back and gently cut down its center and split it at the belly.

4. Using a knife, gently peel the fish fillets back using the bones as your guide.

5. You are now left with the backbone sticking out.

6. Using kitchen shears, gently cut out the backbone from the fish. Using a pair of fish tweezers, pliers, or regular tweezers, pull out the remaining pin bones in the fish.

7. The finished product.

BLACK SEA BASS + CERIGNOLA OLIVES +
CANDIED LEMON + LA QUERCIA PROSCIUTTO

SERVES 4 What's amazing about La Quercia is that despite their Italian name—*quercia* means "oak" in Italian—the company is Iowa-based (not a place you'd instinctively think of when you think of prosciutto), proving once again that something typically thought of as a European specialty can be made just as well by passionate artisans here in America. And it's even more amazing to note that the company is just a touch older than a decade.

FOR THE CANDIED LEMON ZEST

Zest from 3 lemons (see Technique, page 394)

1 cup granulated sugar

FOR THE COCKLE BROTH

1 pound cockles or other fresh clams

½ cup dry white wine

1 cup Chicken Stock (see page 382) or store-bought

1 cup sliced shallots

2 tablespoons sliced garlic

6 sprigs fresh thyme

1 fresh or ½ dried bay leaf

1 cup julienned Vidalia onions

½ cup sea beans (optional)

2 tablespoons chopped fresh curly parsley

2 tablespoons chopped fresh tarragon

½ tablespoon red pepper flakes

FOR THE BLACK SEA BASS

4 (1-pound) black sea bass, butterflied and deboned (see page 68, or have your fishmonger give you fillets)

12 slices quality prosciutto, preferably La Quercia

1 cup sliced, pitted Cerignola olives

½ cup chopped fresh curly parsley

Canola oil

2 ounces (4 tablespoons) unsalted butter

TO ASSEMBLE THE DISH

Mustard oil (see Sources, page 403)

Extra-virgin olive oil

Micro red-veined sorrel (see Sources, page 403)

MAKE THE CANDIED LEMON ZEST

1. Bring a small pot of water to a boil over high heat. Blanch the zest in the boiling water for 1 minute, and immediately transfer to an ice bath. Repeat the blanching and ice bath process 2 more times, using fresh water each time.

2. In a small saucepan, combine the sugar with 1 cup of water and bring to a boil over high heat. Add the blanched lemon zest, reduce the heat to low, and simmer for 20 minutes. Transfer the saucepan to a cooling rack and let the zest and syrup cool to room temperature.

MAKE THE COCKLE BROTH

3. In a medium stockpot, combine the cockles, white wine, chicken stock, shallots, garlic, thyme, and bay leaf with 1 cup of water and bring to a simmer over high heat. Cover, and once the cockles begin to open, after 3 to 5 minutes, remove from the heat immediately. Strain the liquid through a fine-mesh strainer into a large bowl. Remove the cockle meat from the shells and set aside.

4. When ready to serve, in a 4-quart pot, warm the reserved Cockle Broth with the onions over medium heat, and cook until the onions are soft, 7 to 8 minutes. Right before serving, add the sea beans, if using, the reserved cockle meat, parsley, tarragon, and red pepper flakes. Immediately remove from the heat and set aside.

5. Rinse and pat the fish dry. Place 3 slices of the prosciutto, overlapping one another, on top of a piece of plastic wrap. Place the sea bass, skin side down, on the prosciutto.

6. In a medium bowl, mix together the olives, 1 cup of the Candied Lemon Zest, and the parsley. Spoon one-quarter of the mixture down the center of the fish. Roll the fish around the filling into a tight cylinder, wrap it tightly in the plastic wrap, and twist the ends. Repeat with the remaining prosciutto, fish, and olive-lemon-herb mixture. Place the rolled up fish in the refrigerator for at least 1 hour, or up to 6 hours, before cooking.

7. When ready to serve, preheat the oven to 350°F; position the rack in the middle. Remove and discard the plastic wrap from the fish. Add enough oil to a large skillet to cover the bottom of the pan and set it over high heat. Add 1 tablespoon of the butter. Just before the oil starts to smoke, place the fish in the skillet, prosciutto seam side down, and sear for 1 minute. It is important to sear the fish seam side down, because cooking it on the other side first will cause the prosciutto to shrink and unwrap. Gently flip the fish over and sear for another minute. Transfer to a Silpat- or parchment paper–lined half-sheet baking pan. Pour the oil and butter from the skillet on top of the fish. Repeat with the remaining fish and butter. Let the fish sit out for 5 minutes together so it is all roughly the same temperature when it goes into the oven. Bake for 10 to 12 minutes or until a cake tester comes out without force and is warm to the touch. Transfer the fish to a paper towel–lined tray and let it rest for 1 minute. Trim off the ends of the roulade and slice each roulade crosswise into 3 even slices.

ASSEMBLE THE DISH

8. Divide the sea bass slices evenly among 4 warmed bowls. Ladle about $\frac{1}{3}$ cup of the broth around each fish and finish with a drizzle of the mustard and olive oils. Sprinkle with the red-veined sorrel and serve.

Make It Faster *For a slightly simpler execution, you don't need to slice the fish before serving—this is what we do at the restaurant for presentation.*

Note *Sea beans have become increasingly prominent at farmers' markets and specialty stores. Sea beans grow on salt marshes and beaches, have a crunchy texture and a briny flavor, and have an aftertaste slightly reminiscent of asparagus. Often, they are eaten raw, but because of their high sodium content, they are blanched to remove some of their saltiness.*

SERVES 4 This dish started from my desire to make a black trumpet polenta, and just grew from there. For whatever reason, maybe because black is my favorite color, I've always been curious about ways to make food black. I use black garlic and black olive oil (see Sources, page 403), but you don't see a lot of naturally black foods (it probably sends a message of something rotting), other than maybe squid ink, which I hardly ever use.

Besides wanting to make black trumpet polenta, I wanted the whole dish to be completely covered by the emulsion, so you had no idea what was on your plate until you cut into it. I wanted everything to be a surprise: the black trumpet polenta, the squash confit, and the black cod.

FOR THE BUTTERNUT SQUASH CONFIT

4 cups duck fat or olive oil

1 cup diced butternut squash

4 fresh sage leaves

1 fresh or ½ dried bay leaf

Kosher salt

FOR THE ACORN SQUASH EMULSION

4 cups cleaned acorn squash scraps (everything but the seeds), cut into ¼-inch pieces

2 cinnamon sticks

1 star anise

2 whole cloves

5 black peppercorns

1 sprig fresh sage

1 fresh or ½ dried bay leaf

½ cup fresh lime juice

2 ounces (4 tablespoons) unsalted butter

5 grams soy lecithin granules (see Sources, page 403; optional)

1 teaspoon kosher salt

FOR THE BLACK TRUMPET POLENTA

Canola oil

4 cups black trumpet mushrooms

2 ounces (4 tablespoons) unsalted butter

1 head garlic, halved

1 sprig fresh thyme

4 cups whole milk

1 cup polenta

Finely grated zest of 1 lime

Kosher salt

FOR THE BLACK COD

4 (6-ounce) black cod fillets, skin and bloodline removed, skin reserved

Kosher salt

TO ASSEMBLE THE DISH

Lime juice

Finely grated zest of 2 limes

MAKE THE BUTTERNUT SQUASH CONFIT

1. Warm the duck fat in a medium saucepot set over medium heat until it registers 250°F on a deep-frying thermometer. Add the butternut squash, sage, bay leaf, and a couple of pinches of salt. Cook for 5 minutes or until the squash is soft and cooked through. Let the squash cool in the fat. Refrigerate the squash and fat until needed. The confit can be made ahead and refrigerated for up to 4 weeks. Reserve the duck fat for cooking the black cod.

MAKE THE ACORN SQUASH EMULSION

2. Preheat the oven to 300°F. Spread the acorn squash scraps out on a baking sheet and bake for 45 minutes.

3. Place the scraps into a medium pot set over medium heat and cover with 4 cups of water. Add 1 cinnamon stick, star anise, cloves, and peppercorns. Let the liquid simmer for 90 minutes. Strain the liquid through a fine mesh strainer into a nonreactive container. Discard the solids. Add sage, bay leaf, and remaining cinnamon stick. Wrap tightly in plastic wrap and let infuse for 25 minutes. The accumulated moisture that will gather on the inside of the plastic wrap will look like it is raining. Strain.

4. In a small pot, combine the squash broth, lime juice, butter, lecithin (if using), and salt, and bring to a boil over high heat. Remove from the heat, and using an immersion blender, blend until emulsified. Set aside.

and cook for 5 minutes, whisking every minute. The polenta might appear thick at first, but will eventually thin out. Whisk in the mushroom puree. Remove from the heat and set aside. Keep the polenta warm.

MAKE THE BLACK COD

7. While the mushrooms for the polenta cook, make the black cod skins: Preheat the oven to 350°F; position the rack in the middle. Using the back of a spoon, scrape all the meat off the fish skin. Line a baking sheet with a Silpat or parchment paper and spray with nonstick cooking spray. Lay the skins out flat on the lined baking sheet. Cover them with another Silpat or more parchment paper and place another baking sheet on top. Bake the skins for 10 minutes or until crispy. Transfer to a cooling rack and remove the top baking sheet.

8. Rinse and thoroughly pat the fillets dry, and season liberally with salt. In a large sauté pan with high sides set over medium heat, rewarm the reserved duck fat to 110°F. Gently place the cod fillets into the warm duck fat and poach for approximately 24 minutes or until opaque and cooked through. Transfer the fillets to a platter and keep warm.

ASSEMBLE THE DISH

9. Buzz the Acorn Squash Emulsion with an immersion blender until foamy. Divide the Black Trumpet Polenta among 4 plates and top each with a piece of fish and a squeeze of lime juice. Spoon some of the Butternut Squash Confit over the fish, cover the plate with the Acorn Squash Emulsion, and sprinkle with lime zest. Top with a piece of the crispy cod skin, and serve.

Make It Faster *Making the crispy skin guarantees a dramatic presentation. However, you can skip making the crispy skin, and just cook the fish as indicated above, and serve it with polenta. If you're pressed for time, you can also skip the emulsion, since it's mainly used for a dramatic presentation at the restaurant. If you do make the emulsion, keep in mind the role of the lecithin: It helps to keep things smooth. If you choose to skip it, you will not affect the taste of the dish.*

MAKE THE BLACK TRUMPET POLENTA

5. Add enough oil to a large sauté pan to cover the bottom of the pan and set it over high heat. Just before it starts to smoke, add the mushrooms, reduce the heat to medium, and cook the mushrooms until their liquid is nearly evaporated. Add the butter, garlic, and thyme, and cook for 1 minute. Discard the garlic and thyme, and transfer the mushrooms to a blender. Add a few tablespoons of water and blend on high speed until pureed. Set the mushroom puree aside.

6. In a medium pot, bring the milk to a boil over medium-high heat. Reduce the heat to medium and whisk in the polenta, stirring vigorously. Stir in the lime zest and season to taste with salt. Reduce the heat to low

PINK SNAPPER + THAI RED CURRY + SWEET PEAS + BABY FENNEL AND ZUCCHINI

SERVES 4   I picked up this curry sauce from Chef Kazuto Matsusaka and his wife, Vicky, while working at Above, where he was executive chef. I learned a lot from Chef Matsusaka; every day I was introduced to an ingredient I'd never worked with before. There was mirin, miso, ponzu, white soy sauce, uni—just to name a few. The simplicity in what Matsusaka did and the flavors he could extract from just three ingredients helped me to understand that sometimes you don't need forty ingredients and six techniques on one plate. Just let the few elegant ingredients shine. If you look at my food today, Chef Matsusaka's influence is very evident.

FOR THE THAI RED CURRY

Canola oil

1 cup chopped onions

1 cup minced ginger

¼ cup minced garlic

½ cup Thai red curry paste

4 cups plum wine

8 cups heavy cream

6 cups coconut milk

2 cups kaffir lime leaves (wrapped in cheesecloth and tied)

Kosher salt

FOR THE BASMATI RICE CAKES

⅔ cup heavy cream

2 tablespoons cornstarch

⅔ cup cooked basmati rice, room temperature

2 scallions, green parts only, chopped

1 tablespoon canola oil

½ ounce (1 tablespoon) unsalted butter

Kosher salt

FOR THE BABY ZUCCHINI

Olive oil

1 cup crosswise-sliced baby zucchini with tops attached

Kosher salt

FOR THE PEAS AND BABY FENNEL

1 cup shelled English peas

Canola oil

½ cup thinly sliced baby fennel

1 ounce (2 tablespoons) unsalted butter

Granulated sugar

Kosher salt

¼ cup Chicken Stock (see page 382) or store-bought

¼ cup thinly sliced shallots

2 tablespoons chiffonade of fresh mint

FOR THE PINK SNAPPER

4 (5-ounce) pink snapper fillets, skins removed and reserved

Kosher salt

Canola oil

TO ASSEMBLE THE DISH

Raw baby zucchini with tops attached

2 limes, halved

MAKE THE THAI RED CURRY

1. In a large stockpot set over medium heat, warm enough oil to cover the bottom of the pan. Add the onions, ginger, and garlic and cook until the onions are translucent but do not pick up color, 6 to 8 minutes.

2. Add the curry paste and cook for 1 minute, stirring, so that the curry paste does not burn. Add the wine and cook until the pan is dry, about 10 minutes. Add the cream and cook, stirring, until the liquid has reduced by half, about 30 minutes. Add the coconut milk and cook until the liquid has reduced by one-third, about 20 minutes. Transfer the curry to a bain marie (see Technique, page 240) or a nonreactive container and add the kaffir lime leaves. Wrap tightly in plastic wrap and let infuse for 1 hour. The accumulated moisture that will gather on the inside of the plastic wrap will look like it is raining.

3. Unwrap the container and discard the leaves. Using an immersion blender, puree the liquid until smooth and strain it through a fine-mesh strainer into a bowl. Season to taste with salt and set aside. You will need 4 cups of the curry for this recipe; freeze the remainder for use another time (it makes a terrific soup).

MAKE THE BASMATI RICE CAKES

4. In a medium bowl, stir together the heavy cream and cornstarch. Add the rice and scallions, cover, and refrigerate the batter for at least 2 hours.

5. When ready to serve, in a small sauté pan, combine the oil and butter, and heat over high heat until the butter begins to foam. Add the batter in 3-inch-wide and ¾-inch-thick patties and reduce the heat to medium. Cook until the cake edges begin to brown, about 2 minutes. Flip the rice cakes and cook on the other side until the bottom is crispy, about 2 minutes. Transfer the rice cakes to a paper towel–lined tray and season with salt. Set aside.

MAKE THE BABY ZUCCHINI

6. In a large sauté pan set over high heat, warm enough oil to cover the bottom of the pan. Just before it starts to smoke, add the zucchini and cook for 1 minute. Season with salt to taste, remove from the heat, and set aside.

MAKE THE PEAS AND BABY FENNEL

7. Bring a medium pot of water to a boil. Blanch the peas in the boiling water for 1 minute. Immediately transfer to an ice bath and let cool. Drain and set aside.

8. In a large sauté pan set over high heat, warm enough canola oil to cover the bottom of the pan. Just before it starts to smoke, add the fennel and butter; reduce the heat to medium, and cook until the fennel is soft, about 2 minutes. Season to taste with sugar and salt, and add the stock. Cook until the stock has been absorbed and the pan is dry. Stir in the reserved peas and shallots and cook until just warmed through. Remove from the heat and set aside. Right before serving, fold in the mint.

MAKE THE PINK SNAPPER

9. Preheat the oven to 350°F; position the rack in the middle. Scrape all the meat off the snapper skins and spray the skins lightly with cooking spray. Place the skins on a Silpat- or parchment paper–lined half-sheet baking pan and bake for 10 minutes. Transfer to a cooling rack. Place another Silpat or piece of parchment over the skins, and place another half-sheet baking pan on top.

10. Rinse and thoroughly pat the snapper dry. Season the fish with some salt. In a large sauté pan set over high heat, warm enough oil to cover the bottom of the pan until just before it starts to smoke. Add the fillets and cook for 2 minutes on one side. Using a fish spatula, carefully flip the fish onto the other side and cook for 2 minutes or until a cake tester inserted into the fish comes out without force. Transfer the fillets to a plate and set aside. Depending on the size of your sauté pan, you may have to cook your fish in batches.

ASSEMBLE THE DISH

11. Place a Basmati Rice Cake on each of 4 warmed plates, and spoon some Peas and Baby Fennel on the side. Add the Baby Zucchini on the side, and top with a piece of Pink Snapper. Spoon some more of the cooked vegetables over the fish and top with a crispy snapper skin.

12. Buzz the Thai Red Curry with an immersion blender for 20 seconds to emulsify the curry. Spoon the curry around the fish and vegetables. Garnish the plates with the raw baby zucchini and lime halves.

Make It Faster *Make the curry ahead of time. And make just one of the vegetable sides—the baby zucchini is an easy, quick one. Roast the whole snapper with the skin on and serve it family style.*

LINE-CAUGHT FLUKE + FRIED GREEN TOMATOES + WHITE CORN SALAD + BACON AÏOLI

SERVES 4 This is as greenmarket driven as a dish can get. On Saturday mornings, we go to the Tribeca greenmarket and always stop by Blue Moon Fish. In the summer, we get their line-caught fluke before we walk around the rest of the greenmarket and see what else is available. And then we compose a dish based on what's in season. When we first opened, we would do a Saturday night fish special with the fish we'd gotten at the market a few hours before. If you look at the components of this dish, after I picked up the fish, I probably went to the next stand and picked up some corn, and then to the next stand to get some green tomatoes, and so on. And when I got back to the restaurant, I threw it all together and it came out beautifully. This is proof positive that when you have fresh, ripe, in-season ingredients, you get delicious, inspiring results.

FOR THE BACON AÏOLI

1 cup chopped bacon (about 2 to 3 slices, depending on the thickness of bacon)

1 large egg yolk, room temperature

1½ cups canola oil

½ teaspoon cayenne pepper

2¼ teaspoons white wine vinegar

1½ teaspoons chopped fresh chives

½ shallot, brunoise (see page 48)

FOR THE WHITE CORN SALAD

1½ cups champagne vinegar

¼ cup granulated sugar

1 tablespoon kosher salt, plus more as needed

1 fresh or ½ dried bay leaf

1 sprig fresh oregano

2 cups white corn kernels (about 3 ears of corn)

¼ cup brunoise poblano peppers (see page 48)

¼ cup brunoise red peppers (see page 48)

¼ cup brunoise red onions (see page 48)

1 tablespoon chopped fresh oregano

1 teaspoon chopped fresh tarragon

FOR THE FRIED GREEN TOMATOES

2 cups all-purpose flour

1 tablespoon Ararat spice mix (see Sources, page 403)

Kosher salt

2 cups buttermilk

4 large eggs

3 green tomatoes, sliced into ½-inch-thick slices

4 cups Bacon Bread Crumbs (see page 381) or regular bread crumbs

Olive oil

FOR THE FLUKE

4 (5-ounce) fluke fillets, skin removed (see page 59)

Kosher salt

Blended Oil (see page 395)

2 ounces (4 tablespoons) unsalted butter

2 sprigs fresh oregano

Corn shoots (see Sources, page 403; optional)

MAKE THE BACON AÏOLI

1. Preheat the oven to 350°F; position the rack in the middle. Place the bacon on a baking pan and bake for 12 to 15 minutes or until crispy. Reserve the bacon fat in the pan. Set aside but keep the bacon fat warm.

2. In a medium bowl, whisk the egg yolks with 2 teaspoons of water until combined. While whisking, slowly drizzle in the oil and reserved bacon fat until emulsified. Transfer the emulsion to a food processor; add the bacon, cayenne, and vinegar. Transfer to a bowl and fold in the chives and shallot. Taste and adjust the seasonings. Refrigerate until needed.

MAKE THE WHITE CORN SALAD

3. In 2-quart saucepot, combine the vinegar, sugar, salt, bay leaf, and oregano with ½ cup of water and bring to a boil over medium-high heat. Remove from the heat and let the marinade cool to room temperature.

4. Place the corn kernels in a nonreactive container and pour the marinade over. Allow the corn to sit in the marinade for at least 1 hour.

5. Using a slotted spoon, transfer the corn to a large bowl and combine it with both peppers, onions, oregano, and tarragon. Taste and adjust the seasonings. Set aside.

MAKE THE FRIED GREEN TOMATOES

6. In a medium bowl, whisk together the flour, Ararat, and salt until combined. In another medium bowl, whisk together the buttermilk and eggs until combined. Place the Bacon Breadcrumbs into a flat container. Coat the tomato slices in the flour mixture, dip them into the buttermilk-egg mixture, and coat them in the bread crumbs.

7. In a large sauté pan set over high heat, warm enough oil to coat the bottom of the pan. Just before it starts to smoke, add the coated tomatoes and fry until the coating is crispy, about 1 minute per side. Transfer to a paper towel–lined tray and set aside.

MAKE THE FLUKE

8. Thoroughly pat the fillets dry and season with salt. In a large sauté pan set over high heat, warm enough Blended Oil to coat the bottom of the pan, just before it starts to smoke, add 2 fillets and sear for 1 minute on each side, until browned on both sides. Reduce the heat to medium, add half of the butter and oregano, and baste, about 1 minute, until cooked through. Remove from the heat and set aside. Repeat with the remaining fluke, butter, and oregano.

9. Place a dollop of the Bacon Aïoli on each of 4 plates and top with a slice of the Fried Green Tomato. Spoon around some White Corn Salad and top with a piece of fluke. Scatter around the corn shoots, if using, and serve.

Note *Bacon Aïoli will keep, refrigerated, for up to 4 days. Use it for burgers, sandwiches, or for dipping French fries.*

CEDAR QUINAULT TRIBE TROUT + OLD-FASHIONED EGG SAUCE + FRIED HEIRLOOM HOMINY + CHANTERELLES

SERVES 4 The native people of our shores would cook fish tied to cedar planks that were kept around the fire. My father adapted the idea and became famous for his cedar-planked salmon. In a nod to my old man and the Native Americans, here is my take on cedar-planked fish—I like to use Quinault Tribe steelhead trout, which comes directly from the Quinault Indian Reservation and has a very limited season. We pair the trout with a staple in Native American cooking—heirloom hominy from Anson Mills. It takes a while to prepare and you need culinary lime (see Note), but once you try heirloom hominy, there's no turning back.

We get our hedgehog mushrooms from a man named Hans who works at the company Mushrooms & More. He always takes the extra step to find wild mushrooms or berries that I might be looking for.

SPECIAL EQUIPMENT

Cedar shims (make sure you get untreated cedar at the lumber yard or buy cedar planks at a kitchenware store)

FOR THE FRIED HEIRLOOM HOMINY

7 cups spring or filtered water

¼ cup culinary lime (see Sources, page 403)

1 cup heirloom hominy (see Sources, page 403)

Canola oil

2 tablespoons Ararat spice mix (see Sources, page 403)

Kosher salt

FOR THE TROUT

2 ounces (4 tablespoons) unsalted butter, softened

Kosher salt

4 (5-ounce) lake trout or salmon fillets, skin removed

¼ cup mustard powder

FOR THE OLD-FASHIONED EGG SAUCE

⅓ cup white wine vinegar, divided

2 large eggs, preferably farm-fresh

½ cup dry white wine

2 tablespoons whole black peppercorns

2 sprigs fresh thyme

1 shallot, sliced

1 fresh or ½ dried bay leaf

2 cups heavy cream

8 ounces (16 tablespoons) unsalted butter

Kosher salt

Juice of 1 lemon

3 tablespoons chopped fresh curly parsley

1 tablespoon chopped fresh tarragon

FOR THE CHANTERELLES

Blended Oil (see page 395)

2 cups chanterelle mushrooms, cleaned

2 ounces (4 tablespoons) unsalted butter

1 head garlic, halved

3 sprigs fresh thyme

1 cup dry white wine

1 cup Chicken Stock (see page 382) or store-bought

Kosher salt

Freshly ground black pepper

MAKE THE FRIED HEIRLOOM HOMINY (SEE NOTE)

1. Pour the water into a medium enamel- or porcelain-coated pot. Add the culinary lime and stir with a wooden spoon until the lime has dissolved. Bring the lime water to a rolling boil over high heat. As soon as the water comes to a boil, turn off the heat and let the pot stand until the lime water has cooled and cleared, 4 to 5 hours. The water will form a thin, crisp lime skin on its surface, and the liquid beneath will be clear. At the bottom, there will be a layer of cloudy lime solids.

2. Set a fine-mesh strainer over a 4- to 7-quart glass mixing bowl. Gently lift and tilt the pot with lime water and pour the liquid through the strainer, leaving the cloudy solids in the bowl (the lime skin will remain

in the strainer). Allow the solids to settle again, then decant more lime water into the bowl, repeating the process until only about a cup of cloudy solids and water remain at the bottom of the pot. Pour the lime skin and solids down the drain and rinse the pot and sink thoroughly. Return the decanted lime water to the pot. Add the hominy. Let everything settle; skim off and discard any floating kernels. Bring to a boil over high heat, then cover and turn off the heat. Let the hominy stand in the lime water at room temperature overnight.

3. The following day, turn the pot on high heat and bring to a boil. Reduce the heat to low and cook at a gentle simmer until the kernels are soft and chewy and have shed their skins, about 3 hours. To check for doneness, use a wooden spoon to lift a few kernels out of the water, rinse them under cold running water, and taste. If done, the kernels will be soft and slightly chewy. If you taste a hard, starchy center, give the hominy more time, and taste again.

4. Transfer the pot to a sink and run the hominy under hot water to flush out any bits of pericarp (the cellophane-like skin that encases the kernels when they're raw), stirring with a wooden spoon, about 5 minutes. Drain the hominy and rinse it under hot running water, rubbing the kernels between your palms. Cool the hominy, transfer it to an airtight container, and refrigerate until ready to use, up to 1 week, or freeze it for up to 3 months.

5. When ready to serve, lay the hominy out on a paper towel–lined tray until the kernels are completely dry. Add enough oil to a 4-quart saucepot to come 3 inches up the sides. Heat the oil over medium heat until it registers 350°F on a deep-frying thermometer. Add the hominy to the Dutch oven and fry for 30 seconds. Using a slotted spoon, transfer the hominy to a paper towel–lined tray. Season to taste with the Ararat and salt. Set aside.

MAKE THE TROUT

6. Soak the cedar shims in cold water for at least 3 hours or up to 12 hours—you can do this at the same time as you make the lime water for the hominy.

7. About 10 minutes before serving, preheat a broiler to high and place the shims under the broiler (reserve the soaking water), just until they begin to smoke and take on a little color. Return the shims to the soaking water for 5 minutes. Remove and pat dry. Reduce the broiler heat to medium. Brush the "fat" part of the shims with some of the softened butter and sprinkle some salt on top. Brush the fillets with the softened butter and season the bone side with salt. Place the fillet, skin side down, on a shim and sprinkle 1 tablespoon of mustard powder on each fillet. Broil the fish until cooked through, about 3 minutes for medium-rare.

MAKE THE OLD-FASHIONED EGG SAUCE

8. Bring 3 cups of water to a boil in a saucepot. Add the eggs and 3 tablespoons of the vinegar. Reduce the heat enough to maintain a slow, gentle simmer and simmer the eggs for 9 minutes. Immediately transfer the pot to the sink, pour off the hot water, and run the eggs under cold water for 3 minutes. Peel the eggs and separate the yolks from the whites. Using the finest side of a box grater, grate the yolks and whites into separate bowls and set aside.

9. In a nonreactive saucepot, combine the wine, the remaining 2 tablespoons vinegar, peppercorns, thyme, shallot, and bay leaf and bring to a boil over high heat. Reduce the heat to medium and cook until the pan is dry, about 8 to 10 minutes. Add the cream and cook, stirring, until the liquid has reduced by about one-third. Strain the mixture and return it to the pan. Whisk in the butter, 1 tablespoon at a time, waiting for each piece of butter to be fully emulsified before adding the next. Add salt to taste and whisk in the lemon juice. Remove from the eat and keep warm.

10. Right before serving, whisk the parsley, tarragon, grated egg whites, and grated egg yolks into the sauce.

MAKE THE CHANTERELLES

11. Add enough oil to a large skillet to cover the bottom of the pan and set it over high heat. Just before it starts to smoke, add the mushrooms in one even layer, reduce the heat to medium, and cook until the mushrooms begin to brown on the edges, about 3 minutes.

12. Add the butter, garlic halves, and thyme, and cook, stirring, until both the butter and mushrooms are browned, 5 to 10 minutes. Add the wine, and cook until the wine has been absorbed and the pan is nearly dry. Add the stock and cook until it has been absorbed and the pan is nearly dry. Season to taste with salt and pepper, discard the garlic and thyme, and set aside.

ASSEMBLE THE DISH

13. Remove the fish from the broiler and transfer the still-smoking planks (along with the fish) to 4 plates large enough to hold the planks. Ladle the egg sauce over the fish and spoon the chanterelles and Fried Heirloom Hominy around.

Note *Lime is a caustic substance and should not come into prolonged contact with your skin. If you touch culinary lime in either dry or liquid form, rinse the exposed area with cold water. Make sure to carefully and thoroughly rinse all the utensils and pots, as well any surfaces (sink, counters) that came in contact with culinary lime.*

COMMUNITY CATCH
LITCHFIELD FARMS ORGANIC AND NATURAL, LLC
ANDREA ANJERA JR.

When my restaurant was struggling financially, Andrea Anjera Jr., of Community Catch, was one of the few purveyors to extend a line of credit to us and patiently wait until we had money to pay it back. He showed kindness to us that went beyond a business relationship—something I'm particularly grateful for and humbled by.

Andrea also happens to be the guy who procured baby halibut for me—a dish that was so incredibly popular at the restaurant that we served it until the farm raising the fish lost funding and went out of business. It was an amazing product, and I still miss it.

But Andrea and I continue to work together on unique fish that is sustainably sourced and whose origins we can trace, or there is a local connection. That's Andrea's specialty.

While Community Catch, formerly Litchfield Farms, was originally a meat-sourcing business founded by Andrea's grandfather in 1939, when Andrea took over in 2000, he got the company to focus solely on organic and pasture-raised meat.

The decision to move from meat to fish was originally prompted by a conversation Andrea had with his children one day when he was lamenting about how they were the last generation who would be able to eat certain fish. It

After doing some research, Andrea located organic fish producers in the UK and Ireland in 2004, and started to bring in organic salmon, trout, and halibut. A few years later, Community Catch stopped dealing with meat altogether and switched over to only fish.

Today, Andrea works with his extensive network of farmers and harvesters, focuses on traceability and sustainability, sourcing unique, hard-to-find fish. It's a hands-on approach that works well for me and my chefs, as we look at seafood sustainability in the exact same way. We, too, want our children, and their children, and their children to enjoy the same seafood that we do. And it's working with people like Andrea that makes a

SERVES 4 Sauce Proposal was originally called a rather predictable name—Caper-Raisin Emulsion, which is what it is—but as time went by, more and more people asked me if I was married after tasting it. Thus, the name "Sauce Proposal" was born. It sounds a little more fun than its previous name and now it comes with a story. Try making it for your significant other or your crush—and see if you can get a proposal out of it!

FOR THE SAUCE PROPOSAL

5 ounces (10 tablespoons) unsalted butter

¼ cup hazelnuts

Olive oil

½ Vidalia onion, brunoise (see page 48)

3 tablespoons cauliflower florets

3 tablespoons Romanesco cauliflower florets or regular cauliflower florets

Kosher salt

½ cup fresh lime juice

½ cup low-sodium soy sauce

3 tablespoons golden raisins

2 tablespoons chopped capers

2 tablespoons chopped fresh curly parsley

1 tablespoon red pepper flakes

FOR THE CAULIFLOWER PUREE

4 cups roughly chopped cauliflower

3 cups heavy cream

Pinch of kosher salt

FOR THE HALIBUT

4 (5-ounce) East Coast halibut fillets, bloodline and skin removed (see page 59)

1 large egg white

2 tablespoons chopped fresh curly parsley

1 teaspoon red pepper flakes

4 (¼-inch-thick) slices Pullman loaf

Extra-virgin olive oil

Kosher salt

Freshly ground black pepper

MAKE THE SAUCE PROPOSAL

1. Make the brown butter: Add 4 tablespoons of the butter to a sauté pan set over medium heat and cook until the solids brown, 3 to 5 minutes. Immediately transfer the brown butter to an ice bath, whisking to cool down the butter. This step is important because if the brown butter is not whisked while being cooled, it will separate. Refrigerate until ready to use.

2. Preheat the oven to 350°F; position the rack in the middle. Toast the hazelnuts in a shallow baking pan for 10 to 12 minutes or until fragrant. Remove the skins by rubbing the hazelnuts with a kitchen towel. Cool the nuts, then place them in a plastic bag. Using a mallet or a rolling pin, pound the nuts until they are crushed. Set aside 2 tablespoons; reserve the rest for another use (or eat them!).

3. Add enough olive oil to a sauté pan to cover the bottom of the pan and set it over low heat. Add the onion and cook, stirring from time to time, until translucent, 3 to 4 minutes. Remove from the heat, transfer the onions to a plate, and set aside.

4. Return the pan to the stovetop. Add enough olive oil to cover the bottom of the pan and set it over high heat. Just before the oil starts to smoke, add enough cauli-flower and Romanesco florets to cover the bottom of the pan in one layer, reduce the heat to medium, and cook for 2 to 3 minutes. Once the florets begin to brown slightly, add 3 tablespoons of the butter. Let the butter melt, gently shake the pan, season with salt, and transfer the florets to a plate lined with a paper towel. Set the cooked florets aside.

5. In a 2-quart saucepan, bring the lime juice and soy sauce to a boil over high heat. Reduce the heat to low and gradually whisk in the remaining 3 tablespoons butter, 1 tablespoon at a time, until well incorporated and emulsified. Whisk in the reserved brown butter, 1 tablespoon at a time. Remove from the heat and blend with an immersion blender or in a stand blender. Keep the sauce warm.

6. Right before serving, stir in the cooked florets, raisins, capers, parsley, and red pepper flakes. Set aside.

MAKE THE CAULIFLOWER PUREE

7. In a saucepot, combine the cauliflower, cream, and a pinch of salt and cook over medium heat until the cauliflower is cooked through, about 25 minutes. Reserve the cooking liquid. Transfer the cauliflower to a food processor fitted with a blade, or a blender, and pulse a few times. Add the cooking liquid, a couple of tablespoons at a time, until the mixture is smooth and light. If you add too much cooking liquid too fast, your blender might explode, so be sure to add it slowly. Keep warm.

MAKE THE HALIBUT EN CROUTE

8. Preheat the oven to 350°F; position the rack in the middle. Rinse and pat the fish dry. Brush one side of the fillets with the egg white. Sprinkle the parsley and red pepper flakes over the egg white side. Lay the bread slices out and place the fillets over the bread, herb-side down. Trim the bread to fit the filets, and gently flip the fish over so that the bread is on top.

9. Add enough oil to a large skillet to cover the bottom of the pan and set it over medium heat. Season two of the fillets with salt and pepper and add them to the pan, bread-side down. Carefully watch the fish, and once the edges begin to brown, transfer the fish to a Silpat- or parchment paper–lined baking pan, bread side up. Pour the oil from the pan on top of the fish. Repeat with the remaining fillets. Let the fillets sit out for 5 minutes together so they are all roughly the same temperature when they goes into the oven. Bake the fish for about 4 minutes or until a cake tester, when inserted into the fish, comes out without any force.

10. Divide the fish among 4 warmed plates. Spoon the Cauliflower Puree on the side and liberally drizzle the Sauce Proposal over the fish.

BLUE-EYED COD + CUTTLEFISH ANGEL HAIR +
FENNEL + BASIL PESTO

SERVES 4 The blue-eyed cod, also commonly known as blue-eyed trevalla, is a fish commonly found in Australian waters. This mild-tasting fish has deep blue eyes with a golden ring around them, and has a texture, when cooked, somewhere between soft white fish and firmer fish like salmon. To get the blue-eyed trevalla, I work with Sea to Table, a fish distributor that partners with sustainably managed and harvested wild fisheries across the world to deliver fish to restaurants in the United States. I feel good working with a company that wants to ensure that our children and their children might have the opportunity to eat the same fish we did, and that theirs is a thoughtful approach to harvesting the ever-fluctuating fish populations.

FOR BASIL PESTO

3 cups packed basil leaves

2 garlic cloves

½ cup extra-virgin olive oil

½ cup finely grated Parmigiano-Reggiano

1 teaspoon red pepper flakes

FOR THE CUTTLEFISH ANGEL HAIR

1 pound cuttlefish, beaks removed and tentacles reserved

Extra-virgin olive oil

2 tablespoons minced garlic

¼ cup julienned sundried tomatoes (at the restaurant we use Oven-Dried Tomatoes; see page 398)

¼ cup pitted and julienned Cerignola olives

⅓ cup dry white wine

Juice of 1 lemon

½ teaspoon red pepper flakes

1 tablespoon chopped fresh curly parsley

Kosher salt

FOR THE TENTACLES AND FENNEL

Canola oil

4 baby fennel fronds

Kosher salt

FOR THE COD

4 (5-ounce) cod fillets, skin on

Blended Oil (see page 395)

TO ASSEMBLE THE DISH

1 lemon, quartered

Extra-virgin olive oil

MAKE THE BASIL PESTO

1. Bring a 4-quart pot of water to a boil. Blanch the basil in the boiling water for 1 minute, drain, and immediately transfer to an ice bath. Allow the basil to cool, then drain and squeeze out excess water.

2. Transfer the basil to a blender, add the garlic and olive oil, and puree for about 20 seconds. You may need to add a little more oil to get it to go, but do not add a lot or your pesto will not stay green. Immediately transfer the puree to a bowl set over an ice bath and stir until cold. Fold in the cheese and red pepper flakes. Transfer the pesto to an airtight container and refrigerate until needed.

MAKE THE CUTTLEFISH ANGEL HAIR

3. Butterfly the cuttlefish so that their bodies are open flat and trim each cuttlefish into a square. Roll the cuttlefish squares into tight cylinders and wrap the cylinders in plastic, twisting both ends to secure. Freeze until solid, about 2 hours. Using an adjustable mandoline, slice the frozen cuttlefish cylinders crosswise into ⅛-inch-thick slices. (If you don't have a mandoline, skip the freezing process and slice the fish with a knife as thinly as you can.)

4. A few minutes before serving, add enough oil to a large sauté pan to cover the bottom of the pan and set it over high heat. Add the garlic. Watch the garlic carefully, and as soon as it is toasted, turn off the heat and add the cuttlefish, tomatoes, and olives to the pan. Toss well to combine. Add the wine and lemon juice and return the pan to the stovetop over medium heat. Cook the cuttlefish for 30 seconds, scraping the brown bits off the bottom of the pan with a wooden spoon. Remove the pan from the heat and fold in the red pepper flakes, parsley, and salt to taste.

MAKE THE TENTACLES AND FENNEL

5. About 10 minutes before serving, light a grill or preheat a grill pan. Lightly brush the grill with oil. Grill the reserved cuttlefish tentacles over medium-high heat for 3 minutes, turning once, until slightly charred. Alternatively, broil the tentacles on high for about 2 minutes or until slightly charred.

6. A few minutes before serving, warm about 1 inch of oil in a pan set over medium-high heat. Fry the fennel fronds until crispy, about 1 minute. Transfer to a paper towel–lined tray and season with salt.

MAKE THE COD

7. About 10 minutes before serving, preheat the oven to 450°F; position the rack in the middle. Thoroughly pat the fillets dry. Add enough oil to a large ovenproof sauté pan to cover the bottom of the pan and set it over high heat. Just before the oil starts to smoke, add the cod, skin side down, and reduce the heat to medium. Using a fish spatula, very gently press down on the fish so the skin is flush against the bottom of the pan. This cod is a very delicate fish, so be extra-gentle. Cook until the edges begin to brown slightly, about 2 minutes. Transfer the pan to the oven and cook for 3 minutes or until the fish is cooked through and a small piece cut off the fillet reveals flaky, opaque flesh. Remove from the oven, and using a spatula, carefully flip the fish onto the other side. Baste the fish once or twice with the oil in the pan and remove from the heat.

ASSEMBLE THE DISH

8. Divide the pesto among 4 plates and top with the "angel hair" and a piece of cod. Place the fennel and tentacles on the side, and squeeze a bit of the lemon over each plate. Finish everything with a drizzle of olive oil and serve.

SEA TO TABLE

SYDNEY SCHWARZ

Sea to Table was born out of a family vacation the Dimin family took in 1996 to Tobago, where the family fell in love with the daily fresh-caught fish, as well as their sustainable, traditional fishing methods used for many generations.

The Dimin family immediately realized that by providing a direct connection between the fishermen and chefs, something wonderful would happen. The business grew steadily, and today, Sea to Table employs eleven workers full-time who work with various docks

Alaska to the Gulf Coast, from Florida to Montauk. Depending on the season, as well as the catch, Sea to Table works with about one hundred individual fishermen, each of whom the company knows by name. They feel that this kind of personal approach ensures higher quality of the catch and a better, more conscious sea-harvesting.

As you'd expect, Sea to Table provides full transparency to its chefs: from who is producing the food they serve, down to the fisherman who caught the fish.

the catch is delivered to the restaurant—the fish, gently packed in ice, is never frozen.

When I first learned of the concept of getting fish from the dock (any dock!) and into my kitchen, I jumped at the opportunity to work with Sea to Table. Sydney, our sales rep, takes great care to make sure that we are as happy as the fish she sources for us. And with their commitment to sustainability and traceability, Sea to Table works to make sure that future generations will be able

SAFE HARBOR SWORDFISH + FAIRY TALE EGGPLANT CAPONATA + SEA BEANS + ANCHOVY MAÎTRE D' BUTTER

SERVES 4 The swordfish that we get is from a company called Browne Trading, located in Maine. We get this fish only in the summer months, directly from the boat; it is fresh, wild, and line-caught swordfish that is responsibly harvested and tastes absolutely amazing. It is, without a doubt, the best swordfish I've ever tasted. While swordfish tends to be mild, when it sits for too long, it becomes very oily and fishy tasting. This fish comes to us so fresh that we've even served it raw as sashimi—something I've never seen done.

We serve this with Fairy Tale eggplant, which is becoming more popular at farmers' markets. If you've never had Fairy Tale eggplant, please go to your local greenmarket and try to find some.

FOR THE SWORDFISH

½ cup extra-virgin olive oil

¼ cup Shabazi spice mix (see Sources, page 403) or equal parts chili powder, dried parsley, and ground coriander

4 (5-ounce) swordfish steaks

Kosher salt

FOR THE ANCHOVY MAÎTRE D' BUTTER

8 ounces (16 tablespoons) unsalted butter

3 tablespoons minced oil-cured white anchovies

2 tablespoons chopped fresh curly parsley

1 tablespoon minced shallots

1 tablespoon chopped fresh chives

1 teaspoon minced garlic

Finely grated zest of 1 lemon

2 tablespoons kosher salt

FOR THE EGGPLANT CAPONATA

1 tablespoon dried currants

1 tablespoon Sancerre

1 red bell pepper

1 yellow bell pepper

½ cup extra-virgin olive oil, plus more as needed

½ pound Fairy Tale eggplant, sliced crosswise into ¼-inch-thick slices

Kosher salt

Freshly ground black pepper

½ cup cooked chickpeas (canned are fine)

¼ cup tomato concassé (see page 394) or diced tomatoes

¼ cup Balsamic Onions (see page 392), with their cooking liquid

1 tablespoon chiffonade of fresh mint

1 tablespoon chiffonade of fresh basil

TO ASSEMBLE THE DISH

1 cup sea beans (optional)

Kosher salt

25-year-old balsamic vinegar or your best balsamic

MAKE THE SWORDFISH

1. In a small bowl, stir together the olive oil and Shabazi. Place the swordfish steaks in a shallow dish and pour the marinade over them. Cover and refrigerate for at least 6 hours or up to 12.

2. About 45 minutes before serving, remove the fish from the refrigerator and allow it to sit at room temperature for 30 minutes.

3. When ready to assemble the dish, season the swordfish with salt. Light a grill or preheat a grill pan. Grill the fish over medium-high heat, turning once, until a tester inserted into the fish comes out easily and is warm to the touch, about 6 minutes. Alternatively, broil the fish on high until golden brown and cooked through, about 6 minutes. To test for doneness, insert a cake tester in the center of the fish for 10 seconds, and bring it to your bottom lip. If it is warm to the touch, the fish is done.

MAKE THE ANCHOVY MAÎTRE D' BUTTER

4. While the swordfish is marinating, place the butter, anchovies, parsley, shallots, chives, garlic, lemon zest, and salt in the bowl of a stand mixer fitted with the paddle attachment. Mix on high speed for 30 seconds. Separate the mixture into 4 equal parts, and using plastic wrap to help mold and smooth the butter, shape the butter into logs. You will only need 1 log (about 4 tablespoons)

of butter for this recipe. Freeze the rest for later use. You can use the butter any time you make a steak–it's delicious.

MAKE THE EGGPLANT CAPONATA

5. While the swordfish is marinating, cover the currants in the Sancerre and let sit. Preheat the oven to 425°F; position the rack in the middle. Toss the red and yellow peppers in some olive oil and place them on a shallow baking pan. Roast the peppers for 25 to 30 minutes, turning occasionally, until the skins are almost black and the peppers are soft when pierced with a knife. Transfer the peppers to a large bowl, cover tightly with plastic wrap, and allow the peppers to sit for 1½ hours at room temperature.

6. While the peppers are resting, add enough oil to a large sauté pan to cover the bottom of the pan and set it over high heat. Just before it starts to smoke, add the eggplant and reduce the heat to medium. Season the eggplant with salt and pepper; the eggplant will act as a sponge, so you will need to keep adding olive oil to the pan in small amounts. Cook the eggplant until soft and cooked through, about 8 minutes. Set aside to cool to room temperature.

7. Peel, seed, and cut the roasted peppers into medium dice. Transfer the cooled eggplant and peppers to a large bowl and add the chickpeas, tomatoes, and Balsamic Pearl Onions. Right before serving, fold in the basil and mint. Drizzle in the olive oil and ¼ cup of the onions' cooking liquid. Drain the currants and add them to the mixture. Season to taste with salt and pepper and set aside.

ASSEMBLE THE DISH

8. While the fish is coming to room temperature, bring a 2-quart saucepot of unsalted water to a boil and blanch the beans in the boiling water for 10 seconds. Immediately transfer them to an ice bath. Once cool, drain and set aside.

9. Plate the fish on 4 warmed plates. Dab some Anchovy Maître d' Butter on top while the fish is still hot—you want the butter to melt—and spoon some of the caponata on the side, using the liquid as a sauce for the fish. Sprinkle the sea beans, if using, on top and serve.

HOW TO
FILLET A FIN FISH

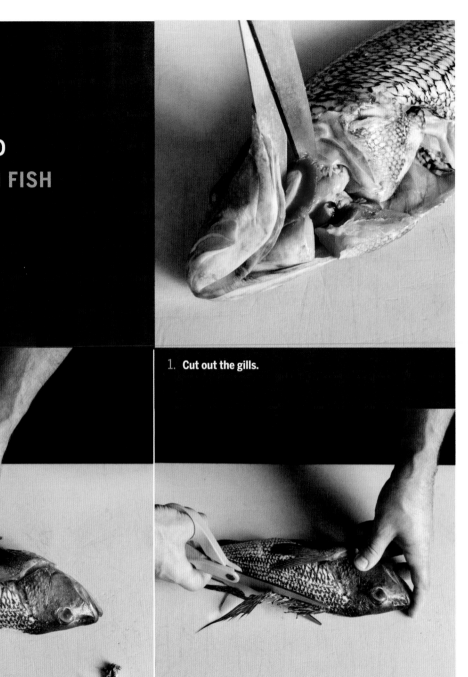

1. Cut out the gills.

2. Cut off all the fins using kitchen shears.

MARC FORGIONE

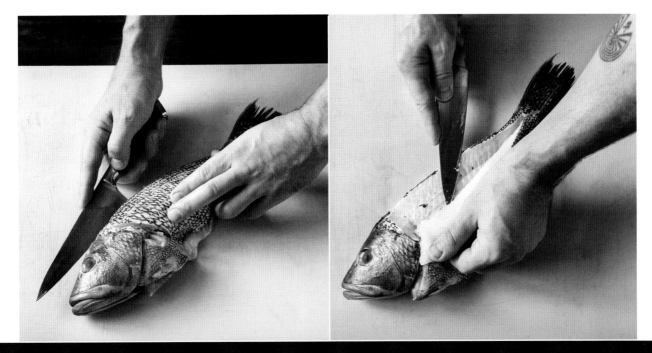

3. Position the fish with its tail facing you, and starting from the head to the tail, with one precise slicing motion, slice down the spine (do not make lots of little incisions; it should be one precise slice) so that half of the side of the fish facing you is now removed from the skeleton.

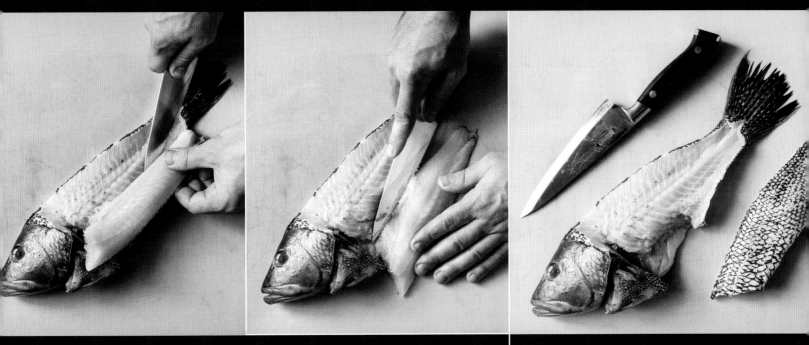

4. Using your finger, gently lift the fillet and with a singular, decisive slice, remove the rest of the side of the fish. Repeat with the other side of the fish, but this time the head of the fish instead of the tail should be facing you.

5. The finished product, with half the fish filleted. Using fish tweezers, pliers, or regular tweezers, pull out the remaining pin bones in the fish.

RED SNAPPER "BÁNH MÌ" + VIETNAMESE SAUSAGE + PICKLED DAIKON + CILANTRO

SERVES 4 I don't know what I did before *bánh mì* sandwiches came into my life. Living across the street from Saigon Bakery has made me slightly addicted to the "Spicy #1," which is the café's pork *bánh mì*. I have to eat at least one a week, or I start to get the shakes. I always wanted to do something with those flavors, and was curious about how they would work with fish. And since I'm sharing this recipe here with you, it's probably clear: The snapper *bánh mì* gives the Spicy #1 a good run for its money. The pickled vegetables in this recipe are great to have on hand; they will spruce up any regular sandwich.

SPECIAL EQUIPMENT

Meat Grinder

FOR THE PICKLED VEGETABLES

1 cup julienned carrots

1 cup julienned daikon radish

1 jalapeño, sliced

4 tablespoons kosher salt

½ cup plus 2 teaspoons granulated sugar

1 cup unseasoned rice wine vinegar

FOR THE SAUSAGE

1 pound pork shoulder with fat, thinly sliced

½ yellow onion, thinly sliced

2 tablespoons fish sauce

2 tablespoons granulated sugar

2 tablespoons olive oil

2 cloves garlic

1 teaspoon toasted sesame oil

1 teaspoon sriracha

Freshly ground black pepper

Canola oil

1 cup brining liquid from Pickled Vegetables

Chiffonade of fresh Thai or regular basil

Chiffonade of fresh mint

FOR THE SNAPPER

4 (5-ounce) red snapper fillets, bloodline and skin removed

2 large egg whites, lightly beaten

2 tablespoons chopped fresh curly parsley

1 teaspoon red pepper flakes

2 cups diced Pullman loaf, crusts removed

Canola oil

Kosher salt

Freshly ground black pepper

TO ASSEMBLE THE DISH

Micro cilantro (see Sources, page 403) or chiffonade of regular cilantro leaves

MAKE THE PICKLED VEGETABLES

1. Combine the carrots, radish, and jalapeño in a bowl with 1 tablespoon of the salt and 2 teaspoons of the sugar, cover, and let sit at room temperature for 20 minutes. Transfer the vegetables to a colander, rinse them under cold water, and squeeze out any excess liquid.

2. In a small nonreactive saucepot, combine the vinegar and the remaining 3 tablespoons salt and ½ cup sugar with ½ cup of water and bring to a boil over high heat. Transfer the pot to an ice bath and let cool. When the marinade is cool to the touch, pour it over the vegetables, cover, and refrigerate for at least 3 hours before serving.

MAKE THE SAUSAGE

3. In a large bowl, combine the pork, onion, fish sauce, sugar, olive oil, garlic, sesame oil, sriracha, and pepper. Cover and refrigerate for 24 hours.

4. Using a meat grinder, grind the meat. Shape it into 2- to 3-inch-diameter patties with your hands; you should have 8 sausage patties.

5. When ready to serve, add enough oil to a sauté pan to cover the bottom of the pan and set it over high heat. Just before the oil starts to smoke, add the patties to the pan, but do not overcrowd the pan (you may need to do

this in batches). Immediately reduce the heat to medium, and cook the sausages until nicely browned on both sides, 3 to 4 minutes per side. Remove the cooked sausage patties from the pan and set aside. Remove the pan from the heat and add 1 cup of the reserved brining liquid (from the Pickled Vegetables), scraping the brown bits off the bottom of the pan with a wooden spoon. Whisk the liquid with the sausage fat until emulsified. Stir in the basil and mint.

MAKE THE SNAPPER

6. Preheat the oven to 350°F; position the rack in the middle. Rinse and pat the fish dry. Brush one side of the fillets with the egg whites. Sprinkle the parsley and red pepper flakes over the egg white side. Press the egg white side of the fish fillets into the bread crumbs.

7. Add enough oil to a large skillet to cover the bottom of the pan and set it over medium heat. Season 2 of the fillets with salt and pepper and add them to the pan, bread side down, just before the oil starts to smoke. Carefully watch the fish, and once the edges begin to brown, transfer the fish to a Silpat- or parchment paper–lined half-sheet baking pan, bread side up. Pour the oil from the pan on top of the fish. Repeat with the remaining fillets. Let the fish sit out for 5 minutes together so they are all roughly the same temperature when they go into the oven. Bake the fish for about 4 minutes or until a cake tester inserted into the fish comes out without any force.

ASSEMBLE THE DISH

8. Divide the pickled vegetables among 4 plates and spoon the sausage and the sauce over the vegetables. Place a snapper fillet on top and garnish with micro cilantro.

BROWNE TRADING COMPANY

LUKE MEYERS

One of the folks we work with on sourcing the freshest, sustainably caught fish is Browne Trading Company. We're lucky to have Luke Meyers, one of their salesmen, working with us on not only sourcing the freshest fish for the restaurant, but also in helping us plan some of our meals. We're always asking questions: Where is the fish coming from? Who is catching it? How is it being caught? So Luke, my chefs, and I are constantly talking about what boat caught which fish and how it was caught. Because tracing the source and sustainability are important to us, Browne Trading is a great partner in helping us adhere to

our principles. Their swordfish, caught by a day boat and which we serve during swordfish season (see page 89), is by far the most delicious and freshest I've ever had! Even people who don't like swordfish change their mind upon tasting the Browne Trading catch!

Established in 1991, Browne Trading places a heavy emphasis on day boat fish that are caught using low-impact fishing methods, such as line fishing, and has minimal impact on non-targeted species. They are deeply committed to sustainable fishing in the Gulf of Maine in order to preserve and protect the long-term viability of

local seafood. Their overseas buyers also focus on procuring day boat fish under Browne Trading's conditional agreement. Traceability is a key aspect of the company's focus: from fishing ground, catch method, vessel, location, and how and when it is transported to Browne Trading facility.

The company employs a handful of salespeople who are deeply knowledgeable not only about the fish that's currently being offered, but also of the preferences of the chefs who they work with.

MAINE MONKFISH + CHICKEN SKIN + VALENCIA BOMBA RICE + OLIVES + SAFFRON + CHORIZO EMULSION

SERVES 4 When I was apprenticing in Europe, I spent two weeks in Spain at a friend's house, and his family made amazing paella in a giant paella pan in their backyard. They added everything to it: seafood, chicken, clams, mussels, chorizo, cod—you name it. Here, I wanted to pay homage to that paella but with my own twist. Instead of chicken, I use only chicken skin, which we wrap the monkfish in. It's all the components of paella but arranged slightly differently. The chorizo becomes a chorizo emulsion, and the rice is brightened up by some preserved lemon rind.

FOR THE CHORIZO EMULSION

Olive oil

2 cups sliced dried, cured chorizo

¼ Vidalia onion, julienned

½ red bell pepper, julienned

½ poblano pepper, julienned

1 garlic clove, thinly sliced

1 teaspoon smoked paprika, plus more as needed

½ cup white wine

3 cups Chicken Stock (see page 382) or store-bought

2 sprigs fresh oregano

1 sprig fresh basil

½ ounce (1 tablespoon) unsalted butter

Juice of ½ lemon, plus more as needed

FOR THE MONKFISH

4 (4x4-inch) pieces chicken skin

4 (5-ounce) monkfish fillets

Kosher salt

3 tablespoons Activa (see Sources, page 403; optional)

Blended Oil (see page 395)

2 ounces (4 tablespoons) unsalted butter

4 sprigs fresh thyme

4 garlic cloves, unpeeled

FOR THE VALENCIA BOMBA RICE

2 to 3 tablespoons extra-virgin olive oil, plus more as needed

1 Spanish onion, brunoise (see page 48)

1 tablespoon tomato paste

3 teaspoons pimentón (Spanish paprika)

1 garlic clove, chopped

3½ cups Lobster Stock (see page 385) or store-bought

Pinch of saffron threads

Kosher salt

1½ cups bomba rice, or another medium-grain Spanish rice

1 cup chopped green olives

1 cup chopped Roasted Peppers (see page 90) or store-bought

3 tablespoons brunoise Lemon Confit Peel (see page 386) or wide strips lemon zest

12 mussels

12 cockles or clams

1 lemon

½ cup chopped fresh curly parsley

TO ASSEMBLE THE DISH

Micro limone (see Sources, page 403)

MAKE THE CHORIZO EMULSION

1. Add enough olive oil to a sauté pan to cover the bottom of the pan and set it over medium heat. Warm the oil until it shimmers. Add the chorizo and cook until it releases its spices and aromatics—the oil will turn red—2 to 3 minutes. You will see some brown bits (*fond*) form at the bottom of the pan.

2. Add the onion, red bell pepper, poblano pepper, and garlic, and deglaze the pan with the vegetables, stirring, letting them sweat until soft, about 5 minutes. Do not let the vegetables pick up color—you might want to reduce the heat to medium-low, depending on the intensity of your burners. Stir in the paprika and cook

for about 1 minute. Add the wine and simmer until the pan is dry, 4 to 6 minutes. Add the stock, oregano, and basil, and simmer until the broth tastes distinctly of chorizo, about 40 minutes.

3. Strain the broth and discard the solids. Return the broth to the stovetop, skim any foam from the surface, and simmer the broth over medium-low heat until it has reduced to about 1 cup.

4. Add the butter, lemon juice, and 2 or 3 dashes of smoked paprika to the broth, and using an immersion blender, whip the liquid until it forms a smooth and uniform emulsion.

MAKE THE MONKFISH AND VALENCIA BOMBA RICE

5. Lay out a piece of the chicken skin on a piece of plastic wrap and place a monkfish fillet toward the bottom edge of the skin. Season both sides with salt and place on a paper towel–lined tray. Repeat with the remaining pieces of chicken skin and monkfish fillets. Refrigerate overnight, uncovered. Remove the tray from the fridge. Sprinkle a little Activa all over the skin and fish, roll the skin around the fish, and then tightly wrap the fish in plastic wrap, twisting the ends to secure and shape the roll. Repeat with the remaining chicken skin and monkfish. Refrigerate for at least 6 hours to set the Activa.

6. About 25 to 30 minutes before serving, in a large sauté pan (or a paella pan, if you have one), warm the oil over high heat. Just before it starts to smoke, add the onion and reduce the heat to medium. Cook the onion, stirring, until soft, about 2 minutes. Reduce the heat to low and stir in the tomato paste and pimentón. Cook, stirring, for about 3 minutes, then add the garlic and cook for 3 to 4 minutes more. Add the stock, saffron, and a pinch of salt. Add the rice, spreading it in a nice, even layer. Raise the heat to medium-high and cook for 4 minutes, stirring every 30 seconds or so. Add the olives, Roasted Peppers, and Lemon Confit, and reduce

the heat to low. Cook, without disturbing the pan, for 8 minutes. Add the mussels and clams, cover the pan, and cook for about 3 minutes or until the mussels and clams open. Discard any shellfish that do not open. Remove from the heat and drizzle olive oil over the rice. Using a fine zester, zest the lemon right over the pan. Stir in the parsley, set aside, and keep warm.

7. About 20 minutes before serving, preheat the oven to 350°F; position the rack in the middle. Add enough oil to a large ovenproof sauté pan to cover the bottom of the pan and set it over high heat. Just before it starts to smoke, add the fish to the pan, seam side down, and reduce the heat to medium. Cook, without moving the fish, until the chicken skin is browned, about 2 minutes. Flip the fish, transfer the pan to the oven, and cook the fish for 4 minutes or until a cake tester inserted into the fish comes out easily and is warm to the touch. While the fish is in the oven, return the emulsion to the stovetop and warm over medium-low heat. Transfer the fish back to the stovetop and flip the fish back to sear side. Turn the heat up to medium and add the butter, garlic, and thyme, and baste the fish for 3 to 4 minutes in the brown butter. Transfer the fish to a plate and allow the fish to rest for 1 minute. Cut each filet into 3 pieces.

ASSEMBLE THE DISH

8. Right before serving, add the monkfish slices to the paella pan, sprinkle with the micro limone, and pour the warm Chorizo Emulsion over the paella.

Make It Faster *Instead of wrapping the monkfish in the chicken skin, you can go the more traditional route and add pieces of chicken to the paella. The Chorizo Emulsion can be made a day ahead, or you can skip it all together, and the rest of the meal should come together pretty fast the following day.*

SMOKED ARCTIC CHAR + SQUASH PICKLES + YELLOW BEETS + HONEYCRISP APPLE TEA + CELERY ROOT

SERVES 4 I love making this dish and think you should absolutely give this a go, but it will make a lot of smoke indoors. So, if you are making this at home, it's best made outside on the grill where the smoke won't set off your smoke alarm. At the restaurant we cook it indoors, but we are equipped to deal with a lot of smoke. Next time you host a cookout in your backyard, consider making it for your guests. It'll be a welcome change to hot dogs and burgers and your friends will be impressed. The squash pickles, on their own, are a great accompaniment to anything grilled: fish, steak, or a burger.

FOR THE SQUASH PICKLES

½ cup diced butternut squash

¼ cup diced delicata squash

½ cup diced yellow beets

¼ cup diced celery root

¼ cup diced firm, tart apples, preferably Honeycrisp

1 shallot, thinly sliced

1½ cups apple cider vinegar

1 tablespoon granulated sugar

1 Thai chile

Kosher salt

1 tablespoon chopped fresh curly parsley

1 teaspoon red pepper flakes

Extra-virgin olive oil

FOR THE APPLE TEA

4 cups fresh apple juice or fresh apple cider (from the greenmarket or freshly juiced)

2 fresh or 1 dried bay leaves

2 cinnamon sticks

2 sprigs fresh rosemary

2 sprigs fresh mint

FOR THE ARCTIC CHAR

4 (5-ounce) arctic char fillets, skin removed and reserved

Cooking spray

1 cup applewood chips

Extra-virgin olive oil

Kosher salt

Canola oil

FOR THE CELERY ROOT PUREE

1 celery root, peeled and roughly chopped

2 cups heavy cream

1 cup Chicken Stock (see page 382) or store-bought

Kosher salt

1 ounce (2 tablespoons) unsalted butter

1 fresh or dried bay leaf

1 cinnamon stick

1 sprig fresh rosemary

MAKE THE SQUASH PICKLES

1. In a medium nonreactive bowl, combine the squashes, beets, celery root, apples, and shallot.

2. In a small nonreactive saucepan, combine the vinegar, sugar, chile, and a pinch of salt with ½ cup of water and bring to a boil over high heat. Immediately pour the marinade over the vegetables. Let cool slightly, cover, and refrigerate overnight.

3. Right before serving, remove the pickled vegetables from the marinade and combine them with the parsley, red pepper flakes, and some olive oil. Taste and adjust the seasonings as needed.

MAKE THE APPLE TEA

4. If you have fresh-pressed the juice, let the juice settle for 1 hour and skim off any foam on the surface. Add the apple juice, bay leaves, cinnamon sticks, rosemary, and mint to a 2-quart nonreactive pot and bring to a boil. Reduce the heat to the lowest setting, and allow the liquid to infuse for 20 minutes, skimming off any impurities that rise to the surface. Strain the liquid through a coffee filter into a bowl and set it aside. If making a day in advance, refrigerate until needed. Right before serving, warm the Apple Tea over medium heat until hot.

5. Preheat the oven to 350°F; position the rack in the middle. Using the back of a spoon, scrape all the meat off the fish skin. Line a half-sheet baking pan with a Silpat or parchment paper and spray with cooking spray. Lay the salmon skins out flat. Cover them with another Silpat or sheet of parchment paper and place another half-sheet baking pan on top. Bake for 7 minutes or until the skin is crispy. Transfer to a cooling rack and remove the top pan.

6. While the char skin chips are baking, soak the applewood chips in a bowl of water for 20 minutes. Line the bottom of a 4-inch deep casserole dish with foil. Place the soaked wood chips into a sauté pan and heat until smoking, about 10 minutes. Transfer the chips to the casserole dish, and make a "basket" out of foil to hang over the edges of the pot so that when you place the fish in it, it will be suspended over the chips. Poke 10 to 12 holes in the "basket" using a paring knife. Pat the fillets dry and season with olive oil and salt. Gently place the fish on top of the perforated foil. Cover the casserole, remove it from the heat, and smoke the fish for about 4 minutes. Refrigerate until ready to serve.

7. About 30 minutes before serving, remove the char from the refrigerator and allow it to rest at room temperature for 20 minutes. Add enough oil to a large sauté pan to cover the bottom of the pan and set it over high heat. Just before it starts to smoke, add the fillets, reduce the heat to medium, and cook until the bottom of the fish is browned, 1 to 2 minutes. Flip the fillets and cook until a cake tester, inserted in the fillet, comes out easily and is warm to the touch, 2 to 3 minutes.

8. While the fish is cooling to room temperature, in a medium pot, combine the celery root, cream, stock, and a pinch of salt and bring to a boil over medium-high heat. Reduce the heat to low, so that the cream is gently simmering. Cook until the celery root is fork-tender, about 20 minutes. Strain through a fine-mesh strainer into a bowl, reserving the cooking liquid, and transfer the celery root to a blender.

9. In a skillet, melt the butter over medium-low heat. Cook until the solids turn brown and the butter smells nutty. Add the brown butter to the blender with the celery root along with a little bit of the reserved celery root cooking liquid, and puree, starting on low speed and gradually increasing to high, until the mixture is light and smooth, about 2 minutes. Pass the puree through a fine-mesh strainer into a bowl, and add the bay leaf, cinnamon stick, and rosemary. Wrap the bowl tightly in plastic wrap and let the puree infuse for 1 hour. Discard the aromatics.

ASSEMBLE THE DISH

10. Divide the fish among 4 warmed large bowls. Serve with the Pickled Squash and Celery Root Puree. Garnish with the char skin chips. At the table, pour the hot Apple Tea into the bowls and serve.

Make It Faster *For a slightly faster preparation, skip the arctic char skin chip and smoke the fish with the skin on.*

CEDAR-PLANKED HAMACHI + LEMON PICKLES + AMERICAN CAVIAR

SERVES 4 This is a play on my dad's signature dish, Cedar-Planked Salmon, which I have also adapted (see page 79). But here, I wanted to do something that was perfect for the summer months: nice, light, and fresh. So instead of cooking the fish through *on* a cedar plank, the plank is actually used to warm the raw fish and impart a little smoke *from* the wood itself. It's a great easy-to-make, simple appetizer that always reminds me of building a fire on the beach and grilling fresh seafood. Life doesn't get better than that.

FOR THE LEMON PICKLES

2 Meyer lemons (regular lemons are fine if Meyer lemons are unavailable)

½ cup champagne vinegar

1 tablespoon granulated sugar

½ teaspoon ground turmeric

FOR THE HAMACHI

4 untreated cedar shims (see Note)

2 (4-ounce) block fillets sushi-grade Hamachi

TO ASSEMBLE THE DISH

Extra-virgin olive oil

Flaky sea salt, such as Maldon

1 lemon, quartered

American caviar

Micro basil (see Sources, page 403) or chiffonade of fresh basil

MAKE THE LEMON PICKLES

1. Thoroughly rinse the lemons and cut them in half crosswise. Using a mandoline, slice the lemon halves into ¹⁄₁₆-inch-thick slices and transfer them to a nonreactive container. Discard the seeds.

2. In a small nonreactive saucepot, combine the vinegar, sugar, and turmeric with 1 cup of water and bring to a boil over high heat. Pour the marinade over the lemon slices and let sit at room temperature for at least 3 hours before serving. If making ahead, refrigerate until ready to use.

MAKE THE HAMACHI

3. Soak the cedar shims in cold water for at least 3 hours. Place the shims under the broiler on high; reserve the soaking water. Toast the wood until browned, 3 to 5 minutes. Return the shims to the water until ready to use.

4. Slice the hamachi into 12 slices, cover, and refrigerate until ready to use.

5. When ready to serve, preheat the broiler and season the planks with some extra-virgin olive oil and salt. Place the planks back in under the broiler until smoking; watch the planks carefully because at this point they could catch fire if left under the broiler for too long. As soon as the planks start to smoke, take them out from under the broiler and squeeze some lemon juice over the planks. Divide the hamachi evenly among the planks and garnish with some caviar, basil, a drizzle of olive oil, and a pinch of flaky sea salt. Dice the Lemon Pickles and serve on the side.

JOHN DORY + BLACK RADISH + RAINBOW CHARD + SWEETBREADS + CHICKEN SKIN CHIPS

SERVES 4 Believe it or not, I got the idea for the chicken skin jus from the excellent cookbook *The Art of Living According to Joe Beef*. At the time, we were making John Dory with the sweetbreads, and needed a savory jus to pull it all together. We were already making monkfish with the chicken skin (see page 97), one of my favorite snacks to eat, so we decided to give chicken skin jus a whirl and it came out great—so flavorful! The jus proved to be the perfect element for John Dory with the sweetbreads—just the thing to bring the whole dish together.

FOR THE SWEETBREADS

½ pound veal sweetbreads

½ cup white wine vinegar

Kosher salt

Canola oil

1 strip bacon

1¼ ounces (2½ tablespoons) unsalted butter

½ carrot, peeled and diced

½ medium onion, peeled and diced

½ celery rib, diced

½ cup dry white wine

1¼ cups Chicken Stock (see page 382) or store-bought

½ cup Veal Stock (see page 382) or store-bought

4 sprigs fresh thyme

1 fresh or ½ dried bay leaf

Blended Oil (see page 395)

2 garlic cloves, unpeeled

FOR THE CHICKEN SKIN JUS

Canola oil

2 pounds chicken skin

4 garlic cloves, unpeeled

1 carrot, coarsely diced

1 onion, coarsely diced

1 celery stalk, coarsely diced

1 tablespoon black peppercorns

2 cups dry red wine

4 cups Chicken Stock (see page 382) or store-bought

4 sprigs fresh thyme

1 fresh or ½ dried bay leaf

Kosher salt

1 tablespoon sherry vinegar

1 teaspoon granulated sugar

FOR THE CHICKEN SKIN CHIPS

4 (6x6-inch) pieces chicken skin

Kosher salt

FOR THE RADISHES

1 black radish, scrubbed

5 red radishes, scrubbed

½ cup (roughly) daikon radish, scrubbed

4 icicle radishes, scrubbed

4 ounces (8 tablespoons) unsalted butter

1 cup Chicken Stock (see page 382) or store-bought

4 teaspoons granulated sugar, plus more as needed

Kosher salt

FOR THE SWISS CHARD

8 ounces yellow Swiss chard

1½ ounces (3 tablespoons) unsalted butter

1 garlic clove, sliced

Kosher salt

FOR THE JOHN DORY

4 (4-ounce) John Dory fillets, skin removed

Kosher salt

1½ ounces (3 tablespoons) unsalted butter

1½ tablespoons Blended Oil (see page 395), plus more as needed

4 sprigs fresh thyme

Radish sprouts (optional)

Flaky sea salt, such as Maldon

1. Soak the sweetbreads in a bowl of water in the refrigerator for at least 8 hours, changing the water at least 2 times. Remove and thoroughly pat the sweetbreads dry.

2. In a small nonreactive saucepot, combine the vinegar and a pinch of salt with 1½ cups of water and bring to a boil. Add the sweetbreads and simmer for 2 minutes. Using a slotted spoon, immediately transfer the sweetbreads to an ice bath and soak for 5 minutes or until cooled. Remove the sweetbreads from the ice bath, pat dry, and transfer to a work surface.

3. Using a paring knife, peel off the outer membranes and any excess fat from the sweetbreads. Set the sweetbreads aside.

4. Add enough oil to a large sauté pan to cover the bottom of the pan and set it over high heat. Just before the oil starts to smoke, season the sweetbreads with salt and add them to the pan. Reduce the heat to medium and do not move the pan until the bottom of the sweetbreads has browned, 5 to 8 minutes. Flip the sweetbreads over and add the bacon to the pan. Cook until the second side of the sweetbreads is browned. Add 1½ tablespoons of the butter. Continue to cook until the butter browns, about 2 minutes, baste sweetbreads with the butter for 1 minute, and transfer to a medium (3- to 4-quart) Dutch oven.

5. Drain the excess fat from the pan, and add the carrot, onion, and celery, scraping any brown bits off the bottom of the pan with a wooden spoon. Add the wine and cook for 2 minutes. Add the chicken and veal stocks, 2 sprigs of the thyme, and the bay leaf. Bring the liquid to a boil and pour it over the sweetbreads. Refrigerate overnight.

6. The next day, remove the sweetbreads from the liquid and trim them into 4 (2-ounce) pieces. Set aside. Discard the cooking liquid.

7. Right before serving, add enough Blended Oil to a large sauté pan to cover the bottom of the pan and set it over high heat. Just before the oil starts to smoke, add the sweetbreads and sear for 1 minute on each side. Add the remaining 1 tablespoon butter, remaining 2 sprigs thyme, and garlic, and baste the sweetbreads in the butter for about 1 minute. Set aside.

8. While the sweetbreads are soaking, preheat the oven to 375°F; position the rack in the middle. Add enough oil to a large ovenproof sauté pan to cover the bottom of the pan and set it over high heat. Just before the oil starts to smoke, add the chicken skin, garlic, carrot, onion, celery, and peppercorns. Reduce the heat to medium and cook until the chicken skin is slightly browned, 7 to 10 minutes. Transfer the pan to the oven and cook, occasionally straining out the fat that collects in the pan, for about 30 minutes or until the skin is crispy.

9. Return the pan to the stovetop. Reduce the oven temperature to 300°F. Turn the stovetop heat to medium, and using a wooden spoon, scrape off any bits that may be sticking to the pan. Once the skins begin to sizzle, add the wine and continue to scrape the brown bits off the bottom of the pan. Cook until the wine has reduced by half. Add the stock and scrape the brown bits off the bottom of the pan using a wooden spoon. Transfer the contents of the pan to a narrow ovenproof saucepot. Add the thyme, bay leaf, and salt to taste; cover and braise in the oven for 1½ hours.

10. Strain the jus through a fine-mesh strainer and discard the solids. Pour the jus back into the pot, return it to the stovetop, and bring it to a boil over high heat. Reduce the heat to medium, so the jus is actively simmering, and skim off any fat that rises to the surface. Taste and adjust the seasonings. Stir in the vinegar and sugar. Strain the jus again and set aside. You should have about 2 cups of jus; you will need 1 cup for this recipe. The remaining jus can be frozen and used for anything from a hearty salad dressing to a sauce for a roasted chicken.

11. Preheat the oven to 350°F; position the rack in the middle. Scrape the excess fat off the skin using a spoon or the back of a knife. Season the skins with salt and transfer them to a Silpat- or parchment paper–lined shallow baking tray. Place another Silpat or piece of parchment paper over the skins and place another shallow baking tray on top. Bake for 30 to 45 minutes or until the skins are crispy (start to check on them after 25 minutes). Set the crisped skins on a cooling rack in a dry place and place a paper towel underneath to catch any dripping fat.

MAKE THE RADISHES

12. Using different sized melon ballers, scoop out black, red, and daikon radishes into assorted size spheres. Keep the radishes separate. Quarter the icicle radishes.

13. In a large sauté pan, add the black radish with 2 tablespoons of the butter and melt the butter over medium heat. When the butter is melted and the pan is heated through, add about ¼ cup of the chicken stock and 1 teaspoon of sugar. Slowly let the stock reduce and the sugar glaze the radishes until they are soft, 8 to 10 minutes. Season to taste with salt and set aside. Repeat the same process for the remaining radishes—because the radishes are of different sizes, the cooking times will vary. Set aside and rewarm slightly over low heat right before serving.

MAKE THE CHARD

14. Remove the stems from the chard leaves and cut the leaves into ½-inch ribbons. Peel the stems and cut them on the bias (they will have slanted diamond shapes).

15. When ready to serve, in a large pan set over medium heat, heat the butter and garlic, and once the garlic is beginning to toast, add the chard stems and leaves with 1 cup of water, and stir together. Season with salt and cover. Cook for about 2 minutes or until the leaves are wilted. Remove from the heat and set aside.

MAKE THE JOHN DORY

16. Pat the fish dry and season with kosher salt. In a large sauté pan, heat the butter and oil over medium-high heat. As soon as the butter begins to brown, add the fish and thyme. Shake the pan to prevent sticking, and cook for 1 to 2 minutes on each side. Watch the butter: If it starts to get too dark, add a little bit more oil.

17. Remove from the heat and divide the fish among 4 warmed plates. Add the Radishes, the Swiss Chard, and the Sweetbreads around the fish. Ladle a little bit of the Chicken Skin Jus over the fish and season with the flaky sea salt. Scatter the radish sprouts, if using, over the fish and top with a Chicken Skin Chip.

Make It Faster *Make the radishes using just one size melon baller and cook them all together instead of separately. Then make the chard and John Dory; skip the sweetbreads. You can make a large batch of Chicken Skin Chips ahead of time, freeze them, and just defrost what you need.*

BASIL-CRUSTED HALIBUT + ECKERTON FARMS CHERRY TOMATOES + SORRENTO OIL EMULSION

SERVES 4 The first version of this dish was made for the opening of BLT Market. Laurent had told me he wanted something that "screamed summer"—this is what I came up with. I wanted to highlight the summer flavors of my childhood: basil and tomatoes. The dish was an instant hit.

It was opening the BLT Market that really got me thinking about moving on and opening my own place. By that time, I had been opening steakhouses for about two years, and when we started creating dishes for Market, it was as if someone shot me with some electricity. I was flexing my creative muscle again and loved the experience.

When I finally opened my own place, this is the version of the dish we made. It makes for an amazing summer meal.

FOR THE SORRENTO OIL EMULSION

¼ cup Sorrento lemon oil (see Sources, page 403) or extra-virgin olive oil

2 ounces (4 tablespoons) unsalted butter, softened

¼ cup fresh lemon juice

¼ cup Mussel Stock (see page 385), Chicken Stock (see page 382), or vegetable stock

Kosher salt

FOR THE MARINATED CHERRY TOMATOES

2 teaspoons coriander seeds

2 cups heirloom cherry tomatoes

¼ red onion, julienned

⅓ cup extra-virgin olive oil

2 tablespoons fresh ginger juice (squeezed from freshly grated ginger)

2 tablespoons chiffonade of fresh basil

1 tablespoon chiffonade of fresh mint

1 tablespoon sherry vinegar

1 clove garlic, minced

Kosher salt

Freshly ground black pepper

FOR THE BASIL CRUST

2 tablespoons pine nuts

1 cup packed fresh basil

1 cup fine bread crumbs

½ cup plus 3 tablespoons grated Parmigiano-Reggiano

4 ounces (8 tablespoons) unsalted butter, softened

3 tablespoons chopped fresh chives

1 small garlic clove, blanched in milk (see page 348)

Kosher salt

Freshly ground black pepper

FOR BASIL PESTO

3 cups packed fresh basil

½ cup extra-virgin olive oil

2 garlic cloves

½ cup grated Parmigiano-Reggiano

1 teaspoon red pepper flakes

FOR THE HALIBUT

4 (5-ounce) halibut fillets

4 fresh basil stems

Kosher salt

½ cup dry white wine

Extra-virgin olive oil

TO ASSEMBLE THE DISH

4 cherry tomatoes on the vine

Flaky sea salt, such as Maldon

Working hard in the office

MAKE THE SORRENTO OIL EMULSION

1. In a small pot, bring the Sorrento lemon oil, butter, lemon juice, and stock to a simmer over medium heat. Remove from the heat and emulsify with an immersion blender until smooth. Set aside.

MAKE THE MARINATED CHERRY TOMATOES

2. In a small skillet over medium heat, toast the coriander seeds until fragrant, 3 to 5 minutes. Transfer to a mortar and pestle and crack. Let cool.

3. Bring a medium pot of water to a boil. Using a paring knife, make a small X incision at the bottom of each cherry tomato. Blanch the tomatoes in the boiling water for 1 minute and immediately transfer to an ice bath. Let the tomatoes cool, then peel the skins off.

4. In a medium bowl, mix together the cracked coriander, peeled tomatoes, onion, olive oil, ginger juice, basil, mint, vinegar, and garlic. Season to taste with salt and pepper, cover, and allow the tomato mixture to sit at room temperature for 4 hours.

MAKE THE BASIL CRUST

5. In a small dry skillet, toast the pine nuts over low heat for about 3 minutes or until golden brown and fragrant. Transfer to a bowl to cool and set aside.

6. Bring a large pot of water to a boil. Blanch the basil for 1 minute, drain, and immediately transfer the basil to an ice bath. Allow the basil to cool, then drain and squeeze out excess moisture.

7. Place the toasted pine nuts, basil, bread crumbs, Parmigiano-Reggiano, butter, chives, garlic, and salt and pepper to taste in a food processor fitted with a blade. Pulse until the ingredients form a fine green puree. Transfer the puree to a half-sheet-pan-size piece of parchment paper, cover the puree with another piece of parchment paper, and using a rolling pin, roll the puree out so it's ⅛ inch thick. If the crust comes out on the sides, scoop it back up, put it back in the center, and roll again. Transfer the crust to a half-sheet baking pan and refrigerate for at least 1 hour or until the butter sets. Once set, cut the crust into pieces corresponding to the fillet shapes and return the cut-out pieces to the refrigerator for at least 2 hours or, preferably, overnight. Freeze the rest of the crust in an airtight container for another use.

8. Bring a large pot of water to a boil. Blanch the basil in the boiling water for 1 minute, drain, and immediately transfer to an ice bath. Let cool, then drain the basil and squeeze out excess moisture.

9. In a food processor fitted with a blade, puree the blanched basil, olive oil, and garlic for about 20 seconds. You might need to add a tiny bit more oil if the mixture is too thick, but add a little bit at a time, because if you add too much, your pesto will not remain bright green. Immediately transfer the pesto to a medium bowl set over a larger bowl of ice water (an ice bath) and stir until cold. Fold in the cheese and red pepper flakes. Transfer to an airtight container and refrigerate until ready to use.

MAKE THE HALIBUT

10. Preheat the oven to 350°F; position the rack in the middle. Rinse and pat the fillets dry. Place the basil stems on a baking sheet. Season the fillets with salt on both sides, and place the fish on top of the basil. Drizzle the wine and olive oil over the fish and transfer to the oven. Check the fillets after 8 minutes by inserting a cake tester, and if it comes out without force, the fish is cooked through. Transfer the fish to a cooling rack.

11. Right before serving, preheat the broiler; position the rack in the middle. Place the fish on a baking sheet. Place a piece of the crust on top of each fillet. Broil the fish for about 30 seconds or until the crust is set and is bright green. Set aside.

ASSEMBLE THE DISH

12. While the fish is baking, bring a small pot of water to a boil. Make a small X incision on the bottom of each tomato. Blanch the tomatoes in the boiling water for 1 minute and immediately transfer to an ice bath. Let the tomatoes cool and, gently, using a paring knife, peel back the skins of the tomatoes three-quarters of the way. You will have 4 peeled cherry tomatoes on the vine with the peeled skin still on, like petals on a flower. Set the peeled tomatoes aside. (This can be done ahead.)

13. Divide the Marinated Cherry Tomatoes among 4 bowls. Place the halibut on top and spoon some Sorrento Oil Emulsion around. Drizzle the Basil Pesto over the tomatoes and sprinkle flaky sea salt on top. Dip the peeled tomatoes on the vine in the pesto and flaky sea salt, and serve them on the side of the fish. Sprinkle with more flaky sea salt to finish and serve with the remaining emulsion on the side.

Make It Faster *This is a beautiful but involved restaurant recipe—at home you might want to make things simpler. Just make the Marinated Cherry Tomatoes ahead of time, and when ready, make the Halibut and maybe skip the Sorrento Oil Emulsion and Basil Crust. If you do make the crust, double or triple your batch, and freeze the extra, so you can re-create the dish in no time. If you don't have time to make your own pesto, or the available basil looks lackluster, find a quality premade pesto and use it instead. Any leftover tomatoes and pesto can be tossed with your pasta the following day for a superb, simple dinner.*

SHELLFISH

"Close your eyes and think of the beach. What I see is blue water, what I feel is the sand, and what I smell are the flavors of the sea. Delicate and briny, perhaps a little sweet, the options and varieties are endless. Each oyster or clam is unlike any other, bearing a distinct flavor and smell that brings you back to the place where it was harvested. From popping open a raw oyster, to steaming a lobster, to making chowders and stews or having a clambake on the beach, no other raw food product can be so rewarding when prepared simply and correctly."

—ED MCFARLAND, ED'S LOBSTER BAR

SERVES 4 Manhattan has its clam chowder and so does New England—this is neither of those. We named ours after Tribeca, where it was created.

This chowder was born in the *Next Iron Chef* finale, the theme of which was Thanksgiving. Olde Salt clams, native to Virginia, are grown off the shores of the beautiful Chincoteague Island. The clams are very briny and salty, making them perfect for chowder where their qualities don't disappear but, instead, shine.

2 to 2¼ pounds sweet potatoes (about 3 to 4), peeled

½ cup dry white wine

1 cup clam juice

5 pounds littleneck clams, preferably Olde Salt or another briny variety, scrubbed and rinsed

2 cups heavy cream

1½ ounces (3 tablespoons) unsalted butter

1¼ cups diced bacon (about 6 slices)

1 large onion, cut into ¼-inch dice

3 garlic cloves, chopped

2 celery stalks, cut into ¼-inch dice

3 sprigs fresh thyme

2 fresh or 1 dried bay leaves

1 pound mussels, cleaned

2 tablespoons chopped fresh curly parsley

2 tablespoons chopped fresh mint

Fine sea salt

Freshly ground black pepper

1 tablespoon Ararat spice mix (see Sources, page 403), plus more for serving

Lime wedges, for serving

1. Thinly slice 1 sweet potato, cut the remaining sweet potatoes into ¼-inch dice, and set both aside. In a large stockpot, combine the wine, clam juice, and ½ cup of water and bring to a boil over high heat. Add the clams, cover, and cook until the clams open, about 10 minutes. Transfer the clams to a large bowl, discarding the ones that did not open. Strain the broth through a fine-mesh strainer and set it aside. When the clams are cool enough to handle, remove the clam meat from the shells and set aside in a bowl. Discard the shells.

2. Place the cream and the sliced sweet potato into a 4-quart pot and bring to a simmer over medium heat. Reduce the heat to low and cook until the potato is fork-tender, 15 minutes. Transfer the potatoes and cream to a blender, puree until smooth, and pass through a fine-mesh strainer into a bowl. Set the puree aside.

3. In a large stockpot set over medium-high heat, melt the butter, add the bacon, and cook. stirring, until crispy. Add the onion, garlic, celery, thyme, and bay leaves. Cook, stirring, until the onion is translucent, about 4 minutes. Add the diced sweet potatoes, the reserved clam broth, and the sweet potato puree. Reduce the heat to medium-low and simmer until the potatoes are fork-tender, 8 to 10 minutes. Discard the thyme and bay leaves. Add the mussels and cook until the mussels open, about 5 minutes. Return the reserved clam meat to the pot, and stir in the parsley and mint. Season to taste with salt and pepper and finish with the Ararat. Ladle the soup into bowls, sprinkle each serving with some more Ararat, and serve with lime wedges.

CRAYFISH BISQUE + BONE MARROW CRACKERS + MORELS + RAMPS

SERVES 4 I made a version of this dish while competing on an episode of *Chopped All-Stars*. For the appetizer round, each of us received a basket, and when I opened mine, there was a small bucket of live crayfish. Believe it or not, I had never cooked with crayfish before. But those crayfish looked like little lobsters, so I treated them as such.

With only twenty minutes to make a dish, I pulled off a bisque start to finish in the time that it might normally take just to prep the ingredients! On the show, I had to incorporate the beef tendon that was also in the basket, but when I made this dish at the restaurant, I decided to use bone marrow instead.

FOR THE BONE MARROW CRACKERS

4 (2-inch) pieces marrow bones

½ cup all-purpose flour

2 teaspoons Amber spice mix (see Sources, page 403)

1 cup ground panko bread crumbs

4 large eggs, lightly beaten

Canola oil

FOR THE MORELS

1 pound fresh morels, cleaned

Canola oil

1 ounce (2 tablespoons) unsalted butter

Kosher salt

2 tablespoons cream sherry

2 sprigs fresh thyme

1 fresh or ½ dried bay leaf

FOR THE CRAYFISH BISQUE

30 crayfish

Canola oil

1 leek, sliced

1 shallot, sliced

1 tablespoon tomato paste

1 cup cream sherry

3 cups Lobster Stock (see page 385) or store-bought

2 cups Veal Stock (see page 382) or store-bought

1 cup heavy cream

3 ramps

Kosher salt

FOR THE VEGETABLES

4 ounces ramps (about ½ to ⅔ bunch)

4 ounces fiddlehead ferns

4 ounces shelled peas (about ½ pound unshelled)

4 ounces shelled, skinned fava beans (about ½ pound unshelled)

TO ASSEMBLE THE DISH

Canola oil

3 ounces (6 tablespoons) unsalted butter

1 teaspoon granulated sugar

Kosher salt

2 teaspoons chopped fresh tarragon

Wood sorrel (optional)

Amber spice mix (see Sources, page 403)

MAKE THE BONE MARROW CRACKERS

1. Soak the marrow bones in a bowl of cold water for 1 hour; drain. Using your thumb, push the marrow out of the bones. Return the marrow to the bowl and add enough fresh water to cover. Refrigerate for 12 hours, changing the water every 3 hours. Remove the marrow from the water and pat dry.

2. In a small bowl, whisk together the flour and Amber until combined. Set the panko in another bowl. Cut each marrow piece into 4 equal slices. Coat the marrow slices in the flour, dip them in the beaten eggs, and then dip them in the panko. Repeat process a second time. Set aside.

3. Separate the morel caps from the stems (reserve the stems for the Crayfish Bisque, below; you will need 1 cup). Slice the caps into ¼-inch rings.

4. Add enough oil to a large sauté pan to cover the bottom of the pan and set it over high heat. Just before the oil starts to smoke, add the mushrooms in one even layer (you may need to do this in batches) and reduce the heat to medium. Once the mushrooms release their liquid and begin to brown, add the butter and cook, stirring, until the mushrooms and butter are nicely browned, 3 to 5 minutes. Season with salt, and add the sherry (it will flame up, so stand back). Deglaze the pan, scraping the brown bits from the bottom of the pan using a wooden spoon. Add the thyme and bay leaf, and reduce until the pan is dry. Remove from the heat and set aside.

MAKE THE CRAYFISH BISQUE

5. Bring a pot of salted water to a boil and blanch the crayfish in the boiling water for 2 minutes. Immediately transfer the crayfish to an ice bath and allow them to cool completely.

6. Remove the tails from the bodies and extract the meat. Devein the tails and refrigerate, covered, until needed.

7. Add enough oil to a large sauté pan to cover the bottom of the pan and set over high heat. Just before it starts to smoke, add the crayfish bodies to the pan, reduce the heat to medium, and let the crayfish get a nice initial sear, 2 to 3 minutes. Using a wooden spoon, crush the bodies and cook them for about 5 minutes. Add the reserved morel stems, leek, and shallot. Using a wooden spoon, stir to deglaze the bottom of the pan. Stir in the tomato paste and cook for about 1 minute. Add the sherry and reduce until the pan is dry. Add the Lobster Stock and reduce the liquid by about half, 15 to 20 minutes. Add the Veal Stock and reduce the liquid by about one-third, about 10 minutes. Add the cream and bring the bisque to a simmer. Gently simmer the bisque for about 5 minutes or until it thickens slightly. Strain the bisque through a fine-mesh strainer into a bowl and add the ramps. Wrap the bowl tightly in plastic wrap and let it sit for 1 hour. The accumulating moisture inside the container will make it look like it is raining. This process will infuse the bisque with the ramp flavor. Strain the bisque again, season to taste with salt, and set aside until needed.

8. Transfer the bisque back to the pot, set it over medium heat, and warm the bisque until almost simmering.

MAKE THE VEGETABLES

9. Bring a pot of salted water to a boil. Blanch the ramps in the boiling water for 1 minute and then transfer to an ice bath. Allow the ramps to cool, then drain and set aside. Repeat the process (using fresh water every time) with the fiddlehead ferns, peas, and favas. Set the vegetables aside.

ASSEMBLE THE DISH

10. Add enough oil to a sauté pan to cover the bottom of the pan and set it over high heat. Just before the oil starts to smoke, add the reserved marrow to the pan, reduce the heat to medium, and sear until the marrow is crispy on both sides, about 1 minute per side.

11. In a sauté pan, melt 2 tablespoons of the butter over medium heat and add the reserved morel caps and blanched vegetables. Cook both until just warmed through, about 2 minutes. Season with the sugar, salt, and tarragon, and divide the mixture among the bowls with the crayfish tails.

12. In a sauté pan, melt the remaining 4 tablespoons of the butter over medium heat and add the reserved crayfish tails. Cook the tails until just warmed through, 2 to 4 minutes. Remove from the heat and divide the tails among 4 warmed bowls. Top with wood sorrel and Bone Marrow Crackers, and sprinkle with Amber.

13. Using an immersion blender, buzz the warmed bisque until emulsified and pour it into the bowls tableside.

Make It Faster *If you're looking for a stunner of a dish to serve to your weeknight guests, the bisque is lovely, delicious, and relatively fast to pull together on a moment's notice. The other components add to the complexity of the dish, but if you're pressed for time, forgo them—it's the bisque you're after.*

OYSTERS + SHALLOTS + TRUFFLES + FOIE GRAS + VEAL

SERVES 4 One of my first real jobs while apprenticing at Michel Guérard was to shuck the oysters for this dish. There, he used the famed Gillardeau Oysters. However, depending on where you're from, just try to get your hands on the freshest oysters available. The recipe may appear complicated, but at the end of the day, it's just oyster bisque with a crunchy little bite on the side.

FOR THE SHALLOT REDUCTION

1 cup brunoise shallots
(see page 48)

1 cup ruby port

2 tablespoons
granulated sugar

1 teaspoon freshly
ground black pepper

1 sprig fresh thyme

1 fresh or ½ dried bay leaf

FOR THE VEAL BON BONS

9 ounces ground
veal shoulder

5 ounces foie gras terrine,
coarsely diced (see
Sources, page 403)

1 tablespoon (½ ounce)
truffle juice, optional (see
Sources, page 403)

1½ tablespoons (½ ounce)
black truffle oil (see Sources,
page 403; optional)

2 tablespoons chopped
fresh curly parsley

¾ ounce black truffle,
brunoise (see page 48)

2 tablespoons veal
demi-glace (see
Sources, page 403)

¼ teaspoon pink curing salt

Kosher salt

Freshly ground white pepper

2 sheets phyllo dough

2 ounces (4 tablespoons)
unsalted butter, melted

FOR THE BEURRE MONTÉ

8 ounces (16 tablespoons)
unsalted butter, cut
into 8 pieces

FOR THE OYSTER BISQUE

24 oysters, preferably a
briny East Coast variety
like Olde Salt or Wellfleet

1 cup heavy cream

1 cup Mussel Stock
(see page 385)

Kosher salt

Lemon wedge (optional)

TO ASSEMBLE THE DISH

½ ounce (1 tablespoon)
unsalted butter

1 cup chiffonade of
baby spinach

MAKE THE SHALLOT REDUCTION

1. In a small pot, combine the shallots, port, sugar, pepper, thyme, and bay leaf, and bring to a boil over medium-high heat. Reduce the heat to low and simmer for about 40 minutes—the mixture will thicken up and become concentrated. Transfer the pot to a cooling rack and let cool to room temperature.

MAKE THE VEAL BON BONS

2. In a large bowl, mix together the veal, terrine, truffle juice (if using), truffle oil, parsley, truffle, demi-glace, and pink salt. Season with salt and pepper. Make a small patty out of some of the meat. Warm a bit of oil in a small sauté pan over medium-high heat, and cook the patty until cooked through, about 2 minutes total. Taste and adjust the seasonings if needed. Repeat with another small patty, if necessary, until the seasonings are just right.

3. Portion the mixture into four 1-ounce balls. Set aside.

4. Lay out the phyllo dough and cut into 12 x 3½-inch strips. Brush the tops with the melted butter. Place a meatball on top of the phyllo dough every 2½ inches. Shape the balls into rectangular logs. Cut the phyllo evenly on either sides of the meat so that each is on an individual piece of phyllo. Wrap the phyllo around the logs and twist the ends to close. Place phyllo logs in the refrigerator to set until ready to use.

MAKE THE BEURRE MONTÉ

5. In a medium pot, bring 1 cup of water to a boil over high heat. Reduce the heat to medium and whisk in the butter, piece by piece, making sure that each piece is emulsified before adding the next. It is important that each piece of butter is fully incorporated into the mixture before another is added. If the butter mixture starts to break, whisk in a few drops of warm water. Set aside and keep warm.

MAKE THE OYSTER BISQUE

6. Shuck the oysters over a large bowl, reserving their juices. Set aside the oysters. Strain the oyster juice through a fine-mesh strainer into a bowl and measure out 1 cup. Place the strained juice, heavy cream, and Mussel Stock in a medium pot, and bring to a boil over high heat. Reduce the heat to medium and whisk in 2 cups of the Beurre Monté. Add salt to taste; depending on your oysters, you may or may not need to add a squeeze of fresh lemon. Set aside.

ASSEMBLE THE DISH

7. In a medium pot set over medium heat, bring the Oyster Bisque to a simmer and add the reserved oysters. Immediately remove from the heat and let the bisque and oysters stand for 3 minutes. In a nonstick pan, heat the butter over medium-high heat and add the Veal Bon Bons. Sear all four sides of each bon bon until crispy.

8. Using a slotted spoon, remove the oysters from the bisque and divide them among 4 warmed bowls. Return the bisque to the stovetop over medium-high heat, and simmer for 1 minute. Ladle some of the bisque over the oysters, making sure that the tops of the oysters are showing. Using a fork, dot the tops of the oysters with the Shallot Reduction. Strain the remaining bisque through a fine-mesh strainer into a bowl, and froth the bisque using an immersion blender. Spoon the bisque around the oysters in each bowl, plant a bon bon on the rim of each bowl (if you don't have a rim, serve them on the side), sprinkle with the spinach chiffonade, and serve.

Make It Faster *You can also ask your fishmonger to shuck the oysters for you and have them reserve the juices.*

RIGHTEOUS FOODS

KEITH SWENSON

Keith Swenson walked away from a career on Wall Street after losing a roommate in one of the towers on September 11, 2001. He found his way back to a career in finance again, but that only lasted a few years. Simply put, he no longer saw the purpose of

He connected with college friends, Travis and Ryan Croxton from Rappa-hannock River Oysters, who wanted to get their oysters to New York restau-rants and were looking for a reliable and trustworthy distributor. And so Keith's sister, Amy Swenson, started

My restaurant was one of Righteous Foods' first customers. One night, Amy hand-delivered some oysters to the Monkey Bar where my dad was a consulting chef at the time, and I just happened to be there that night. I tried a few of the Olde Salt oysters and

SERVES 4 Believe it or not, this is my very first published recipe. It came out in *Bon Appétit* in 2006, while I was with BLT. I know it might sound weird to combine scallops and blue cheese, but there's something about the combination of the sweet scallops, spicy port reduction, fruit, and cheese that makes it all come together.

SPECIAL EQUIPMENT

4 (6-inch) skewers

FOR THE PORT REDUCTION

2 cups ruby port

¼ cup granulated sugar

2 tablespoons cracked black pepper

1 sprig fresh mint

FOR THE APPLE NAGE

½ cup mild honey

½ cup fresh lime juice

⅓ cup olive oil

½ apple (preferably Honeycrisp), brunoise (see page 48)

¼ cup brunoise celery root (see page 48)

¼ cup fresh apple juice

¼ cup mustard oil (see Sources, page 403)

1 tablespoon ground coriander

1 tablespoon chopped fresh cilantro

1 tablespoon honey vinegar (see Sources, page 403)

10 drops green Tabasco

Kosher salt

FOR THE DEVILS ON HORSEBACK

12 dates, butterflied

4 ounces Fourme d'Ambert or another strong blue cheese

6 thin bacon strips, halved (see Sources, page 403)

Canola oil

FOR THE BAY SCALLOPS

36 bay scallops

Canola oil

Kosher salt

¾ ounce (1½ tablespoons) unsalted butter

TO ASSEMBLE THE DISH

Fourme d'Ambert or another strong blue cheese

Micro celery (see Sources, page 403) or chiffonade of fresh celery leaves

MAKE THE PORT REDUCTION

1. In a 2-quart saucepot, combine the port, sugar, pepper, and mint and bring to a boil over high heat. Reduce the heat to medium-low, and cook until the liquid has reduced and is thick enough to coat the back of a spoon, about 30 minutes. Remove from the heat and let cool to room temperature. Do not refrigerate.

MAKE THE APPLE NAGE

2. In a medium bowl, mix together the honey, lime juice, olive oil, apple, celery root, apple juice, mustard oil, coriander, cilantro, honey vinegar, and Tabasco. Season to taste with salt. Set aside.

MAKE THE DEVILS ON HORSEBACK

3. Stuff the dates with the cheese and very tightly wrap a bacon slice around each date. Take 4 (6-inch) skewers and put 3 dates on each one.

4. Heat 1 inch of oil in a sauté pan until it registers 350°F on a deep-frying thermometer. Gently add the dates and fry until the bacon is crispy. Gently push the dates off of the skewers onto clean paper towels and set aside.

MAKE THE BAY SCALLOPS

5. Thoroughly pat the scallops dry. In a large sauté pan set over high heat, warm enough oil to cover the bottom of the pan. Just before it starts to smoke, season one-third of the scallops (12 scallops) with salt and add them to the pan in one even layer. (You will do 2 more batches of scallops. It is very important that you season the scallops *right* before you cook them. Otherwise, the salt will

make the scallops produce liquid and they will not sear properly.) Immediately, lower the heat to medium, and do not move the pan. Once the edges of the scallops begin to brown, after about 30 seconds, add ½ tablespoon of the butter and roll the scallops in the butter on the heat for 30 seconds. Transfer the cooked scallops to a tray and repeat with the remaining scallops and butter.

ASSEMBLE THE DISH

6. Divide the scallops among 4 warmed plates. Drizzle the Apple Nage around them and brush the plate with Port Reduction. Crumble some cheese on top and sprinkle with the celery leaves. Divide the Devils on Horseback among the plates and serve.

+ You will probably wind up with some extra nage. Save it and use it as a salad dressing—it's delicious and will keep for a few days!

MANILA CLAMS + PARMIGIANO-REGGIANO–CUCUMBER BROTH + SEA BEANS

SERVES 4 My younger brother, Bryan, came up with this dish, which appeared on our original bar menu. It's a great way to cook clams in the summertime when the cucumbers are in season—they add a refreshing, herbal note to the clams. We made a version of this dish this for the *Iron Chef America* Brothers Battle where the secret ingredient was Parmigiano-Reggiano cheese. You'd never think cheese and clams go together—but the combination is truly beautiful.

FOR THE MANILA CLAMS AND CLAM BROTH

2 pounds Manila clams, rinsed and scrubbed

2 cups Chicken Stock (see page 382) or store-bought

1 cup dry white wine

1 tablespoon red pepper flakes

3 sprigs fresh thyme

1 fresh or ½ dried bay leaf

2½ cups fresh cucumber juice (from Korean or Kirby cucumbers)

2 cups finely grated Parmigiano-Reggiano

½ cup crème fraîche

½ cup heavy cream

½ teaspoon finely grated garlic

A few dashes Tabasco sauce or other hot sauce

Juice of ½ lemon

3 tablespoons chiffonade of fresh basil, plus more for serving

3 tablespoons chopped fresh curly parsley, plus more for serving

2 cups sea beans, cleaned (optional)

FOR THE TOAST

4 (¾-inch-thick) slices rustic country bread

4 garlic cloves, halved

Extra-virgin olive oil

Kosher salt

Freshly ground black pepper

MAKE THE MANILA CLAMS AND CLAM BROTH

1. In a large stockpot, combine the clams, stock, wine, pepper flakes, thyme, and bay leaf and bring to a lively simmer over medium heat. Reduce the heat to low, cover, and gently simmer until the clams open, 3 to 4 minutes. Strain the broth immediately through a fine-mesh strainer into a large bowl; set the clams aside.

2. To the bowl with the clam broth, add the cucumber juice, cheese, crème fraîche, heavy cream, garlic, and Tabasco. Taste and adjust the seasonings. Refrigerate for at least 30 minutes or until cold. Using an immersion blender, puree the mixture until smooth and emulsified. Add the lemon juice, basil, and parsley, stir, and set aside.

MAKE THE TOAST

3. Rub the bread slices with the garlic halves. Drizzle them with some olive oil and season with salt and pepper. Light a grill or preheat a grill pan. Grill the bread over high heat, turning occasionally, until toasted, 2 to 3 minutes per side. Alternatively, place the bread on a baking sheet and cook under a broiler for about 1 minute or until slightly toasted—the bread should still be a little soft. Drizzle the bread with more olive oil and set aside.

ASSEMBLE THE DISH

4. Divide the toast among 4 bowls. Return the clams to the pot with the broth, add the sea beans, if using, and warm the broth over medium heat until warmed through, 2 to 4 minutes. Ladle the clams with the broth and sea beans over the bread and scatter some basil and parsley on top before serving.

MARC FORGIONE

LA BOÎTE À ÉPICE

LIOR LEV SERCARZ

"Years ago, I was in one kitchen, and these days I'm in fifty," muses Lior Lev Sercarz, the owner of a gourmet bakery and spice company, La Boîte à Épice, tucked away on 11th Avenue in New York City's Midtown West.

Sercarz attributes the success of his business partly to the size of his company and his hands-on approach with the chefs who are his clients. Part of the charm is the structure: When chefs call, they immediately get Sercarz. "They don't get a voicemail or a dial-zero-for-an-operator," Sercarz says. "They get me. I'll go see chefs at eleven p.m. or seven a.m. When chefs ask me for something, they know that I will do it if I can. If I say that I cannot, they know that I cannot."

Born to a Tunisian father and a Transylvanian mother in Dan, a kibbutz in Israel, Sercarz grew up surrounded by culinary traditions from Europe, the Middle East, and Africa. This made Israel an ideal place to be exposed to various different herbs and spices.

Sercarz worked as a chef in Israel and then spent five years in Lyon with the Paul Bocuse Institute. It was while living in France that Sercarz met Olivier Roellinger, well known all over the world for his cuisine and his masterful use of spices in cooking, as well as his knowledge of the spice trade. Roellinger gradually became a mentor, of sorts, to Sercarz, teaching him about the industry and encouraging him to build his own business down the road.

It was while Sercarz was working at Daniel, a fine dining restaurant in New York City, that his idea of working with spices started to develop. When Sercarz realized he did not want to have his own restaurant, he was at the same time realizing there was a serious dearth of knowledge of the spice world: how the spices are grown, traded, and used in the kitchen either by a professional chef or a home cook. Together, those two epiphanies made him think of doing something related to the culinary industry but not a restaurant, per se.

As he was thinking about growing the spice blend business, as fate would have it, Sercarz's first client was Laurent Tourondel, and I was serving as corporate chef for Tourondel at the time. Tourondel and I commissioned some spice blends for BLT Market, and a relationship was born.

When I left the BLT restaurant group to open my own restaurant, Sercarz was the first purveyor I called, and La Boîte à Épice spice blends were used in the restaurant's dishes from day one.

All of the spice blends have names. Some are named for important people in the world of spices, such as Pierre Poivre, a personal idol of Sercarz. Some spice blends are named for a place: Ararat, for example. Some blends are named for a dominant ingredient or a flower—it always has to do with either an ingredient, a place, or a person.

These days Sercarz likes to think of himself as a silent partner in chefs' kitchens, helping to elevate chefs' creations with his unique spice blends. Sercarz creates custom blends for his clients, when asked, or can source a hard-to-find spice via his extensive network of contacts. Selecting and sourcing the right spices is a long, meticulous process. With a lot of options in the market, you need to have a discerning palate and an understanding of seasons, geography, and agriculture.

With Sercarz flying all over the world to source the best spices and creating his unique spice blends, he has followed in his mentor's footsteps, except, he quips, "He is in France, and I'm here, and I'm still twenty years behind him."

LIOR LEV SERCARZ of La Boîte à Épice

CUTTLEFISH + PAPAS BRAVAS + CHORIZO + SPICY MAYONNAISE

SERVES 4 *Papas bravas* is a traditional *tapa* in Barcelona, made with spicy and garlicky potato cubes and served at virtually every tapas-style meal. The dish is a perfect complement to cuttlefish, which is a cousin of squid, and spicy, porky chorizo.

FOR THE CUTTLEFISH

1½ pounds cuttlefish

1 cup extra-virgin olive oil

2 tablespoons Amber spice mix (see Sources, page 403)

Finely grated zest of 2 lemons

Kosher salt

Olive oil

½ cup white rioja

Juice of 2 lemons

2 tablespoons chopped fresh curly parsley

1 tablespoon chopped fresh cilantro

1 tablespoon red pepper flakes

Freshly ground black pepper

FOR THE SPICY MAYONNAISE

½ recipe Mayonnaise (see page 380) or 1 cup store-bought

3 tablespoons sriracha, plus more to taste

FOR THE CHORIZO

¼ pound pork shoulder, cubed

1 garlic clove

3 tablespoons Cataluña spice mix (see Sources, page 403)

Kosher salt

FOR THE LEMON DRESSING

¼ cup extra-virgin olive oil

2 tablespoons fresh lemon juice

¼ teaspoon cracked black pepper

½ small garlic clove, chopped

Kosher salt

FOR THE PAPAS BRAVAS

4 large Yukon Gold potatoes (about 3 pounds), peeled

4 cups canola oil

TO ASSEMBLE THE DISH

Kosher salt

Smoked paprika

Flaky sea salt, such as Maldon

Amber spice mix (see Sources, page 403)

Micro basil (see Sources, page 403) or chiffonade of fresh basil

MARINATE THE CUTTLEFISH

1. Clean the beaks from the cuttlefish, and remove the tentacles from the bodies (you will need them later). If the cuttlefish tentacles seem a bit large and unwieldy to you, feel free to use squid tentacles instead. Place the cuttlefish in a medium bowl and combine with the olive oil, Amber, and lemon zest. Cover and refrigerate for at least 2 hours and up to 12 hours.

MAKE THE SPICY MAYONNAISE

2. Stir together the Mayonnaise and sriracha until well combined. Set aside. If making ahead, cover and refrigerate until ready to use.

MAKE THE CHORIZO

3. Using a meat grinder or a meat grinding attachment to your stand mixer set with the medium die, grind the pork and garlic clove and fold in the Cataluña. If you don't have a meat grinder, ask your butcher to grind the meat, and combine it with a minced garlic clove at home. Season with salt.

4. Add enough oil to a small sauté pan to cover the bottom of the pan and set it over high heat. Break off a tiny piece of the chorizo, form it into a small patty, and just before the oil begins to smoke, add it to the pan. Reduce the heat to medium and cook the chorizo, flipping once, until cooked through, about 1 minute. Taste and adjust the seasonings, if necessary. Repeat the process until the seasonings are where you want them.

5. Shape the chorizo into (2- to 3-inch) patties. Add enough oil to a sauté pan to cover the bottom of the pan and set it over high heat. Just before the oil begins to smoke, add the chorizo patties (you may need to do this in batches) and cook until the bottoms of the patties are nicely browned, about 3 minutes. Do not overcrowd the pan or your patties will steam instead of brown. Flip the patties and cook until the other side is nicely browned as well and the chorizo is cooked through, about 3 minutes. Transfer the chorizo to a plate and set aside.

MAKE THE LEMON DRESSING

6. In a medium bowl combine the oil, lemon juice, pepper, garlic, and salt to taste. Set aside.

MAKE THE PAPAS BRAVAS

7. Cut the potatoes into medium dice and transfer to a bowl with cold water to prevent discoloration.

8. Warm the oil in a Dutch oven until the temperature reaches 300°F. Drain the potatoes, pat dry with paper towels, and blanch in the oil, about 2 minutes. Transfer to a paper towel–lined tray and refrigerate until ready to assemble the dish. Reserve the frying oil until you assemble the dish.

MAKE THE CUTTLEFISH

9. Remove the cuttlefish from the marinade, pat them dry, and season with salt. Add enough oil to a large sauté pan to cover the bottom of the pan and set it over high heat. Just before it starts to smoke, add the cuttlefish and place a heavy weight on top (a foil-wrapped brick or a foil-wrapped sauté pan). Reduce the heat to medium and cook for 3 minutes—the fish should be caramelized on the bottom. Remove the weight and turn off the heat. Add the wine, lemon juice, parsley, cilantro, and red pepper flakes, and deglaze the pan, scraping the brown bits off the bottom of the pan. Pour the contents of the pan into a warmed bowl and set aside.

10. Brush the reserved tentacles with olive oil and season them with salt and pepper. Light a grill or preheat a grill pan. Grill the tentacles over high heat, turning occasionally, until cooked through, 4 to 5 minutes. Set aside. (Alternatively, place the tentacles on a half-sheet baking pan and cook under a broiler for about 1 minute, or until slightly charred. Remove from the oven and set aside.)

ASSEMBLE THE DISH

11. Reheat the oil you used to fry the potatoes to 350°F. Re-fry the potatoes until crispy, 2 to 3 minutes. Transfer to a paper towel–lined tray and immediately season with salt and smoked paprika.

12. Divide the potatoes among 4 plates; dot the Spicy Mayonnaise around the potatoes. Divide the cuttlefish among the plates, placing it on top of the potatoes, and plate the tentacles and chorizo around. Drizzle some Lemon Dressing on the cuttlefish and sprinkle with flaky sea salt and Amber. Scatter basil around and serve.

Make It Faster *The Spicy Mayonnaise and Lemon Dressing come together very quickly and you can make them well in advance. Since the Papas Bravas take some time to cook, you can skip them and instead serve the mayonnaise and dressing with your favorite spicy side.*

"HANGTOWN FRY" + CRISPY OLDE SALT OYSTERS + SMOKED PAPRIKA AÏOLI + PICKLED RED ONIONS + NORTH COUNTRY BACON

SERVES 4 According to the El Dorado County Museum, "No dish epitomizes California and its Gold Rush more than Hangtown Fry." Hangtown Fry was invented during the Gold Rush in the 1850s in Placerville, California, known at the time as Hangtown. Some sources say it was invented by a gold prospector who struck it rich one day and requested the most expensive dish on the menu, thus marrying the most expensive ingredients available at the time: eggs, bacon, and oysters. Another story tells of an inmate sentenced to die, who requested an oyster omelette for his last meal, knowing full well that the oysters would have to be brought from a hundred miles away, thus delaying his execution by a day. Whatever the story, I think pairing oysters, bacon, and eggs is just a great combo. At the restaurant, we like to use Olde Salt oysters. Their briny, salty flesh is a perfect fit for bacon and eggs.

FOR THE AÏOLI

½ recipe Mayonnaise (see page 380), or 4 ounces store-bought

2 tablespoons Ararat spice mix (see Sources, page 403)

1 shallot, minced

3 tablespoons chopped fresh chives

Juice of 1 lemon

FOR THE CRISPY SHALLOTS

Canola oil

3 shallots, thinly sliced

½ cup all-purpose flour

Kosher salt

FOR THE OYSTERS

12 oysters, shucked

2 cups buttermilk

2 cups fine cornmeal

2 tablespoons Ararat spice mix (see Sources, page 403), plus more as needed

1 tablespoon chili powder

1 tablespoon kosher salt

FOR THE OMELETTES

Canola oil

½ cup chopped bacon (about 5 strips)

2 tablespoons chopped fresh chervil

1 tablespoon chopped fresh curly parsley

1 tablespoon chopped fresh tarragon

8 large eggs, preferably farm fresh

Kosher salt

Freshly ground black pepper

½ cup Pickled Red Onions (see page 386) or raw onions

TO ASSEMBLE THE DISH

Micro celery (see Sources, page 403) or chiffonade of fresh celery (optional)

Smoked paprika

MAKE THE AÏOLI

1. In a medium bowl, combine the Mayonnaise, Ararat, shallot, chives, and lemon juice. Set aside.

MAKE THE CRISPY SHALLOTS

2. Add enough oil to a Dutch oven to come 1½ inches up the sides and heat the oil over medium-high heat until it registers 300°F on a deep-frying thermometer. Toss the shallots in the flour until well coated. Using a strainer, shake the excess flour off. Fry the shallots for about 30 seconds or until crispy. Transfer the shallots to a paper towel–lined tray and season with salt.

3. Use the same oil as for the Crispy Shallots. Heat the oil until it registers 350°F on a deep-frying thermometer. While the oil is heating, soak the oysters in buttermilk for 10 minutes. Meanwhile, in a medium bowl, combine the cornmeal with Ararat, chili powder, and salt. Remove the oysters from the buttermilk using a slotted spoon, and shake off the excess buttermilk. Toss the oysters in the cornmeal mixture, shake off the excess, and fry for 30 seconds or until crispy. Transfer the oysters to a paper towel–lined tray. Season with salt and Ararat to taste.

MAKE THE OMELETTES

4. Add enough oil to a large skillet to cover the bottom of the pan and set it over high heat. Just before the oil begins to smoke, add the bacon. Reduce the heat to medium and render the lardons until crispy, about 12 minutes. Using a slotted spoon, transfer the cooked lardons to a paper towel–lined plate and let cool completely. Reserve the rendered bacon fat.

5. Preheat the oven to 375°F; position the rack in the middle. In a small bowl, combine the chervil, parsley, and tarragon. Set aside.

6. Divide the eggs among 4 bowls. Divide the herb mixture among the bowls, and season with salt and pepper.

7. Warm a small nonstick ovenproof pan over high heat and add 1 tablespoon of bacon fat. Add one-quarter of the lardons and one-quarter of the Pickled Red Onions. Once the mixture begins to sizzle, add one of the egg mixtures. Cook for 30 to 40 seconds, to make sure the omelette isn't sticking to the pan. Transfer the pan to the oven and cook the eggs for 2 minutes or until the eggs are set and a toothpick inserted into the eggs comes out clean. Remove from the heat and set aside. This works better if you have 2 nonstick ovenproof pans going at the same time. If you decide to use a large nonstick pan to fit all 8 eggs, you will need to adjust the cooking time. It should take about 4 minutes, but will depend on the size of your pan.

ASSEMBLE THE DISH

8. Spoon some Aïoli on each of 4 slightly warmed plates and top with the oysters. Place an omelette on top and top with celery chiffonade, if using, and the Crispy Shallots. Dust with the smoked paprika and serve.

SERVES 4 This is a perfect example of something that sounds crazy on paper but ends up tasting magical on your plate.

I was trying to come up with a barbecue baked oyster for a summer appetizer. The original idea came from a story I heard about Chef Mark Miller making grilled oysters with barbecue sauce and limes. While I liked my first stab at it, it was still missing something, but I wasn't quite sure what that something was.

At the time, we were using grated pepper jack cheese for a staff meal and it was sitting out on the counter and I grabbed a handful, sprinkled a little on top of the oysters, and broiled them. I was shocked when I tasted the finished dish—pepper jack and oysters wound up being a perfect pairing!

No longer just a summer starter, these oysters have been on our menu ever since. And while they are good any time of year, in the summer, with a cold beer, these make for a very good time.

FOR THE BACON POWDER

4 strips bacon

FOR THE OYSTERS

2 ounces (4 tablespoons) unsalted butter

1 red bell pepper, brunoise (see page 48)

1 jalapeño pepper, brunoise (see page 48)

½ red onion, finely diced

2 tablespoons Ararat spice mix (see Sources, page 403), plus more as needed

¼ cup all-purpose flour

1½ cups whole milk

Kosher salt

Freshly ground black pepper

¼ cup coarsely shredded pepper jack cheese

2 tablespoons chopped fresh curly parsley

2 tablespoons chopped fresh chives

1 dozen oysters, shucked, preferably Hummock Island or other East Coast variety

1 cup Homemade Barbecue Sauce (see page 387) or store-bought

Lime wedges, for serving

Cilantro sprigs, for serving

MAKE THE BACON POWDER

1. Preheat the oven to 350°F; position the rack in the middle. Place the bacon in a shallow baking pan and bake for 12 to 15 minutes or until crispy. Transfer the bacon to a paper towel and blot to remove excess fat. Let cool, mince, and set aside in a warm place on a paper towel–lined plate. As the minced bacon dries, it will become crispy again.

MAKE THE OYSTERS

2. First, make the pepper jack béchamel: In a large sauté pan, melt the butter over medium-high heat until it foams. Add the peppers and onion and cook until soft, 4 to 5 minutes. Stir in the Ararat and cook for 1 minute. Whisk in the flour, reduce the heat to medium, and cook for 1 minute. Whisk in the milk and transfer the mixture to a saucepot set over medium heat. Stir every minute or so for about 15 minutes or until you can't taste the flour and the sauce is thick and coats the back of a spoon. If the mixture appears too thick, whisk in a little more milk to loosen it up. Season with salt

and pepper to taste, and fold in the cheese, parsley, and chives. Remove from the heat and let cool completely. Spoon some of the pepper jack béchamel over each oyster and brush with the barbecue sauce on top.

3. Cook the oysters in a shallow baking dish under the broiler for 2 to 3 minutes or until the béchamel is bubbling. Remove the oysters from the oven and sprinkle with reserved Bacon Powder and a bit more Ararat. Serve with lime wedges and cilantro sprigs.

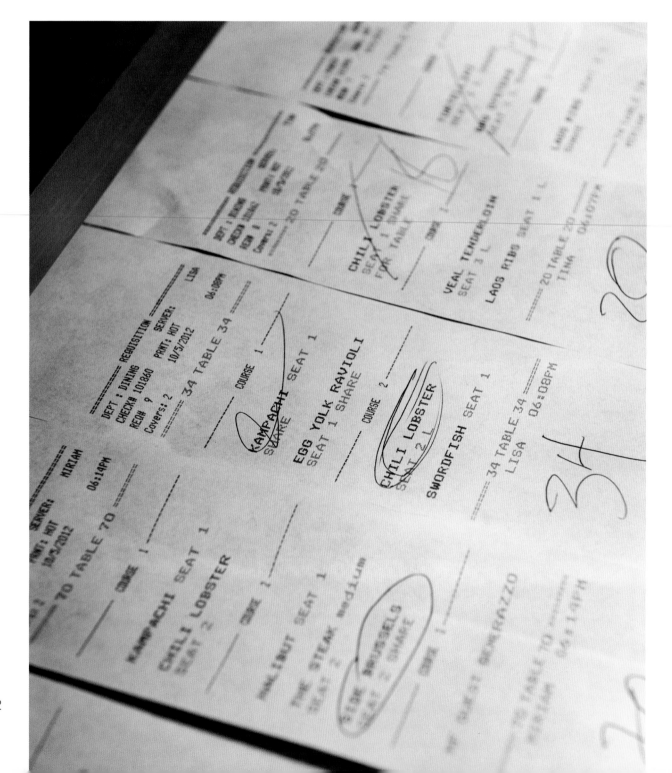

When Jordan Elkin and Brian McGovern started Homarus, neither had a background in seafood or food, unless you count dining out a background in food. Jordan, whose brother is a rabbi and who grew up in a kosher household, had a background in real estate, while his partner, Brian, came out of NYU film school.

The two of them had an idea to open up a lobster shack, and that was before the lobster shack trend had taken hold of New York. Jordan even spent some time working at a Shake Shack to better understand all the moving pieces of a food joint. But with the economy being in recession, they couldn't raise adequate financing to open up a physical space. And that's when the two started to think about a wholesale lobster concept.

The business model was simple: Drive up to Rockland, Maine, get the lobsters from the boats, drive back to New York, and sell them to restaurants. Oh, and work harder than anybody else. Since they opened in 2009, there hasn't been a single day that the business has been closed. They are a seven-days-a-week, 365-days-a-year shop. For the first two years of operation, neither Jordan nor Brian took any vacation time. With a small business that needed growing, there were no days off. These days, when Jordan needs to take off for Jewish holidays, Brian picks up the slack; and the reverse happens around Christmastime when Jordan doesn't mind working the holiday.

BRIAN and JORDAN of Homarus

Jordan attributes part of their success to their youth and energy: "The seafood business is very competitive and set in its ways. A lot of old people, old trucks, old boats. My partner and I are younger, and it's helped—revving up the energy. Good attitude and smiles go a long way."

Both men live in Manhattan and are familiar with the restaurant and the nightlife scene. They started selling door to door, first visiting a couple of places and gradually building their business up to 175 restaurants. Homarus's clients fall in all kinds of categories—from top restaurants to trendy low-key joints—and Homarus has yet to lose a single client.

I met Jordan through my then–sous chef, Barry Frish, whose parents are good friends with Jordan's in-laws. From the get-go, I felt a connection with Jordan and Brian. On top of selling a great product, these guys always make me laugh, and they understand that it's not just business—it's also a life that we live. Call me old school, but I like having a personal relationship with someone I work with. Clearly, so do they.

HOW TO
KILL AND PREP
A LOBSTER FOR
CHILI LOBSTER

1. Firmly grip the lobster and stab the lobster head with the tip of the blade all the way down until the knife meets the cutting board.

2. In one motion, pull the blade through the rest of the body until the lobster is halved.

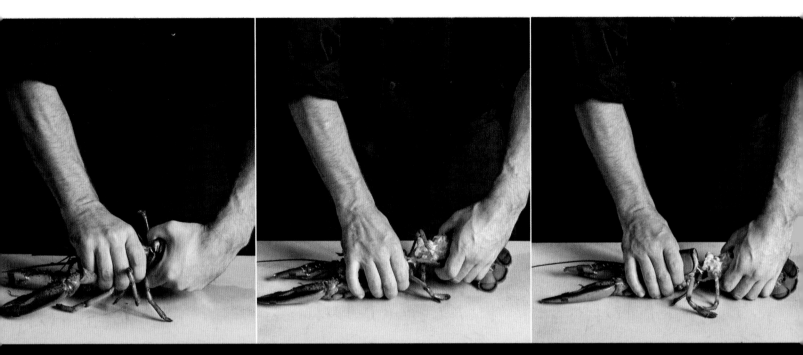

3. Using both hands, twist the tail away from you, and pull to release.

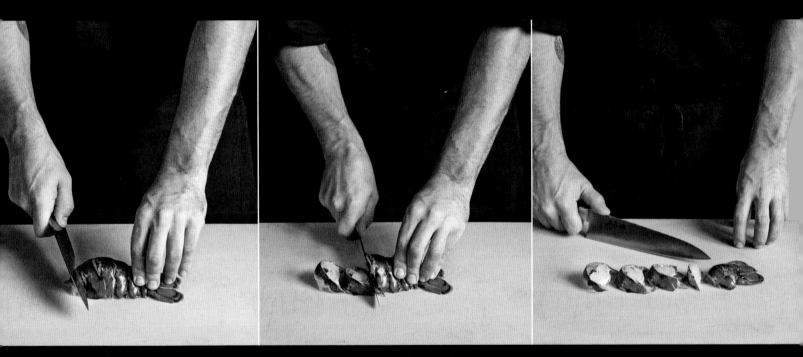

4. Lay the tail out and slice through each shell segment to cut the tail into pieces.

SERVES 4 This has become a dish that, along with the Chicken Under a Brick (see page 213), we've sort of become known for. But it didn't become wildly popular until Sam Sifton, the dining critic for the *New York Times* at the time, wrote his review of the restaurant, devoting a whole paragraph to Chili Lobster, and adding it to his list of recommended dishes. After that, Chili Lobster got on everyone's radar and has since remained one of our most popular offerings on the menu. On any given night, we go through anywhere from 30 to 50 lobsters, and when you're doing 130 covers, 30 to 50 is quite a big chunk!

4 (1½-pound) lobsters

2 cups Lobster Stock (see page 385) or store-bought

¼ cup sriracha

2 tablespoons low-sodium soy sauce

6 ounces (12 tablespoons) unsalted butter

Juice of 2 limes

Kosher salt

¼ cup canola oil

2 tablespoons chopped fresh ginger

2 tablespoons chopped onion

4 thick slices brioche or sourdough bread

Freshly ground black pepper

2 tablespoons chiffonade of fresh mint

2 tablespoons sliced scallions, green parts only, soaked in ice water

1. Bring a large pot of salted water to a boil. Remove the tails from the lobster bodies and cut the tails into 1-inch pieces while they are still in their shells. Remove the claws and place them in the pot of boiling water. Simmer for 4 minutes. Transfer the claws to an ice bath. Once cool, remove the meat from the claws and knuckles and set the meat aside. (See page 134 for instructions.)

2. Bring the Lobster Stock to a simmer and add the sriracha and soy sauce. Piece by piece, using a hand blender or a whisk, whisk in 6 tablespoons of the butter until emulsified. Finish with the lime juice and season with salt. This sauce may seem too spicy at first but the sweetness from the lobster will help balance it out.

3. Season the lobster tails with salt on both sides. In a wok or a large sauté pan set over high heat, heat just enough oil to cover the bottom of the pan. Just before it starts to smoke, add the lobster tails, turn the heat down to medium, and cook for 1 minute, undisturbed. Add the ginger and onion and cook for 30 seconds, stirring. Add the lobster stock emulsion and deglaze the pan, scraping the brown bits off the bottom of the pan with a wooden spoon. Turn the heat down to low and cook for 1 more minute or until the lobster is cooked through. Remove the lobster meat from the sauce and distribute it among 4 plates.

4. Add the claw and knuckle meat and reduce the remaining sauce until it thickens slightly, about 2 minutes. While the sauce is reducing, butter the bread slices with the remaining 6 tablespoons butter and season with salt and pepper. Cut each bread slice diagonally— you should wind up with 8 triangular slices. Toast the bread in a toaster oven until toasted and golden brown.

5. Taste the lobster sauce and add more salt and pepper, if needed. Add the claw and knuckle meat to each bowl. Finish with the mint chiffonade and sliced scallions. Divide the sauce evenly among the four bowls and serve the lobster with Texas toast on the side—you will want it all to mop up the sauce afterward.

SOFT-SHELL CRABS + PICKLED RAMPS + SQUASH BLOSSOMS + SAUCE CAJUN

SERVES 4 This is a play on *fritto misto*, one of the first dishes that I was actually allowed to cook while doing a *stage* in France for one of Michel Guérard's restaurants; they wanted to see if I could keep up during service. Each *fritto misto* had eight different elements that were fried *à la minute* in a plug-in home fryer. And everything moved fast, fast, fast. As we say in the kitchen, "Sink or swim."

FOR THE MUSSEL REDUCTION

2 cups Mussel Stock
(see page 385)

2 cups muscat

1 cup dry vermouth,
preferably Noilly Prat

1 cup dry white wine

1 sliced shallot

FOR THE SAUCE CAJUN

1¾ cups Mayonnaise (see page 380) or store-bought

1 teaspoon Thai
green curry paste

1 teaspoon teriyaki sauce

¾ teaspoon minced
fresh ginger

½ teaspoon minced,
blanched lime zest
(see page 394)

¼ teaspoon ground turmeric

¼ teaspoon chopped
fresh tarragon

Kosher salt

FOR THE TEMPURA BATTER

One (8-ounce) package
tempura batter mix

¾ cup cold club soda

1 ice cube

FOR THE SOFT-SHELL CRABS AND VEGETABLES

4 squash blossoms

1 gallon canola oil

8 Pickled Ramps, bulbs
only (see page 389)

4 fennel fronds

4 scallions, trimmed
to 4 inches

4 large fresh mint leaves

4 small soft-shell crabs,
cleaned (see below)

2 lemons, halved, for serving

MAKE THE MUSSEL REDUCTION

1. In a stockpot, combine the Mussel Stock, muscat, vermouth, wine, and shallot and bring to a boil over high heat. Reduce the heat to low and simmer, uncovered, until the liquid has reduced to approximately 1 cup, about 1 hour. Transfer the reduction to a cooling rack and let cool to room temperature.

MAKE THE SAUCE CAJUN

2. In a large bowl, whisk together the Mayonnaise, ¼ cup of the Mussel Reduction, curry paste, teriyaki sauce, ginger, lime zest, turmeric, tarragon, and salt until combined. Set the sauce aside.

MAKE THE TEMPURA BATTER

3. In a medium bowl, whisk together the tempura batter mix and club soda until combined. Add the ice cube and let it gradually melt into the batter—the batter will be a little lumpy.

MAKE THE CRABS AND VEGETABLES

4. Halve the squash blossoms, and remove the insides and outer stems.

+ To clean soft-shell crabs, remove the fibrous gills by gently lifting the top shell at the left outer edge (just enough to reach in a finger and thumb). Repeat on the other side. Flip the crab over and remove the central apron on the end: Grab and tug the apron down, then cut off and discard. Finally, snip off the mouth and eyes in one cut.

5. Divide the oil between 2 large Dutch ovens, and warm the oil over medium-high heat until the temperature reaches 350°F on a deep-frying thermometer (see Note).

6. Dip the ramps in the Tempura Batter, and gently lower them into the hot oil. Fry the ramps until crispy, about 1 minute. Transfer to a cooling rack set over a paper towel–lined tray. Repeat with the squash blossoms, fennel fronds, scallions, and mint. Save the crabs for last. Dip each crab in the batter, and gently lower it into the hot oil. Be careful—the crabs sometimes pop, so wear protective clothing and be alert. Fry the crabs until crispy, 1 to 2 minutes. Do not overcrowd the Dutch oven—depending on your pot size, you may be able to fry 2 crabs at a time, but no more than that. Transfer the crabs to a paper towel–lined tray; repeat with the remaining crabs. Season the vegetables and crabs with salt, divide among 4 plates, and serve with the Sauce Cajun and a squirt of lemon.

+ If you are making this and expecting company, and would like to get a bit of a head start, you can make the vegetables slightly ahead. Lay the fried vegetables out in a single layer on a paper towel–lined tray—they should hold their own for 15 to 20 minutes.

Note   *You will want to use 2 Dutch ovens because after half of your battered items are fried, the oil in the first Dutch oven needs to be discarded. Since it takes a while to get the oil to the right temperature, you want the second batch to be ready to go when the first batch is all used up.*

SERVES 4 This is a play on an American backyard classic: potato salad. This simple side is present at just about every summer get-together—no summer barbecue is complete without it. Here, with the addition of oyster emulsion and caviar, we turn it into a very elegant starter. It's fun to serve at the beginning and get everyone excited for the rest of the meal. It's also a great way to kick off a New Year's party—just be sure to have plenty of Champagne to go around.

FOR THE POTATO SALAD

12 ounces Yukon Gold potatoes (1 large or 2 medium)

¼ cup crème fraîche

¼ cup sparkling water

2 tablespoons chopped Blanched Lemon Zest (see page 394)

2 tablespoons minced shallots

2 garlic cloves, minced

1 tablespoon fresh lime juice

¼ cup extra-virgin olive oil

Kosher salt

½ cup heavy cream

FOR THE OYSTER EMULSION

4 oysters, preferably a briny East Coast oyster such as Olde Salt or Wellfleet

8 ounces crème fraîche

Juice of ½ lime

1 teaspoon freshly grated horseradish

Kosher salt

TO ASSEMBLE THE DISH

Osetra caviar (optional)

Finely chopped rock chives (see Sources, page 403) or regular fresh chives

Extra-virgin olive oil

MAKE THE POTATO SALAD

1. Place the potatoes in a medium pot, add cold water to cover, and bring to a boil over high heat. Reduce the heat to medium and cook the potatoes until fork-tender, 15 to 20 minutes. Drain and carefully peel the hot potatoes, either wearing a pair of latex gloves or by holding down the potato with one fork and carefully peeling it with another. Once peeled, transfer the potatoes to a large bowl and mash them with a fork until the texture is mostly smooth but a few lumps remain.

2. Add the crème fraîche, sparkling water, Blanched Lemon Zest, shallots, garlic, and lime juice, and mix until well combined. Drizzle in the olive oil and season to taste with salt, but keep in mind that if you plan to serve this with caviar, the caviar itself is salty, so season accordingly.

3. In a cold, clean bowl, using a handheld mixer or a whisk, beat the heavy cream until stiff peaks form. Gently fold the whipped cream into the potato mixture and refrigerate for at least 2 hours and up to 6 hours before serving.

MAKE THE OYSTER EMULSION

4. Rinse and shuck the oysters, reserving the shells. In a blender, combine the oysters, crème fraîche, lime juice, horseradish, and salt to taste and puree. Strain the mixture through a fine-mesh strainer into a bowl, pressing on the solids to extract all the liquid, and refrigerate the liquid for at least 1 hour. Using an immersion blender, buzz the chilled liquid. The liquid will separate into foam and liquid, and the foam is what you want. Skim off the foam and set it aside in a bowl. Discard the liquid underneath.

ASSEMBLE THE DISH

5. Spoon some of the potato salad into the oyster shells (there will be leftover potato salad). Top the potato salad with some caviar, if desired, and some of the oyster foam. Sprinkle the chives over the salad and drizzle with a bit of olive oil. Serve the remaining potato salad on the side.

Make It Faster *If you want to just make a delicious potato salad, this is a great one to make, even without the oyster emulsion.*

> **+** Whenever you make any potato salad, it's very important to work with still-warm potatoes. Warm potatoes are better at absorbing other ingredients like oil and cream, resulting in a creamier, more luxurious-tasting salad.

huître

Marché pour 4 personnes

---

24 huîtres plates belons (taille double zéro) ou
24 huîtres « spéciales » portugaises

---

150 g de beurre ramolli à la température de la cuisine
Poivre
1 cuillère à soupe de jus de citron

---

70 g de carottes   ) épluchés
80 g de blancs de poireaux (et lavés
20 g de beurre

) 1 litre d'eau
(10 g de gros sel

24 feuilles de laitue
Sel et poivre

---

1 casserole plate ou sauteuse
1 grande casserole
1 petite casserole
1 cuillère à café
1 passoire doublée d'un linge étamine
4 plats à huîtres ou
4 assiettes plates recouvertes de gros sel
1 fouet

Huîtres ch

« HUÎTRES EN HABIT AU BEURR

PRÉPARATION DE LA JULIENN ET DE LA LAITUE :

1. Tailler en très fine **julienne** * — bâ
gueur et 1 mm de section — les carot
reaux. Faire chauffer dans la casserole
et y faire revenir vivement, pendant
asse_____nnée de sel et poivre. Tenir
_____ du four préalablement chau
_____6).

_____les feuilles de laitue 1
_____plie du litre d'eau bou
_____goutter sur un linge.

___ON DES HUÎTRES :
_____nnier.

_____de la cuillère à café, détac
_____uilles en se tenant au-des.
_____ur jus filtré dans la petite ca

_____ver les coquilles concaves, les
_____plats à huîtres ou sur les assiettes
_____n les enfonçant bien pour éviter qu
tenir au chaud à l'entrée du four, p
julienne (1).

5. **Pocher** les huîtres 30 secondes
casserole contenant leur eau filtrée (3
leur eau de cuisson.

6. **Emmailloter** les huîtres dans les
formant des sortes de petits baluchon
coquilles respectives (4); les tenir au c
du four maintenu à doux.

WHITE GAZPACHO + LAUGHING BIRD SHRIMP + GRAPE AND MINT CEVICHE

SERVES 4 Most Americans don't know that the original gazpacho was made with green grapes, not tomatoes; and the tomato version followed the grape one. But I hadn't tried white gazpacho until I went to Spain in my twenties. I fell hard for it and have been making various iterations ever since.

White gazpacho is one of the most refreshing summer meals there is—and on very hot days, it's a relief to know you can make something so delicious without having to turn on your stove. Spanish food and tapas have been gaining popularity in the last few years, so now white gazpacho can be found on many different menus, not just Spanish ones.

FOR THE GRAPES

1 cup extra-virgin olive oil

½ cup sliced seedless green grapes

½ cup sliced seedless red grapes

¼ cup chiffonade of fresh mint

Kosher salt

FOR THE GAZPACHO

½ cup plus 2 tablespoons Marcona almonds

¼ cup extra-virgin olive oil, plus more as needed

Kosher salt

Amber spice mix (see Sources, page 403)

2 cups large-dice stale country bread

4 garlic cloves, sliced

10 ounces seedless green grapes

7 ounces Greek whole-milk yogurt, strained overnight (see Note)

2 large seedless cucumbers, peeled and chopped

4 teaspoons sherry vinegar

FOR THE LAUGHING BIRD SHRIMP

2 cups white wine vinegar

6 tablespoons granulated sugar

3 teaspoons red pepper flakes

½ tablespoon kosher salt

24 Laughing Bird shrimp or rock shrimp, halved lengthwise

2 cups extra-virgin olive oil

2 teaspoons Amber spice mix (see Sources, page 403), plus more for serving

TO ASSEMBLE THE DISH

Micro cilantro (see Sources, page 403) or cilantro leaves

Amber spice mix (see Sources, page 403)

MAKE THE GRAPES

1. Combine the olive oil, green and red grapes, mint, and salt in a medium bowl. Refrigerate until ready to use.

MAKE THE GAZPACHO

2. Preheat the oven to 350°F; position the rack in the middle. Spread the almonds on a quarter-sheet baking pan. Toast the almonds until golden and fragrant, 10 minutes. Take 2 tablespoons of the almonds and toss with just enough olive oil to coat and a pinch of salt and Amber while warm. Set aside. Transfer remaining almonds to a rack and let cool to room temperature.

3. While the almonds are toasting, soak the bread in cold water for 10 minutes.

4. Bring a small pot of water to a boil over high heat. Blanch the garlic in the boiling water for 1 minute. Immediately transfer to an ice bath and let cool. Repeat the blanching and shocking process 2 more times. Squeeze the excess water from the garlic with your hands and transfer the garlic to a blender.

5. Squeeze the excess water from the bread and break up the soaked bread with your hands. Add the bread, ½ cup of toasted plain almonds, grapes, yogurt, cucumbers, and vinegar to the blender. Season with salt and

puree until smooth. You might need to add a couple of tablespoons of water if the mixture looks too stiff. With the blender motor running, slowly drizzle in the ¼ cup of oil and allow the mixture to emulsify. Pass the mixture through a fine-mesh strainer into a bowl and refrigerate for at least 3 hours before serving. The colder your gazpacho is, the better.

MAKE THE LAUGHING BIRD SHRIMP

6. In a medium nonreactive pot, combine the vinegar, sugar, pepper flakes, and salt with 1½ cups of water and bring to a boil over medium-high heat. Remove from the heat and let cool until just warm to the touch. Add the shrimp to the pot, and let the shrimp sit in the liquid for 30 minutes. Using a slotted spoon, transfer the shrimp to a medium bowl, and cover with the olive oil and Amber. Refrigerate until cool.

ASSEMBLE THE DISH

7. Ladle the gazpacho among 4 chilled bowls. Divide the Laughing Bird shrimp and the grapes among the bowls, and drizzle some of the olive oil from the shrimp over the soup. Sprinkle with the seasoned almonds, and garnish with cilantro and a pinch of Amber.

Note *To strain Greek yogurt, set a strainer lined with cheesecloth over a bowl. Add the yogurt, cover, and place in the refrigerator overnight.*

CASCO BAY COD + PEI MUSSELS + MAYAN SHRIMP + UNI CREAM

SERVES 4 I love being inspired by other chefs. A little while back, I had dinner at the John Dory, a fantastic restaurant in New York, run by a chef I really respect—April Bloomfield. At John Dory, Bloomfield makes this amazing oyster pan roast and serves it with uni (sea urchin) toast. After trying it, I was inspired to make something at my place that featured uni front and center. In fact, in this dish, uni gets featured twice: There's uni butter and uni cream—perfect flavors to complement the briny mussels and sweet shrimp.

FOR THE UNI BUTTER

4 ounces uni

4 ounces (8 tablespoons) unsalted butter

Finely grated zest of 1 lemon

1 teaspoon kosher salt

FOR THE UNI CREAM

½ cup dry white wine

4 pounds littleneck clams, scrubbed and rinsed

3 sprigs fresh thyme

1 small celery root, thinly sliced, plus 1 cup diced celery root (about 1 pound in total)

2 cups heavy cream

1½ ounces (3 tablespoons) unsalted butter

1 large onion, peeled and cut into ¼-inch dice

3 garlic cloves, peeled and chopped

2 celery stalks, cut into ¼-inch dice

2 tablespoons Vadouvan curry powder (see Sources, page 403)

2 fresh or 1 dry bay leaves

8 ounces uni

FOR THE COD

4 (3-ounce) cod fillets, skin on, preferably Casco Bay

Kosher salt

Blended Oil (see page 395)

TO ASSEMBLE THE DISH

1 pound Prince Edward Island mussels

2 pounds littleneck clams, scrubbed and rinsed

4 head-on Mayan shrimp, shells removed and deveined

2 tablespoons chopped celery leaves

Baguette slices

Micro celery (see Sources, page 403) or chiffonade of fresh celery leaves (optional)

4 uni fillets

MAKE THE UNI BUTTER

1. In the bowl of a stand mixer fitted with the paddle attachment, combine the uni, butter, lemon zest, and salt. Whip the butter on high until light and fluffy, about 2 minutes. Pass the butter through a tamis or a wide fine-mesh strainer. Transfer to a covered container and refrigerate until needed.

MAKE THE UNI CREAM

2. In a large pot, combine the wine with 1½ cups of water and bring to a boil. Add the clams and thyme and cook, covered, until the clams open, about 10 minutes. Transfer the clams to a large bowl (or several large bowls) and set aside. Discard the clams that did not open. Strain the cooking liquid into a separate bowl, discard the thyme, and set aside. You can either discard the cooked clams or use them for something else (at the restaurant we use them for family meal).

3. In a medium saucepot, combine the sliced celery root and cream and bring to a simmer over medium-high heat. Reduce the heat to medium-low so the liquid is at a gentle simmer, and cook until the celery root is cooked through, 12 to 15 minutes. Transfer the celery root to a blender with ½ cup of the cooking liquid, and puree until smooth. Pass the celery root cream through a fine-mesh strainer into a bowl and set aside.

4. In a medium sauté pan, melt the butter over medium heat. Add the onion, garlic, celery, Vadouvan, and bay leaves, and cook, stirring, until the onion is translucent, about 4 minutes. Add the reserved clam cooking liquid, the reserved celery root cream, and the diced celery root. Cook until the diced celery root is fork-tender, about 8 minutes. Strain the liquid through a fine-mesh strainer and transfer half of the strained liquid to a blender; reserve the cooked vegetables. Add the uni to the blender and puree the mixture on high speed until smooth. Add the other half of the liquid to the blender and puree until smooth. Pass the uni cream through a fine-mesh strainer into a pot. Set aside and keep warm.

MAKE THE COD

5. Preheat the oven to 450°F; position the rack in the middle. Pat the fish dry with paper towels and season both sides with salt.

6. Add enough Blended Oil to a large ovenproof sauté pan to cover the bottom of the pan and set it over high heat. Just before it starts to smoke, add the fish, skin side down, and reduce the heat to medium. Cook for about 5 minutes or until the bottom of the fish is nicely browned. Transfer the pan to the oven and cook the fish for 2 minutes. Return the fish to the stovetop over medium heat, flip the fish, and baste the fish once or twice with the oil in the pan. Transfer to a cooling rack.

ASSEMBLE THE DISH

7. Add the mussels and the remaining 2 pounds of clams to the pot with the Uni Cream. Once they begin to open, add the shrimp and cooked vegetables and at the last second, add the chopped celery leaves.

8. While you're finishing the soup, light a grill or preheat a grill pan. Grill the bread over high heat until charred on one side, about 2 minutes. Alternatively, place the bread in a shallow baking pan and cook under a broiler for about 1 minute or until charred on top. The bread should be crispy on one side and soft on the other. As soon as the bread comes off the heat, spread some of the Uni Butter over it.

9. Divide the Uni Cream among 4 warmed bowls, making sure that the seafood is evenly distributed. Top each bowl with a piece of cod and scatter the micro celery around, if using. Place an uni fillet over each piece of fish, and serve with the toasted baguette slices.

DIVER SEA SCALLOPS + BUTTERNUT SQUASH RISOTTO + CHORIZO SALT

SERVES 4 Diver scallops got their name because unlike regular scallops, which are most commonly harvested by using scallop dredges or bottom trawls, diver scallops are hand-harvested by individual divers. This method is considered to be more ecologically friendly, as hand-harvesting does not damage the undersea environments as the dredges do; and diver scallops tend to be fresher because they take less time to reach the consumer than with alternative scallop harvesting methods, which can take up to two weeks. Diver scallops are considered to be a seasonal item (December through April) with a short harvesting window. So if you happen to see a diver scallop on a menu in the off-season, you might want to look into it.

FOR THE CHORIZO OIL

½ cup Blended Oil (see page 395)

3 tablespoons of sliced cured chorizo (see Sources, page 403)

2 tablespoons smoked paprika

FOR THE CHORIZO SALT AND EMULSION

Canola oil

2 links cured chorizo (see Sources, page 403)

½ cup brunoise red peppers (see page 48)

½ cup brunoise onions (see page 48)

3 tablespoons smoked paprika

1 tablespoon chili powder

1 cup dry white wine

4 cups Chicken Stock (see page 382) or store-bought

1 sprig fresh thyme

1 fresh or ½ dried bay leaf

1 ounce (2 tablespoons) unsalted butter

1 teaspoon soy lecithin granules (see Sources, page 403; optional)

FOR THE BUTTERNUT SQUASH

Canola oil

1 cup diced butternut squash

Kosher salt

¼ cup dry white wine

1 cinnamon stick

FOR THE BUTTERNUT SQUASH RISOTTO

1 sprig fresh thyme

1 fresh or ½ dried bay leaf

5 to 6 cups hot Chicken Stock (see page 382) or store-bought

½ cup brunoise Vidalia onions (see page 48)

2 cups Arborio rice

1½ cups dry white wine

½ cup fresh butternut squash juice or fresh carrot juice

¼ cup chopped fresh chives

3 tablespoons cream cheese

2 tablespoons chiffonade of fresh sage

1 tablespoon brunoise shallots (see page 48)

1 teaspoon white truffle oil, optional

Kosher salt

¼ cup finely grated Parmigiano-Reggiano

2 tablespoons diced chorizo

FOR THE DIVER SCALLOPS

12 diver sea scallops (size U/10; see page 149)

Blended Oil (see page 395)

3 tablespoons (1½ ounces) unsalted butter

3 sprigs fresh thyme

3 leaves fresh sage

TO ASSEMBLE THE DISH

Olive oil

Sage leaves

MAKE THE CHORIZO OIL

1. Add the Blended Oil, chorizo, and paprika to a 1-quart pot and warm the oil over medium-high heat until the temperature registers 250°F on a deep-frying thermometer. Remove from the heat and let sit for 2 hours in a warm place. Strain the oil through a coffee filter and set aside.

MAKE THE CHORIZO SALT AND EMULSION

2. While the Chorizo Oil infuses, add enough oil to a large sauté pan to come 1 inch up the sides. Warm the oil until it registers 300°F on a deep-frying thermometer. Trim the skin off the chorizo links; set chorizo aside. Fry the chorizo skin in the oil until crispy, about 10 seconds. Transfer to a paper towel–lined tray and leave in a warm place for 2 hours. Chop the chorizo skin to the consistency of flaky sea salt.

3. Slice the chorizo into ¼-inch slices. Add enough oil to a 3-quart saucepot to cover the bottom of the pot and set it over high heat. Just before it starts to smoke, add the chorizo, reduce the heat to medium, and cook the chorizo until crispy. Add the red peppers, onions, paprika, and chili powder, and cook until the spices are fragrant and the vegetables are soft. Add the wine, and cook until the wine has reduced by half. Add the stock, thyme, and bay leaf. Reduce the heat to low and simmer for 1½ hours. Strain the broth through a fine-mesh strainer. Add the butter and lecithin, if using, and using an immersion blender, whip the liquid until smooth and emulsified. Measure out 1½ cups for the recipe and set aside. Discard the rest—you need all this liquid for the emulsification to take place, but only 1½ cups for the dish itself.

MAKE THE BUTTERNUT SQUASH

4. Add enough oil to a large sauté pan to cover the bottom of the pan and set it over high heat. Just before it starts to smoke, add the squash, reduce the heat to medium, and season with salt. Add the white wine and cinnamon stick. Reduce the heat to low and cook until the pan is dry and the squash is cooked through, about 3 minutes. Transfer the squash to a plate, cover, and set aside. (The squash can be made in advance.)

+ Don't cook more than four sea scallops at the same time in a medium pan. You want them perfectly cooked, and overcrowding ruins them.

MAKE THE BUTTERNUT SQUASH RISOTTO

5. Using kitchen twine, tie the thyme and bay leaf into a bundle. In a 4-quart pot, warm the stock over high heat until it is hot. Make sure the stock remains hot.

6. In a 4-quart pot, heat 3 tablespoons of the Chorizo Oil over medium-high heat until shimmering. Add the onions, reduce the heat to medium, and cook until translucent, about 3 minutes. Add the rice and stir to coat. Cook until the rice starts to toast, about 3 minutes. Add the wine, and cook until the pan is dry. Add 1 cup of the hot stock and the thyme–bay leaf bundle. Stir with a wooden spoon until the rice has absorbed the stock. Continue to add the stock 1 cup at a time, stirring until the stock has been absorbed before adding the next cup. Cook until the rice is just about cooked, but is still al dente. Add the Butternut Squash, squash juice, chives, cream cheese, sage, shallots, truffle oil, and salt to taste. Fold in the Parmigiano-Reggiano and diced chorizo. Taste and adjust the seasonings. Remove from the heat, cover, and keep warm.

MAKE THE DIVER SCALLOPS

7. Preheat the oven to 400°F; position the rack in the middle. Thoroughly pat dry the scallops. Add enough Blended Oil to a large ovenproof sauté pan to cover the bottom of the pan and set it over high heat. Just before it starts to smoke, add 4 scallops to the pan and immediately reduce the heat to medium. Transfer the pan to the oven for 90 seconds and then immediately return it to the stovetop over medium heat. Add 1 tablespoon of the butter, 1 sprig of thyme, and 1 sage leaf. Flip the scallops and baste them for 10 seconds. Transfer the cooked scallops to a paper towel–lined tray. Repeat with the remaining scallops, butter, thyme, and sage leaves.

8. Add enough olive oil to a medium sauté pan to come ½ inch up the sides. Set the pan over medium heat and warm the oil until tiny bubbles begin to form. Gently slide the sage leaves into the oil—they will produce a lot of bubbles as they fry. When the bubbles stop forming, the sage leaves are done. Transfer the leaves to a paper towel–lined plate using a slotted spoon.

9. Divide the Butternut Squash Risotto among 4 warmed plates. Evenly distribute the Diver Scallops over the risotto and season with the Chorizo Salt. Spoon the Chorizo Emulsion around and sprinkle the fried sage leaves on top.

Make It Faster *The Chorizo Emulsion is the longest-cooking component of this dish. Instead, you can just make the risotto and cook the scallops, which would make the meal perfectly doable for a weeknight dinner.*

Note *The recipe makes more Chorizo Oil than you need for the dish, but since it keeps indefinitely, it's a great flavor enhancer to keep on hand to add to any savory meal. Store it in a squeeze bottle at room temperature.*

SCALLOPS

Scallops come in all shapes and sizes. Their number usually indicates how many are in a pound. For example, designating scallops as "20/30" means that there are 20 to 30 scallops in 1 pound of scallops. Thus, the smaller the number is, the larger the scallops are, and the fewer of them make up a pound.

Sometimes, you might also see designations like "U/15" or "U/10." In this case, the U stands for "under," suggesting that it would take fewer than 15 (or 10) scallops to make a pound. Sea scallops are large and reach between 1½ and 2 inches in diameter. Much like steak, they can be pan seared so the outside gets crispy and caramelized while the inside stays tender and rare.

Bay scallops, known for their sweet and delicate texture, are among the smallest of scallops, often listed as "70/120," meaning it would take between 70 and 120 scallops to make up a pound. You can find bay scallops anywhere from Cape Cod to the Gulf of Mexico, and sometimes in Nova Scotia. In New York, bay scallops mostly inhabit the small bays and harbors of Peconic Bay on the eastern end of Long Island, and have also been found in Great South Bay, Moriches Bay, and Shinnecock Bay. Harvested between July and late September, bay scallops prefer to inhabit shallow coastal bays and estuaries with sandy and muddy bottoms and eelgrass beds.

The vast majority of scallops are harvested by boats dragging chain nets across the ocean floor—this can be very disruptive to the delicate sea ecosystems and many unsuspecting sea dwellers can get caught and die in the process.

Diver scallops, on the other hand, are harvested by divers who jump into the water and collect them by hand. While the term "diver" itself does not imply size, the divers generally tend to go for the largest scallops they can find. You will most likely see diver scallops in the 10/30 range. Diver scallops are more ecologically sound because the divers tend to go for the bigger, more mature scallops, letting the younger ones live on, thus allowing the scallop

SEA SCALLOPS + DICKSON'S TASSO + POMMES FONDANT + SUGAR SNAP PEAS + MUSTARD OIL EMULSION

SERVES 4 Dickson's Farmstand Meats, located in Chelsea Market in New York, is a terrific small meat shop offering a selection of artisanal meats and meat products. They focus on grass-fed (and finished), organic, heritage breeds, and work with small farmers to source their products.

One day, I was at the Food Network headquarters, which also happens to be located at the Chelsea Market, and on my way out, stopped by Dickson's to get a sandwich. The meat in the sandwich was so delicious that I went back the next day to pick up samples of everything, including the Tasso ham, which I loved so much that I wanted to use it in a dish.

Tasso ham is a thick hunk of fatty pork, cured in a blend of spices, and is a specialty of southern Louisiana. Technically, Tasso ham isn't "ham," per se, since it's not made out of pork shoulder. But since the cut is typically fatty and has a great deal of flavor, it's called ham nonetheless.

SPECIAL EQUIPMENT

Wooden skewers

FOR THE EMULSION

½ cup Chicken Stock (see page 382) or store-bought

½ cup fresh lemon juice

¼ cup mustard oil (see Sources, page 403)

¼ cup extra-virgin olive oil

4 ounces (8 tablespoons) unsalted butter, cut into pieces

Kosher salt

FOR THE PEAS

½ cup shelled green peas

1 cup (about 3½ ounces) sugar snap peas

Olive oil

¼ cup finely diced bacon (2 to 3 strips)

2 teaspoons chopped garlic

3 ounces (about 5) cipollini onions, sliced

1 large pinch granulated sugar

¼ cup Chicken Stock (see page 382) or store-bought

½ head chiffonade of Bibb lettuce

1 ounce (2 tablespoons) unsalted butter

Kosher salt

Freshly ground black pepper

FOR THE POTATOES

2 Idaho potatoes, peeled and immersed in water

4 ounces (8 tablespoons) Clarified Butter (see page 390)

1½ ounces (3 tablespoons) unsalted butter

4 sprigs fresh thyme

½ cup chopped leeks, white parts only

1 cup Veal Stock (see page 382) or Chicken Stock (see page 382) or store-bought

Kosher salt

Freshly ground black pepper

FOR THE SCALLOPS

12 sea scallops, shucked and tough muscle removed

12 thin slices Tasso ham

Canola oil

TO ASSEMBLE THE DISH

1 tablespoon chiffonade of fresh mint

Flaky sea salt, such as Maldon

Baby fennel fronds or curly parsley

Chili oil

1. In a small saucepot, combine the stock, lemon juice, mustard oil, and olive oil, and bring to a boil over medium-high heat. Add the butter, and using an immersion blender, blend until the mixture is light and frothy. Season to taste with salt and set aside.

MAKE THE PEAS

2. Bring a 4-quart pot of salted water to a boil. Add the green peas and cook for 1 minute. Transfer to an ice bath and let cool. Repeat with the sugar snap peas. Drain and set aside.

3. Add enough oil to a large skillet to cover the bottom of the pan and set it over high heat. Just before the oil starts to smoke, add the bacon, reduce the heat to medium, and render the lardons until crispy, 5 to 7 minutes. Add the garlic and cook until toasted, 1 to 2 minutes. Add the cipollini onions and sugar and cook until both have slightly caramelized, about 3 minutes. Add the stock and deglaze the pan, scraping the brown bits off the bottom of the pan with a wooden spoon. Add the lettuce and cook for 1 minute. Add the blanched peas and butter and cook until warmed through, 2 to 3 minutes. Season to taste with salt and pepper and set aside.

+ Leeks can be tricky to clean and are often *very* gritty. To properly clean them, halve the leeks down the middle and remove the tough outer layers. Run the halved leeks under cold, running water, chop them, and soak them in a bowl of cold water for 5 minutes. The remaining dirt and sand will fall to the bottom of the bowl. Scoop the leeks out using a slotted spoon or a spider, leaving the grit at the bottom.

MAKE THE POTATOES

4. Using a medium melon baller, scoop out potato balls from the peeled potatoes. Transfer the potato balls to a large bowl filled with cold water until ready to use. Transfer the potatoes to a paper towel–lined tray and pat them dry. Be sure to get as much water off as possible or the oil will spatter.

5. In a large skillet, warm the Clarified Butter over high heat. Just before it starts to smoke—you may need to cook the potatoes in batches, so divide the Clarified Butter accordingly—add the potatoes and shake the pan to make sure the potatoes aren't sticking to the pan. Reduce the heat to medium, and cook the potatoes until well browned all over. Add the unsalted butter and thyme and cook for 1 minute. Add the leeks and stir to combine. Add the stock and cook until the stock is almost completely absorbed and the potatoes are fork-tender. Season to taste with salt and pepper, transfer the potatoes and leeks to a large bowl, and set aside.

MAKE THE SCALLOPS

6. Wrap each scallop in a slice of Tasso. Place 3 wrapped scallops on a wooden skewer with the seam side on the outside.

7. Add enough oil to a large sauté pan to cover the bottom of the pan and set it over high heat. Just before the oil starts to smoke, add the wrapped scallop skewers, seam side down, and sear on each side for 30 seconds. (Bear in mind that you are not searing the top and bottom of the scallops—just the sides that are wrapped in ham; use the skewer to roll the sides over the pan.) Remove from the pan and set aside.

ASSEMBLE THE DISH

8. Fold the mint into the peas. Divide the potatoes and peas among 4 warmed plates. Divide the scallops among the plates and sprinkle with flaky sea salt. Spoon the emulsion around the scallops and garnish with fennel fronds and chili oil.

Make It Faster *Make the scallops with the emulsion and just one other component, peas or potatoes.*

LITTLENECK CLAMS + PORK-FENNEL SAUSAGE + BELL PEPPERS + ONIONS

SERVES 4 One of my all-time favorite flavor combinations is your classic American-Italian marriage of sausage and peppers. I had wanted to feature the dish on our menu and was playing around with those two ingredients, but wanted to create something a little off the beaten (expected) path, and worthy of a restaurant feature. Believe it or not, clams go especially well with pork; and the fennel in the sausage is a wonderful complement to their briny, saline notes. Onions and peppers add a subtle sweetness, offsetting the salty sausage. Slightly sophisticated, this is fun to make—and even more fun to eat!

FOR THE ONIONS AND PEPPERS

3 red bell peppers

3 yellow bell peppers

Olive oil

1 Vidalia onion, julienned

Kosher salt

FOR THE PORK-FENNEL SAUSAGE

½ cup fennel seeds

1 pound cubed pork shoulder

2 garlic cloves

2 teaspoons pink curing salt

1 tablespoon kosher salt

FOR THE CLAMS

Olive oil

2 pounds littleneck clams

2 cups dry white wine

1 cup Chicken Stock (see page 382) or store-bought

4 cups 10-Minute Tomato Sauce (see page 380) or canned

4 cups outer broccoli rabe leaves, stems removed

¼ cup chiffonade of fresh basil

Extra-virgin olive oil

4 (¾-inch-thick) slices rustic country bread

Kosher salt

Freshly ground black pepper

MAKE THE ONIONS AND PEPPERS

1. Turn the broiler to high; position the rack in the top. In a large bowl, toss the peppers in olive oil. Transfer them to a shallow baking pan and broil them until the skins are almost black and the peppers are soft, about 10 minutes. Transfer to a bowl, cover tightly with plastic wrap, and let stand for 1½ hours at room temperature. Peel, seed, and julienne the peppers and set them aside.

2. Add enough oil to a large sauté pan to cover the bottom of the pan and set it over high heat. Just before the oil starts to smoke, add the onion, reduce the heat to medium, and cook, stirring, until soft. Add the peppers and stir to combine with the onion. Transfer to a parchment paper–lined tray and let cool.

MAKE THE PORK-FENNEL SAUSAGE

3. In a small, dry skillet, toast the fennel seeds over low heat until fragrant, about 3 minutes. Remove from the heat, transfer to a small bowl, and let cool. Using a meat grinder, or a meat grinding attachment to your stand mixer, grind together the pork, garlic, fennel seeds, and both salts. Set aside. If you do not own a meat grinder, ask your butcher to grind the meat and combine it with the remaining sausage ingredients at home.

Blowing off some steam

MAKE THE CLAMS

4. Add enough olive oil to a large stockpot to cover the bottom of the pot and set it over high heat. Just before the oil starts to smoke, add the reserved sausage and sear it on one side, breaking up the meat with a wooden spoon. Cook until the meat browns, about 10 minutes. Add the clams and the Onions and Peppers and cook for 30 seconds. Add the wine and stock and cook for 30 seconds more. Reduce the heat to medium and add the tomato sauce. Cover and cook until the clams open, 8 to 10 minutes. Remove the lid and stir in the broccoli rabe leaves and basil.

5. Drizzle some olive oil over the bread slices and season them with salt and pepper. Light a grill or preheat a grill pan. Grill the bread over high heat, turning once, until toasted, 2 to 3 minutes. Alternatively, place the bread on a half-sheet baking pan and cook under a broiler for about 1 minute—the bread should still be a little soft, but have slight color on top. Drizzle with more olive oil and set aside.

6. Discard any clams that did not open. Divide the clams in tomato sauce among 4 bowls, with grilled bread on the side. Drizzle with more extra-virgin olive oil before serving.

Make It Faster *If making your own sausage meat isn't your thing, you can always cook with your favorite prepared sausage instead. The rest of the components come together quickly. Onions and Peppers can be made a day in advance, so when you throw the whole dish together, your dinner should be ready in half an hour.*

DIVER SEA SCALLOP + ROE VINAIGRETTE + OSETRA CAVIAR + SCALLOP BACON + RAMPS

SERVES 4 While I risk sounding totally cliché, ramps are one of my favorite ingredients. I know it's not wildly original, but I love them nonetheless. Partly, it's because ramps are one of the harbingers of spring; when they show up at greenmarkets, chefs and home cooks everywhere rejoice. Ramps' arrival means that the long, cold winter is finally over.

It also means you no longer have to contend with just root vegetables. Soon, there will be asparagus, overwintered broccoli rabe, and much, much more.

Ramps are also mysterious. Still a wild, foraged product, the ramp has a short, blink-and-you'll-miss-it season.

But what I really love is their amazing, mild garlic flavor. We originally made this as a starter for our ramp tasting menu at the restaurant. It's a delicious way to kick off dinner.

SPECIAL EQUIPMENT

1 cup applewood chips

FOR THE RAMP CHIMICHURRI

8 ramps, cleaned
and trimmed

1 recipe Chimichurri
Sauce (see page 242)

FOR THE ROE VINAIGRETTE

4 diver sea scallops
in the shell

2 tablespoons extra-
virgin olive oil

2 tablespoons fresh
lemon juice

1 tablespoon mustard oil
(see Sources, page 403)

2 teaspoons mild honey

FOR THE SCALLOP BACON

1 cup canola oil

Kosher salt

Freshly ground black pepper

Smoked salt, crushed in
a mortar and pestle

FOR THE SCALLOPS

Extra-virgin olive oil

Kosher salt

TO ASSEMBLE THE DISH

2 lemons, halved

Osetra caviar (optional)

4 small ramps, cleaned
and trimmed

MAKE THE RAMPS

1. Bring a medium pot of salted water to a boil. Cut the ramps in half, separating the white bulb parts from the green tops. Blanch the ramp greens for 15 seconds and immediately transfer them to an ice bath. Allow the greens to cool, then strain them and squeeze out all the excess liquid. Finely chop the ramp greens, mince the ramp bulbs, and combine the two in a small bowl. Add the chopped ramps to the Chimichurri Sauce. Set aside until needed.

MAKE THE ROE VINAIGRETTE

2. Open the scallop shells, but do not separate the scallops from the bottom shell. Remove the red roe sack and skirt (it is the outermost edge and looks wavy, like a skirt) from the shells, and rinse both under cold water. Place the roe and skirts in separate containers and refrigerate until needed.

3. Rinse the scallops on the half shell under the cold water and transfer them to a towel set over a sheet pan. Place another towel on top and refrigerate until needed.

4. In a small nonreactive bowl, mix the olive oil, lemon juice, mustard oil, and honey until well combined. Add the reserved scallop roe, cover, and refrigerate for 1 hour.

5. Using a whisk, emulsify the chilled mixture, pass it through a fine-mesh strainer into a bowl, and refrigerate until needed.

MAKE THE SCALLOP BACON (SEE "MAKE IT FASTER," BELOW)

6. Soak the applewood chips in water for 20 minutes.

7. In a small pot, warm 1 cup of oil over medium heat until it registers 300°F on a deep-frying thermometer. While you wait for the oil to come to temperature, season the reserved scallop skirts with salt and pepper.

8. Line the bottom of a 4-quart saucepot with foil. Place the soaked wood chips over the foil. Make a "basket" out of foil to hang over the edges of the pot so that when you place the scallop skirts in it, they will be suspended over the wood chips. Poke 8 to 10 holes in the "basket" with a paring knife. Remove the "basket" from the pot and set it nearby. Place the pot over high heat until the wood chips begin to smoke and smell fragrant, 8 to 10 minutes. Reduce the heat to medium, and gently slide the "basket" over the pot. Gently lower the scallop skirts into the "basket," cover the pot, and smoke the scallop skirts for about 10 minutes. Transfer the smoked scallop skirts to a parchment paper–lined tray to cool.

9. Once the oil has come up to temperature, fry the smoked scallop skirts until crispy, 1 to 2 minutes. Transfer the fried scallop skirts to a paper towel–lined tray and season with smoked salt. The skirts will curl up and get crispy, and resemble little pieces of bacon. Set aside in a dry place.

MAKE THE SCALLOPS

10. Preheat the oven to 350°F; position the rack in the middle. Remove the scallops on the half shell from the refrigerator and let stand at room temperature for 15 minutes. Bake the scallops for about 5 minutes or until warm to the touch. As soon as the scallops come out of the oven, drizzle them with a little olive oil and add a pinch of salt to each scallop.

ASSEMBLE THE DISH

11. Spoon enough of the Ramp Chimichurri to cover the top of each scallop. You will have extra Ramp Chimichurri left over; set it aside for an omelette the next morning. Spoon the Roe Vinaigrette around the scallops, and give a generous squeeze of lemon. Spoon a bit of the caviar on top, if using. Place the Scallop Bacon over the caviar and garnish each plate with a raw ramp.

Make It Faster *If your kitchen doesn't come with windows or good ventilation, you might want to consider skipping the Scallop Bacon, as it will get smoky, and just make the Roe Vinaigrette and the scallops.*

VEGETABLES

"Colorful and multidimensional, vegetables allow us to distinguish the nuances of each growing season in our region. A walk through the greenmarket supplies inspiration for an entire menu, and each plant has a particular story to tell. Vegetable combinations are stealing the spotlight more frequently than ever, at home and in our restaurants, giving us a chance to celebrate the responsible, solid, and committed work of farmers we rely on to grow an inspired community."

—MICHAEL ANTHONY

RED BEET RAVIOLI + MIDNIGHT MOON GOAT CHEESE + WALNUTS + WATERCRESS

SERVES 4 There is no pasta in this dish. Instead, the beets are thinly sliced, then baked at a low temperature to soften them. As a result, their texture becomes delicate, almost like fresh pasta sheets. At the restaurant, we use Coach Farm goat cheese, but any fresh goat cheese will do. The walnuts are a natural pairing to the beets and the watercress provides a necessary bite for a little contrast.

FOR THE CANDIED WALNUTS

2 cups walnuts

1 cup granulated sugar

1 tablespoon ground cinnamon

FOR THE WALNUT VINAIGRETTE

1 cup extra-virgin olive oil

½ cup sherry vinegar

¼ cup walnut oil

Kosher salt

Freshly ground black pepper

FOR THE WATERCRESS AND ENDIVE SALAD

3 cups watercress tops (preferably wild) with 2 inches of the stem left intact

12 red endive leaves

FOR THE BEET RAVIOLI SHEETS

1 extra-large beet (1¼ to 1½ pounds), trimmed and peeled

Extra-virgin olive oil

FOR THE GOAT CHEESE FILLING

1 pound fresh goat cheese, room temperature

2 tablespoons chopped fresh chives

2 tablespoons chopped fresh curly parsley

1 tablespoon minced shallots

Kosher salt

Freshly ground black pepper

TO ASSEMBLE THE DISH

½ pound fresh goat cheese

Walnut oil

MAKE THE CANDIED WALNUTS

1. Preheat the oven to 325°F; position the rack in the middle. Spread the walnuts out on a baking sheet and toast them in the oven for 10 minutes or until fragrant. Set the walnuts aside while you make the sugar glaze.

2. In a medium pot, combine the sugar with 1 cup of water and bring to a boil over medium heat. Add the cinnamon, reduce the heat to low, and simmer for 4 minutes, until you smell the cinnamon and sugar caramelizing. Fold in the walnuts and cook for 30 seconds more. Transfer the coated nuts to a Silpat- or parchment paper–lined baking sheet and spread them into an even layer. Allow the nuts to cool to room temperature, then crush the nuts using your hands or a mallet.

MAKE THE WALNUT VINAIGRETTE

3. Using a fork, in a small bowl blend the olive oil, sherry vinegar, and walnut oil. Season to taste with salt and pepper. The vinaigrette will look "broken," not uniform or emulsified.

MAKE THE WATERCRESS AND ENDIVE SALAD

4. In a large bowl, toss the watercress and endive together. Set aside.

MAKE THE BEET RAVIOLI SHEETS

5. Preheat the oven to 350°F; position the rack in the middle. Using an adjustable mandoline, slice the beet into 1/16-inch-thick slices. You will need 24 slices. Using a ring cutter, cut each slice into a 2½-inch circle. Lay the cut circles on a Silpat-lined baking sheet and brush them with a little olive oil. Bake the beet circles for 10 minutes or until soft. Transfer to a cooling rack and let cool. Set aside.

MAKE THE GOAT CHEESE FILLING

6. In the bowl of a stand mixer fitted with the paddle attachment, combine the goat cheese, chives, parsley, shallots, salt, and pepper, and mix on low speed until

well combined. Transfer the mixture to a pastry bag fitted with a #8 tip. Line a large cutting board or a counter with parchment paper. Lay 12 of the beet circles on the paper. Pipe the filling onto the circles, leaving a ½-inch unfilled border around the filling. Repeat until all 12 circles are filled. Place the remaining beet circles on top of the filled beet circles, and using the dull side of a ½-inch ring cutter (see page 187), gently mold the ravioli into shape and press the edges of the beet circles together. Using a 2-inch ring cutter, cut the ravioli into shape.

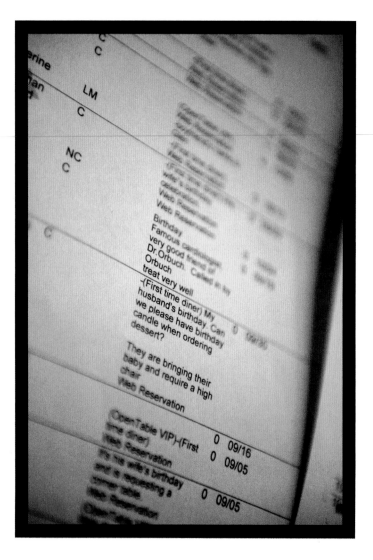

7. Divide the ravioli among 4 chilled plates—you should have 3 ravioli per plate. Place the Watercress and Endive Salad on top of the ravioli and around each plate, and drizzle the Walnut Vinaigrette over. Crumble the goat cheese and sprinkle some Candied Walnuts on top and around the ravioli. Drizzle some walnut oil on top before serving.

Make It Faster *Instead of making the ravioli, make a beet and goat cheese salad instead. Simply wrap the beets in foil and roast at 400°F until you can easily pierce the beet with a knife, then thinly slice the beets as if for ravioli. Make the Candied Walnuts and the Walnut Vinaigrette; Toss the beets and the walnuts with the watercress and endive, add the goat cheese and the accompanying herbs, and dress with the vinaigrette for a simple, delicious salad.*

EGGPLANT + BLACK PEPPER OLIVE OIL + BURRATA + TOMATO CONFIT

SERVES 4 I got the idea for this dish when I was on *The Next Iron Chef*, battling Chef Marco Canora. He made this amazing Eggplant Parmigiano-Reggiano that the judges absolutely loved. When I got back to New York, it happened to be eggplant season, and I started to play around with various combinations. In the end, I loved how the eggplant worked with tomato confit and creamy, runny burrata. Thank you, Marco, for the inspiration.

FOR THE BLACK PEPPER OLIVE OIL

3 tablespoons cracked black pepper

1 cup extra-virgin olive oil

FOR THE TOMATO CONFIT

4 large heirloom tomatoes, such as Purple Cherokee

3 garlic cloves, thinly sliced

Extra-virgin olive oil

Granulated sugar

Kosher salt

Freshly ground black pepper

12 sprigs fresh thyme

4 fresh or 2 dried bay leaves

2 tablespoons chiffonade of fresh basil

FOR THE EGGPLANT

1 large Italian eggplant (about 1½ pounds), peeled

Kosher salt

½ cup extra-virgin olive oil

12 fresh basil leaves

12 slices garlic

FOR THE BURRATA

2 balls fresh burrata

Extra-virgin olive oil

Flaky sea salt

FOR THE GARLIC CROUTONS

1 cup medium-diced Pullman bread

¼ cup extra-virgin olive oil

1 tablespoon minced garlic

2 teaspoons chopped fresh curly parsley

Finely grated zest of 1 lemon

1 tablespoon red pepper flakes

Kosher salt

Freshly ground black pepper

TO ASSEMBLE THE DISH

Assorted basil leaves and tops

Parmigiano-Reggiano shavings

Flaky sea salt, such as Maldon

MAKE THE BLACK PEPPER OLIVE OIL

1. In a small, dry skillet, toast the black pepper over low heat for about 3 minutes or until fragrant. Transfer the pepper to a small saucepot and add the oil. Warm the oil and peppercorns over medium heat until a deep-frying thermometer registers 180°F. Remove the pot from the heat and allow the oil to infuse at room temperature for 4 hours before using. Strain the oil through a coffee filter into a bowl and set aside.

MAKE THE TOMATO CONFIT

2. Preheat the oven to 275°F; position the rack in the middle. Line a baking sheet with parchment paper. Slice the tomatoes crosswise into ½-inch-thick slices and lay them on the lined baking sheet. Sprinkle the garlic slices evenly over the tomatoes, drizzle them with olive oil, and season with some sugar, salt, and pepper. Scatter the thyme and bay leaves on top. Bake for about 1 hour or until the tomatoes are wilted and look a little dry. Transfer to a cooling rack and let cool to room temperature. Leave the oven on. Discard the thyme and bay leaves. Remove the skins from the tomatoes and roughly chop the tomato flesh. Place the tomatoes and the pan juices in a medium bowl. Add the basil, toss to combine, and set the mixture aside in a cool place. If making the eggplant via Sous-Vide Alternative Instructions, raise the oven temperature to 300°F; otherwise, raise the heat to 350°F.

3. SOUS-VIDE COOKING INSTRUCTIONS (see step 4 for Sous-Vide Alternative Instructions): Fill an immersion circulator with water and heat the water to 180°F. Cut the eggplant into large seedless cubes (discard the core with the seeds)—you should have about 16 pieces—and toss them with some salt. Divide the eggplant, olive oil, basil, and garlic equally among 4 vacuum-seal bags. Press out the extra air from the bags and seal. Poach the eggplant in the immersion circulator for about 45 minutes. Transfer the bags to an ice bath and cool the eggplant for 10 minutes. Set aside.

4. SOUS-VIDE ALTERNATIVE INSTRUCTIONS: In an ovenproof pot set over medium heat, warm the oil until the temperature registers 180°F on a deep-frying thermometer. Cut the eggplant into large seedless cubes (discard the core with the seeds)—you should have about 16 pieces—and toss them with some salt. Add the eggplant, basil, and garlic to the oil and transfer the pot to the oven. Bake for about 30 minutes or until the eggplant is soft. Transfer to a cooling rack and set aside to cool. Raise the oven temperature to 450°F. When the eggplant is cool, transfer it to a fine-mesh strainer and drain, discarding the basil and garlic.

MAKE THE BURRATA

5. Cut the burrata balls in half, drizzle them generously with olive oil, and season with some flaky sea salt. Set aside at room temperature.

MAKE THE GARLIC CROUTONS

6. Line a baking sheet with parchment paper. Place the bread cubes and oil in a cold skillet and turn the heat to medium. Shake the pan a little bit so the cubes do not stick together. Cook until the bread is evenly toasted on all sides. Add the garlic and toss to coat. Cook until the garlic is toasted. You must watch the pan carefully—you do not want to burn the garlic. As soon as it is toasted, add the parsley, and immediately transfer the mixture to the lined baking sheet. Sprinkle the bread cubes with the lemon zest and red pepper flakes, and season with salt and black pepper. Set aside.

ASSEMBLE THE DISH

7. Place the cooked eggplant in a 9 x 13-inch baking dish. With the oven preheated to 450°F, bake the eggplant for about 10 minutes or until the eggplant is heated through and lightly browned. Add the reserved burrata to the eggplant and bake for an additional 3 minutes. Transfer to a cooling rack and set aside.

8. In a small saucepot, warm the Tomato Confit over medium heat until warm but not simmering.

9. Divide the cooked eggplant and burrata among 4 warmed bowls and drizzle with the Black Pepper Olive Oil. Spoon ¼ cup of the Tomato Confit into each bowl and add the Garlic Croutons on top. Sprinkle each serving evenly with basil leaves and tops, Parmigiano-Reggiano shavings, and flaky sea salt, and serve.

SPRING "CAESAR" SALAD + WHITE FRISÉE + SNOW AND SNAP PEAS + PARMIGIANO-REGGIANO–LEMON DRESSING

SERVES 4 Did you know that the original Caesar salad dressing contained no anchovies? The salad, which is one of my favorite things to eat, was invented at Hotel Cesar in Tijuana, Mexico, by a chef who was an Italian immigrant. In the 1920s, at the height of Prohibition, Los Angeles socialites were coming to Tijuana in droves to drink and party, and many stayed at this upscale hotel on the water.

The story is that the salad was a result of kitchen resourcefulness on the part of the chef; the kitchen had ran out of fresh vegetables, and the chef had to come up with a salad with what was in the pantry: Parmigiano-Reggiano cheese, eggs, lemon, garlic, and lettuce. Originally, the salad was served without forks. Hotel guests were brought a large plate of lettuce leaves, the ends of which were left undressed so the guests could pick them up with their hands and not bother looking all that civilized.

While our dressing is closer to the original in that it, too, contains no anchovies, that's purely a coincidence. I learned of the traditional dressing recipe well after I had started making this salad at the restaurant as an attempt to create something a little lighter for the spring.

FOR THE CAESAR DRESSING

2 large eggs

2 tablespoons Dijon mustard

2 garlic cloves

⅔ cup extra-virgin olive oil

¾ cup finely grated Parmigiano-Reggiano

¼ cup fresh lemon juice

Kosher salt

Freshly ground black pepper

FOR THE CROUTONS

2 garlic cloves, halved lengthwise

4 (1-inch-thick) slices country bread, such as filone

Extra-virgin olive oil

Kosher salt

Freshly ground black pepper

FOR THE SALAD

2 cups (about 7 ounces) snow peas

2 cups (about 8 ounces) sugar snap peas

4 cups white frisée, stems and green parts, trimmed

3 tablespoons chiffonade of fresh mint

Kosher salt

Freshly ground black pepper

1 lemon, halved

Extra-virgin olive oil

1 cup finely grated Parmigiano-Reggiano

Red pepper flakes

MAKE THE CAESAR DRESSING

1. In a 2-quart pot, bring 3 cups of water to a boil over high heat. Reduce the heat to medium-low until the water is simmering and gently lower the eggs into the pot. Cook the eggs in the simmering water for 6 minutes. Immediately transfer the eggs to an ice bath and allow them to cool for 4 minutes. Crack and peel the eggs and transfer to a food processor fitted with a blade. Add the mustard and garlic, and pulse a few times until the ingredients are just combined. With the motor running, slowly drizzle in the oil until emulsified. Add the cheese and lemon juice and pulse a couple of times to combine. Taste for seasoning and add salt and pepper as needed. Transfer the dressing to a bowl, cover, and refrigerate until ready to use.

2. Light a grill or preheat a grill pan over medium-high heat. Rub the garlic halves all over the bread slices. Drizzle the bread with olive oil and season with salt and pepper.

3. Grill the bread for 3 to 4 minutes, turning once, until charred. Alternatively, broil the bread on high for 1 minute or until slightly charred. The bread should still have some softness inside, but the outside should be crisped. Let the toasted bread cool for a few minutes before cutting it into bite-size pieces. Set aside.

MAKE THE SALAD

4. Bring a pot of salted water to a boil. Trim both types of peas and remove the inedible stringy spine. Blanch the snow peas in the boiling water for 1 minute; remove them with a slotted spoon and transfer to an ice bath. Repeat the blanching process with sugar snap peas. Julienne the cooled snow peas and slice the sugar snap peas into bite-size pieces.

5. In a large salad bowl, toss together both peas, the frisée, and the mint. Drizzle with the Caesar Dressing, season with salt and pepper, and toss to combine.

6. Divide the salad among 4 chilled plates. Scatter the Croutons all around. Add a squeeze of the lemon and drizzle olive oil onto each plate. Sprinkle each plate with Parmigiano-Reggiano and a pinch of the red pepper flakes before serving.

PASTA

"Pasta is easily one of my favorite foods, it satisfies the soul and fills the belly like no other food I can think of; it is also one of the most challenging foods to perfect. Doing pasta well takes time and practice. I get as much joy out of making it as I do out of eating it, and that's the secret when it comes to making great pasta—you need to learn how to enjoy the process and pay close attention, and when it's ready to serve, it must be eaten immediately. As my nonna always used to say, 'Pasta waits for no one.'"

—MARCO CANORA

SERVES 4 AS A MAIN COURSE, 6 AS AN APPETIZER This dish reminds me of the time Adam Platt, one of the restaurant critics for *New York* magazine (who gave us one star, by the way), came in to eat. While my sommelier was pouring wine at the table next to him, he overheard Adam's guest comment that these agnolotti were one of the best pastas she had eaten all summer. However, in his review, he trashed us in every way, shape, and form. As a matter of fact, he didn't even give us a full review—we got a couple of paragraphs at the end of someone else's. Thanks a lot, Adam, we really appreciate your thorough assessment.

The olive oil we use in this dish comes from Tre Olive, a very small producer in Calabria owned by the Maruca family—which also happens to be the family of one of my best friends.

For a dramatic presentation, if you own a siphon (see photo on page 173), try putting all the ingredients on top of the siphon and the tomato water on the bottom. Light a flame on the siphon and watch the tomato water beautifully rise and infuse with the aromatics.

The agnolotti sound a bit tricky to make at first, but once you make them once, you'll see just how manageable the recipe is. This makes for a terrific summer afternoon lunch or a Sunday dinner.

FOR THE TOMATO CONSOMMÉ

5 pounds mixed heirloom tomatoes (including cherry tomatoes), quartered

1 jalapeño, sliced

10 fresh basil leaves

3 garlic cloves

Pinch of kosher salt

Pinch of granulated sugar

FOR THE AGNOLOTTI

½ recipe Pasta Dough (see page 388)

1 cup ricotta cheese, preferably sheep's-milk, drained overnight

1½ tablespoons brunoise shallots (see page 48)

1½ tablespoons chopped fresh basil

1 teaspoon red pepper flakes

½ large egg yolk, room temperature

Finely grated zest of 1 lemon

Kosher salt

Freshly ground black pepper

All-purpose flour or cornmeal, for dusting

TO ASSEMBLE THE DISH

1 cup cherry tomatoes

Pinch of red pepper flakes

1 spring onion, shaved

Chiffonade of fresh basil (ideally a mix of opal, lemon, and Greek bush basils)

Basil oil (see page 395; optional)

Tre Olive olive oil (see Sources, page 403)

Flaky sea salt, such as Maldon

MAKE THE TOMATO CONSOMMÉ

1. Place the tomatoes, jalapeño, basil, garlic, salt, and sugar in a food processor and process until pureed (work in batches, if necessary). Set a large fine-mesh strainer lined with several layers of cheesecloth over a stockpot or a deep bowl. (You will need about 1 foot of space between the bottom of the strainer and bottom of the pot or bowl.) Pour the tomato mixture into the strainer and tie the ends of the cheesecloth together. Refrigerate and let strain for 12 hours. (If your refrigerator does not have enough space for the stockpot or bowl, divide the tomato mixture in half and strain in 2 smaller containers side by side.) Transfer the strained consommé to a medium pot. You should have about 4 to 4½ cups of the consommé, depending on how juicy or watery the tomatoes are.

2. While the Tomato Consommé is straining, make the Pasta Dough. Allow it to rest for 1 hour before using. In a large bowl, whisk together the ricotta, shallots, basil, red pepper flakes, egg yolk, and lemon zest. Season to taste with salt and pepper. Transfer the filling to a pastry bag fitted with a ½-inch plain tip and set aside.

3. Divide the Pasta Dough into 2 or 3 pieces. Run the dough through a pasta machine on the widest setting. Fold the dough in half, rotate it a quarter turn, and run it through on the same setting. Repeat this process two more times, decreasing the thickness setting each time. The pasta sheets should be at least 5 inches wide and thin enough that you can see the silhouette of your hand (and the light) through them, but not so thin that they are transparent. Because the dough dries out quickly, cover the pasta sheets you're not immediately filling with a dry kitchen towel.

4. Working quickly, one sheet at time, fill and shape the agnolotti. Lay a sheet of pasta lengthwise on a lightly floured work surface. Pipe a line of filling ¾ inch from the bottom edge, leaving a ¾-inch border on the left and right sides. Fold the bottom portion of the dough over the filling and press the edge lightly to seal the dough. Do not run your finger down the dough or you risk ripping the pasta. Press to tightly seal the left and right edges of the dough, pressing out any air pockets. You will have ½ inches of pasta overhanging the filled "tube." Using a crimped pastry wheel, separate the tube of filled pasta from the pasta sheet and cut a small portion from the left and right sides to leave a crimped edge.

5. Working your way down the "tube" of filled pasta in 1-inch increments, pinch the pasta between your thumb and forefinger, leaving a ¾-inch-wide sealed area. It is important to leave this much space so the agnolotti do not fall apart when you separate them from one another. Working quickly, separate the agnolotti from one another by running the pastry wheel down the center of the sealed area between each "pillow." Place the finished agnolotti on a baking sheet dusted with flour or cornmeal, making sure they do not touch one another. Repeat the procedure with the remaining dough sheets and filling. You should have approximately 48 agnolotti. Reserve 24 agnolotti and freeze the rest for later use.

ASSEMBLE THE DISH

6. Bring a small pot of lightly salted water to a boil. Cut a small X at the top of each cherry tomato. Blanch the tomatoes in the boiling water for 30 seconds and immediately transfer them to an ice bath to cool. When the tomatoes have cooled, peel the tomatoes and set aside. Bring a large pot of salted water to a boil over high heat. While the water heats up, gently heat the Tomato Consommé in a small saucepot over low heat, but do not allow it to boil.

7. Add the agnolotti to the boiling water and cook for 30 seconds, or until they float to the top. Using a slotted spoon, gently transfer the agnolotti to 4 warmed bowls, dividing them evenly among the bowls. Ladle the Tomato Consommé over the agnolotti to cover. Add a pinch of the red pepper flakes to each and top with some shaved onion and basil chiffonade. Drizzle the basil oil, if using, and the olive oil over each portion, and sprinkle with a pinch of flaky sea salt.

Make It Faster *To make the dish move a little faster, you could make a quick tomato sauce with fresh tomatoes, garlic, and basil and serve it with the agnolotti. It will still taste amazing.*

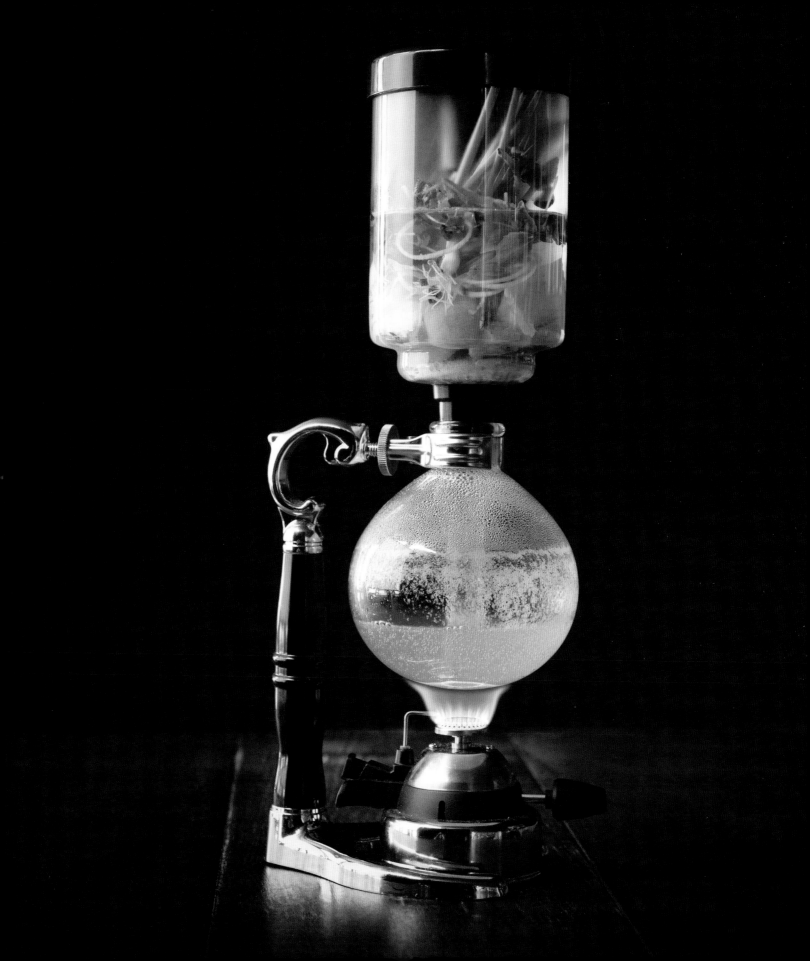

Ian Purkayastha is not what you'd call an average teenager. When he first showed up at my restaurant talking about truffles, I thought he was trying to sell us candy. But once we started talking, I realized Ian was trying to sell us truffles, as in the mushroom! His business, despite his youth, turned out to be the real deal. Ian started buying truffles around the age of sixteen and hasn't stopped since.

Originally from Houston, Texas, Ian's family moved to Arkansas when he was fourteen years old. Moving from a cosmopolitan place to a small town was a culture shock for Ian, who missed living in a big, bustling city.

He struggled to make new friends and fit in at his new school. He felt lonely in Arkansas. But at some point, Ian's uncle showed him how to forage for wild mushrooms, and Ian became obsessed with all things fungus.

On one visit back to Houston, Ian tried truffles for the first time in a restaurant. "Immediately," he recalls, "I wanted to get my hands on some truffles and cook with them at home."

After a little research, Ian bought some summer truffles directly from a company in France. He used his savings, because, he laughs, "My parents weren't going to pay for truffles for their fifteen-year-old son."

Truffles have a short shelf life, and a pound of them is quite a lot for one person. When the truffles arrived, Ian thought, "Why not try to sell a portion of them and recoup some of what I spent?"

So Ian went to the three best restaurants in Arkansas and was able to sell almost all of the truffles, pocketing a good profit at the end of the day. When all was said and done, he was able to enjoy both the truffles that he kept for himself and a small financial gain.

There was another thing, too: Ian enjoyed going out to restaurants, cold-calling, meeting chefs, and trying new foods. He decided that for the remainder of the summer, he was going to start a company, Tartufi Unlimited (*tartufi* means "truffles" in Italian), and import truffles for restaurants. What was intended to be a summer project turned into a yearlong venture. During the day, Ian would be in school, and in the evenings, he was doing homework and running a truffle import business out of his room.

A year later, Ian, at the time a senior in high school, was hired by PAQ, an Italian truffle importer, to establish an American footprint. He set up a shipping center out of his parents' garage and started to ship truffles all over the country. After graduating high school, Ian moved to New York to work for PAQ. Within two years, PAQ had dozens of clients and business was booming.

In 2012, feeling the need to strike out on his own, Ian started Regalis Foods, shipping truffles, truffle products, and other luxury food items, such as Israeli and Bulgarian caviar, to his clients. Ian is still working around the clock with the help of a few full-time employees. He personally shows up to restaurants with zip-top bags full of truffles, briefly chats with chefs, and departs. Personal contact is very important to him. Clearly, he's not sitting on his laurels.

Not too shabby for a kid who's not even twenty yet. With his passion and energy for the business, I look forward to seeing how he grows in the future.

IAN PURKAYASTHA of Regalis Foods

MOREL LASAGNA + BABY WHITE ASPARAGUS + SUMMER TRUFFLE + TASSO HAM

SERVES 4 This is my interpretation of a dish from the '50s and '60s that James Beard used to love called "Asparagus in Ambush"—a very simple hors d'oeuvre composed of asparagus spears, béchamel, and hollowed-out bread. The first time I ever tasted baby white asparagus "in ambush" was at the Greenbrier in Virginia when I was ten years old. I had absolutely no idea what it was, but it was the first time, as far as I can remember, that I was excited by food. Here is my interpretation of the classic dish.

FOR THE TASSO HAM

12 paper-thin slices Tasso ham (see Sources, page 403)

FOR THE SHALLOT REDUCTION

4 ounces (8 tablespoons) unsalted butter

8 ounces shallots, brunoise (see page 48)

½ cup dry white wine

¼ cup dry vermouth

2 cups heavy cream

FOR THE LASAGNA FILLING

1 pound morel mushrooms, cleaned and stemmed

Canola oil

¼ cup sliced shallots

1½ ounces (3 tablespoons) unsalted butter

Kosher salt

3 tablespoons cream sherry

¼ cup Tomato Concassé (see page 394) or peeled, seeded, and coarsely diced tomatoes

2 tablespoons chopped fresh curly parsley

1 sprig fresh thyme

1 fresh or ½ dried bay leaf

FOR THE LASAGNA

1 recipe Pasta Dough (see page 388)

All-purpose flour

2½ ounces (5 tablespoons) unsalted butter

2 sprigs fresh thyme

1 cup baby white asparagus (see Sources, page 403)

1 cup Tomato Concassé (see page 394) or peeled, seeded, and coarsely diced tomatoes

1 tablespoon chopped fresh curly parsley

Micro parsley leaves (we use micro mitsuba; see Sources, page 403)

1 summer truffle (optional)

Parmigiano-Reggiano shavings

Olive oil

MAKE THE TASSO HAM

1. Preheat the oven to 350°F; position the rack in the middle. Bake the ham slices in a single layer (you may need to do this in batches) on a Silpat- or parchment paper–lined baking sheet for 8 to 10 minutes, checking on the ham slices often to make sure they don't curl. Transfer to a cooling rack and let cool.

MAKE THE SHALLOT REDUCTION

2. In a large skillet, melt the butter over medium-low heat until foaming. Add the shallots and sweat them until soft and translucent, 5 to 6 minutes. Add the white wine and vermouth and simmer for 3 to 4 minutes. Add the cream, reduce the heat to low, and stir every 4 minutes or so to make sure the cream is not scorching on the bottom of the pan. Simmer the mixture until it has reduced by half, 12 to 14 minutes. Remove the reduction from the heat. Reserve half of the reduction for use in the Lasagna Filling and freeze the rest for later use.

+ Summer truffles are truffles that are harvested in the summer. They have paler flesh and a less pronounced aroma than their winter-harvested cousins.

175

MAKE THE LASAGNA FILLING

3. Slice the morels into ¼-inch rings. Add just enough oil to a large sauté pan to coat the bottom of the pan and set the pan over high heat. Just before the oil starts to smoke, add the mushrooms to the pan in one even layer (you may need to do this in batches). Reduce the heat to medium and cook the mushrooms until they release their liquid and begin to brown. Add the shallots and butter and cook until the butter and mushrooms are brown, 7 to 10 minutes. Season with salt and deglaze the pan with sherry (the sherry might flame up, so stand back). Stir in the reserved Shallot Reduction and the Tomato Concassé, parsley, thyme, and bay leaf. Transfer the morel filling to a baking pan lined with parchment paper and allow it to cool. Set aside.

MAKE THE LASAGNA

4. Make the Pasta Dough. Allow it to rest 1 hour before using. Lightly dust a work surface with flour. Using a pasta machine or a pasta roller attachment for your stand mixer, roll the Pasta Dough on the #1 setting of the machine (about 2.5mm). Cut the dough into sixteen 3x5-inch strips.

5. Bring a large pot of salted water to a boil. In a large skillet over medium heat, add the butter and thyme, and brown the butter until it smells nutty and fragrant. Reduce the heat to medium-low and add the asparagus and Tomato Concassé. At the same time, add the pasta to the boiling water. Cook the pasta for 20 seconds, then drain, reserving 1 cup of the pasta water, and transfer the pasta to the skillet with the brown butter, asparagus, and tomatoes. Add the cooled Lasagna Filling and toss everything together with a few spoonfuls of the reserved pasta water (use more if needed). Add the chopped parsley, and remove from the heat. Discard the thyme.

6. Place 1 pasta sheet on each of 4 plates and top each sheet with some of the asparagus-morel mixture. Layer another sheet of pasta on top, and repeat until each plate has 4 pasta layers. Top equally with the Tasso ham and micro parsley. Shave the truffle on top, if using, and finish with the Parmigiano-Reggiano shavings. Drizzle with a little of your favorite olive oil.

"Family Meal": an important part of a working restaurant

TRE OLIVE

MIKE MARUCA

Olive oil, like wine, has a *terroir*—meaning that it reflects the tasting notes of the region in which it originated depending on type of soil, climate, and proximity to water. Sicilian olive oils tend to be robust and peppery, while Ligurian ones are delicate and grassy.

Chances are that if you are buying olive oil at your local grocery store, you are getting blended oil—oil that doesn't come from a single origin grove. That's because large olive oil manufacturers buy their oil in bulk from many oil makers and combine them in their facilities before pouring the oil into bottles. The result might not highlight distinct tasting notes from any particular region.

I've known Mike Maruca and his family since college—we've been good friends for years. We even backpacked through Europe together after graduation, and I visited his family's olive groves in Calabria, which they've been tending since 1934 when the family opened up their first olive mill.

For decades, his family was harvesting olive oil from local farmers from a single estate and pressing them into fine extra-virgin olive oil. The family would then sell large quantities of that oil to a wholesaler at a discount because they were buying in bulk. The wholesaler would then take that oil and blend it with olive oils from Africa, Turkey, and other countries, and sell it to big store brands like Bertolli.

In 1970, Mike's parents emigrated from Calabria to Western Massachusetts in search of better job opportunities, but most of the family remained in Italy tending to the olive trees. Mike and his family made frequent trips to visit their relatives, and Mike grew up knowing his Italian cousins pretty well.

In 2009, during a visit to the family groves, three cousins, including Mike, started to discuss how they could avoid selling their oil to the large companies who often diluted it with lesser-quality oil. They decided to start bottling their single-estate oil and try to sell it directly to the consumer. Thus, Tre Olive (*tre* meaning "three" in Italian, for the three cousins) was born.

When I first tasted Tre Olive oil, I knew it was the oil I had to carry at my restaurant, and we've been doing so ever since. Their oil is exceptional—slightly peppery but also round, sweet, and well balanced, with incredible body. Because it's from a single estate, you can fully taste the *terroir* of the region; if you close your eyes, it's like an instant, momentary trip to Calabria.

SWEET CORN RAVIOLI + DAY-BOAT MAINE LOBSTER + LEMON VERBENA EMULSION

SERVES 4 In the summer, it doesn't get more American than lobster and corn, and this is my favorite twist on this classic combination of flavors. This pasta recipe is one that you should source from the greenmarket as much as you possibly can. During the height of summer, corn is just stunning, and the store-bought stuff just doesn't begin to compare. Lemon verbena, ample at the greenmarket in summertime, adds a distinct seasonal note to this all-American combo of lobster and fresh summer corn.

FOR THE LEMON VERBENA STOCK

3 ears corn

1 cup dry white wine

1 large sprig lemon verbena or basil

FOR THE SWEET CORN RAVIOLI

2 cups corn kernels (reserved from the corn used in the Lemon Verbena Stock)

3¾ cups Chicken Stock (see page 382) or store-bought

3 leaves fresh lemon verbena, bound together

½ cup polenta

½ cup (4 ounces) cream cheese

½ cup finely grated Parmigiano-Reggiano

1 tablespoon chiffonade of fresh basil

1 tablespoon chiffonade of fresh mint

¼ teaspoon red pepper flakes

Kosher salt

Freshly ground black pepper

Olive oil

¼ Vidalia onion, brunoise (see page 48)

½ cup Arborio rice

½ cup dry white wine

1 sprig fresh thyme

1 fresh or ½ dried bay leaf

1 recipe Pasta Dough (see page 388)

All-purpose flour

3 large egg yolks, lightly beaten

FOR THE LOBSTER

2 (1¼-pound) lobsters

Kosher salt

Canola oil

½ cup dry white wine

TO ASSEMBLE THE DISH

4 ounces (8 tablespoons) unsalted butter

¼ cup chiffonade of fresh basil

2 tablespoons chiffonade of fresh lemon verbena

Corn shoots (see Sources, page 403)

MAKE THE LEMON VERBENA STOCK

1. Preheat the oven to 350°F; position the rack in the middle. Remove the kernels from the cobs and set the kernels aside. Cut the cobs in half, place them in a shallow baking pan, and roast for 30 minutes or until browned. Transfer the cobs to a 3-quart saucepot set over medium heat and add the wine and 3 cups of water. Bring the liquid to a simmer, reduce the heat to low, and cook, covered, for 1 hour. Transfer the pot to a bain marie (see page 240) or a nonreactive container. Add the lemon verbena, cover the top of the container tightly in plastic wrap, and let the stock infuse for 1 hour. The accumulated moisture that will gather on the inside of the plastic wrap will look like it is raining. This is where the infusion of flavor takes place. Strain the liquid through a fine-mesh strainer, reserving the cobs, and set aside.

MAKE THE SWEET CORN RAVIOLI

2. Using a juicer, press 1¼ cups of the reserved corn kernels—you should get about ½ cup of corn juice. Alternatively, if you don't own a juicer, puree 1¼ cups of corn kernels in a blender, transfer the pureed corn to a kitchen towel or cheesecloth, and squeeze out the juice so that you get ½ cup of corn juice. Set aside the remaining ¾ cup corn kernels—you will need them for the ravioli as well as for assembling the dish.

3. In a 4-quart pot, bring 2 cups of the stock to a boil over high heat. Add the lemon verbena, cover, and remove from the heat. Let the broth infuse for 10 minutes.

Discard verbena and return the pot to the stovetop. Over low heat, slowly whisk in the polenta and cook, whisking constantly, for 5 minutes. Remove from the heat, cover, and let sit in a warm place for 10 minutes. Whisk in the cream cheese, Parmigiano-Reggiano, reserved corn juice, remaining ¾ cup corn kernels, basil, mint, red pepper flakes, salt, and pepper. Cover and set aside.

4. In a small pot, bring the remaining 1¾ cups of chicken stock to a boil over high heat. Remove from the heat, and keep warm.

5. Add enough olive oil to a large sauté pan to cover the bottom of the pan and set it over high heat. Just before the oil starts to smoke, add the onion, reduce the heat to medium, and cook, stirring, until soft, about 5 minutes. Do not let the onion pick up color. Add the rice and cook, stirring, for 1 minute. Add the wine and cook, stirring, until it has been absorbed. Add the thyme and bay leaf, and ladle in the hot stock, 1 ladle at a time, allowing for the stock to be absorbed before adding more. Cook until the rice is al dente. Taste and adjust the seasonings.

6. Transfer the risotto to a meat grinder set to medium die setting and grind it through. Transfer the ground risotto to the bowl with the polenta mixture and mix to combine. Set the risotto-polenta batter over an ice bath and let cool completely. Once cool, transfer the mixture to a pastry bag fitted with a ½-inch plain tip and set aside.

7. Make the Pasta Dough. Allow it to rest 1 hour before using. Lightly dust the surface of the counter with some flour. Using a pasta machine or a pasta roller attachment for your stand mixer, roll the Pasta Dough on the #1 setting of the machine (about 2.5 mm). Cut the dough into 12x5-inch strips. Divide the strips into 2 parts: tops and bottoms. Brush the bottom strips with some of the beaten egg yolks and pipe 2 tablespoons of risotto-polenta filling every 2 inches or so—the diameter of filling should be about 1½ inches.

8. Place the top pasta sheets over the bottom ones, and using the dull side of a 2½-inch ring cutter, press down to shape the ravioli. Using a 2-inch ring cutter, cut out the ravioli. Alternatively, you can do this using a ravioli mold. Set aside 16 ravioli and freeze the remainder for another use. Transfer the ravioli to a lightly floured, parchment paper–lined baking sheet—you may need more than 1 sheet. Note: If making ravioli ahead of time, flash-freeze the ravioli on a baking sheet for 20 minutes before placing them in a tightly sealed container and freezing them until needed.

MAKE THE LOBSTER

9. Bring a large pot of salted water to a boil. First, kill the lobsters by stabbing them through the head with a chef's knife. (This might seem cruel, but it is actually the most humane way to kill them—the lobsters die instantly.) Remove the tails from the lobster bodies and cut the tails into 1-inch pieces while they are still in their shells; set aside. Remove the claws from the lobster bodies and freeze the bodies for another use (such as a Lobster Stock; see page 385). Place the claws in the pot of boiling water and cook for 4 minutes, then transfer the claws to an ice bath. Once cool, remove the meat from the claws and knuckles and set the meat aside in a bowl.

10. Season the lobster tail pieces with salt on both sides. In a large sauté pan set over high heat, heat just enough oil to cover the bottom of the pan. Just before it starts to smoke, add the lobster tail pieces, reduce the heat to medium, and cook, undisturbed, for 1 to 2 minutes. Add the wine, reduce the heat to medium, and cook for 1 to 2 minutes more, until cooked through. Transfer the lobster tails to a plate to cool. Once they are cool enough to handle, poke the meat out with a fork and set it aside in the bowl with the claw meat, discarding the shells or reserving them for another use.

ASSEMBLE THE DISH

11. When ready to serve, bring a large pot of salted water to a boil over high heat; reduce the heat to medium and keep the water at a simmer while you prepare the rest of the dish.

12. In a medium skillet, melt the butter over medium heat, about 1 to 2 minutes. Once the butter browns, remove the pan from the heat and stir in 1 cup of the Lemon Verbena Stock. Return the skillet to the stovetop over

medium-high heat and reduce the stock by about half, until it thickens slightly, 1 to 2 minutes. Add the reserved corn kernels and lobster meat. Reduce the heat to medium, and cook for 90 seconds to 2 minutes.

13. Raise the heat under the pot of salted water to high, make sure the water is at a rolling boil, and add the ravioli. Cook for 20 seconds, and using a slotted spoon, immediately transfer to the pan with the lobster meat.

Ladle in a little bit of the pasta water to bind the ingredients together. Shake the pan to emulsify the sauce. Stir in the basil and lemon verbena. Garnish with the corn shoots. Divide among 4 warmed plates and serve.

Make It Faster   *Make the Lemon Verbena Stock and the lobster. Combine it with wide fresh egg pasta that either you make yourself or purchase at your local fine foods store. Add some fresh corn kernels in the last minute of cooking.*

TORTELLINI D'AVANZI   +   TRUFFLE BALSAMIC VINEGAR   +   PIERRE POIVRE   +   TRUMPET ROYALE

SERVES 4 This is a perfect example of taking leftovers, or *avanzi* in Italian, and making something delicious out of them. We usually wind up with some leftover veal breast after trimming it to perfect portions, and we didn't want to waste perfectly delicious meat that wasn't perfectly cut. One day, my sous-chef, Barry, decided to make tortellini with filling from the veal breast scraps, and the dish took off from there. It became one of our best sellers and a classic on the menu. The truffle-infused balsamic vinegar is a beautiful product brought to us by our "truffle boy," Ian, from Regalis (page 174). The balsamic is aged with truffle scraps in Modena and then bottled up. Not bad for a dish that started out as leftovers and ended up on the tasting menu.

FOR THE VEAL BREAST CONFIT

8 ounces veal breast

½ recipe The Cure
(see page 391)

1 recipe Onion Brûlé
(see page 393)

3 tablespoons whole
black peppercorns

2 tablespoons fennel seeds

2 sprigs fresh thyme

1 sprig fresh rosemary

1 fresh or ½ dried bay leaf

8 cups canola oil

2 heads garlic, halved

1 medium carrot

FOR THE VINAIGRETTE

¾ cup extra-virgin olive oil

¼ cup truffle-infused
balsamic vinegar or your
best balsamic vinegar

1 tablespoon Pierre
Poivre spice mix (see
Sources, page 403)

1 tablespoon flaky sea
salt, such as Maldon

1 teaspoon minced garlic

FOR THE TORTELLINI

1 recipe Pasta Dough
(see page 388)

5 tablespoons cream cheese

2 tablespoons Red Wine
Sauce (see page 392)

2 tablespoons rendered
bone marrow (from Marrow-
Potato Puree, see page
272) or melted butter

1 tablespoon chopped
fresh curly parsley

1 tablespoon minced shallots

1 tablespoon chopped
fresh chives

Kosher salt

1 large egg, lightly beaten

TO ASSEMBLE THE DISH

1 fresh trumpet royale
mushroom

Canola oil

Fresh flat-leaf parsley leaves

16 slices Parmigiano-
Reggiano

Flaky sea salt, such
as Maldon

Pierre Poivre spice mix
(see Sources, page 403)
or smoked paprika

MAKE THE VEAL BREAST CONFIT

1. Pat the veal dry and rub The Cure all over. Refrigerate, uncovered, overnight. Make the Onion Brûlé.

2. Preheat the oven to 300°F; position the rack in the middle. Rinse the veal under cold water, pat dry, and set aside in a roasting pan. Let sit for about 30 minutes or until it reaches room temperature. Meanwhile, make a sachet with the peppercorns, fennel seed, thyme, rosemary, and bay leaf using folded-over cheesecloth.

3. In a large stockpot, combine the oil, onion brulé, garlic, carrot, and herb-spice sachet and warm over medium-high heat until the oil temperature registers 200°F on a deep-frying thermometer. Pour the contents of the stockpot over the veal. Cover the roasting pan with parchment paper, and then wrap it in foil. Transfer the roasting pan to the oven and cook the veal for about 2 hours, or until the meat is tender. Let the veal cool overnight, refrigerated, in the oil.

4. Place the roasting pan on the stovetop and, over medium-low heat, warm the pan just enough to pull out the veal. Remove the bones from the meat if there are any and set the meat aside. Stir the liquid with a fork to mix it up, and set aside 3 tablespoons of the cooking liquid for the tortellini. Strain the remaining oil and reserve it for another use.

MAKE THE VINAIGRETTE

5. While the veal breast cooks, in a medium bowl, combine the olive oil, vinegar, Pierre Poivre, flaky sea salt, and garlic. Stir to combine well and set aside.

MAKE THE TORTELLINI

6. Make the Pasta Dough. Allow it to rest for 1 hour before making the Tortellini. In a large bowl, combine the reserved Veal Breast Confit (or use whatever leftover cooked meat you have on hand), cream cheese, reserved confit cooking liquid, Red Wine Sauce, bone marrow, parsley, shallots, chives, and salt, and mix thoroughly. Taste and adjust the seasonings, if needed.

7. Make the tortellini: Roll out the Pasta Dough, either by hand or using a pasta machine, to about ⅛ inch thick. Using a 2-inch ring cutter, cut the dough into discs. You should get about 48 discs. Place ¼ teaspoon of the filling into the center of each round. Fold the top over and press the edge gently to seal. Lightly brush the edges with the beaten egg. Fold back around your finger and turn down the edge to form a tortellino. Transfer the tortellini to a lightly floured tray and refrigerate or freeze until needed. You may have some extra Pasta Dough left over. If that is the case, cut it into fettuccine, place in a tightly sealed container, and reserve for later use.

ASSEMBLE THE DISH

8. Place a large stockpot of salted water over high heat and bring it to a boil. While the water heats up, using either a mandoline or a truffle slicer, slice the trumpet as thinly as possible—you will need 16 nearly see-through slices. Set aside.

9. Meanwhile, lay out two pieces of parchment paper and very lightly brush both pieces with oil. Lay out the parsley leaves over one of the pieces of parchment so that the leaves are flat against the paper. Place the second parchment piece, oil side down, over the leaves, and transfer to the microwave. Microwave the leaves in 30-second intervals for a total of about 90 seconds to 2 minutes, until crispy. Check on the leaves after each interval to see if they are crisp. Once done, remove the leaves from the parchment and set them aside.

10. Add the tortellini to the boiling water and cook for 1 to 2 minutes. Drain and transfer the tortellini to a large bowl and toss with a little bit of the Vinaigrette to coat the pasta. Divide the tortellini among 4 warmed bowls and spoon some more of the Vinaigrette on top. Add the sliced trumpet mushroom, Parmigiano-Reggiano, and crispy parsley. Sprinkle with flaky sea salt and Pierre Poivre, and serve.

SERVES 4 Carbonara has always been one of my favorite pastas, so I knew when we opened the restaurant, I wanted to do something with that idea for one of our pasta dishes. This is one of those dishes where you get to play with your food and not get in trouble. The visual effect of the egg yolk oozing out of the ravioli is something that makes people happy every time.

FOR THE SPECK STOCK

4 ounces thinly sliced speck
(see Sources, page 403)

4 ounces Parmigiano-
Reggiano rind

½ tablespoon black
peppercorns

1½ sprigs fresh thyme

½ fresh or small piece
dried bay leaf

FOR THE SPECK LARDONS

Blended Oil (see page 395)

2 cups speck lardons

FOR THE CHANTERELLES

1 pound chanterelles,
cleaned and halved

Kosher salt

Freshly ground black pepper

Canola oil

1½ ounces (3 tablespoons)
unsalted butter

1 head garlic, halved

3 sprigs fresh thyme

1 fresh or ½ dried bay leaf

½ cup dry white wine

½ cup Chicken Stock (see
page 382) or store-bought

FOR THE PASTA DOUGH

1 recipe Pasta Dough
(see page 388)

FOR THE RICOTTA FILLING

1 cup Homemade
Ricotta (see page
394) or store-bought,
preferably sheep's-milk

¼ cup cracked black
peppercorns

Finely grated zest of 1 lemon

FOR THE RAVIOLI

1 large egg yolk, whisked

4 large egg yolks

TO ASSEMBLE THE DISH

1 cup fresh peas

Kosher salt

3 tablespoons chopped
fresh curly parsley

Affilia cress (see Sources,
page 403), pea shoots, or
chopped fresh curly parsley

Pecorino shavings

Flaky sea salt, such
as Maldon

Freshly ground black pepper

MAKE THE SPECK STOCK

1. In a medium pot set over high heat, combine the speck, Parmigiano-Reggiano rind, peppercorns, thyme, and bay leaf with 5 cups of water. Bring to a boil over high heat, reduce the heat to low, and simmer for about 1 hour or until the stock is generously flavored with speck. Strain through a fine-mesh strainer into a bowl, discard the solids, and set aside. When ready to serve, warm the Speck Stock until simmering.

MAKE THE SPECK LARDONS

2. Add enough Blended Oil to a large sauté pan to cover the bottom of the pan and set it over high heat. Just before the oil starts to smoke, add the speck, and once it begins to render fat, reduce the heat to medium. Cook until the lardons are crispy, 7 to 8 minutes. Transfer the lardons to a paper towel–lined tray. Reserve the rendered fat.

MAKE THE CHANTERELLES

3. Season the mushrooms with salt and pepper. Add enough oil to a large sauté pan to cover the bottom of the pan and set it over high heat. Just before the oil starts to smoke, add the mushrooms in one even layer and reduce the heat to medium. You may need to do this in batches. Once the mushrooms begin to sear, add the butter, garlic, thyme, and bay leaf, and toss together to combine. Cook, stirring from time to time, until the butter begins to brown. Add the wine and deglaze the pan, scraping the brown bits off the bottom of the pan using a wooden spoon. Cook until the pan is dry, 5 to 8 minutes; add the chicken stock and cook until the stock reduces and the pan is dry, 5 to 8 minutes. Transfer the mushrooms to a parchment paper–lined tray and set aside in a warm place until ready to use.

4. Allow the Pasta Dough to rest 1 hour before making the Ravioli.

MAKE THE RICOTTA FILLING

5. While the Pasta Dough rests, in a food processor fitted with a metal blade, combine the ricotta, peppercorns, and lemon zest. Whip the filling in the food processor until smooth. Transfer to a pastry bag fitted with a plain tip or to a resealable plastic bag with one corner snipped off. Refrigerate until ready to use.

MAKE THE RAVIOLI

6. Divide the Pasta Dough into two or three pieces. Run one piece of dough through a pasta machine (cover the remaining dough in the meantime) starting at the thickest setting (usually a 1 on the pasta machine). Fold the sheet in half and run it through the machine again. Switch the machine to the next setting and run the sheet through again. Continue running the sheet through the machine until you reach the desired thickness for fettuccine (usually a 4 or 5). Repeat with the remaining pieces of dough. Cut the pasta to the strips of the same length (about 4x8 inches); you should have 4 strips of pasta. Using the dull side of a 3-inch ring cutter, push down to make 4 indents on two of the sheets. Brush the two sheets of pasta with the indents with some of the beaten egg yolks. Pipe about 2 tablespoons of Ricotta Filling into the center of the indents. With the back of a spoon, make a well in the center of each portion of filling and add an egg yolk to each one. It is imperative that the yolks remain unbroken. Cover with the other two sheets of pasta, and again using the dull side of the ring cutter, push down to seal. (Make sure there is no extra air inside the ravioli.)

ASSEMBLE THE DISH

7. Bring a small pot of water to a boil. Blanch the peas in the boiling water for 1 minute, drain, and transfer to an ice bath. Allow the peas to cool. Drain and set aside.

8. Bring a large stockpot of water to a boil and generously salt the water; it should taste like the sea. In a large sauté pan set over medium heat, combine the cooked Chanterelles and reserved speck fat and heat until warm. Stir in the blanched peas and cook for 1 minute until the peas are warmed through. Add 1½ cups of the Speck Stock to the mushrooms and peas.

9. Add the Ravioli to the boiling water and cook for 20 seconds. Transfer the ravioli to the sauté pan and toss everything together. Season to taste with salt and add the parsley. Divide the ravioli among 4 bowls (1 raviolo per bowl), and spoon some of the pea mixture around but not on top. Sprinkle with the Affilia cress, some pecorino shavings, flaky sea salt, and freshly ground black pepper. Serve and instruct your guests to cut the ravioli into as many pieces as possible and mix everything together.

Make It Faster   *The Speck Stock adds a delicious layer of flavor, working to enhance the taste of the lardons, but if you're in a pinch, chicken stock or water should be just fine.*

SERVES 4 (MAKES ABOUT 20 RAVIOLI) In 2011, inspired by the idea of Shanghai soup dumplings, we started making panna cotta ravioli. With the help of a little gelatin, you can take anything—juice, cheese, soup—and turn it into a semisolid state. And when you encase it in ravioli and warm the ravioli up, the semisolid filling melts again, so when you bite into it, there's a nice burst of a creamy soup.

Making a gelée out of olive oil is a little bit tricky; you have to add some unusual components to make it want to solidify a bit. We kept the measurements for those components in grams because precision is key in these kinds of recipes, and grams are far more accurate as units of measurement than ounces. I highly recommend that you keep a digital scale in your kitchen—you will find that it's easier and more precise, and you'll have fewer dishes to wash in the end.

FOR THE OLIVE OIL EN GELÉE

300 grams Isomalt (see Sources, page 403)

240 grams granulated sugar

70 grams glucose (see Sources, page 403)

46 grams powdered gelatin

600 grams extra-virgin olive oil

FOR THE PARMIGIANO-REGGIANO PANNA COTTA RAVIOLI FILLING

2 cups whole milk

1½ cups (11 ounces) grated Parmigiano-Reggiano

½ tablespoon white truffle oil

2 gelatin sheets

FOR THE MEZZALUNA

1 recipe Pasta Dough (see page 388)

All-purpose flour

1 large egg

FOR THE BALSAMIC REDUCTION

1 cup balsamic vinegar

¼ cup granulated sugar

1 teaspoon cracked black peppercorns

3 fresh mint leaves

FOR THE SOPPRESSATA SALT

Canola oil

10 thin slices soppressata picante

TO ASSEMBLE THE DISH

12 thin slices soppressata picante

Extra-virgin olive oil

Flaky sea salt, such as Maldon

Micro basil (see Sources, page 403) or chiffonade of fresh basil

MAKE THE OLIVE OIL EN GELÉE

1. Combine the Isomalt, sugar, and glucose with 1¼ cups (288 grams) of water in a saucepan. Cook over medium-high heat, stirring, until dissolved. Whisk in the gelatin, remove from the heat, and add the olive oil, whisking to emulsify. Pour the liquid into a quarter-sheet pan (9 x 13 inches), transfer to the refrigerator, and chill until set, 1 to 2 hours.

2. Release the gelée sides from the pan by running a paring knife around the edge of the pan. Place a cutting board lined with parchment paper (with the paper facing the gelée) over the pan, and carefully but quickly invert the pan so the gelée is over the parchment paper. Using a 2-inch ring cutter, cut 12 gelée discs. Using a small offset spatula, very gently transfer the gelée discs to a parchment paper–lined tray. Cover and refrigerate until needed.

MAKE THE PARMIGIANO-REGGIANO PANNA COTTA RAVIOLI FILLING

3. In a 2-quart saucepot, combine the milk, cheese, and truffle oil, and bring to a lively simmer over medium-high heat, stirring often so that the cheese does not stick to the bottom. While the milk warms, bloom the

gelatin sheets in a small bowl filled with cold water for about 2 minutes. Wring out excess moisture from the sheets, and discard the water. Remove the milk-cheese mixture from the heat and whisk in the bloomed gelatin sheets until dissolved. Strain the mixture through a fine-mesh strainer onto a parchment paper–lined half-sheet (13 x 18) baking pan. Transfer the pan to the freezer until the liquid sets, 1 to 2 hours. Transfer the pan to the refrigerator until ready to use.

MAKE THE MEZZALUNA

4. Make the Pasta Dough. Allow it to rest 1 hour before making the Mezzaluna. Lightly dust the surface of the counter with some flour, and lightly beat the egg in a small bowl. Using a pasta machine or a pasta roller attachment for your stand mixer, roll out the Pasta Dough, starting on the thickest setting and progressing to the thinnest setting of the machine. Lay the sheets out over the floured counter. Using a 2-inch ring cutter, cut out 20 discs from the dough. Using a small melon baller, scoop out the Parmigiano-Reggiano Panna Cotta Ravioli Filling and place one ball in the center of each dough circle. Using a pastry brush, brush the top half of the pasta circles with the egg wash, fold up the pasta to create half-moon ravioli, and press the edges together to seal. Transfer the half-moons to a lightly floured half-sheet baking pan and freeze until needed. Repeat with any remaining pasta dough and filling. You will use 20 mezzaluna for this recipe; freeze the remainder for up to 3 months for later use.

MAKE THE BALSAMIC REDUCTION

5. Place the vinegar, sugar, peppercorns, and mint in a small nonreactive saucepot and bring to a boil over high heat. Reduce the heat to low and gently simmer the liquid for 10 to 15 minutes or until it is thick enough to coat the back of a spoon. Remove the pot from the heat and allow the liquid to cool. Strain through a fine-mesh strainer into a bowl and keep at room temperature.

MAKE THE SOPPRESSATA SALT

6. Add 1 inch of oil to a small skillet. Warm the oil over medium-high heat until it registers 300°F on a deep-frying thermometer. Add the soppressata slices and fry until crispy, about 2 minutes. Transfer the soppressata to a paper towel–lined tray and let cool completely. Mince until the soppressata has the consistency of flaky sea salt. Set aside in a dry place.

ASSEMBLE THE DISH

7. Bring a large pot of salted water to a boil. While the water warms up, using a 2-inch ring cutter, cut out 12 soppressata discs. Place 3 soppressata circles on each of 4 plates. Place a disc of the Olive Oil en Gelée on top of the soppressata on each plate.

8. Add the mezzaluna to the boiling water and cook for 30 seconds. Using a slotted spoon, transfer the pasta to a mixing bowl and toss with enough extra-virgin olive oil to coat. Let the pasta cool slightly before dividing them evenly among the plates, placing them on top of the gelée disc (if the mezzaluna are too hot, they will melt the gelée). Sprinkle with flaky sea salt and garnish with basil. Drizzle the Balsamic Reduction around the mezzaluna and make a small pile of the Soppressata Salt on the side. Serve and eat each mezzaluna with a little reduction and a pinch of Soppressata Salt.

Make It Faster *If you're keen on making your own ravioli, but want to skip the gelée part, be my guest. Make the ravioli and Balsamic Reduction and just serve the ravioli drizzled with your best extra-virgin olive oil.*

SPAGHETTI ALLA BOTTARGA + PRESERVED MEYER LEMON

SERVES 4 Bottarga is nothing more than pressed, salted fish roe, typically from grey mullet, tuna, or swordfish; and while it sounds like nothing special, it's an amazing secret weapon, packed with loads of flavor, that every cook should have in his kitchen. Our bottarga comes from Sardinian grey mullet, but there is also excellent domestic bottarga available. While bottarga is very expensive, a little of it goes a long way, and it has a long shelf life if you keep it tightly wrapped. Its flavor is unlike anything else and can't be replicated by any other ingredient. Slightly metallic tasting (in a pleasant way), bottarga has a clean ocean salinity much like an oyster, and brightens up anything from pasta to simple ricotta crostini. Here, it transforms a plate of simple spaghetti. An impressive accomplishment for humble salty fish eggs!

SPECIAL EQUIPMENT

Bigoli press

FOR THE BOTTARGA BREAD CRUMBS

Extra-virgin olive oil

4 cups coarse bread crumbs, such as panko

1 cup thinly shaved bottarga, preferably Sardinian grey mullet

¼ cup chopped fresh curly parsley

Finely grated zest of 2 lemons

Pinch of red pepper flakes

FOR THE SPAGHETTI

½ cup whole milk

½ ounce (1 tablespoon) unsalted butter, melted

3 large eggs, preferably farm-fresh

4 cups all-purpose flour, plus more as needed

½ teaspoon kosher salt

TO ASSEMBLE THE DISH

1 Preserved Meyer Lemon (see page 391) or store-bought

1 celery stalk

1 (2-inch) piece bottarga

¼ cup extra-virgin olive oil, plus more as needed

Finely grated zest of 1 lemon

Red pepper flakes

Juice of 1 lemon

Micro celery (see Sources, page 403) or chiffonade of celery leaves

MAKE THE BOTTARGA BREAD CRUMBS

1. Add enough oil to a large sauté pan to cover the bottom of the pan and set it over high heat. Just before it starts to smoke, add the bread crumbs and reduce the heat to medium. Stir constantly until the bread crumbs start to brown all over, about 2 minutes. Stir in the bottarga. Keep stirring until the bread crumbs are evenly toasted, 5 to 6 minutes. Remove from the heat and stir in the parsley, lemon zest, and red pepper flakes. Taste and adjust the seasonings, if you like, and set aside.

MAKE THE SPAGHETTI

2. In a small saucepan, warm the milk and butter over low heat until the butter is melted and the liquid is warm to the touch. Transfer the warmed milk mixture to a large bowl and whisk in the eggs, one by one, fully incorporating each egg before adding the next egg. Add the flour and salt, and using a fork, mix well until thoroughly combined. Transfer the dough to a lightly floured large bowl and knead for 2 to 3 minutes. Wrap the dough in plastic wrap and refrigerate for at least 1 hour or up to 1 day.

3. Set up a bigoli press with the small die and make spaghetti. Set the pasta aside on a floured tray or counter while you assemble the dish.

4. If using homemade Preserved Meyer Lemons, cut the white pith and flesh from 1 lemon. Discard the flesh, and finely julienne the skin. Soak the julienned zest in cold water for at least 30 minutes, changing the water another 2 times before using. If using store-bought preserved lemons, discard the flesh, and just finely julienne the skin, minus the soaking.

5. Using a mandoline or a very sharp knife, peel and slice the celery, on a slight bias, as thinly as you possibly can. Transfer the celery to a bowl filled with ice water. Set aside.

6. Using a truffle slicer or a mandoline, slice the bottarga as thinly as you can, over a plate, without it falling apart. Drizzle with some olive oil and set aside.

7. Bring a large pot of lightly salted water to a boil. In a large skillet (the largest you have—think 6-quart sauté pan), heat the Bottarga Bread Crumbs with ¼ cup olive oil until warm. Blanch the pasta in the boiling water for 15 to 20 seconds. Immediately transfer the pasta to the skillet with the bread crumbs. Let a little pasta water fall in to bind the pasta to the sauce. Toss everything together until well combined. Your skillet will be full, so toss carefully.

8. Divide the pasta among 4 warmed bowls. Drizzle olive oil around the bowl. Scatter the lemon zest all over the pasta and sprinkle with the red pepper flakes. Spoon the reserved celery slices and bottarga slices around and on top of the pasta and drizzle lemon juice everywhere. Top with micro celery and the reserved julienned preserved lemon.

Make It Faster *Fine foods stores will sell you excellent fresh pasta, preserved lemons in a jar (though it's very worthwhile, and easy, to make your own), and bottarga. If you want to make your own pasta, but lack a bigoli press, you can either make whatever pasta you like using your pasta machine or roll out sheets of pasta and cut the pasta by hand. Either way, it makes for a simple, seductive, delicious meal.*

SERVES 4 At the restaurant we make these cavatelli fresh every day. They are absolutely delicious, but do not hold well overnight, and I don't like to freeze them—they never taste the same once thawed. Since we always have these cavatelli on hand, it's an added bonus that there's always some cavatelli left for a late-night snack at the end of service.

SPECIAL EQUIPMENT

Cavatelli machine

FOR THE GREEN GARLIC CONFIT

2 green garlic stalks

3 fresh basil leaves

Extra-virgin olive oil

FOR THE BOLOGNESE

3 sprigs fresh thyme

1 sprig fresh basil

1 fresh or ½ dried bay leaf

2 (28-ounce) cans tomatoes, preferably San Marzano

2 pounds lamb belly

6 garlic cloves

Olive oil

4 cups Veal Stock (see page 382) or store-bought

Kosher salt

Red pepper flakes

FOR THE CAVATELLI

2 cups packed fresh curly parsley leaves

1 cup packed fresh mint leaves

1½ cups (8 ounces) semolina flour

1½ cups (8 ounces) 00 flour, plus additional for dusting

1 pound fresh ricotta

2 large eggs, room temperature

FOR THE HERBED RICOTTA

1 cup fresh ricotta, preferably sheep's-milk

2 teaspoons chopped fresh mint

2 teaspoons chopped fresh curly parsley

Kosher salt

Freshly ground black pepper

TO ASSEMBLE THE DISH

Fresh mint leaves

Fresh basil leaves

Kosher salt

Parmigiano-Reggiano

Clay pepper flakes (see Sources, page 403) or red pepper flakes

MAKE THE GREEN GARLIC CONFIT

1. Cut the garlic on the bias into 1-inch pieces. Place the garlic and basil leaves in a pot, add enough olive oil to cover, and heat over medium heat until the oil temperature registers 180°F on a deep-frying thermometer. Remove the pot from the heat, set aside, and let sit for 2 hours. The garlic should be soft, but still hold its shape.

MAKE THE BOLOGNESE

2. Place the thyme, basil, and bay leaf on a piece of double-plied cheesecloth and tie the corners together to form a sachet. Crush the tomatoes with your hands, and measure out 4 cups. Reserve the tomato juices and set both aside.

3. Using a meat grinder or a meat grinding attachment to your stand mixer, grind the lamb belly with 2 of the garlic cloves. Alternatively, you can ask your butcher to grind the meat and mix it with 2 of finely minced garlic cloves at home.

4. Add enough oil to a large saucepot to cover the bottom of the pan and set it over high heat. Just before the oil starts to smoke, add the ground lamb, reduce the heat to medium-high, and do not move the meat, or break it up, until you get a good sear—this is where a lot of flavor comes from. Once the meat has browned on the bottom, break it up with a wooden spoon. Cook the meat until browned all over. You may need to drain off the fat a couple of times from the pot. If so, just return the pot back to the stove. Add the stock and cook until the stock has reduced by about half.

5. Meanwhile, in a separate saucepot, add enough oil to cover the bottom of the pot and heat over medium-high until shimmering. While the oil heats up, thinly slice the remaining 4 garlic cloves. Add the garlic to the pan and raise the heat to high. Be sure to watch and shake the pan the entire time so that the garlic does not stick to the bottom of the pan. Once the garlic is brown and fragrant, add the reserved crushed tomatoes with their reserved juices, reduce the heat to low, and simmer for 10 minutes so that the sauce thickens up. Add the tomato sauce and herb sachet to the lamb mixture. Bring the sauce to a simmer and reduce the heat to low. Cover the pot and cook the sauce for 1 hour to let the flavors develop.

6. Remove the sachet, and using an immersion blender, buzz the sauce just enough to break up the meat, but not too much or the sauce will have a strange texture. Taste and season to taste with salt and a pinch of red pepper flakes. Keep warm. If making ahead, refrigerate or freeze until needed.

MAKE THE CAVATELLI

7. Bring a pot of salted water to a boil. Prepare an ice bath. Place the parsley and mint in a large strainer and set the strainer in the boiling water for 10 seconds. Remove the strainer and immediately place it in an ice bath to stop the cooking. Once cold, squeeze out any excess water from the herbs. Transfer the herbs to a blender and puree until smooth. Add a couple of tablespoons of water, if necessary, to achieve the desired consistency. Set aside.

8. In a large bowl, sift together the semolina and 00 flours and set aside. In another bowl, mix together the ricotta, eggs, and herb puree. Transfer the flours and ricotta-egg mixture to the bowl of a food processor fitted with a blade and pulse together until a dough forms.

9. Turn the dough out onto a slightly floured surface, and using your hands, knead for 1 minute, or until the dough is smooth and elastic. Press the dough into a disc, wrap tightly in plastic wrap, and let the dough rest at room temperature for at least 30 minutes.

10. On a lightly floured surface, roll the dough into logs a little less wide than a quarter and transfer them to a lightly floured tray. Run the logs through a cavatelli machine, and toss the shaped cavatelli in a little semolina flour to prevent sticking. Refrigerate the cavatelli until ready to use.

MAKE THE HERBED RICOTTA

11. While the cavatelli dough sits, place the ricotta, mint, parsley, salt, and pepper in the bowl of a food processor fitted with a blade and whip until smooth. Set aside; cover and refrigerate if necessary.

ASSEMBLE THE DISH

12. Bring a large pot of water to a boil. While the water heats up, warm the Bolognese sauce and add the basil and mint leaves. When the water comes to a rolling boil, add enough salt so that the water tastes like seawater. Blanch the cavatelli in the boiling water for 1 minute and immediately transfer the pasta to the sauce and cook together for 1 minute.

13. Divide the cavatelli among 4 warmed bowls and garnish with a scoop of herbed ricotta and freshly grated Parmigiano-Reggiano. Sprinkle the clay pepper flakes on top and serve.

"BAKED POTATO" CRÈME FRAÎCHE RAVIOLI + POTATO BROWN BUTTER + PANCETTA + TRUFFLE

SERVES 4 This is a play on a loaded baked potato. Everything you would normally put on top of the potato is stuffed inside of the ravioli and the potato is turned into the garnish. It's a really fun and delicious pasta dish.

FOR THE PANCETTA SALT

4 slices pancetta

FOR THE BAKED POTATO STOCK

2 russet potatoes, scrubbed clean

2 teaspoons kosher salt

⅓ cup whole black peppercorns

6 sprigs fresh thyme

2 fresh bay leaves

FOR THE RAVIOLI

2 gelatin sheets

1 cup heavy cream

1 cup sour cream

1½ tablespoons chopped fresh chives

1 tablespoon crème fraîche

½ tablespoon minced shallots

½ tablespoon finely grated Parmigiano-Reggiano

Finely grated zest and juice of ½ lemon

¼ teaspoon black truffle oil

Kosher salt

Freshly ground black pepper

Red pepper flakes

1 recipe Pasta Dough (see page 388)

All-purpose flour

3 large egg yolks, lightly beaten

TO ASSEMBLE THE DISH

1 leek, julienned

Canola oil

½ cup all-purpose flour

Kosher salt

1 russet potato, diced

2 ounces (4 tablespoons) unsalted butter

2 shallots, julienned

2 tablespoons chopped fresh chives

1 tablespoon red pepper flakes

½ cup scallion threads

Black truffle oil

Black truffle (optional)

MAKE THE PANCETTA SALT

1. Preheat the oven to 350°F; position the rack in the middle. Bake the pancetta in a shallow baking pan for 12 minutes or until crispy. Transfer the pancetta to a parchment paper–lined tray and let cool. Mince the pancetta by hand until it resembles flaky sea salt, and let dry in a warm place. Leave the oven on.

MAKE THE BAKED POTATO STOCK

2. Pierce the potatoes with a fork in several places to allow steam to escape. Place the potatoes on the oven rack and bake for 40 minutes to 1 hour or until fork-tender. Remove from the oven (leave the oven on) and cut crosswise into ½-inch slices. Place the potato slices on a baking sheet and bake for 20 to 25 minutes or until crispy. Transfer the potato slices to a large saucepot and cover with 4 cups of cold water. Add salt to the water and bring it to a simmer. Simmer for 1 hour, 45 minutes. Add the peppercorns, thyme, and bay leaves, and transfer to a nonreactive container. Wrap tightly in plastic wrap and let infuse for ½ hour. The accumulated moisture that will gather on the inside of the plastic wrap will look like it is raining inside. Strain the potato stock through a fine-mesh strainer into a bowl and set aside until ready to use.

MAKE THE RAVIOLI

3. Bloom the gelatin sheets in ice water until soft, about 3 minutes. Once soft, squeeze out any excess liquid. In a small saucepan, bring the heavy cream to a simmer over medium heat. Add the bloomed gelatin and whisk until incorporated. Pass the mixture through a fine-mesh strainer into a bowl and set aside.

4. In a medium bowl, mix together the sour cream, chives, crème fraîche, shallots, Parmigiano-Reggiano, lemon zest, and truffle oil. Season to taste with salt, pepper, and red pepper flakes. Fold in the heavy cream mixture until well combined. Transfer the filling to a pastry bag fitted with a ½-inch plain tip and set aside.

5. Make the Pasta Dough. Allow it to rest for 1 hour before making the ravioli. Lightly dust the surface of the counter with some flour. Using a pasta machine or a pasta roller attachment for your stand mixer, roll the Pasta Dough on the #1 setting of the machine (about 2.5 mm). Cut the dough into 12x5-inch strips. Divide the strips into 2 parts: tops and bottoms. Brush the bottom strips with some of the beaten egg yolks and pipe 2 tablespoons of the ravioli filling every 2 inches or so—the diameter of filling should be about 1½ inches.

6. Place the top pasta sheets over the bottom ones, and using the back end of a 2½-inch ring cutter, press down to shape the ravioli. Using a 2-inch ring cutter, cut out the ravioli. Alternatively, you can do this using a ravioli mold. Set aside 16 ravioli and freeze the rest for another time. Transfer the ravioli to a lightly floured, parchment paper–lined baking sheet—you may need more than 1 sheet. Note: If making ravioli ahead of time, flash-freeze the ravioli on a baking sheet for 20 minutes before placing them in a tightly sealed container and freezing them until needed.

ASSEMBLE THE DISH

7. While you make the pasta, soak the leek in cold water for 1 hour, drain, and dry it in a salad spinner. About 40 minutes later, heat 1 inch of oil in a skillet set over medium-high heat until the oil temperature registers 300°F on a deep-frying thermometer. At the same time, bring a medium pot of salted water to a boil. Toss the leek in the flour until it is well coated and gently add it to the oil. Fry the leek until crispy, about 30 seconds, then transfer to a parchment paper–lined tray and season to taste with salt. Set aside.

8. Add the potato to the boiling water, reduce the heat to medium, and cook the potato at an active simmer until fork-tender, about 4 minutes. Strain the potato and transfer to an ice bath.

9. When ready to serve, bring a large pot of water to a rolling boil and add enough salt so that the water tastes like seawater. In a sauté pan, heat the butter and potato over medium heat until the butter browns. Add 1 cup of the Baked Potato Stock, shallots, and chives. Drop the ravioli in the water and cook for 3 minutes. Immediately transfer the ravioli to the pan with the butter and potatoes, toss together, and cook for about 30 seconds. Divide the pasta among 4 warmed plates. Garnish with red pepper flakes, scallion threads, reserved fried leeks, Pancetta Salt, truffle oil, and truffle (if using).

POULTRY + DUCK

"I grew up in Berkeley, and my grandparents raised chickens nearby in Cotati, California. Our farm was surrounded by turkey farmers, ranchers raising sheep, and other livestock. I was weaned on chickens, so to speak. I attended cooking school in Paris and while there I ate delicious poultry—goose, mallards, poussin, and so on. It was in England a couple of years later where I developed an affinity to game birds. In-season grouse, woodcock, pheasant, and the like would appear on menus. It was a taste that I loved. Later at Michael's in Santa Monica, I was lucky to have purveyors that delivered me delicious quail, pigeons, and ducks. But the chickens we received were not in the same league. It was only when I moved to New York and Marc's dad introduced me to a superior bird that I found chicken nirvana. These chickens were magnificent: They were healthy and extremely tasty. I believed these chickens were truly the equal to the poulet de Bresse I had eaten in France, maybe better. So by the sourcing of these fine birds, and with the amazing assistance of Larry Forgione, I was able to serve a nice charcoal-grilled chicken, which caught New York by surprise. New Yorkers pride themselves on the best of all things, and my JW Chicken at Jams, at $23 (1984 prices) seemed to captivate them; and so solidified my reputation."

—JONATHAN WAXMAN

DUCK SAUSAGE + SWISS CHARD + CORNBREAD + DRIED CURRANTS

SERVES 4   This was one of the dishes that came out of the *Next Iron Chef* finale. When I found out the theme of the battle was Thanksgiving, I immediately decided to cook a meal using those ingredients that appeared at the very first Thanksgiving in 1621. This duck sausage dish was a hit with the judges: Donatella Arpaia actually called it "one of those perfect bites"! However, during the actual cooking segment, we were nervous that the sausage part might have gone horribly awry. My sous-chef, Barry, is quoted in his television debut as saying, "Chef, I think we might have a problem." When he removed the sausage from the water, he thought that the sausage hadn't set. This, as you can imagine, would have been catastrophic for the season finale. Good for all of us (but mostly him), there was no problem and the sausage had set beautifully. This is a great recipe to try your hand at if you don't have an immersion circulator, but are fascinated with the process. You can poach the sausage in simmering water for ten minutes; in order to keep the temperature constant, keep a bowl of ice cubes by the stove.

FOR THE DUCK SAUSAGE

1 (8-ounce) duck breast, skin on, cut into medium cubes

1 garlic clove

1 teaspoon kosher salt

1 teaspoon Pierre Poivre spice mix (see Sources, page 403) or smoked paprika

1 teaspoon sriracha

1 teaspoon maple syrup

FOR THE CURRANT REDUCTION

1 cup ruby port

¼ cup dried red currants

5 leaves fresh mint

2 teaspoons freshly ground black pepper

FOR THE CORNBREAD

4 ounces (8 tablespoons) unsalted butter, plus more for the pan

1 cup all-purpose flour

¾ cup finely ground cornmeal

2 tablespoons granulated sugar

1 teaspoon baking powder

Pinch of kosher salt

½ cup whole milk

3 large eggs

FOR THE DUCK SKIN CRACKLINS

Skin from 1 duck breast

2 tablespoons mild honey

2 teaspoons low-sodium soy sauce

FOR THE SWISS CHARD

4 large Swiss chard leaves, thick stems removed

TO ASSEMBLE THE DISH

½ ounce (1 tablespoon) unsalted butter

Flaky sea salt, such as Maldon

Micro watercress (optional)

Red radishes, julienned

MAKE THE DUCK SAUSAGE

1. In a medium bowl, combine the duck with the garlic, salt, and Pierre Poivre. Pass the mixture through a meat grinder. (If you don't own a meat grinder, you can ask your butcher to coarsely grind the duck and mix it with minced garlic, salt, and the Pierre Poivre.) Combine the duck mixture with the sriracha and maple syrup. Cover and refrigerate overnight.

2. Preheat an immersion circulator filled with water until the water temperature registers 190°F. Shape 4 sausages

out of the ground duck mixture and wrap each sausage tightly in plastic wrap. Place each sausage into a small vacuum-seal bag and seal the bags.

3. Poach the duck sausage in the immersion circulator for 10 minutes. (Alternatively, you can place the sausages in 4 resealable bags, squeeze out as much air as possible, seal the bags, and poach for 10 minutes in a pot of 190°F water. Monitor the water temperature throughout the cooking time and keep a bowl of ice cubes nearby in case you need to lower the water temperature.) Transfer the bag(s) to an ice bath, and chill until the sausage is set, 10 to 15 minutes. You can make the sausage up to 2 days ahead and refrigerate it until needed.

MAKE THE CURRANT REDUCTION

4. In a small, nonreactive saucepan, combine the port, currants, mint, and pepper over medium-high heat. Bring to a simmer, lower the heat to medium, and reduce until the liquid resembles thick syrup, about 25 minutes. Remove from the heat and set aside. Do not refrigerate.

MAKE THE CORNBREAD

5. Preheat the oven to 350°F; position the rack in the middle. Place a piece of buttered parchment paper, butter side down, in a 9 x 13 x 1-inch baking pan and lightly butter the top of the parchment. Set aside.

6. In a large bowl, whisk together the flour, cornmeal, sugar, baking powder, and salt until thoroughly combined. In a small saucepan set over medium-low heat, melt the butter. Do not let the butter boil. In a medium bowl set over a towel, whisk together the milk and eggs until well combined. Slowly drizzle the melted butter into the milk-egg mixture, whisking continuously until emulsified. Add the dry ingredients to the wet ingredients and mix to incorporate, until you get a thick batter. Pour the batter into the baking pan and smooth out the top with an offset spatula. Gently tap the pan against the counter a couple of times to remove any air bubbles. Bake the cornbread for 10 to 15 minutes or until a toothpick inserted into the center of the bread comes out clean.

7. Transfer the cornbread to a cooling rack (keep the oven at 350°F) and let cool to room temperature. Using a 2-inch ring cutter, cut the cornbread into discs. You need 12 cornbread discs; you will get about 24. Transfer the cornbread discs to an airtight container.

MAKE THE DUCK SKIN CRACKLINS

8. Using the back of a knife, scrape off any excess fat from the duck skin. Place the skin on a Silpat or parchment paper–lined baking sheet. Place another Silpat or piece of parchment paper over the skin and top with another sheet pan of the same size. Bake at 350°F until the skin is crispy, 45 minutes to 1 hour. Keep in mind that the fat will render and will be in between the baking pans. Transfer the duck skin to a cooling rack set over a baking pan; leave the oven on. Strain the rendered duck fat and reserve it for another use (you can use it in place of butter or oil, and whatever you cook in duck fat will be that much more delicious).

9. While the duck skin is in the oven, in a small pot, combine the honey and soy sauce and bring to a boil over medium heat. Immediately remove from the heat and set aside. Brush the crispy duck skin with the honey-soy mixture, and let cool in a dry place.

MAKE THE SWISS CHARD

10. Bring a large pot of salted water to a boil. Blanch the chard leaves in the boiling water for 10 seconds. Immediately drain the leaves and transfer them to an ice bath. Let cool, and squeeze out any excess water. Lay the leaves flat on the counter or a flat surface.

ASSEMBLE THE DISH

11. Squeeze the duck sausages out of the plastic bags and distribute them among the chard leaves, placing them in the center of the leaves. Roll the leaves around the sausages like a spring roll. Transfer the wrapped sausages to a shallow baking pan and warm in the oven until heated through, about 8 minutes. Transfer the sausages to a cutting board and slice each sausage into 3 pieces.

12. In a large sauté pan, melt the butter over medium-high heat until it foams. Add 12 cornbread discs and cook until lightly browned on each side, 2 to 3 minutes per side (you may need to do this in batches). Divide the cornbread discs among 4 warmed plates. Top each cornbread disc with a piece of sausage. Sprinkle some flaky sea salt over the sausages, and drizzle the Currant Reduction on top. Top with micro watercress, if desired, radishes, Duck Skin Cracklins, and a drizzle of the reserved duck fat.

HOW TO
TRUSS A CHICKEN

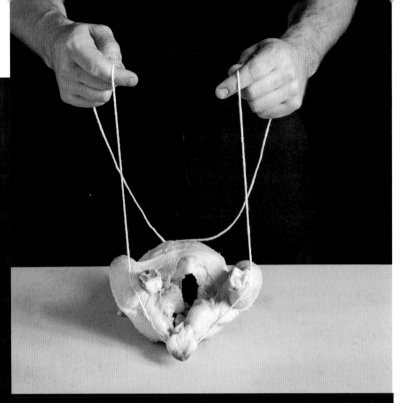

1. Position the chicken with the neck cavity facing toward you, breast side up. Cut a 4-foot-long piece of kitchen twine.

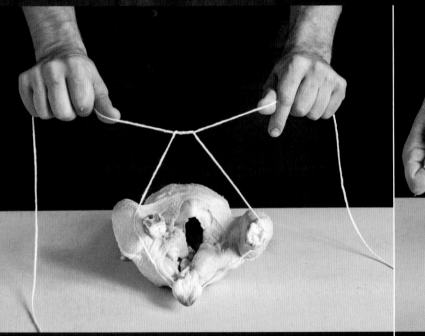

2. Place the kitchen twine under the chicken (closer to where the legs are) and make a butcher's knot (twisting the string twice before making an actual knot).

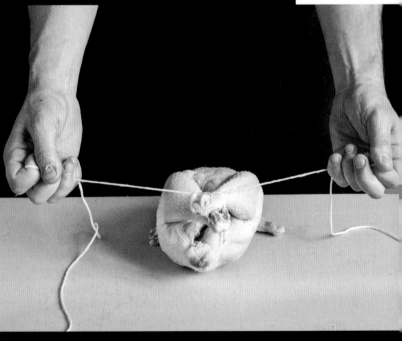

3. Pull the knot tight, so that the ends of the drumsticks come together.

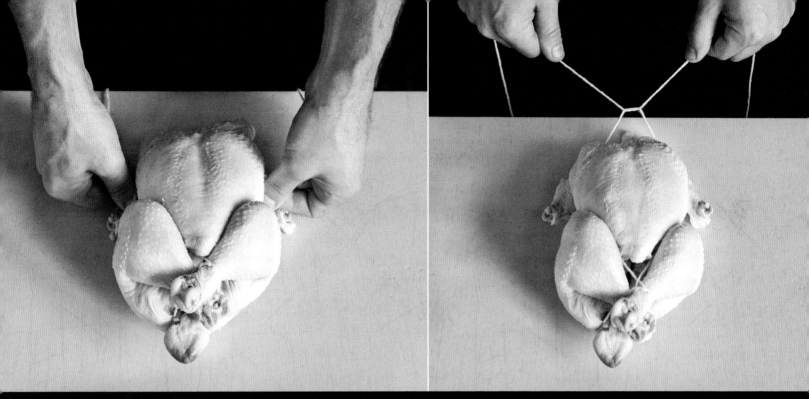

4. Holding the two strings in your hands, cross the ends of the string (so the left goes into your right hand and vice versa) and then hook the string underneath the wings and into the wing pit of the chicken. Make another butcher's knot by the neck cavity, and gently pull on the ends of the string so that the skin from the neck gets tighter and tighter. Finish everything off with another regular knot, and you have a trussed chicken!

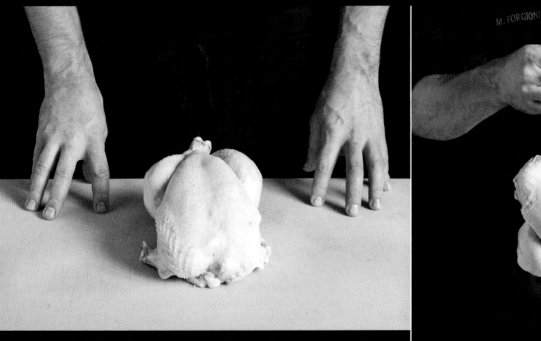

5. A trussed chicken.

6. Marc holding a trussed chicken.

TRUFFLE-STUFFED BELL AND EVANS CHICKEN + NATURAL JUS

SERVES 4 One year, I found myself in San Juan over Christmas, and it was the first time I had been away from my family during the holiday. Despite being alone, I didn't want the holiday to be any less special—I was on a gorgeous island, surrounded by incredible ingredients. So I decided to make something festive and a little decadent: a truffle-stuffed chicken!

This is a perfect meal to make when you just want to celebrate life and are full of joy. It's both comforting and exotic—which makes it perfect for a Christmas dinner. A beautiful, succulent bird, luxurious truffles, and flavorful jus—what else do you we need in life except, maybe, someone to share the chicken with?

You can choose one of the many sides in this book to serve with this chicken; we recommend the Basic Potato Puree and the Mustard Greens, but feel free to play around and find the sides you like the best.

FOR THE CHICKEN JUS

4 cups Small Game Jus (made with chicken, see page 383) or store-bought chicken stock

FOR THE CHICKEN STUFFING

¼ cup Mushroom Duxelles (see page 396)

6 ounces (12 tablespoons) unsalted butter, softened

½ cup and 2 tablespoons panko bread crumbs

2 tablespoons minced shallot

1 tablespoon chopped black truffle

1 tablespoon chopped fresh rosemary

Kosher salt

FOR THE CHICKEN

One (4- to 5-pound) air-chilled chicken, preferably a quality brand like Bell and Evans

Kosher salt

Freshly ground black pepper

Black truffle oil

2 sprigs fresh sage

2 sprigs fresh rosemary

2 sprigs fresh thyme

2 fresh or 1 dried bay leaf

1 head garlic, halved

2 thick slices country bread, such as filone

TO ASSEMBLE THE DISH

1 recipe Basic Potato Puree (see page 396)

1 recipe Mustard Greens (see page 259)

1 black truffle

MAKE THE CHICKEN JUS

1. Cook the Small Game Jus over medium-high heat until it has reduced to about 2 cups, 30 to 45 minutes. Set aside until ready to use. (If using stock instead, see "Make It Faster," below.)

MAKE THE CHICKEN STUFFING

2. In a large bowl, mix together the Mushroom Duxelles, butter, panko, shallot, truffle, rosemary, and salt to taste until well combined. Set aside.

MAKE THE CHICKEN

3. Preheat the oven to 450°F; position the rack in the middle. Using a sharp carving knife, remove the wishbone and wings from the chicken (you can reserve these parts to make Small Game Jus). Thoroughly pat the chicken dry inside and out with paper towels. Season the inside with salt, pepper, and a few drops of the truffle oil. Using your fingers, gently separate the skin from the breast (make sure you do this for the whole breast), creating one big air pocket between the skin and breast (be careful not to rip the skin). Place

some of the Chicken Stuffing in between the skin and breast and press down on the skin to evenly distribute the stuffing—you want to wind up with about a ¼-inch-thick coat of the stuffing all around the breast. Stuff the sage, rosemary, thyme, bay leaves, and garlic inside the bird. Truss the chicken and season the outside with salt and pepper, and let the chicken sit at room temperature for at least 25 and up to 40 minutes.

4. Place the bread slices on a baking sheet and place the chicken on top of the bread. Roast the chicken for 20 minutes or until the breast skin is beginning to get golden brown and blister slightly. Reduce the oven temperature to 350°F and roast for an additional 20 to 30 minutes or until the chicken is golden brown and the juices run clear when the chicken is pierced under the thigh or until the internal thigh temperature registers 190°F on a meat thermometer. You can also test the doneness by trying to twist the drumstick. When it gives easily, the chicken is done.

ASSEMBLE THE DISH

5. Transfer the chicken to a carving board and allow it to rest at least 15 minutes before carving. Meanwhile, warm the Chicken Jus over medium-low heat until just simmering. Take the leftover juices in the pan from the chicken and add them to the jus. Carve the chicken, and serve with the Basic Potato Puree and Mustard Greens or your favorite sides for roasted chicken. Shave some of the black truffle on top and serve with the jus.

Make It Faster *If you definitely want a jus of sorts but don't have time to start with the Small Game Jus, find a store-bought chicken stock you like, and reduce it by half to get a concentrated flavor.*

JURGIELEWICZ DUCK BREAST + PICKLED PEACHES + BRAISED ALMONDS + CANDIED BACON

SERVES 4 We get our peaches from the guys over at Red Jacket Orchards—their peaches are incredible: juicy, fragrant . . . everything you could possibly want in a summer peach! We decided to lightly pickle them and pair them with duck—and it worked beautifully. For the pickled peaches, you want a slightly underripe (read: firm) peach in order for it to hold its form. This would also work well with Honeycrisp apples. And here's a tip for the candied bacon: It will keep for a few days, so when you make it, I recommend making more than what you need.

FOR THE CANDIED BACON

1 cup granulated sugar

1 tablespoon sriracha

12 slices bacon

FOR THE BRAISED ALMONDS

2 cups Marcona or plain almonds

2 cups Veal Stock (see page 382) or store-bought

½ cup Homemade Barbecue Sauce (see page 387) or store-bought

2 sprigs fresh thyme

1 fresh or ½ dried bay leaf

Pinch kosher salt

2 cups chiffonade of mustard greens

FOR THE PICKLED PEACHES

1 peach

1 teaspoon coriander seeds

1 teaspoon cumin seeds

1 teaspoon whole white peppercorns

1 teaspoon whole black peppercorns

1 teaspoon cumin seeds

1 sprig fresh thyme

1 fresh or ½ dried bay leaf

1 cup apple cider vinegar

1 tablespoon granulated sugar

1 teaspoon ground turmeric

1 teaspoon kosher salt

¼ jalapeño, sliced

FOR THE DUCK

½ recipe Duck Glaze (see page 391)

1 cup mild honey

2 tablespoons low-sodium soy sauce

1 sprig fresh rosemary

One (1-inch) knob ginger, sliced

Olive oil

4 duck breasts, preferably White Pekin

Kosher salt

Freshly gound black pepper

TO ASSEMBLE THE DISH

Kosher salt

1 ounce (2 tablespoons) unsalted butter

Smoked flaky sea salt or regular flaky sea salt (Maldon makes both)

Basil oil (see page 395) or your best extra-virgin olive oil

MAKE THE CANDIED BACON

1. Preheat the oven to 180°F; position the rack in the middle. In a small saucepot set over high heat, combine the sugar and sriracha with 1 cup of water and bring to a boil. Remove the syrup from the heat and set aside.

2. Using a pastry brush, brush the bacon slices with the syrup on both sides. Place a baking rack over a baking sheet and spray both with nonstick cooking spray. Transfer the bacon slices to the rack. Bake for 4 hours or until the bacon is crispy and glazed—it should look almost like glass. Transfer to a cooling rack set in a dry place and let the bacon cool for 1 hour. Set aside until needed. Raise the oven temperature to 200°F.

MAKE THE BRAISED ALMONDS

3. In a medium ovenproof saucepot, combine the almonds, stock, barbecue sauce, thyme, bay leaf, and salt with 1 cup of water. Cover and transfer the pot to the oven. Braise for about 4 hours or until the almonds are soft. Drain and transfer the almonds to a cooling rack and allow them to cool for 10 minutes. Transfer to a bowl, toss with the mustard greens, and set aside.

MAKE THE PICKLED PEACHES

4. Quarter and pit the peach. Slice into thin half-moon slices. Transfer the slices to a nonreactive container.

5. In a small, dry pan, toast the coriander, cumin, and peppercorns over low heat until fragrant, about 3 minutes. Transfer the toasted spices to a piece of double-plied cheesecloth, add the thyme and bay leaf, and tie the edges of the cheesecloth together to form a sachet.

6. In a small saucepan, combine the vinegar, sugar, turmeric, salt, and spice sachet with ½ cup of water and bring to a boil over high heat. Pour the pickling liquid over the peach slices, add the jalapeño, and let sit for 4 hours at room temperature.

MAKE THE DUCK

7. In a medium, deep saucepot set over medium-high heat, combine the Duck Glaze, honey, soy sauce, rosemary, and ginger. Bring to a boil, remove from the heat, and set aside. Be careful: As honey heats up, it rises.

8. Add enough oil to a large sauté pan to cover the bottom and set it over high heat. Season the duck with salt and pepper. Just before the oil starts to smoke, place the duck breasts (do not crowd the pan), skin side down, and reduce the heat to medium-low. Continuously drain and reserve the fat from the pan to ensure searing while the fat is rendering. Cook the duck for about 8 minutes or until the skin is crispy and the fat renders out. Add the glaze to the pan along with ¼ cup of the reserved fat and cook for 1 minute. (If you are working in batches, portion out your glaze accordingly.) Flip the duck and baste with the glaze and fat for 1 minute more. Transfer the duck to a plate, skin side up, and pour the contents of the pan over the meat.

ASSEMBLE THE DISH

9. In a small saucepot, warm 16 peach slices with 1 cup of their pickling liquid over medium heat. Using a slotted spoon, transfer the peaches to the bowl with the reserved almonds and mustard greens, toss together, and season with salt. Divide among 4 warmed plates. Reserve the warmed pickling liquid.

10. Add the butter to the reserved pickling liquid and whisk to emulsify. Drizzle the emulsion around the peaches, almonds, and mustard greens. Slice the duck breasts and plate the slices on top. Place one or two pieces of the Candied Bacon over each duck breast, and finish with a pinch of the smoked flaky sea salt, basil oil, and a little glaze from the duck.

JOE JURGIELEWICZ & SON, LTD.

JOEY JURGIELEWICZ

Joey calls himself the International Duck Promoter—and it is his goal to get more people to eat duck. And with Jurgielewicz duck, he will most definitely succeed. It is, by far, the best duck I've ever tasted.

Twenty-six years ago, Joey's father, a Cornell veterinary school graduate, started raising white Pekin duck. Decades prior, Joey's grandfather had a duck farm under the same name, but it had been sold years earlier. While working at a veterinary practice, Joey's father missed raising ducks. "It was always the ducks, the ducks, the ducks," Joey laughs. So after being a practicing veterinarian for a few years, Joey's father decided to return to his family trade—and start a duck farm, Joe Jurgielewicz & Son.

He found the perfect farm space in the Blue Mountains in Pennsylvania, Because it's a small, family-run farm, Joey and his family take care of everything: from picking up the eggs at five in the morning, to hatching them in their own hatchery, to raising, processing and distributing them throughout North America. There is work, real work, every single day.

"Just because it's Christmas," says Joey, "doesn't mean that the ducks will stop laying eggs. They don't take days off, and neither do we."

Pekin duck is an American duck that is actually the same breed of duck that has been raised and eaten in China for over 2,000 years. It just happens to be the best breed of duck for the North American environment.

It is also moist, tender, and flavorful. When people turn up their noses at the thought of duck, they are thinking of gamy, poor-quality duck—most definitely not Jurgielewicz bird.

If you treat the animal right, if you feed it the best food, you will get an amazing product. And when you bring it into the kitchen, magic will happen.

Even before he started to work on his father's farm, while still in college, Joey had a quart of rendered duck fat in his mini fridge in his dorm room. At first, his roommates thought it was disgusting, but pretty soon Joey realized that they were quietly raiding his duck fat supply to roast vegetables or fry eggs. Without even trying, he had quietly started a duck revolution that has now become his life's mission.

HOW TO
PREP A CHICKEN FOR CHICKEN UNDER A BRICK

1. **Here is your chicken.**

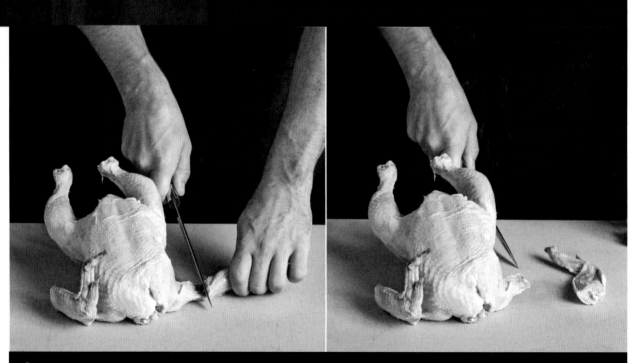

2. **Cut each wing off at the joint.**

MARC FORGIONE

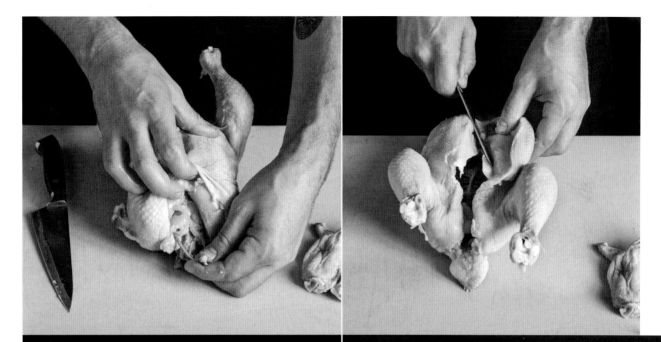

3. Remove the wishbone.

4. With the breast side up, working down breastbone and plate, slice against the bone in a single smooth motion (peeling back the breast).

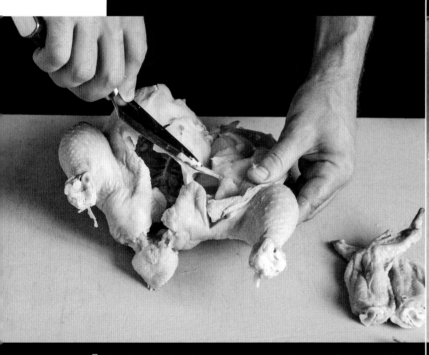

5. Continue to slice the breast away from the bone all the way down to the thigh bone (the breast is going to turn into the thigh and you need to keep them connected—be careful not to tear them apart.

6. Separate the breast/thigh/leg from the carcass so it is one connected half of the chicken. Repeat with the other side of the chicken.

7. **Remove the drumstick at the joint from the chicken half.**

8. **With the chicken half skin side down, slice into the thigh and remove the thigh bone.**

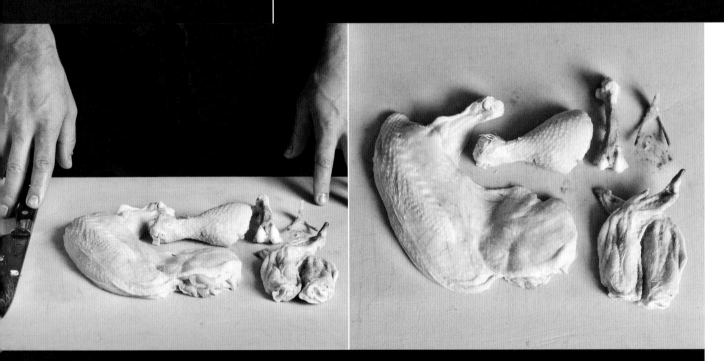

9. **Now your chicken half is ready to go. (You can repeat with the other chicken half.)**

MARC FORGIONE

CHICKEN UNDER A BRICK

SERVES 2 This chicken is a perfect example of what happens when there aren't enough cooks in the kitchen and you need to make do with what you have. In 2009, we were short-staffed, going through a recession, and just trying to survive. I wore many hats—the butcher, the meat cook, just to name a few—and didn't have time to season the chickens when the orders were coming in during dinnertime. To manage, I started to season the skin in the mornings when I got in, and the chickens would sit in the fridge all day, curing in the salt. This act of pure necessity turned our chicken into one of the most ordered dishes—and something we've become known for. I also learned that this was the very trick Zuni Café had used in creating their famed roasted chicken (which happens to be the best chicken I've ever had). By sitting in the fridge all day, the salt penetrates the skin, seasoning it, and the dry refrigerator air allows the skin to dry. Dry chicken skin combined with a hot pan gives you the tastiest, crispiest chicken skin you can possibly imagine.

SPECIAL EQUIPMENT

1 brick wrapped in tin foil; cast-iron skillet

FOR THE CHICKEN

One (3-pound) chicken

Kosher salt

Freshly ground black pepper

2 lemons

2 cups Chicken Stock (see page 382) or store-bought

1 sprig fresh rosemary

Canola oil

4 ounces (8 tablespoons) unsalted butter

3 tablespoons chopped capers

3 tablespoons chopped shallots

2 tablespoons chopped fresh curly parsley

Red pepper flakes

FOR THE ROSEMARY POTATOES

2 sprigs fresh thyme

1 fresh or ½ dried bay leaf

6 medium Yukon Gold potatoes

½ head garlic

Kosher salt

Blended Oil (see page 395)

1½ ounces (3 tablespoons) unsalted butter

1 tablespoon chopped fresh curly parsley

1 tablespoon chopped fresh rosemary

Freshly ground black pepper

Pinch of red pepper flakes

FOR THE CRISPY SHALLOTS

1 recipe Crispy Shallots (see page 128)

FOR THE SPICY BROCCOLI RABE

1 bunch broccoli rabe

Olive oil

Kosher salt

1 teaspoon red pepper flakes

PREPARE THE CHICKEN:

1. The day before cooking, separate the drumsticks from the chicken and reserve in the refrigerator, covered. Debone the chicken (see page 210 or have your local butcher do this for you), remove the wings, and fillet the breast and thigh meat, leaving the two intact.

2. Thoroughly dry the breast and thigh meat. Season the chicken skin side with salt. Season the flesh side with salt and pepper. Using a Microplane grater, finely zest 1 lemon, so that the zest falls directly on the chicken flesh (that way the oils from the peels are not wasted and land directly on the chicken). Refrigerate the seasoned breast and thigh meat, uncovered, overnight or up to 24 hours.

3. Peel the other lemon without getting any of the pith. In a medium pot set over medium heat, combine the stock, rosemary, and lemon peel, and bring to a simmer. Add the reserved drumsticks, and gently poach in the simmering chicken stock for 30 minutes. Transfer the drumsticks to a dish and cover with the poaching liquid. Allow to sit at room temperature for 45 minutes, and place in the refrigerator and allow the drumsticks to cool overnight in the poaching liquid.

MAKE THE ROSEMARY POTATOES

4. Before you start cooking the chicken on day 2, using kitchen twine, tie the thyme and bay leaf together. Set aside. Place the potatoes in a large pot and cover generously with cold water. Add the garlic, the herb bundle, and a healthy pinch of salt. Place the pot over medium-high heat and cook the potatoes until fork-tender, 30 to 40 minutes. Remove the potatoes from the water and let cool to room temperature.

5. Once the potatoes are cool enough to handle, cut each potato in half lengthwise and gently smash each one—they should look like little pancakes.

6. While the chicken is in the oven, add enough oil to a large sauté pan to coat the bottom of the pan. Heat over high heat until the oil is shimmering. Add the potatoes, lower the heat to medium, and cook the potatoes until a nice crust begins to form on the bottom. Add the butter and toss it with the potatoes. Once the butter begins to brown and the potatoes are golden brown all over, add the parsley and rosemary, and season to taste with salt, black pepper, and red pepper flakes. Transfer the potatoes to a warmed plate.

COOK THE CHICKEN

7. Remove the drumsticks from the poaching liquid and thoroughly pat them dry. Season the drumsticks with salt and set aside.

8. Preheat the oven to 425°F; position the rack in the middle. Remove the cured breast and thigh meat from the refrigerator and let it rest at room temperature for at least 15 minutes prior to cooking.

9. To an ovenproof skillet large enough to hold the whole chicken, add enough oil to cover the bottom of the pan. Set the pan over high heat. Just before it starts to smoke, add the chicken (minus the drumsticks), skin side down, and shake the pan to prevent sticking. Immediately reduce the heat to medium. Place a brick on top of the chicken so that it is pushing down on all sides. Once the edges begin to brown, transfer the chicken to the oven and roast for 15 to 18 minutes. The chicken skin should look golden brown and begin to crisp up.

10. Transfer the chicken back to the stovetop and add the drumsticks to the pan. Raise the heat to medium, remove the brick, and cook the chicken until the skin is crispy, about 5 minutes.

MAKE THE CRISPY SHALLOTS

11. Prepare the Crispy Shallots as directed on page 128.

MAKE THE SPICY BROCCOLI RABE

12. While the chicken is in the oven, bring a large pot of salted water to a boil over high heat. Trim the stems and discard the wilted outer leaves. Blanch the broccoli rabe in the boiling water for 10 seconds. Transfer the broccoli rabe to a large plate and let cool to room temperature. Set aside. When ready to serve, add enough olive oil to a skillet to cover the bottom of the pan and warm it over medium heat. Add the broccoli rabe and cook until warmed through. Season with salt and the red pepper flakes and stir to combine. Remove from the heat and set aside.

FINISH THE CHICKEN

13. Place the chicken on top of the Rosemary Potatoes, skin side up, and add the drumsticks to either side.

14. Add the butter, capers, and shallots to the pan that the chicken was cooked in and cook until the solids begin to brown. Stir in the parsley and red pepper flakes.

15. Place the Spicy Broccoli Rabe on top of the chicken. Pour the caper butter over the contents of the plate and serve immediately. Top with crispy shallots.

SERVES 4 While grape jelly is still the most popular pairing in a peanut butter sandwich, strawberry jelly can give grape jelly a run for its money. When I was a kid, there were always both kinds in my mom's pantry, and I always preferred the strawberry to the grape. To this day, I think that strawberries and peanut butter are a perfect pairing, and I put them together here.

FOR THE BALSAMIC REDUCTION

1 cup balsamic vinegar

¼ cup granulated sugar

1 teaspoon freshly ground black pepper

One (1-inch) piece ginger root, sliced

FOR THE PEANUT SAUCE

2 tablespoons canola oil

1 tablespoon Thai red curry paste

1 cup pale ale

¼ cup unsulfured molasses

¼ cup creamy peanut butter

2 tablespoons fresh lemon juice

1 tablespoon plus 1 teaspoon cider vinegar

1 teaspoon chili powder

1 teaspoon minced garlic

1 teaspoon dry mustard powder

1 teaspoon cayenne pepper

1 fresh or ½ dried bay leaf

FOR THE CASHEW CRUMBLE

½ cup raw cashews

1 tablespoon Vadouvan curry powder (see Sources, page 403)

Blended Oil (see page 395)

FOR THE SQUABS

4 squabs

One (2-ounce) foie gras terrine, sliced

Kosher salt

Canola oil

4 (½-inch thick) slices brioche, cut to the same size as the squab breasts

FOR THE STRAWBERRY SALAD

½ cup sliced baby fennel

1 cup sliced strawberries

1 tablespoon chiffonade of fresh mint

1 tablespoon chiffonade of fresh Thai basil

Extra-virgin olive oil

White balsamic vinegar

Kosher salt

Freshly ground black pepper

TO ASSEMBLE THE DISH

Thai basil flowers or chiffonade of Thai or regular basil (optional)

Fennel fronds

Flaky sea salt, such as Maldon

MAKE THE BALSAMIC REDUCTION

1. In a nonreactive saucepan, combine the vinegar, sugar, pepper, and ginger and bring to a boil over high heat. Reduce the heat to low and gently simmer the liquid until it is thick enough to coat the back of a spoon, 10 to 15 minutes. Strain the reduction through a fine-mesh strainer while it is still hot, and allow it to cool to room temperature.

MAKE THE PEANUT SAUCE

2. While the Balsamic Reduction cooks, in a small saucepot, warm the oil over low heat until shimmering. Add the curry paste and cook for 2 minutes, to wake up the spices. Add the beer, molasses, peanut butter, lemon juice, vinegar, chili powder, garlic, mustard, cayenne, and bay leaf, and bring the liquid to a gentle simmer. Cook at a gentle simmer for 10 minutes. Remove and discard the bay leaf, and using an immersion blender, puree the mixture until smooth. Pass the mixture through a fine-mesh strainer into a bowl and set aside.

3. While the Balsamic Reduction and Peanut Sauce cook, preheat the oven to 350°F; position the rack in the middle. Toss the cashews with the curry powder and just enough Blended Oil to coat, and transfer the nuts to a shallow baking sheet. Bake for about 8 minutes or until the cashews are toasted and fragrant. Transfer the nuts to a small bowl and let cool completely.

4. Place the cooled cashews in a food processor fitted with a metal blade, and process the nuts for 5 seconds. Transfer them to a paper towel–lined tray, and set aside in a dry place until ready to use.

MAKE THE SQUAB

5. Cut off the squab breasts (see Note) and gently separate the skin from the flesh with either your pinky or the back of a small spoon, being careful not to tear the skin. Place a layer of the foie gras terrine underneath the skin on the flesh and season the breasts with salt.

6. SOUS-VIDE COOKING INSTRUCTIONS (see step 8 for Sous-Vide Alternative Instructions): Preheat an immersion circulator filled with water until the water temperature registers 140°F. Place the breasts, skin-side up, in a single layer into a medium-size vacuum-seal bag. Seal the bag and poach in the immersion circulator for 30 minutes. Remove the bag from the water and let sit for 4 minutes before removing the squab breasts from the bag. Reserve the cooking liquid that pools inside the bag.

7. Add enough oil to a sauté pan to cover the bottom of the pan and set it over high heat. Just before the oil begins to smoke, add the squab breasts, skin side down. Reduce the heat to medium and cook until the skin is browned and crispy, 2 to 3 minutes, basting the breasts with the pan juices as the squab cook. Set the squab breasts aside. (Proceed to step 9.)

8. SOUS-VIDE ALTERNATIVE INSTRUCTIONS: Preheat the oven to 375°F; position the rack in the middle. Add enough oil to an ovenproof sauté pan to cover the bottom of the pan and set it over high heat. Just before the oil begins to smoke, add the squab breasts. Reduce the heat to medium, and cook the breasts until browned on both sides, 2 to 3 minutes per side. Transfer the pan to the oven and bake the squab breasts until cooked through, about 12 minutes. Remove from the oven and allow the squab breasts to rest while you prepare the rest of the dish.

9. Place the brioche slices in a sauté pan, set over medium heat, and toast on both sides, 1 to 2 minutes. Set the toasted brioche slices aside.

MAKE THE STRAWBERRY SALAD

10. Soak the baby fennel in ice water for 30 minutes, drain, and pat dry. In a nonreactive bowl, combine the fennel, strawberries, mint, and basil. Right before serving, drizzle the salad with some oil and vinegar, and season to taste with salt and pepper.

ASSEMBLE THE DISH

11. Drizzle a little Balsamic Reduction over 4 plates and spoon some of the Peanut Sauce in the center of each. On each plate, layer a slice of toasted brioche, followed by the Strawberry Salad, and top with the squab breasts. Finish with the Cashew Crumble and basil flowers, if using, and sprinkle with the fennel fronds and flaky sea salt.

Make It Faster *Make the squab in the oven and serve it with the Peanut Sauce and Strawberry Salad.*

Note *You will have the rest of the squab left over—no need for it to go to waste. Remove the legs and confit them for another use, maybe Tortellini d'Avanzi (see page 182). You can also make a jus (see Small Game Jus, page 383) from the bones and keep it in the freezer to flavor sauces or make rich gravy.*

Salt, pepper, and patience

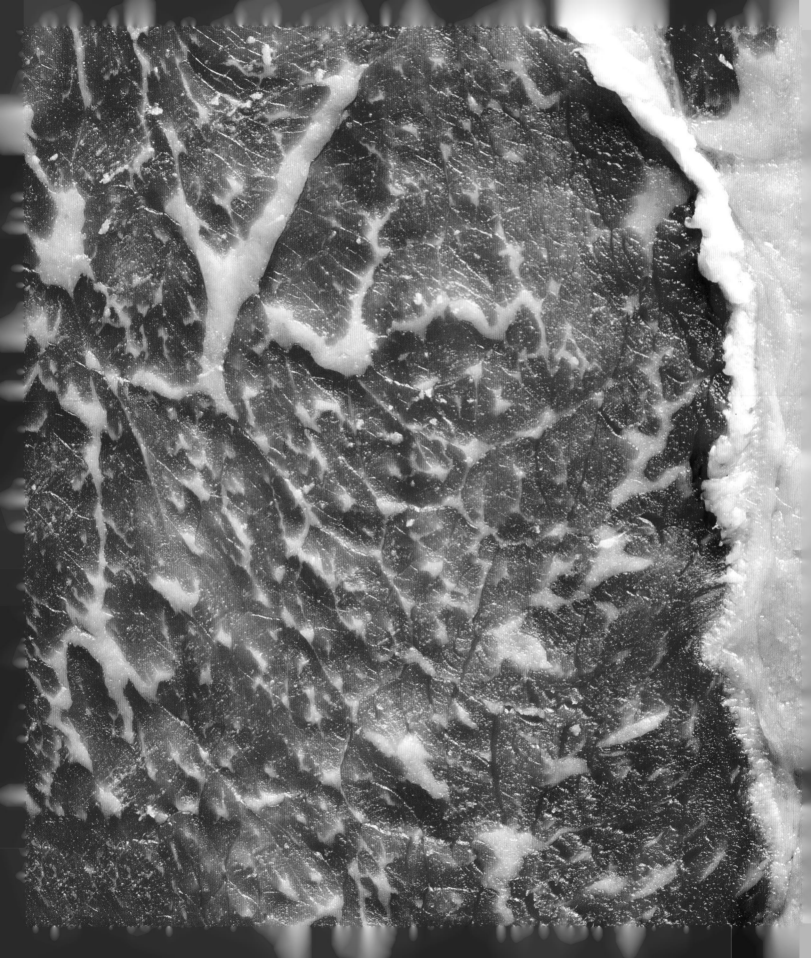

MEAT

"As you may know, nothing gets me more excited than perfectly cooked meat. The magical smells of a fatty rib eye hitting the grill, or the hours of magical aromas produced by the slow smoking of a pork shoulder are what I live for, not only as a chef but what I crave as an eater. I mean, don't get me wrong, vegetables are great, and who could pass up perfectly cooked seafood, but nothing cures a man's primal cravings much like meat!"

—MICHAEL SYMON

WAGYU BEEF + BAKED AROMATIC SEA SALT + BÉARNAISE VINAIGRETTE

SERVES 2 I created this dish for my uncle George, who came in for dinner one night back when I was a chef at BLT Prime. I served it to him as a midcourse, and didn't think to tell him that the salt bricks weren't supposed to be eaten—something Uncle George realized after one unsuccessful attempt to cut into the bricks. We serve our Wagyu beef with a béarnaise vinaigrette, and if you happen to have any of it left over, it is just amazing drizzled over grilled asparagus. Just be sure to not eat the salt bricks.

FOR THE WAGYU BEEF

One (6-ounce) Wagyu beef filet

Micro parsley (see Sources, page 403) or fresh flat-leaf parsley leaves

FOR THE BÉARNAISE VINAIGRETTE

2½ cups white wine vinegar

1 cup diced shallots

4 sprigs fresh tarragon, leaves and stems separated

2 tablespoons cracked black peppercorns

FOR THE SALT BRICKS

2 cups coarse sea salt

3 large egg whites

2 tablespoons chopped fresh rosemary

2 tablespoons chopped garlic

2 tablespoons minced Preserved Meyer Lemons (see page 391) or store-bought

2 tablespoons cracked black peppercorns

2 tablespoons cracked pink peppercorns

PREPARE THE WAGYU BEEF

1. Pat the beef dry and wrap it tightly in plastic wrap. Refrigerate the meat for about 1 hour.

MAKE THE BÉARNAISE VINAIGRETTE

2. In a small nonreactive saucepan, combine the vinegar, shallots, tarragon stems (reserve the leaves), and peppercorns. Bring the mixture to a simmer over medium heat, reduce the heat to low, and simmer until the mixture has reduced to about ⅓ cup, about 40 minutes. Remove from the heat, discard the tarragon stems, and set aside. Keep the reduction warm.

MAKE THE SALT BRICKS

3. While the Béarnaise Reduction is simmering, preheat the oven to 300°F; position the rack in the middle. In a large bowl, mix together the sea salt, egg whites, rosemary, garlic, Preserved Meyer Lemons, and black and pink peppercorns. Add water slowly, until the mixture has the consistency of wet sand. Mold the mixture into 2 rectangular bricks and smooth out the edges with a rubber spatula. Transfer the bricks to a shallow baking pan and bake until they are "set," about 20 minutes. Transfer the bricks to a cooling rack and let cool completely.

ASSEMBLE THE DISH

4. Preheat the broiler. Warm the Salt Bricks under the broiler for 3 minutes. Chop the reserved tarragon leaves. Transfer the filet to a cutting board, remove and discard the plastic wrap, and slice the filet into twelve ½-ounce (⅛-inch) slices. Place 1 salt block on each of 2 serving plates. Place 6 slices of beef on each block, brush the Béarnaise Vinaigrette over the beef, garnish with the chopped tarragon leaves and micro parsley, and serve immediately.

PROSCIUTTO-WRAPPED FIGS + MARCELLI'S SOFT PECORINO + ROSEMARY-GINGER REDUCTION

SERVES 4 Figs and prosciutto are a natural pairing, playing off of each other's contrasting flavors. Here, we decided to stuff the figs with this amazing pecorino from Bob Marcelli's family farm in Abruzzo, Italy. When most people think about pecorino, they think of pecorino Romano, which is a drier sheep's-milk cheese with a high salt content. Pecorino, however, is just an indication that the cheese is made with sheep's milk and can be either hard, soft, or in between. Marcelli's pecorino is a unique cheese: soft, runny, and unabashedly stinky. It's one of the best cheeses I've ever had and I recommend that everyone try to find it. However, if you can't find Marcelli's cheeses, particularly this one, find another sheep's-milk cheese that is soft enough to be scooped with a spoon.

SPECIAL EQUIPMENT

4 (6-inch) skewers

FOR THE ROSEMARY-GINGER REDUCTION

1 cup ruby port

½ cup granulated sugar

3 tablespoons cracked black pepper

One (1-inch) piece ginger, peeled and sliced

1 sprig fresh mint

1 sprig fresh rosemary

1 fresh or ½ dried bay leaf

FOR THE FIGS

12 fresh black Mission figs

6 ounces Marcelli's Pecorino Gregoriano (see Sources, page 403) or other soft, runny, sheep's milk cheese

6 paper-thin slices Prosciutto di Parma

Extra-virgin olive oil

TO ASSEMBLE THE DISH

Pecorino

Micro arugula (see Sources, page 403) or chiffonade of arugula

Olive oil

Freshly ground black pepper

MAKE THE ROSEMARY-GINGER REDUCTION

1. In a nonreactive saucepan, combine the port, sugar, pepper, ginger, mint, rosemary, and bay leaf and bring to a boil over high heat. Reduce the heat to low and simmer until the liquid has reduced considerably and coats the back of a spoon, about 30 minutes. Transfer to a cooling rack, and let cool to room temperature. Pass the reduction through a fine-mesh strainer into a bowl, discard the aromatics, and set aside until ready to use. Do not refrigerate the reduction or it will be too thick to use.

MAKE THE FIGS

2. With a paring knife, make an incision at the bottom of the figs, cutting two-thirds of the way down. Stuff a small piece of cheese inside each fig and pinch the edges of the figs back together so they look as if they were never cut.

3. Halve the prosciutto slices lengthwise—you should have twelve 5- to 6-inch-long strips. Roll a prosciutto strip around each fig so that the "fat" part of the strip is on top of the fig. Secure 3 figs onto a 6-inch skewer; repeat with the remaining figs. Refrigerate the skewers, covered, for at least 1 hour or up to 1 day. Light a grill or preheat a grill pan. Brush the figs with olive oil and grill on medium heat for 3 minutes on each side or until the prosciutto is crispy. Alternatively, you can broil the figs for 1 minute on each side or until the prosciutto is crispy.

ASSEMBLE THE DISH

4. Brush some of the Rosemary-Ginger Reduction in the center of 4 plates. Slide the figs off the skewers and divide them evenly among the plates over the reduction. Top with pecorino and arugula, drizzle with olive oil, and finish with a pinch of black pepper.

BUFFALO TARTARE + HOTTISH SAUCE + YOUNG ONION + LOCAL RADISH

SERVES 4 Buffalo meat, in general, is starting to make a comeback. Believe it or not, at one point in time, this country had more buffalo than people, and the buffalo was considered sacred. The Native American tribes used every single scrap of the animal: the bones, the hair, the skin, and, of course, the meat. It's a shame that *our* forefathers didn't have the same respect for the buffalo that the Native Americans did.

This Hottish Sauce can be used for anything. I highly recommend it as a condiment for a steak or a burger, a salad dressing, a sauce for grilled fish—you name it. It's especially good with this tartare. Make a generous batch—you'll be glad you did.

FOR THE HOTTISH SAUCE

Canola oil

2 white onions, diced

1 green bell pepper, seeded and diced

1 red bell pepper, seeded and diced

4 garlic cloves, finely diced

1 jalapeño, finely diced

½ cup chili powder

½ teaspoon cayenne

2 cups good-quality tomato juice

½ cup red wine vinegar

2 teaspoons Dijon mustard

FOR THE BUFFALO TARTARE

8 ounces trimmed buffalo tenderloin, finely diced

Extra-virgin olive oil

FOR THE RADISH AND SPRING ONION SALAD

½ cup sliced radishes

½ cup sliced spring onions

1 tablespoon chopped fresh chives

Flaky sea salt (such as Maldon)

Extra-virgin olive oil

TO ASSEMBLE THE DISH

Kosher salt

Extra-virgin olive oil

Juice of 2 limes

Chive blossoms

Flaky sea salt, such as Maldon

Toasted or grilled bread

MAKE THE HOTTISH SAUCE

1. In a large sauté pan set over medium heat, warm enough oil to cover the bottom of the pan. Add the onions, peppers, garlic, and jalapeño, and sweat the vegetables for 3 to 4 minutes, until limp. Add the chili powder and cayenne, and toast the spices for about 1 minute. Add the tomato juice, vinegar, and mustard, reduce the heat to low, and cook until the sauce reaches the consistency of ketchup, 10 to 15 minutes. Transfer the mixture to a blender and puree until completely smooth. Taste and adjust the seasonings, if needed.

MAKE THE BUFFALO TARTARE

2. In a large bowl, toss the buffalo meat with just enough olive oil to coat. Cover and refrigerate until ready to plate.

"Man knows that all healing plants are given by Wakan-Tanka, therefore they are holy. So, too, is the buffalo holy, because it is the gift of Wakan-Tanka."

—FLATIRON, OGLALA SIOUX CHIEF

MAKE THE RADISH AND SPRING ONION SALAD

3. Soak the radishes and onions in a bowl with ice water for 30 minutes. Transfer the vegetables to a paper towel–lined tray and refrigerate until ready to use.

4. Right before serving, place the radishes and onions in a bowl, add the chives, olive oil, and salt, and toss until the vegetables are coated.

ASSEMBLE THE DISH

5. Add ⅓ cup of the Hottish Sauce and some salt to the tartare and mix to combine. Mold the tartare into 4 (2-ounce) molds or just divide the tartare among 4 chilled plates.

6. Measure out about ½ cup of the Hottish Sauce and thin it out with some olive oil and lime juice. Drizzle the sauce around the plate and spoon the Radish and Spring Onion Salad on top. Sprinkle with some chive blossoms and flaky sea salt, and serve with toasted bread on the side.

Note *This recipe makes about 4 cups of sauce, which is more than you need. You can refrigerate the remaining sauce and use it over another tartare or as a barbecue sauce. Try adding pineapple or mango to make it more interesting!*

RED WINE–BRAISED SHORT RIBS + ROAST GARLIC–POTATO PUREE + BRUSSELS SPROUTS

SERVES 4 In the winter, few things taste as good and comforting as braised short ribs. The meat cooks slowly, and by the time it reaches your plate, it is tender and falling off the bone. Serve this dish family style in a Dutch oven: Bring the covered pot straight from the oven to the table, and lift the lid only after everyone has gathered around to eat. The aroma from the pot will get everyone instantly hungry and make the dinner experience that much more delicious.

FOR THE SHORT RIBS

4 (1-pound) short ribs on the bone

Kosher salt

12 sprigs fresh thyme

4 sprigs fresh rosemary

2 celery stalks

3 fresh or 1½ dried bay leaves

3 bacon slices

⅓ cup vegetable oil, or more as needed

4 ounces (8 tablespoons) unsalted butter

3 garlic heads, halved horizontally

20 garlic cloves, halved

8 shallots, diced

5 medium carrots, peeled and cut into 1-inch pieces

2 medium onions, peeled and cut into eighths

20 whole black peppercorns, cracked

⅓ cup tomato paste

⅓ cup all-purpose flour

6 cups dry red wine, such as Cabernet Sauvignon

6 cups ruby port

5 cups Veal Stock (see page 382) or store-bought

2 cups Chicken Stock (see page 382) or store-bought

¼ cup granulated sugar

Freshly ground black pepper

4 fresh or 2 dried bay leaves

Flaky sea salt, such as Maldon

FOR THE BRUSSELS SPROUTS

Canola oil

2 pounds Brussels sprouts, trimmed, sliced lengthwise in half

1 cup prosciutto lardons

1 cup mild honey

1 tablespoon granulated sugar

3 tablespoons chopped fresh curly parsley

Kosher salt

FOR THE GARLIC BUTTER

¼ cup minced garlic

2 ounces (4 tablespoons) unsalted butter

1 tablespoon fresh thyme leaves

TO ASSEMBLE THE DISH

1 recipe Basic Potato Puree (see page 396)

MAKE THE SHORT RIBS

1. Thoroughly pat the ribs dry and season them liberally with salt. Refrigerate the ribs, uncovered, overnight.

2. Let the ribs sit at room temperature for 40 minutes before cooking. Meanwhile, preheat the oven to 300°F; position the rack in the middle. Make a bouquet garni: place 8 sprigs of the thyme, the rosemary, celery, and 2 fresh or 1 dried bay leaf on the overlapping pieces of bacon and wrap the bacon around. Using a piece of kitchen twine, tie the bouquet garni tightly and set aside.

3. Add enough oil to a large ovenproof heavy-bottomed pot or Dutch oven to cover the bottom of the pot and set it over high heat. Just before it starts to smoke, add the ribs, and reduce the heat to medium-high. Brown the ribs on all sides, 2 to 3 minutes per side. Add the butter and halved garlic heads and cook until the butter browns. Transfer the ribs to a platter and set aside. Remove half of the butter from the pot and discard.

Return the pot to the stovetop and add the bouquet garni. Cook for 1 minute, until the bacon begins to brown. Add the garlic cloves, shallots, carrots, onions, and peppercorns to the pot and cook until the vegetables brown slightly, about 5 minutes. Stir in the tomato paste and cook for 2 minutes. Stir in the flour and cook for 1 minute. Add the wine, and 3 cups of port. Cook until the mixture has reduced by one-third. Return the ribs to the pot, add the veal and chicken stocks, and bring to a simmer. Place a piece of parchment paper over the pot, and cover tightly with a lid. Transfer the pot to the oven and cook for about 4 hours.

4. While the ribs cook, make the port reduction. In a medium pot set over medium heat, combine the remaining 3 cups of port, sugar, a pinch of black pepper (4 to 5 turns on your pepper mill), and salt to taste. Bring the liquid to a simmer and cook until it reduces by half, and the reduction thickens and coats the back of the spoon. Remove from the heat and set aside.

5. Remove the ribs from the Dutch oven to a plate. Strain the remaining sauce using a fine-mesh strainer into a pot. Bring to a boil and turn down to a simmer, skimming off any fat. Add the port reduction. Return the ribs to the Dutch oven and pour the sauce over the ribs (if you have the time, let them sit overnight if not, they can be served immediately with the bay leaves on top of the meat).

6. If cooling the ribs overnight, about 1 hour and 15 minutes before serving, preheat the oven to 350°F; position the rack in the middle. Place the ribs and their sauce in an ovenproof dish, place the bay leaves on top, and sprinkle with flaky sea salt. Cover to dish and warm the ribs in the oven for 30 to 40 minutes. Uncover and cook for 30 minutes more or until the meat is soft and warmed through.

MAKE THE BRUSSELS SPROUTS

7. Add enough oil to a large skillet to cover the bottom of the pan and set the skillet over high heat. Add the Brussels sprouts, cut side down, and cook until the edges start to caramelize, 2 to 3 minutes. Add the prosciutto, reduce the heat to medium, and cook until the prosciutto is crispy, about 4 minutes. Add the honey and sugar, and cook until the honey turns into a nice glaze. (If the glaze gets too sticky, add a couple of tablespoons of water.) Stir in the parsley and season to taste with salt.

MAKE THE GARLIC BUTTER

8. Before reheating the ribs, in a small saucepot, warm the garlic and butter over medium heat until the garlic begins to brown. Stir occasionally to make sure the milk solids are not sticking to the bottom of the pan. Stir in the thyme and remove from the heat.

ASSEMBLE THE DISH

9. Drizzle the Garlic Butter all over the ribs and cover the pot. Serve the ribs in their cooking vessel, family style: Bring the whole pot to the table and open the lid so everyone can smell the infused butter combining with the ribs. Serve with the Brussels Sprouts and Basic Potato Puree on the side.

Make It Faster *For a simpler at-home meal, make the ribs with just one of the sides—the ribs are the real draw of this dish.*

PRIME HANGER STEAK + POMMES BOULANGÈRES +
TORPEDO SHALLOTS + SPINACH

SERVES 4 Pommes boulangères is a classic, rustic French gratin. It is said that the dish was traditionally prepped by a baker's wife and brought over to the bakery where the baker could cook the dish in the bread oven and have a hot meal (hence the name *boulangère,* meaning "baker's wife").

As for hanger steak—sometimes it gets a bad rap as a cheap and chewy cut, but if cooked right, it's probably my favorite cut. The trick to a tender hanger steak (one that most people don't know) is just to cut against the grain.

FOR THE SHALLOTS

4 torpedo shallots

¼ cup extra-virgin olive oil

¼ cup sherry vinegar

Kosher salt

Freshly ground black pepper

Olive oil

FOR THE POMMES
BOULANGÈRES

2½ ounces (5 tablespoons)
unsalted butter

Olive oil

3 cups chopped bacon (about
15 strips), cut into lardons

½ cup sliced garlic

3 cups julienned
Vidalia onions

3 tablespoons chiffonade
of fresh sage

2 tablespoons chopped
fresh curly parsley

2 cups Veal Stock (see page
382) or store-bought

2 cups Chicken Stock (see
page 382) or store-bought

4 large baking potatoes,
peeled and sliced ⅛ inch
thick, soaked in cold water
(for no more than 10 minutes)

Kosher salt

Freshly ground black pepper

6 sprigs fresh thyme

4 fresh or 2 dried bay leaves

2 teaspoons ground
juniper berries

FOR THE SPINACH

¼ cup thinly sliced garlic

Canola oil

1 pound fresh spinach

FOR THE HANGER STEAKS

4 (10-ounce) center
cut hanger steaks

Kosher salt

Freshly ground black pepper

Olive oil

2 ounces (4 tablespoons)
unsalted butter

12 garlic cloves, skin on

12 sprigs fresh thyme

Flaky sea salt, such
as Maldon

MAKE THE SHALLOTS

1. Preheat the oven to 375°F; position the rack in the middle. In a medium bowl, toss the shallots with the extra-virgin olive oil and the vinegar. Bake for 35 minutes, or until the shallots are soft. Reduce the oven temperature to 350°F. Season the shallots to taste with salt and pepper. Add enough olive oil to a medium skillet to cover the bottom of the pan and set it on the stovetop over high heat. Just before the oil starts to smoke, add the shallots and sear until nicely browned on all sides. Remove the pan from the heat and set aside. Keep the oven on.

MAKE THE POMMES BOULANGÈRES

2. Use 3 tablespoons of the butter to generously grease a hotel pan (20¾ x 12¾ x 4 inches) or a 6-quart casserole dish.

3. Add enough oil to a large skillet to cover the bottom of the pan and set the skillet on the stovetop over high heat. Just before it starts to smoke, add the lardons. Reduce the heat to medium-low and cook until crispy, about 10 minutes. Add the garlic and cook until crispy, 3 to 4 minutes. Add the onions and cook until the onions are soft, 6 to 7 minutes. Stir in the sage and parsley and cook for 30 seconds more. Add the veal and chicken stocks, raise the heat to high, and bring the broth mixture to a boil. Remove from the heat and set aside.

4. Layer the potatoes in a single layer on the bottom of a 3-quart oven proof dish or hotel pan, overlapping each one slightly, and season with salt and pepper. Ladle some of the broth mixture on top. Repeat the process until you either get to the top of the pan or run out of potatoes. Ladle the remaining broth mixture on top and sprinkle with the thyme, bay leaves, and juniper berries. Cover the pan with foil and bake for 30 minutes, remove the foil, and cook for another 30 to 45 minutes or until fork-tender.

5. Transfer the casserole to a shallow baking pan, cover with a piece of parchment paper, and place a pan on top with a weight inside (a can of beans will do). Refrigerate for at least 3 hours or up to overnight.

6. When ready to serve, preheat the oven to 350°F; position the rack in the middle. Remove the top pan, and discard the parchment and foil. Invert the potatoes onto a carving board with a blood groove (to collect and pool the cooking juices), and tap the bottom of the pan to release the potatoes. Reserve the juices. Cut the block of potatoes into pieces of the size and shape you desire.

7. Warm the Pommes Boulangères pieces, along with the reserved juices, in a baking pan with the remaining 2 tablespoons of the butter, about 10 minutes or until warmed through.

MAKE THE SPINACH

8. When ready to serve, add the garlic and a splash of oil to a cold skillet and cook over medium heat until the garlic is crispy, 2 to 3 minutes. Add the spinach and cook until the spinach is wilted, 2 to 3 minutes. Remove from the heat and set aside.

MAKE THE HANGER STEAKS

9. Thoroughly pat the steaks dry and season them with salt and pepper. Add enough olive oil to a large sauté pan to cover the bottom of the pan and set it on the stovetop over high heat. Just before it begins to smoke, add 2 of the steaks to the pan and sear them on all sides until caramelized, 4 to 5 minutes. Add 2 tablespoons of the butter, 6 garlic cloves, and 6 sprigs of thyme to the pan. Baste the steaks and roll them around in the fat, being careful not to burn the butter. Reduce the heat to medium and cook until the butter browns. You might need to add a splash of olive oil to the pan if it looks like the butter is starting to burn. Transfer the steaks to a platter and allow them to rest for at least 5 minutes before carving. Reserve the pan drippings. Repeat with the remaining steaks, butter, garlic, and thyme. Let the steaks sit for 10 minutes before carving.

ASSEMBLE THE DISH

10. Divide the steaks and Pommes Boulangères among 4 warmed plates. Spoon the Spinach and Shallots around the steak and potatoes, drizzle with the reserved pan drippings, and sprinkle with flaky sea salt before serving.

CREEKSTONE RANCH FLATIRON STEAK + POTATO MILLE-FEUILLE + MOUNTAIN HUCKLEBERRIES + MAYTAG BLUE CHEESE

SERVES 4 Berries aren't exactly the first things that come to mind when you think of steak, but that is exactly what happened here. A little while back, I got some wild huckleberries from our mushroom purveyor, Mushrooms & More, and when I tasted them, they reminded me of bordelaise, which is my favorite sauce for a steak. So, I wanted to do something that would incorporate the berries with the steak, but still retain their natural sweetness and texture. And from there, the dish just kind of shaped itself and grew organically as I kept tasting, and tasting, and building around it.

At the restaurant, we halve the steak lengthwise and sprinkle a little Activa (see Sources, page 403) over one of the halves, like a confectioners' sugar dusting. We place the other steak half on top and the Activa essentially binds the two slices of steak together, making for a dramatic restaurant presentation. If you want to keep things simple at home, just follow the recipe below, but if you want to re-create the restaurant presentation, try our method with Activa and simply adjust the cooking time.

FOR THE ROAST GARLIC BUTTER

1 cup extra-virgin olive oil

10 garlic cloves

4 ounces (8 tablespoons) unsalted butter, softened

3 tablespoons chopped fresh curly parsley

1 tablespoon kosher salt

FOR THE PORT-WINE REDUCTION

Canola oil

2 cups sliced shallots

1 cup sliced white button mushrooms

3 tablespoons cracked black pepper

2 tablespoons granulated sugar

8 cups dry red wine

4 cups ruby port

3 cups Veal Stock (see page 382) or store-bought

4 sprigs fresh thyme

2 fresh or 1 dried bay leaves

1 cup mountain huckleberries, or substitute blueberries or blackberries

FOR THE POTATO MILLE-FEUILLE

1½ ounces (3 tablespoons) unsalted butter

Canola oil

10 garlic cloves, sliced

1 Vidalia onion, julienned

¼ cup chopped fresh summer savory

2 tablespoons chopped fresh curly parsley

2 tablespoons chopped fresh rosemary

2 cups Veal Stock (see page 382) or store-bought

2 cups Chicken Stock (see page 382) or store-bought

4 large Idaho potatoes (4 to 5 pounds), peeled and sliced 1/16 inch thick

1½ cups crumbled Maytag or other blue cheese, plus more for serving

Kosher salt

Freshly ground black pepper

6 sprigs fresh thyme

2 fresh or 1 dried bay leaves

FOR THE STEAKS

4 (10-ounce) flatiron steaks

Kosher salt

Freshly ground black pepper

Canola oil

4 ounces (8 tablespoons) unsalted butter

6 sprigs fresh thyme

Cloves from 1 head garlic, unpeeled

FOR THE SAUTÉED GREENS

Olive oil

3 garlic cloves, chopped

2 pounds baby spinach or other seasonal baby greens

1 teaspoon freshly ground nutmeg

Kosher salt

1. In a saucepot set over medium heat, warm the olive oil and garlic until the oil reaches 275°F. Cook until the garlic is soft and lightly browned, 3 to 4 minutes. Strain the garlic, reserving the oil. (The reserved oil will be great when you are making garlic bread, so be sure to save it. It will keep for 2 weeks.) Transfer the garlic to a stand mixer fitted with the paddle attachment. Add the butter, parsley, and salt, and mix on medium speed until the garlic is well incorporated. Transfer to a container, cover, and refrigerate until needed.

MAKE THE PORT-WINE REDUCTION

2. Add enough oil to a large nonreactive stockpot to cover the bottom of the pot and set it over high heat. Just before the oil starts to smoke, add the shallots, mushrooms, and pepper, and reduce the heat to medium. Sweat the vegetables until brown bits (a *fond*) form on the bottom of the pan, and add the sugar. Add the wine and port, and deglaze the pan, scraping the brown bits off the bottom of the pan. Simmer the liquid until it has reduced to about 3 cups. Add the stock and cook until the liquid has reduced to 3 cups. Be sure to skim any impurities that float to the surface. Transfer the liquid to a bain marie or a nonreactive container. Add the thyme and bay leaves, and wrap the top tightly in plastic wrap. Let the reduction infuse for 1 hour. The accumulated moisture that will gather on the inside of the plastic wrap will look like it is raining. Strain the liquid through a fine-mesh strainer into a saucepan and set aside. When ready to serve, warm the Port-Wine Reduction until simmering. Right before serving, stir in the huckleberries and cook them in the reduction for 30 seconds. Remove from the heat and set aside.

MAKE THE POTATO MILLE-FEUILLE

3. Preheat the oven to 425°F; position the rack in the middle. Generously butter a half-size hotel pan (12¾ x 10½ x 4 inches) or a 2-quart ovenproof dish with the butter.

4. Add enough oil to a large sauté pan to cover the bottom of the pan, add the garlic, and set it over high heat. Once the garlic starts to turn brown, reduce the heat to medium. Add the onion and cook, stirring, until soft,

about 5 minutes. Stir in the savory, parsley, and rosemary, and cook until fragrant, about 2 minutes. Add the stocks, raise the heat to high, and bring the liquid to a boil. Remove the garlic-herb stock from the heat and set aside.

5. Layer the potato slices in the greased hotel pan in a single layer, overlapping slightly. Sprinkle them with some blue cheese and ladle some of the garlic-herb stock over. Make sure that when you ladle the stock, you get the garlic and herbs, not just the liquid. Season with salt and pepper. Repeat until you run out of potatoes or reach the top of the pan. Place the thyme and bay leaves on top and finish with some more of the garlic-herb stock. Cover the pan tightly with foil and bake for 20 minutes. Reduce the oven temperature to 350°F and remove the foil from the pan. Bake for 1 hour or until the potatoes feel tender when pierced with a paring knife. Transfer the pan onto a baking pan or a heatproof tray. Place a piece of parchment paper on top and place another hotel pan over the potatoes. Place a weight in the top hotel pan (a can of beans will do). Refrigerate overnight. To release the mille-feuille, run a knife around the perimeter of the potatoes. Place the hotel pan over low heat to loosen the juices. Invert the potatoes onto a carving board with a blood groove, reserving the cooking liquid. Cut the potatoes into pieces of the desired size.

6. Place a large nonstick pan over medium-high heat and add enough oil to cover the bottom of the pan. Just before the pan begins to smoke, add the pieces of *mille-feuille* cut side down and sear for 30 to 45 seconds, until lightly browned. Repeat on all cut sides.

MAKE THE STEAKS

7. Preheat the oven to 350°F; position the rack in the middle. Thoroughly pat the meat dry. Season both sides liberally with salt and pepper. Add enough oil to a large ovenproof sauté pan to cover the bottom of the pan and set it over high heat. Just before the oil starts to smoke, add half of the steaks to the pan and cook for 1 minute. Reduce the heat to medium-high and cook the meat, without moving it, for about 4 minutes. Check the bottom to see if the steaks are charred to your liking, and if they are, transfer the steaks to a plate or a cutting

board, and let them rest while you repeat the same process with the remaining steaks. Let the second batch of steaks rest 5 minutes before placing all 4 steaks onto a shallow roasting sheet, charred side up, and placing everything in the oven for 3 to 4 minutes for medium-rare. Transfer the steaks back to the cutting board and return the pan to the stovetop. Working in 2 batches, flip the steaks back onto the seared side. Add half of: the butter, thyme, and garlic and raise the heat to high. Baste the steaks with the butter for 1 to 2 minutes. If the butter starts to burn, reduce the heat and add a splash of oil to the pan to lower the overall temperature. Transfer the steaks to a carving board. Repeat with the remaining steaks, butter, thyme, and garlic. Let the steaks rest for at least 7 minutes before serving. While the steaks rest, warm up the Potato Mille-Feuille. Reserve the butter from the pan in which you cooked the steaks—you will need it when you assemble the dish.

MAKE THE SAUTÉED GREENS

8. While the potatoes are reheating, add enough oil to a large sauté pan to cover the bottom of the pan. Add the garlic and set over high heat. Turn the heat down to medium. When the garlic begins to brown, immediately add the spinach. Very important: Watch the pan here and rely on your sense of smell to tell you when the garlic is ready to come off the heat. Garlic goes from perfectly cooked to burnt in a matter of seconds, so be ready with the spinach in your hand. Cook, stirring, until the spinach is wilted, 1 to 2 minutes. Season with the nutmeg and salt to taste. Remove from the heat.

ASSEMBLE THE DISH

9. Divide the Sautéed Greens among 4 warmed plates and top them with the steaks and reserved steak butter. Serve with the Potato Mille-Feuille, Roast Garlic Butter, and Port-Wine Reduction. Crumble some blue cheese on top.

COOKING WITH FAT

Fat is not the devil everyone makes it out to be. Fat is one of the key taste components—it makes food taste good, and I enjoy cooking with it. The key is moderation. At the restaurant we save all our fat. After a couple of days, if we have enough fat, instead of making confit pork shoulder with duck fat, which is what a lot of people do, we can confit the pork in pork fat.

The meat station at the restaurant has three containers: duck fat, beef fat, and pork fat, and we cook and baste the respective meats in their own fat. Beef fat tastes good on beef, pork fat tastes good on pork, and so on.

Fat doesn't just enhance the taste of meat, but also adds depth and flavor to eggs or potatoes, just to name a few. See Potato Brown Butter (page 196) for a perfect example.

Not only do we cook with fat, but we encourage others to do the same. Which brings me to this recommendation: Save your fat, and use it in place of butter or oil to cook with whenever the mood strikes you. Not only will it make a difference in how your food tastes, but also you'll be using every scrap of the animal without wasting a thing.

SERVES 4 It's funny how sometimes a dish comes together starting with a side and then everything else—the protein, vegetable, sauce—will get built around it. This is such a case. Vichyssoise, which is a French potato-leek soup, is one of my favorite things to eat. Normally, it is served cold, but I actually enjoy it hot, which is a bit untraditional. So instead of making it as expected, I turned it into croquettes. Once I had the croquettes down, I started to think about what would go well with them, and built the rest of the dish around this side. This is one of the dishes in the book that relies pretty heavily on a digital scale and precision is very important, especially when making the croquettes. If you don't own a digital kitchen scale already, I very much recommend one—it is a very useful and inexpensive gadget to have in the kitchen.

FOR THE BORDELAISE

3 tablespoons canola oil

¾ cups chopped button mushrooms

3 shallots, sliced

1 garlic clove, chopped

2 tablespoons whole black peppercorns

1 tablespoon granulated sugar

½ cup red wine vinegar, plus more as needed

4 cups dry red wine

1 cup ruby port

1 sprig fresh thyme

1 fresh or ½ dried bay leaf

4 cups Veal Stock (see page 382) or store-bought

1 cup Chicken Stock (see page 382) or store-bought

Kosher salt

FOR THE CHESTNUTS

Canola oil

2 cups diced bacon (10 slices)

4 garlic cloves, sliced

2 cups sliced chestnuts

5 tablespoons mild honey

2 cups Veal Stock (see page 382) or Chicken Stock (see page 382) or store-bought

2 tablespoons chopped fresh curly parsley

1 tablespoon chopped fresh sage

Kosher salt

FOR THE VICHYSSOISE CROQUETTES

5 large Idaho potatoes (about 2 pounds 3 ounces)

4 ounces (8 tablespoons) unsalted butter

½ cup (3½ ounces) finely chopped leeks

1 large egg, lightly beaten

1½ cups plus 2 tablespoons all-purpose flour

5 large eggs, room temperature

2 teaspoons kosher salt, plus more as needed

3 cups canola oil

FOR THE RIB EYE

4 (8-ounce) boneless rib eye steaks (tied to keep shape)

Kosher salt

Freshly ground black pepper

Canola oil

4 ounces (8 tablespoons) unsalted butter

6 sprigs fresh thyme

1 head garlic, halved

TO ASSEMBLE THE DISH

1 recipe Maître d'Hôtel Butter (see page 386)

Flaky sea salt, such as Maldon

Tahoon cress (see Sources, page 403) or chiffonade of watercress

1. In a 3-quart saucepot, warm the canola oil over medium heat. Add the mushrooms, shallots, and garlic, and cook until the shallots are translucent, about 4 minutes. Add the peppercorns and cook for 1 minute. Stir in the sugar and cook for 1 minute more. Add the vinegar and deglaze the pan, scraping the brown bits off the bottom of the pan with a wooden spoon. Cook until the vinegar has been absorbed. Add the wine, port, thyme, and bay leaf. Raise the heat to medium-high, and cook until the liquid has reduced by half, 15 to 20 minutes. Add the stocks and strain through a fine-mesh strainer.

2. Return the liquid to the stove over medium heat. As the liquid cooks, it will start to separate. When it does, skim off any excess fat, tilting the pot slightly to make it easier to skim. Season to taste with salt, and add more vinegar if you like.

3. Strain the sauce again and set it aside; you should have about 3 cups of the finished sauce, but you will only need 1 cup for this recipe. Freeze the rest for the next time you make a steak.

MAKE THE CHESTNUTS

4. Add enough oil to a large skillet to cover the bottom of the pan and set it over high heat. Just before it starts to smoke, add the bacon, reduce the heat to medium-low, and render the lardons until crispy, about 8 minutes. Once the bacon is crispy, add the garlic and cook until crispy. Watch it very closely—the garlic cooks very fast and goes from cooked to burnt in mere seconds. As soon as the garlic is crispy, add the chestnuts and toss to coat in the oil. Add the honey and cook until the chestnuts are caramelized, 3 to 5 minutes. Add the stock and cook until the stock has almost all cooked off. Stir in the parsley and sage. Taste and season with salt. Remove from heat and set aside.

MAKE THE VICHYSSOISE CROQUETTES

5. Preheat the oven to 300°F; position the rack in the middle. Bake the potatoes for 1½ hours or until fork-tender. While the potatoes are still warm, split the potatoes and scoop out their centers. Measure out 2 pounds 3 ounces (1000 grams) of potato and push it through a food mill into a large bowl.

6. In a small skillet, melt 1 tablespoon of the butter with leeks over medium heat and add to the potatoes. Whisk in the beaten egg and set the potato mixture aside in a warm place.

7. Make the pâte à choux: In a 4-quart pot, melt the remaining butter with 2 teaspoons of water over medium-high heat. Stir in the flour, and reduce the heat to medium. Keep stirring vigorously. The batter will eventually come together in a ball, but that doesn't mean it is done. You must cook out the flour by stirring every 10 seconds for about 3 minutes. You want to cook out the flour from the pâte so your batter isn't grainy. If the edges start to brown, lower the heat a bit and continue to stir. Once done, transfer the batter to the bowl of a stand mixer fitted with the paddle attachment. With the mixer on medium speed, add the 5 eggs, one at a time, waiting until each egg is fully incorporated before adding the next, and, finally, add the salt.

8. Weigh the potato mixture and weigh the pâte à choux. Measure it out so you have a 2-to-1 ratio of potato to pâte. It is more precise if you work in grams. Transfer both to the bowl of a stand mixer fitted with the paddle attachment and mix on medium speed for 15 seconds or until just combined—do not overwork the mixture. Lightly flour your hands and roll the mixture into golf ball–size croquettes. You should wind up with 15 to 20 croquettes. Transfer the croquettes to a floured tray and refrigerate until needed.

9. When ready to serve, add the oil to a 4-quart saucepot, and heat over medium-high heat until the oil registers 300°F on a deep-frying thermometer. Gently add 12 croquettes to the hot oil, and fry until crispy and golden on the outside, 2 to 3 minutes. Using a slotted spoon, transfer the croquettes to a paper towel–lined tray and season with salt.

MAKE THE RIB EYE

10. Preheat the oven to 350°F; position the rack in the middle. Thoroughly pat the meat dry. Season both sides liberally with salt and pepper. Add enough oil to

a large ovenproof sauté pan to cover the bottom of the pan and set it over high heat. Just before the oil starts to smoke, add half of the steaks to the pan and cook for 1 minute. Reduce the heat to medium-high and cook the meat, without moving it, for about 4 minutes. Check the bottom to see if the steaks are charred to your liking, and if they are, transfer the steaks to a plate or a cutting board, and let them rest while you repeat the same process with the remaining steaks. Be sure to let the second batch of steaks rest 5 minutes before placing all 4 steaks onto a shallow roasting sheet, charred side up, and placing everything in the oven for 6 to 8 minutes for medium-rare. Transfer the steaks back to the cutting board and return the pan to the stovetop. Working in 2 batches, return the steaks to the pan, seared side up. Add half of each: the butter, thyme, and garlic, and raise the heat to high. Baste the steaks with the butter for about 2 minutes. If the butter starts to burn, reduce the heat and add a splash of oil to the pan

to lower the overall temperature. Transfer the steaks to a carving board. Repeat with the remaining steaks, butter, thyme, and garlic. Let steaks rest for at least 10 minutes before serving.

ASSEMBLE THE DISH

11. In a small saucepan, combine 1 cup of the Chestnuts mixture with the reserved Bordelaise Sauce and warm over medium heat until heated through.

12. Divide the remaining chestnut mixture among 4 warmed plates, placing it in the center of each plate. Remove the strings from the steaks and place the steaks on top of the chestnuts. Spoon the warmed bordelaise around and top the steaks with Maître d' Butter. Sprinkle some flaky sea salt over the steaks, divide the croquettes among the plates, and finish with Tahoon cress or watercress chiffonade.

MAKING IT RAIN

Take a bunch of basil and smell it—that's one smell. Now, take a bunch of basil and boil it in water for half an hour. Smell it. Now take a bunch of basil, put it into a warm sauce, cover it with plastic, and leave it in there for 15 minutes. Unwrap it and smell it. You'll notice that the smell of the basil cooked by the last process is not the same as the others. The last process doesn't kill the flavor—instead, it enhances it.

Herbs are only fragrant for so long. There are stronger herbs like thyme and rosemary that might hold up better, but the reason we "make it rain" is to better extract the flavor. And you can do it with spices, cumin, coriander, basil, mint, oregano, lemon verbena—their flavors peak at a certain point, so we extract as much as we can and then get rid of the spent herbs.

1. Pour the hot liquid into a bain marie or a nonreactive container.

2. Add the aromatics/herbs.

3. Place a piece of plastic wrap over the bain marie.

4. Using another piece of plastic wrap twisted into a "rope," tie the plastic on top of the container tightly so there is no air escaping.

5. The top of the plastic wrap will form a bubble and moisture will accumulate on the inside of the plastic wrap. It will look like it is raining inside.

6. Strain the infused broth.

28-DAY DRY-AGED PRIME CREEKSTONE FARMS TOMAHAWK CHOP + POTATO BROWN BUTTER + CHIMICHURRI + VIDALIA ONIONS

SERVES 2 One night, in the spring of 2011, I decided to rent a party bus for the whole staff to go check out the Pat LaFrieda meat facilities. As we were walking around, I noticed this gorgeous bone, and when I asked Pat what it was, he told me it was a Tomahawk Chop. I ordered a couple of pieces the next day, and fell in love with the cut. It's got a perfect fat-to-meat ratio and the bones give the steak so much flavor. While the menu will change weekly and with the seasons, one of the things that always remains is the Tomahawk Chop.

FOR THE CHIMICHURRI SAUCE

¾ cup extra-virgin olive oil

½ cup chopped fresh curly parsley

½ cup chopped fresh cilantro

3 tablespoons minced shallots

1 tablespoon red pepper flakes

1 tablespoon minced garlic

Kosher salt

¼ cup sherry vinegar

FOR THE POTATO PUREE

1 recipe Basic Potato Puree (see page 396)

FOR THE TOMAHAWK

One (40-ounce) dry-aged Tomahawk Chop, about 2½ inches thick

Kosher salt

Freshly ground black pepper

Canola oil

4 ounces (8 tablespoons) unsalted butter

1 head garlic, halved horizontally

6 sprigs fresh thyme

FOR THE GRILLED VIDALIA ONIONS

1 Vidalia onion, cut into ½-inch-thick rings

Olive oil

Kosher salt

Freshly ground black pepper

TO ASSEMBLE THE DISH

Flaky sea salt, such as Maldon

Smoked salt

Freshly ground black pepper

MAKE THE CHIMICHURRI SAUCE

1. In a medium bowl mix together the olive oil, parsley, cilantro, shallots, red pepper flakes, garlic, and salt. Cover and refrigerate for at least 2 hours or up to 1 day. Right before serving, add the sherry vinegar.

MAKE THE POTATO PUREE

2. Start making the Basic Potato Puree. You will need the butter from the steak to finish it, so keep the puree warm until you cook the steak.

3. While the steak is resting, whisk just enough of the reserved steak butter into the Potato Puree until the mixture is emulsified. Cover the puree and keep warm until ready to serve. Reserve the remaining steak butter for when you assemble the dish.

MAKE THE TOMAHAWK

4. Preheat the oven to 350°F; position the rack in the middle. Pat the steak dry and season both sides liberally with salt and pepper. Let the steak come to room temperature before cooking.

5. Add enough oil to a large, ovenproof sauté pan to cover the bottom of the pan and set it over high heat. Just before the oil starts to smoke, add the steak and sear for 1 minute. Reduce the heat to medium-high and cook the steak, without moving it, for about 4 minutes.

Check the bottom of the steak to see if it is charred to your liking; if it is, flip it over and cook the other side for 1 to 2 minutes. Transfer the steak to a baking sheet and cook in the oven for about 10 minutes for medium-rare. Return the steak to the pan over medium heat and add the butter, garlic, and thyme. Raise the heat to high and baste the steak in the butter for about 2 minutes. (If the butter starts to burn, reduce the heat, and add bit of oil to the pan to lower the overall temperature of the butter.) Transfer the steak to a plate and let it rest for 10 minutes before serving. Reserve the browned steak butter in the pan. When ready to serve, slice the steak across the grain.

MAKE THE GRILLED VIDALIA ONIONS

6. While the steak is resting, toss the onions rings with some olive oil, 2 tablespoons of the Chimichurri Sauce, salt, and pepper. Light a grill or preheat a grill pan. Grill the onions over high heat, turning occasionally, until cooked through, 4 to 5 minutes. Alternatively, place the onions on a baking sheet and cook under a broiler set on high for 1 to 2 minutes or until the desired char is achieved. Set aside until ready to assemble the dish.

ASSEMBLE THE DISH

7. Divide the sliced steak between 2 warmed plates and sprinkle with some flaky sea salt. Spoon some of the Chimichurri Sauce on top of the steak, drizzle with the reserved steak butter, and sprinkle with smoked salt and black pepper. Serve with the Potato Puree, Grilled Vidalia Onions, and more Chimichurri Sauce on the side.

Make It Faster *This is a dish that actually comes together pretty quickly, and the Chimichurri Sauce is easy to throw together and can be made ahead of time; just remember to wait until serving to add the sherry vinegar. You can always follow your preferred potato puree recipe if the one here seems a bit too involved.*

+ The reason you add vinegar to the chimichurri at the last minute is because the vinegar, if allowed to rest too long, will ruin the bright green color of the sauce.

SERVES 2 Sometimes restaurant presentation isn't realistic for the home cook. But at other times, breathtaking presentation just *looks* complicated and can be easily done in a home kitchen. We do an amazing presentation of this rack of lamb in the restaurant, and it's dead simple to re-create at home for your guests. All you need is a lot of sea salt to create a crust for the lamb. The salt layer creates a perfect encasing for a flavorful, moist lamb, every time. And when your guests crack the salt crust, they will become instantly hungry from the fragrant steam coming off the lamb.

FOR THE TOMATO CONSERVE

3 tablespoons coriander seeds

Concassé of 3 tomatoes (see page 394) or 3 tomatoes, seeded and coarsely chopped

Concassé of 3 green tomatoes (see page 394) or 3 green tomatoes, seeded and coarsely chopped

1 cup unseasoned rice wine vinegar

½ cup packed light brown sugar

2 tablespoons chopped fresh ginger

1 cinnamon stick

1 fresh or ½ dried bay leaf

Kosher salt

1 teaspoon Chios spice mix (see Sources, page 403) or a blend of dried tarragon, parsley, basil, and bit of mint

2 tablespoons chiffonade of fresh mint

FOR THE ASPARAGUS

24 spears pencil-thin asparagus, trimmed

Extra-virgin olive oil

Kosher salt

Freshly ground black pepper

FOR THE POTATO AND SPRING ONION PUREE

2 large Idaho potatoes, scrubbed

2 large Yukon Gold potatoes, scrubbed

1 head garlic, halved

Kosher salt

5 spring onion bulbs

2 cups heavy cream

6 sprigs fresh thyme

1 cup whole milk, plus more as needed (see Make It Faster below)

8 ounces (16 tablespoons) unsalted butter, diced

FOR THE SALT-CRUSTED LAMB

4 cups coarse sea salt

1 cup kosher salt

2 tablespoons chopped fresh rosemary plus 4 sprigs fresh rosemary

2 tablespoons chopped garlic

2 tablespoons minced Preserved Meyer Lemons (see page 403) or store-bought

2 large egg whites (about ¼ cup)

4 sprigs fresh mint

One (2½- to 3-pound) rack of lamb, chin bone removed and frenched

6 sprigs thyme

2 fresh or 1 dried bay leaves

TO ASSEMBLE THE DISH

1 recipe Lamb Jus (see Small Game Jus, page 383; use lamb bones)

Chive oil (see page 395) or extra-virgin olive oil

Micro red veined sorrel, (see Sources, page 403); optional

MAKE THE TOMATO CONSERVE

1. In a small skillet, toast the coriander seeds over low heat until fragrant, about 3 minutes. Transfer the toasted coriander to a mortar and pestle and crack the seeds. In a nonreactive medium saucepot, combine the toasted coriander, tomatoes, rice wine vinegar, brown sugar, ginger, cinnamon stick, bay leaf, and a pinch of salt and bring to a simmer over medium heat. Reduce the heat to low and cook until the mixture has a syrupy consistency, about 20 minutes. Transfer the mixture to a medium nonreactive container, and fold in the Chios and mint. Cover and allow the conserve to cool to room temperature.

+ Contrary to a common restaurant practice, I don't like to blanch asparagus before grilling or broiling it. I prefer the taste of slightly charred asparagus that hasn't been blanched.

2. Drizzle the asparagus with olive oil and toss to lightly coat. Season with salt and pepper. Light a grill or preheat a grill pan. Grill the asparagus over medium-high heat for 2 minutes, turning once. Alternatively, preheat a broiler, and place the asparagus on a baking sheet. Broil the asparagus for 1 minute or until lightly charred.

MAKE THE POTATO AND SPRING ONION PUREE

3. Because the potatoes will finish cooking at different times, you will need to use two pots. Place the Idaho potatoes in one pot and the Yukon Golds in another. Place a garlic half in each pot. Cover the potatoes with cold water and generously salt the water—it should taste like seawater. Bring to a simmer over medium heat and cook until the potatoes are fork-tender. Start checking on the potatoes after 20 minutes.

4. While the potatoes are cooking, julienne the spring onions. In a medium saucepot, combine the onions with the cream and a pinch of salt. Tie the thyme sprigs into a bundle and add to the onion-cream mixture. Bring the mixture to a simmer over medium heat, reduce the heat to low, and cook until the onions are soft, about 15 minutes. Strain the mixture through a fine-mesh strainer and discard the thyme. Discard the cream or reserve it to use in place of the milk for the puree. Transfer the onions to a blender, puree until smooth, and set them aside. In a small pot, bring the milk to a boil over medium heat, remove from the heat, and set aside.

5. Drain the cooked potatoes, and while they are still hot, peel them, either wearing latex gloves or using two forks. If peeling with forks, hold one potato securely with a fork while pulling the skin off with the other. While the potatoes are hot, push them through a food mill into a large bowl or mash them finely with a potato masher or a fork. Using a hand (or a stand) mixer fitted with a whisk, whip the potatoes until fluffy. Work quickly: The potatoes must not get cold. Add the pureed spring onions and whisk to incorporate. Piece by piece, whisk in the butter. If the mixture starts to get stiff, add a splash of the warm milk or the reserved onion-infused cream, and continue whisking and adding in the butter until no more butter remains. You may need more warm milk than what you have on hand, depending on the size and starch content of the potatoes.

6. Pass the mixture through a fine-mesh strainer directly into a pot. Season to taste with salt, and place a piece of buttered parchment paper over the potatoes. Keep warm.

MAKE THE SALT-CRUSTED LAMB

7. While the potatoes cook, preheat the oven to 375°F; position a rack in the middle. In a medium bowl, mix together the salts, chopped rosemary, garlic, Preserved Lemons, and egg whites. Add enough water so that the mixture resembles wet sand. Spread some of the salt crust over a Silpat- or parchment paper–lined baking sheet in a layer wide enough for the lamb to rest on, and place the rosemary and mint sprigs over the salt crust layer. Place the lamb on top, top with the thyme and bay leaves, and bury the rest of the lamb in the salt mixture, leaving the bones sticking out at the top. Wrap the bones in foil (to prevent them from burning) and transfer the lamb to the oven. Bake the lamb for 25 minutes or until a meat thermometer registers 115°F when inserted into the center of the lamb. Transfer the lamb to a cooling rack and let rest for at least 10 minutes.

8. When ready to serve, bring the lamb tableside and use a spoon or the back of a knife to crack the salt crust and dust any excess salt off the meat. Reserve any juices that pool.

ASSEMBLE THE DISH

9. Divide the lamb chops and asparagus among 4 warmed plates. Add the Lamb Jus, and drizzle the chive oil over the lamb and asparagus. Spoon some Potato and Spring Onion Puree on the side and sprinkle sorrel leaves, if using, around the plate.

Make It Faster *The puree here is a restaurant-style potato puree. To make this faster and a bit easier at home, peel and roughly chop the potatoes, cook them in salted boiling water, and after draining them, mash them with pieces of butter and warm milk. Broil the asparagus and make the lamb. Skip the chive oil and use your best extra-virgin olive oil to finish the plate. It will still taste absolutely delicious and is a perfect weeknight dinner option.*

PAT LAFRIEDA MEAT PURVEYORS

PAT LAFRIEDA

For me, working with Pat LaFrieda goes beyond a mere business relationship. He and his company proved to be a lifeline when my restaurant was struggling financially and we owed some purveyors—including him—a lot of money. But instead of pulling his business, Pat stuck with us and patiently waited for us to pay our debts. I don't think I can ever properly express my gratitude to Pat for going beyond the "it's not personal—it's business" practice and treating me and my staff with so much consideration. I'll always, *always* be grateful.

On any given day, Pat's company deals with hundreds of restaurants and makes more than eight hundred deliveries. LaFrieda works with hundreds of farms across the country, selecting only those farms that have the highest standards in raising and slaughtering animals. Most of their beef and pork is harvested out of one facility using the Temple Grandin method, which has shown to cause animals the least amount of distress before slaughter.

The original LaFrieda meat business got its start in Italy in the late 1800s with Pat LaFrieda's great-grandfather. As a kid, he learned the trade in Naples, and then in 1906 brought his wife and children to the United States and opened up retail butcher shops in Queens and Brooklyn. In the 1920s, one of his sons started a restaurant supply company, which became LaFrieda Meats, which, eventually, was passed on to his younger brother, Pat, who was Pat LaFrieda Jr.'s grandfather, then to Pat's father, and then to Pat himself, making Pat the third generation of Pat LaFrieda Meat Purveyors.

The meat industry is not glamorous: the hours, the temperature in the meat lockers—it's a tough environment, and Pat's father was hoping his son would finally get to leave the meat business and pursue an easier lifestyle. Starting at the age of ten and all through high school, Pat helped his father at work on weekends. His father would take him to a slaughterhouse, which was his way of trying to scare Pat out of the business. And it worked to a point, but at the same time, it appealed to Pat. "My family was in the business of supplying good meat to restaurants—there's no downside to our trade."

Pat went on to prep schools and then to college, and then on to Wall Street where he was a stockbroker. He thought he'd love it, but instead he found himself hating every single minute. He missed being cold in the meat lockers and he hated the corporate culture of banking. So Pat left the job he hated and returned to the family trade. He was well prepared for what awaited him. In college, he had joined the Army Reserves, where he learned a strong work ethic. He knew he could handle the late hours, how to beat sleep deprivation and work all night. At first, Pat's father resisted it, but eventually gave in and allowed Pat to come on board full-time. And since Pat has been growing the company business at a steady 15 percent per year, his father is far from complaining. In fact, he's probably glad things worked out the way they did.

PAT LAFRIEDA

SERVES 4 When I was living in France, one of my favorite snacks was merguez on a baguette. They used to sell them at the summer *fêtes* (festivals) filled with French fries and lightly coated with mayo. Ever since that summer, I had wanted to incorporate merguez into a dish where it played a prominent role. If you don't feel like making the whole thing, the orzo salad, on its own, makes a fantastic summer lunch or a dinner side.

FOR THE LAMB BELLY

1 recipe The Cure
(see page 391)

1 lamb belly (about
3½ pounds)

2 tablespoons Activa (see
Sources, page 403)

2 tablespoons chopped
fresh curly parsley

1 tablespoon chopped
fresh rosemary

2 teaspoons chopped garlic

1 teaspoon cracked
black peppercorns

1 sprig rosemary
(for non-sous-vide
cooking; see step 3)

Olive oil (for non-sous-
vide cooking; see step 3)

2 cups all-purpose flour

Kosher salt

Freshly ground black pepper

2 cups whole milk

4 large eggs

3 cups bread crumbs

Canola oil

FOR THE BLACK OLIVE SALT

1 cup oil-cured black olives

FOR THE MERGUEZ

1 pound lamb belly,
coarsely diced

¼ cup harissa

3 tablespoons extra-
virgin olive oil

1 garlic clove

2 tablespoons kosher
salt, plus additional

1 teaspoon pink curing salt

Canola oil

FOR THE FETA BALLS

10 sheets gelatin

500 grams feta cheese

240 grams feta liquid

25 grams methylcelluose
F50 (see Sources, page 403)

FOR THE ORZO SALAD

3 cups orzo

Extra-virgin olive oil

4 cups Chicken Stock (see
page 382) or store-bought

1 fresh or ½ dried bay leaf

Kosher salt

2 tablespoons sherry vinegar

¼ cup Oven-Dried
Tomatoes (see page 398)
or sun-dried tomatoes

2 tablespoons minced Lemon
Confit peel (see page 386)
or finely grated lemon zest

¼ cup chopped oil-
cured black olives

12 leaves dandelion greens

3 tablespoons chopped
fresh curly parsley

FOR THE LAMB LOIN

Extra-virgin olive oil

One (3-pound) lamb loin,
preferably Colorado lamb

2 ounces (4 tablespoons)
unsalted butter

4 sprigs fresh thyme

1 head garlic, halved

TO ASSEMBLE THE DISH

Extra-virgin olive oil

MAKE THE LAMB BELLY

1. Rub The Cure all over the lamb belly. Refrigerate, un-covered, for 3 hours. Rinse the belly under cold water and pat dry. Gently pound the belly and sprinkle the flesh side with the Activa. In a small bowl, combine the parsley, rosemary, garlic, and peppercorns, and rub the mixture all over the flesh side of the belly. Make a roll with the belly so that the flesh side is on the inside and, using kitchen twine, tie firmly to secure. Refrigerate for at least 6 hours so that the Activa sets.

> ✚ The reason we lay out warm food over parchment paper on metal baking sheets is that sometimes the metal imparts a slightly metallic taste to the food. Parchment paper helps to keep the flavors pure.

2. SOUS-VIDE COOKING INSTRUCTIONS (see step 3 for Sous-Vide Alternative Instructions): Fill an immersion circulator with water and preheat to 180°F. Place the lamb belly in a vacuum-seal bag, seal the bag, and poach the belly for 8 hours.

3. SOUS-VIDE ALTERNATIVE INSTRUCTIONS: Preheat the oven to 300°F; position the rack in the middle. Place the lamb belly in a Dutch oven, add the rosemary, and cover completely with olive oil. Cook the lamb belly for 3 hours or until the meat is tender.

4. When the lamb belly is cooked, remove from either the immersion circulator or the oven, and let cool until the meat is warm to the touch. Slice the lamb belly into ¾-inch-thick slices.

5. When ready to serve, set up a breading station. Place the flour in a tray and season with salt and pepper. In another tray, lightly beat the milk and eggs together until combined. Place the bread crumbs in a third tray and season to taste with salt. Dredge the lamb belly slices in the seasoned flour, then in the egg wash, letting the excess drip off, and, finally, in the bread crumbs.

6. Add enough canola oil to a large sauté pan to cover the bottom of the pan and set over medium heat. Warm the oil until it shimmers. Add the breaded belly slices and fry until lightly toasted on both sides, 2 to 3 minutes per side. Transfer the slices to a parchment paper–lined tray.

MAKE THE BLACK OLIVE SALT

7. While the Activa sets the lamb belly, preheat the oven to 350°F; position the rack in the middle. Lay the olives out on a shallow, parchment paper–lined baking pan, transfer to the oven, turn the oven off, and leave overnight. In the morning, your olives should be toasted and dried out.

8. Transfer the olives to the bowl of a food processor fitted with a metal blade and pulse until the olives resemble the texture of coarse sea salt. Transfer the ground olives back to the baking pan and let sit, in a dry place, for 2 hours. Set aside until ready to use.

MAKE THE MERGUEZ

9. While the Activa sets the lamb belly, in a large non-reactive bowl, combine the diced lamb belly, harissa, olive oil, and garlic. Cover and refrigerate overnight. The next day, using the small die on the meat grinder, grind the mixture. Season the meat with the kosher and pink salts and form a small patty. (If you don't have a meat grinder, ask your butcher to grind the meat. Combine the ground meat with the harissa, olive oil, and minced garlic clove, and cover and refrigerate overnight. Season with the salts the following day.)

10. Add enough canola oil to a small sauté pan to cover the bottom of the pan and set it over high heat. Just before it starts to smoke, add the patty and cook until it is well browned and cooked through, 2 to 3 minutes. Taste the patty and adjust the seasonings, if necessary, in the remaining merguez mixture. If necessary, repeat the test-patty cooking process. When your seasonings are where you want them, refrigerate the meat until ready to use.

MAKE THE FETA BALLS

11. In a medium bowl, bloom the gelatin in ice water for 2 minutes. Meanwhile, place the feta cheese and feta liquid in a blender and blend on high until smooth. Add the methylcellulose to the blender and blend until combined.

12. Remove the gelatin sheets from the ice water and wring out all of the excess moisture. Place the gelatin in a bowl set on top of a pot of simmering water until the gelatin is completely melted, about 2 minutes. Add the melted gelatin to the blender and blend on high until combined.

13. Pour the mixture into a mixing bowl and freeze for 1 hour.

14. Using your hands, form the mixture into small, golf ball–size balls (about 45 grams each), and wrap each feta ball tightly in plastic wrap; keep frozen until needed. When ready to serve, bring a pot of water to a boil and gently slide the feta balls into the boiling water, still in the plastic wrap, and cook for about 2 minutes.

MAKE THE ORZO SALAD

15. Preheat the oven to 350°F; position the rack in the middle. In a large bowl, toss the orzo with just enough olive oil to coat and spread it out in an even layer on a shallow baking tray. Bake for 3 to 5 minutes or until lightly toasted. This is a very important step: The orzo needs to be toasted.

16. While the orzo is toasting, in a 4-quart pot, bring the stock and bay leaf to a boil and season with salt. Add the toasted orzo to the stock, reduce the heat to medium, and cook until orzo is tender, 5 to 7 minutes. Drain the orzo, toss with a drizzle of extra-virgin olive oil to prevent sticking, and lay it out in a flat layer on parchment paper. Set aside.

17. When ready to serve, add enough oil to a large sauté pan to cover the bottom of the pan and set it over high heat. Just before the oil starts to smoke, add the Merguez mixture in one large "patty" and cook until the edges begin to caramelize, 2 to 3 minutes. Be vigilant: The spices in harissa will burn if you do not pay attention. Once the merguez has slightly browned on the bottom, break the sausage up into smaller pieces. Once all of the meat is browned, add the toasted orzo and toss the mixture together. Add the sherry vinegar and deglaze the pan, scraping the brown bits off the bottom of the pan with a wooden spoon. Add the Oven-Dried Tomatoes and Lemon Confit peel. Just before serving, transfer the salad to a large bowl and fold in the olives, dandelion greens, and parsley.

MAKE THE LAMB LOIN

18. About 30 minutes before serving, preheat the oven to 350°F; position the rack in the middle. Add enough oil to a large sauté pan to cover the bottom of the pan and set it over high heat. Just before the oil starts to smoke, add the lamb loin and sear for 1 minute. Reduce the heat to medium, and cook until the bottom is browned, 4 to 6 minutes. Add the butter, thyme, and garlic to the pan and baste for 1 minute.

19. Transfer the lamb to a roasting pan with a rack and pour about two-thirds of the rendered lamb fat over the meat (reserve the remaining fat). Bake for 12 to 14 minutes or until a thermometer inserted into the center of the lamb registers 115°F. Transfer the lamb to a carving board and let the meat rest for 15 minutes before slicing.

ASSEMBLE THE DISH

20. Slice and arrange the lamb loin on 4 warm plates. Divide the Orzo Salad among the plates. Unwrap the Feta Balls, place them on top of the Orzo Salad, and drizzle with olive oil. Finish with the Lamb Belly and Black Olive Salt.

+ Activa is a coagulant, helping the meat to become glued to itself. It's used in restaurant presentations. If you're making this at home and you don't want to use it or can't find it, skip it, but take extra care to make sure that the meat stays put.

VEAL TENDERLOIN + BOUDIN NOIR + SALT-AND-PEPPER FINGERLINGS + SPRING GARLIC + PORCINI + MUSTARD REDUCTION

SERVES 4 When we first opened the restaurant, we didn't have an immersion circulator for the first five months. We simply couldn't afford anything extra. The absence of the immersion circulator would suggest that sous-vide cooking was out of our reach, but we didn't let it derail us. We simply made our own, makeshift immersion circulator by poaching the meat in a reliable bag in softly simmering water and keeping a constant eye on the thermometer, adding cubes of ice to the water whenever the temperature would start to climb. And it worked out fine. The tenderloin in this recipe needs to be cooked sous-vide to set, so if, like most people, you don't own an immersion circulator, the makeshift sous-vide method will work very well for you here. This is our signature meat course for the tasting menu. It started off with the sausage being stuffed inside the tenderloin, which is a pretty classic move. But I wanted to try something different: We were making our own breakfast sausage—and it had no casing. The first time we did it, in the winter of 2011, we used water instead of blood, but like the version with the blood better, so this is the version we offer here. While this isn't traditional boudin noir, we liked our creation so much, we decided to keep it.

FOR THE MUSTARD REDUCTION

3 tablespoons canola oil

Veal scraps from tenderloin

¾ cup chopped button mushrooms

3 shallots, sliced

1 garlic clove, chopped

2 tablespoons whole black peppercorns

1 tablespoon granulated sugar

½ cup red wine vinegar, plus more as needed

4 cups dry red wine

1 cup ruby port

1 sprig fresh thyme

1 fresh or ½ dried bay leaf

4 cups Veal Stock (see page 382) or store-bought

1 cup Chicken Stock (see page 382) or store-bought

Kosher salt

1 ounce (2 tablespoons) unsalted butter

1 tablespoon grainy mustard

FOR THE PEARL ONIONS

1 cup red pearl onions, peeled and halved

½ cup red wine vinegar

1 tablespoon cracked black peppercorns

2 teaspoons kosher salt

1 teaspoon granulated sugar

1 fresh or ½ dried bay leaf

FOR THE FINGERLING POTATOES

1 pound fingerling potatoes

8 sprigs fresh thyme

3 fresh or 1½ dried bay leaves

2 ounces (4 tablespoons) unsalted butter

5 garlic cloves, unpeeled

2 tablespoons Blended Oil (see page 395)

Kosher salt

Freshly ground black pepper

FOR THE TENDERLOINS

One (454-gram / 1-pound) pork belly

5 garlic cloves: 2 peeled, 3 unpeeled

100 grams pork blood (ask your butcher)

20 grams kosher salt

20 grams Vadouvan curry powder (see Sources, page 403)

15 grams Chios spice mix (see Sources, page 403)

20 grams ground cinnamon

3 tablespoons chopped fresh curly parsley

120 grams Activa (optional)

2 (283-gram / 10-ounce) veal tenderloins

Canola oil

43 grams (3 tablespoons) unsalted butter

2 sprigs fresh thyme

1 sprig fresh rosemary

1 cup chopped fresh
curly parsley

3 tablespoons
minced shallots

2 tablespoons chopped
fresh rosemary

1 tablespoon chopped
fresh thyme

1 garlic clove, minced

1 teaspoon pink
peppercorns, crushed

Extra-virgin olive oil

FOR THE GRILLED GREEN
GARLIC

4 stalks green garlic

Extra-virgin olive oil

Kosher salt

Freshly ground black pepper

FOR THE PORCINI
MUSHROOMS

1 pound small porcini
mushrooms or other
small mushrooms,
cleaned and halved

Kosher salt

Freshly ground black pepper

Canola oil

1½ ounces (3 tablespoons)
unsalted butter

1 head garlic, halved

3 sprigs fresh thyme

1 fresh or ½ dried bay leaf

½ cup dry white wine

½ cup Chicken Stock (see
page 382) or store-bought

TO ASSEMBLE THE DISH

1½ ounces (3 tablespoons)
unsalted butter

1 tablespoon chopped
fresh curly parsley

12 celery leaves

Flaky sea salt, such
as Maldon

MAKE THE MUSTARD REDUCTION

1. While the Tenderloins cook, in a 3-quart saucepot, warm
the oil over medium heat until shimmering. Add the
veal scraps and cook until nicely browned, 5 minutes.
Add the mushrooms, shallots, and garlic, and cook until
the shallots are translucent, about 4 minutes. Add the
peppercorns and cook for 1 minute. Stir in the sugar and
cook 1 more minute. Add the vinegar and deglaze the
pan, scraping the brown bits off the bottom of the pan
using a wooden spoon. Cook until the pan is dry, and
add the wine, port, thyme, and bay leaf. Raise the heat
to medium-high and cook until the liquid has reduced
by about half, about 20 minutes. Add the stocks and
cook until the liquid has reduced to about 2 cups and
has the consistency of syrup. Strain through a fine-mesh
strainer, return the reduction to the stove over medium
heat, and skim off any excess fat, tilting the pot slightly
to make it easier to skim. Season to taste with salt, and
taste for balance—you may want to add a bit more vinegar depending on your preferences. Strain the sauce
again and set aside. You will have about 3 cups of sauce;
you need 1 cup of sauce for this recipe. The rest can be
frozen and used another time you make the dish, or
served with another meat dish.

2. When ready to serve, warm the reduction over medium
heat, and whisk in the 2 tablespoons of butter until
emulsified. Stir in the mustard until fully incorporated.
Set aside.

MAKE THE PEARL ONIONS

3. While the Mustard Reduction is cooking, add the onions to a nonreactive bowl.

4. In a nonreactive saucepot, combine the vinegar, pepper, salt, sugar, and bay leaf with ¼ cup of water, and
bring to a boil. Pour the marinade over the onions, and
let stand at room temperature for at least 1 hour before
serving.

MAKE THE FINGERLING POTATOES

5. Bring a medium pot of salted water to a boil. Add the
potatoes, 4 sprigs of the thyme, and 2 fresh or 1 dried
bay leaves, and cook at an active simmer over medium
heat until the potatoes are fork-tender. Strain, and
while the potatoes are hot, peel the potatoes using a
paring knife (you may need to wear latex gloves).

6. Transfer the potatoes to a large skillet, add the butter, garlic, and Blended Oil, and raise the heat to medium-high. Once the butter begins to brown, lower the heat to medium so it does not burn, add the remaining 4 sprigs thyme, and roll the potatoes in the butter, so that they are browned all the way around. Season with salt and pepper and once the potatoes are crispy all the way around, remove from the heat and set aside.

MAKE THE TENDERLOINS

7. Using a meat grinder or a meat grinding attachment to your stand mixer, grind the pork belly and 2 peeled garlic cloves to medium grind. (Alternatively, you can ask your butcher to grind your pork and combine it with finely minced garlic at home.)

8. In a stand mixer fitted with a paddle attachment, whip the ground pork and slowly add the blood to emulsify. Add the salt, curry, Chios, cinnamon, parsley, and Activa, if using, and mix for another 5 seconds or so, just to combine.

9. Trim the tails and tops off the tenderloins so that they are about the size of a cigar (you should have about 3 per tenderloin. Reserve the scraps for the Mustard Reduction; see recipe below). Place a large piece of plastic wrap on the counter. Make a 7 x 3-inch rectangle out of the blood sausage meat on the plastic wrap. Place the tenderloin pieces, with ½ inch in between, in the center, and sprinkle enough Activa, if using, to cover the meat. Roll the meat into a tight cylinder, wrap with the plastic wrap, and tie the ends tightly. Repeat with more blood sausage and the other tenderloin pieces.

10. SOUS-VIDE COOKING INSTRUCTIONS (see step 11 for Sous-Vide Alternative Instructions): Fill an immersion circulator with water and preheat to 140°F. Place the tenderloins in 2 vacuum-seal bags, seal the bags, and poach the veal for 2 hours. Transfer the tenderloins to an ice bath and allow the meat to cool, in the bag, for at least 10 minutes or until ready to assemble the dish.

11. SOUS-VIDE ALTERNATIVE INSTRUCTIONS: Place the wrapped tenderloins into a resealable plastic bag and squeeze out as much air as possible. Fill a pot halfway with water and over medium heat, bring the water to 140°F. Reduce the heat to its lowest setting, place the resealable bag in the water, and carefully watch the thermometer so that the temperature of the water remains around 140°F. Have a bowl of ice cubes ready so that you can add them to the water when the temperature starts to go above 140°F. Cook for about 2 hours; then transfer the bag to an ice bath and allow the meat to cool, in the bag, for at least 10 minutes or until ready to assemble the dish.

12. When ready to serve, add enough oil to a large sauté pan to cover the bottom of the pan and set it over high heat. Just before the oil starts to smoke, remove the tenderloins from the sealed bags, pat them dry, and add them to the pan, seam side down. Reduce the heat to medium and add the butter, 3 unpeeled garlic cloves, thyme, and rosemary. Baste the tenderloins for 2 minutes and remove from the pan. Let the meat rest for 10 minutes before slicing. Pour some of the pan drippings over the meat and discard the remainder.

MAKE THE MEAT MARINADE

13. While the tenderloins cook and the Mustard Reduction reduces, in a small bowl, combine the parsley, shallots, rosemary, thyme, garlic, and peppercorns. Add enough extra-virgin olive oil to cover the mixture and create a slurry. Set aside.

MAKE THE GRILLED GREEN GARLIC

14. Trim the garlic stalks, removing any dirt and tough outer layers. Cut the stalks into 5-inch pieces. Rinse the garlic under cold, running water and transfer to a container or a resealable plastic bag. Add the Meat Marinade and let the garlic sit at room temperature for 1 hour.

15. Remove the garlic from the marinade and season with olive oil, salt, and pepper. Light a grill or preheat a grill pan. Grill the garlic over high heat, turning occasionally, until slightly charred and cooked through, 4 to 6 minutes. Alternatively, place the garlic under a broiler for 1 minute or until slightly charred. Remove from the heat, cut on the bias into 1-inch pieces, and set aside.

MAKE THE PORCINI MUSHROOMS

16. Season the mushrooms with salt and pepper. Add enough oil to a large sauté pan to cover the bottom of the pan and set it over high heat. Just before the oil starts to smoke, add the mushrooms and reduce the heat to medium. Once the mushrooms begin to sear, add the butter, garlic, thyme, and bay leaf, and toss together to combine. Cook, stirring from time to time, until the butter begins to brown. Add the wine and deglaze the pan, scraping the brown bits off the bottom of the pan using a wooden spoon. Cook until the pan is dry, 5 to 8 minutes; add the stock and cook until the stock reduces and the pan is dry, 5 to 8 minutes. Transfer the mushrooms to a parchment paper–lined tray and set aside in a warm place until ready to use.

ASSEMBLE THE DISH

17. When ready to serve, while the Tenderloins rest, return the sauté pan to the stovetop, add the butter, and over medium heat, add the Porcini Mushrooms and Fingerling Potatoes, and stir gently from time to time until warmed through. Add the Grilled Green Garlic and Pearl Onions and cook, stirring gently, until warmed through.

18. Slice the tenderloins into 12 pieces and divide evenly among 4 warmed plates. Add the Fingerling Potatoes, Grilled Green Garlic, Pearl Onions, and Porcini Mushrooms. Stir the parsley into the Mustard Reduction and drizzle the reduction and tenderloin pan drippings around, garnish with the celery leaves, and sprinkle some flaky sea salt to finish.

HAMPSHIRE PORK TENDERLOIN + SPECK + MUSTARD GREENS + GNOCCHI À LA ROMAINE

SERVES 4 When many see the word *gnocchi*, they think only of potato gnocchi, but gnocchi, which means "dumplings" in Italian, don't need to contain potatoes at all. They can be, and are frequently, made with regular or semolina flour, and, at times not very much of it either. Ricotta gnocchi, for example, contain either very little flour or none at all.

The gnocchi here are done in the Roman style, with semolina flour. Since most people don't keep pork scraps at home, ask your butcher if he has any scraps lying around, or ask for the cheapest cut of pork—which is usually the belly or the shoulder. To slightly expedite this at home, ask your butcher to dice the meat for you.

FOR THE PORK JUS

Canola oil

1 pound pork scraps, chopped into large pieces and fat trimmed

4 chicken wings

1 large carrot, diced

1 large celery stalk, diced

1 large onion, diced

1 firm, tart apple, preferably Honeycrisp

3 tablespoons whole black peppercorns

2 teaspoons kosher salt, plus more as needed

2 tablespoons cider vinegar

1 tablespoon sugar

1 tablespoon tomato paste

3 cups Chicken Stock (see page 382) or store-bought

1 cup Veal Stock (see page 382) or store-bought

3 sprigs fresh thyme

1 sprig fresh rosemary

1 cinnamon stick

1 fresh or ½ dried bay leaf

FOR THE GNOCCHI

2 cups whole milk

2 cups Chicken Stock (see page 382) or store bought

1 sprig fresh rosemary

1 cup polenta, preferably Sclafani brand

Kosher salt

¾ cup grated Parmigiano-Reggiano, plus more as needed

1 tablespoon chopped fresh curly parsley

1 teaspoon red pepper flakes

FOR THE TENDERLOIN

12 slices speck

3 tablespoons chopped fresh chives

Freshly ground black pepper

4 (6-ounce) trimmed Hampshire pork tenderloins

Blended Oil (see page 395)

2 ounces (4 tablespoons) unsalted butter

4 garlic cloves, unpeeled

1 sprig fresh rosemary

2 sprigs fresh thyme

FOR THE MUSTARD GREENS

Blended Oil (see page 395)

2 tablespoons chopped bacon

1 ounce (2 tablespoons) unsalted butter

2 garlic cloves, sliced

1 pound mustard greens, roughly chopped

1 teaspoon red pepper flakes

Kosher salt

TO ASSEMBLE THE DISH

Petite mustard greens (optional)

Smoked salt (see Sources, page 403)

MAKE THE PORK JUS

1. Preheat the oven to 400°F; position the rack in the middle. In a roasting pan set over two burners on high heat, warm enough oil to cover the bottom of the pan. Just before it starts to smoke, add the pork and wings, and transfer the pan to the oven. Roast the meat for about 20 minutes or until nicely caramelized.

2. Return the roasting pan to the stovetop, and over medium heat, add the carrot, celery, onion, apple, peppercorns, and salt, and deglaze the pan, scraping the brown bits off the bottom of the pan with a wooden spoon. Cook for 4 to 5 minutes or until the vegetables soften a bit. Add the vinegar and sugar and cook until the pan is dry, 2 to 4 minutes.

3. Stir in the tomato paste, and transfer the contents to a large stockpot. Add the stocks and 2 cups of water, and simmer over medium-high heat, skimming off the initial foam that forms at the surface. Bring the liquid to a boil, reduce the heat to low, and simmer, uncovered, until the liquid has the consistency of a thick sauce, about 2 hours. Taste and adjust the seasonings if needed.

4. Remove the pot from the heat and add the thyme, rosemary, cinnamon stick, and bay leaf. Wrap the top of the pot tightly with plastic wrap and let the jus infuse for 1 hour. The moisture that will gather inside will make it look like it is raining. Strain the liquid through a fine-mesh strainer and return it to the stockpot. Return the pot to the stovetop over medium heat and bring the liquid to a simmer. Skim off any excess fat that rises to the surface, remove from the heat, and set aside until ready to use.

5. Just before serving, warm the Pork Jus over medium heat until almost simmering.

MAKE THE GNOCCHI

6. In a 2-quart saucepot, combine the milk, stock, and rosemary and bring to a boil. Reduce the heat to low so that the milk is gently simmering, and discard the rosemary. Whisk in the polenta and a generous pinch of salt. Cook the polenta, whisking constantly, until it is no longer grainy (instant polenta will be immediately smooth). Remove from the heat, and whisk in the Parmigiano-Reggiano.

7. Spray 2 Silpats or pieces of parchment paper with non-stick cooking spray and place one in a baking pan. Pour the polenta over, and smooth out the top with an offset spatula. Place the second Silpat or piece of parchment paper over the polenta, sprayed side down, and place

another baking pan on top, gently pressing down to smooth out the top of the polenta. Transfer the pans to the refrigerator for about 4 hours or until set. Remove the trays from the refrigerator and invert the bottom tray onto a kitchen counter to release the polenta.

8. Using a 2-inch ring cutter, cut out 8 discs or make half-moons (by cutting each disc in half) of polenta and set aside on a Silpat- or parchment paper–lined tray. Sprinkle some more Parmigiano-Reggiano on top.

9. When ready to serve, preheat the broiler on high and broil the gnocchi until the cheese is bubbling and the gnocchi are heated through, 1 to 2 minutes. Sprinkle the parsley and red pepper flakes on top.

MAKE THE TENDERLOIN

10. SOUS-VIDE COOKING INSTRUCTIONS (see step 12 for Sous-Vide Alternative Instructions): Fill an immersion circulator with water and heat the water to 140°F. Place a piece of plastic wrap on a kitchen counter. Place 3 pieces of speck on top of the wrap, slightly overlapping one another. Make sure that the fat faces in the same direction. Sprinkle about one-quarter of the chives over the speck and add a pinch of black pepper. Place a tenderloin at the bottom of the speck strip, and roll the tenderloin in the strip. Wrap the tenderloin-speck roll tightly in the plastic wrap and twist the ends to make a compact "log." Repeat with the remaining speck, chives, pepper, and tenderloins.

11. Transfer the tenderloins into vacuum-seal bags, seal the bags, and place them in the immersion circulator. Poach the meat for 2 hours. Immediately transfer the bags to an ice bath until they cool completely and refrigerate. When ready to sear the pork, remove from the fridge at least 20 minutes before

12. SOUS-VIDE ALTERNATIVE INSTRUCTIONS: Preheat the oven to 350°F; position the rack in the middle. Add enough Blended Oil to a large ovenproof sauté pan to cover the bottom of the pan and set it over high heat. Just before the oil starts to smoke, add the tenderloins (you may have to do this in 2 batches) and sear each side until nicely browned, about 4 minutes per side. Transfer the pan to the oven and cook the meat for about 10 minutes

or until the meat reaches an internal temperature of 125°F to 130°F on a meat thermometer. Transfer the meat to a plate and allow the tenderloins to rest in a warm place for at least 10 minutes.

13. When ready to serve, add enough Blended Oil to a large sauté pan to cover the bottom of the pan and set it over high heat. Just before the oil starts to smoke, unwrap the pork tenderloins and add them to the pan; reduce the heat immediately. If the meat was cooked sous-vide, cook the tenderloins until nicely browned before adding the butter, garlic, rosemary, and thyme, and baste with the butter for 1 minute. If the meat has been seared and roasted, immediately add the butter, garlic, rosemary, and thyme, and baste the tenderloins for 1 minute. Transfer the meat from the pan onto a plate set in a warm place (such as on top of an oven that's been warmed and turned off), and let the tenderloins sit for at least 5 minutes before serving. Reserve the butter from the pan.

MAKE THE MUSTARD GREENS

14. Add enough Blended Oil to a medium skillet to cover the bottom of the pan and set it over high heat. Just before the oil starts to smoke, add the bacon and butter, reduce the heat to medium, and cook until the bacon is crispy, 4 to 6 minutes. Add the garlic and cook until the garlic is toasted, about 1 minute; the garlic cooks very quickly so watch it carefully. Add the mustard greens, red pepper flakes, a few pinches of salt, and 1 tablespoon of water. Stir to distribute, and cook until the greens are wilted and the water has evaporated, about 1 minute. Transfer the contents of the pan to a paper towel–lined plate and set aside.

ASSEMBLE THE DISH

15. Divide the mustard greens among 4 warmed plates. Slice the Tenderloin and place them on top of the greens. Top with the Gnocchi, and sprinkle with some petite greens, if using, and some smoked salt. Spoon the Pork Jus around and drizzle some of the reserved pan butter on the pork.

Don't forget to baste!

BACON-CRUSTED HAMPSHIRE PORK CHOP + SMOKE-WHIPPED POTATOES + PICKLED PEPQUINO

SERVES 4 Never in a million years did I think I was going to put a deep-fried pork chop on the menu. But during the restaurant's early days, I was so busy as a meat cook that I didn't have time to sear the meat on the stovetop. Being short on kitchen staff, we decided to give deep-frying a try, and it turned out to be one of our most popular dishes—the pork chops would come out incredibly tender and juicy. And they go perfectly with some pickled pepquinos.

I was one of the first folks to get my hands on some pepquino melons from Koppert Cress (see Sources, page 403), and I thought they would make terrific pickles. If you decide to get pepquinos, make a large batch of pickles and serve them alongside anything meaty: a steak, a burger, or a nice pâté. Or you can serve your favorite pickles here in case pepquinos prove to be elusive.

FOR THE PICKLED PEPQUINO MELONS

2 cups halved pepquino melons

¼ cup sliced baby fennel

¼ cup halved, peeled red pearl onions

2 tablespoons plus ¼ teaspoon kosher salt

2 cups white wine vinegar

⅓ cup granulated sugar

¼ cup capers

2 teaspoons turmeric

3 sprigs fresh thyme

1 fresh or ½ dried bay leaf

FOR THE PORK CHOPS

½ recipe Brine (see page 389)

4 (12-ounce) bone-in Hampshire pork chops

2 cups whole milk

4 large eggs

2 cups all-purpose flour

1 teaspoon kosher salt, plus more as needed

Freshly ground black pepper

1 recipe Bacon Bread Crumbs (see page 381) or regular bread crumbs

Canola oil

FOR THE SMOKED POTATO PUREE

2 Idaho potatoes (2 pounds), scrubbed

2 large Yukon Gold potatoes (1½ pounds), scrubbed

1 head garlic, halved widthwise

6 sprigs fresh thyme

Kosher salt

2 cups Smoked Onion (see page 390)

2 cups heavy cream

2 cups whole milk, plus more as needed

8 ounces (16 tablespoons) unsalted butter, diced

1 recipe Chlorophyll (see page 389)

TO ASSEMBLE THE DISH

2 ounces (4 tablespoons) unsalted butter

2 tablespoons chopped fresh curly parsley

1 tablespoon red pepper flakes

Micro mustard greens (see Sources, page 403) or chopped fresh curly parsley (optional)

Smoked salt (see Sources, page 403) or flaky sea salt, such as Maldon

MAKE THE PICKLED PEPQUINO MELONS

1. Place the melons, fennel, and onions in a large nonreactive bowl. Sprinkle ¼ teaspoon of salt over and toss to combine. Set aside while you prepare the pickling solution.

2. In a 2-quart nonreactive pot, combine the vinegar, sugar, capers, turmeric, remaining 2 tablespoons salt, the thyme, and the bay leaf with 1 cup of water and bring to a boil over medium-high heat. Remove the pot from the heat, and immediately pour the liquid over the vegetables. Allow the vegetables and pickling liquid to come to room temperature, then cover and refrigerate overnight.

3. Pour the Brine over the meat and refrigerate for 3 hours.

4. When ready to serve, remove the pork chops from the Brine and thoroughly pat dry with paper towels. Preheat the oven to 300°F; position the rack in the middle. In a large bowl, mix together the milk and eggs. In a separate medium bowl, season the flour with 1 teaspoon of salt and some pepper. Set up a breading station. Place the seasoned flour in one tray, the milk-egg mixture in another, and the Bacon Bread Crumbs in a third tray. Dredge the chops in the flour, then the egg wash (letting the excess drip off), and finally, in the bread crumbs.

5. In a large, ovenproof sauté pan, warm 1 inch of oil over medium-high heat until it registers 350°F on a deep-frying thermometer. Fry the pork chops until the coating is crispy, 2 to 3 minutes. Alternatively, add enough oil to a sauté pan to cover the bottom of the pan and set it over high heat. Just before the oil starts to smoke, add the pork chops and cook until the coating is crispy, 2 to 3 minutes.

6. Transfer the pork chops to the oven and bake for 8 minutes or until the internal temperature of the meat registers between 125°F and 130°F on a meat thermometer. Set aside to cool.

MAKE THE SMOKED POTATO PUREE

7. Because the potatoes will be done cooking at different times, you will need to cook them separately. Place the Idaho potatoes in one pot and the Yukon Golds in another. Divide the garlic halves and thyme sprigs between the pots. Cover the potatoes with cold water and add a pinch of salt to each pot. Bring the water to a boil over high heat, reduce the heat to medium, and simmer until the potatoes are fork-tender. Start checking on the potatoes after about 20 minutes.

8. While the potatoes are cooking, place the Smoked Onion and cream in a medium pot and bring to a boil over medium-high heat. Reduce the heat to low and simmer until the onion is soft, about 7 minutes, stirring from time to time to prevent the cream from burning on the bottom. Strain the mixture; discard the cream or reserve it for another use. Transfer the onion to a blender, puree it until smooth, and set aside. Place the milk in a small pot and bring it to a boil over medium-high heat. Remove from the heat and set aside.

9. Drain the potatoes, and while hot, carefully peel them using either latex gloves or two forks. If using forks, hold a potato with one fork while pulling the skin off with the other. While the potatoes are hot, push them through a food mill into a large bowl. Add the pureed Smoked Onion to the potatoes and whisk everything together until thoroughly combined. Piece by piece, whisk in the butter. If the mixture starts to get stiff, add a splash of the warm milk, and continue whisking and adding in the butter until no more butter remains. You may need more warm milk than what you have on hand, depending on the size and the starch content of the potatoes.

10. Pass the mixture through a fine-mesh strainer directly into a pot. Season to taste with salt. Place a piece of buttered parchment paper on top of the puree, and keep warm. (You may want to finish cooking the pork chops at this point.) Right before serving, whisk in the Chlorophyll.

ASSEMBLE THE DISH

11. In a medium sauté pan set over medium heat, add the butter and cook until the solids are brown and the butter smells nutty. Remove the brown butter from the heat and whisk in 1 cup of the pepquino pickling liquid, stirring until the mixture is emulsified. Return the pan to the stovetop, and over low heat, whisk in the parsley and red pepper flakes. Remove from the heat and set aside.

12. Divide the Smoked Potato Puree among 4 warmed plates. Place a Pork Chop on top of the puree; spoon some pepquino pickles and pickling liquid on top. Scatter micro greens over (if using), and season with some smoked salt. Serve with the brown butter–pickling liquid emulsion on the side.

Make It Faster *If you're in a bind, or want to make this for a weeknight dinner, make the pork chop by brining it for a few hours in the morning before you leave for work, and then at night, make your favorite mashed potatoes and serve with whatever pickles you have on hand.*

VENISON LOIN + BLACK TRUMPET MUSHROOMS + RAISINS + GIN + KABOCHA SQUASH

SERVES 4 This was one of the dishes I made for the *Next Iron Chef* season finale. When I found out that we were cooking a Thanksgiving meal, I immediately knew I was going to be doing something to honor the Native Americans who were present at the original Thanksgiving feast.

I looked back on the previous year: a tough twelve months, both mentally and emotionally. Upon an invitation from a friend, I had started attending Native American ceremonies and they helped me to answer a lot of questions I was asking at the time. These rituals, in so many ways, put things in perspective and kept me grounded. The decision to honor Native Americans was a split-second one: I immediately remembered the advice my mom gave me when I was getting ready to leave to tape the show—"Always go with your gut." Not only did it feel right: It felt like the only choice I had. Not only did Native Americans help the Pilgrims through the first years of life on American shores, but they also helped *me* through a difficult time in my life. In a manner, this was *my* way of showing thanks.

So I cooked a Thanksgiving meal using the ingredients present at the very first Thanksgiving in 1621. Unlike the traditional Thanksgiving meal of today, the Pilgrims didn't serve turkey, cranberry sauce, or mashed potatoes. Instead, they ate venison, duck, oysters, and the like.

It was a risky move, making a truly traditional Thanksgiving meal, but I listened to my gut, and it clearly worked out for me in the end.

FOR THE STUFFING

3 tablespoons golden raisins

2 tablespoons dry gin, such as Bulldog

Olive oil

2 cups dried small-dice brioche

1 ounce (2 tablespoons) unsalted butter

8 ounces black trumpet mushrooms

2 tablespoons finely diced onions

2 tablespoons finely diced celery root

2 tablespoons chopped fresh curly parsley

2 tablespoons chopped fresh sage

1 teaspoon smoked ground cinnamon (see Sources, page 403) or plain ground cinnamon

1 tablespoon sliced garlic

¾ cup Veal Stock (see page 382) or store-bought

Kosher salt

Freshly ground black pepper

FOR THE VENISON

2 (14-ounce) venison loin cuts, halved

12 ounces caul fat, soaked and rinsed

5 tablespoons Activa (optional)

Kosher salt

Freshly ground black pepper

Olive oil

4 ounces (8 tablespoons) unsalted butter

4 sprigs fresh rosemary

4 sprigs fresh thyme

2 tablespoons dried juniper berries

FOR THE SAGE CHIPS

Canola oil

12 small sage leaves

FOR THE KABOCHA SQUASH
PUREE

1½ cups (about ¾
pound) kabocha squash,
peeled, seeded, and cut
into small pieces

2 cups heavy cream

1 cinnamon stick

Kosher salt

Peel from 1 lemon from
Lemon Confit (see page 386)

TO ASSEMBLE THE DISH

1 recipe Venison Jus (see
page 384), or 3 cups store-
bought beef demi-glace

Flaky sea salt, such
as Maldon

Celery leaves

MAKE THE STUFFING

1. Soak the raisins in the gin in a small bowl. Set aside while you prepare the rest of the stuffing.

2. Add enough olive oil to a large sauté pan to cover the bottom of the pan and set over medium-high heat. Add the bread cubes and cook until browned on all sides. Transfer the bread cubes to a large bowl and set aside.

3. Add 2 tablespoons of oil and the butter to the skillet. Add the mushrooms, onions, and celery root, and cook until cooked through, about 5 minutes. Stir in the parsley, sage, and cinnamon. Transfer the mushroom-vegetable mixture to the bowl with the bread cubes and set aside.

4. Warm 3 tablespoons of oil in the skillet. Add the garlic and cook until the garlic is crispy, 30 seconds to 1 minute; watch the garlic carefully, as it can go from cooked to burnt very quickly. Transfer the garlic chips to a paper towel–lined tray and let cool. Combine the garlic chips with the bread cube mixture.

5. In a small pot, bring the stock to a boil over high heat, and add it to the bread mixture as needed until the consistency is that of Thanksgiving stuffing. Drain the raisins and fold them into the stuffing. Season to taste with salt and pepper. Set aside.

PREPARE THE VENISON

6. Pat the meat dry and butterfly the venison pieces so that each piece looks like an open book. Gently pound out each piece to ½-inch thickness. Cut the caul fat into 4 equal pieces. Lay out a piece of plastic wrap over the counter and place a piece of caul fat on top of the plastic wrap. Place a piece of the venison meat on top of the caul fat so that it looks like an open book. Spoon some of the stuffing on top of the meat, sprinkle a little Activa all over, if using, and roll each venison half into a tight sausagelike cylinder. Wrap this cylinder tightly in the plastic wrap, and twist each end to make a tight and compact roll. Repeat this with the remaining venison, caul fat, and stuffing to make a total of 4 cylinders. You should have a little bit of the stuffing left over—set it aside.

7. Place each of the rolled-up venison cylinders in a vacuum-seal bag and seal the bags. Refrigerate the meat for at least 6 hours or up to overnight.

8. SOUS-VIDE COOKING INSTRUCTIONS (see step 11 for Sous-Vide Alternative Instructions): About 1½ hours before serving, fill an immersion circulator with water and preheat to 133°F. Place the bags in the water and poach for 1 hour. Allow the venison to rest for about 7 minutes, remove from the bags, pat dry, and season with salt and pepper. Add enough oil to a large sauté pan to cover the bottom of the pan and set it over high heat. Just before the oil starts to smoke, add one loin and sear until well-browned on all sides, about 1 minute per side. Reduce the heat to medium, and add 2 tablespoons of butter, a sprig of rosemary, a sprig of thyme, and ½ teaspoon of the juniper berries. Baste with the infused butter for 1 minute. Transfer to a carving board and allow the meat to rest for 5 minutes before slicing. Repeat with the remaining loin rolls.

9. SOUS-VIDE ALTERNATIVE INSTRUCTIONS: Preheat the oven to 350°F; position the rack in the middle. Pat the meat dry and season with salt and pepper. Add enough oil to a large sauté pan to cover the bottom of the pan and set it over high heat. Just before the oil starts to smoke, add one venison roll, reduce the heat to medium, and cook until browned on all sides. Repeat with the remaining loins. Transfer the loins to a roasting pan, place in the oven and cook for 10 to 12 minutes. Return one loin to the sauté pan over medium heat, and add 2 tablespoons of butter, a sprig of rosemary, a sprig of thyme, and ½ teaspoon of the juniper berries. Baste with the infused butter for 1 minute. Transfer to a carving board and allow the meat to rest for 5 minutes before slicing. Repeat with the remaining loin rolls.

10. Warm ½ inch of oil in a medium skillet to 300°F. Add the sage leaves and fry until crispy. You will see a lot of bubbles around the leaves as they cook—when the bubbles begin to subside, the sage leaves are done. Transfer to a paper towel–lined tray and set aside in a dry place.

MAKE THE KABOCHA SQUASH PUREE

11. In a large pot, combine the squash, cream, cinnamon stick, and a pinch of salt and bring to a simmer over medium heat. Cook until the squash is soft and can be mashed with a fork, 20 to 25 minutes. Remove and discard the cinnamon stick and transfer the squash to a blender with ¼ cup of the cooking liquid. Add the lemon peel and puree until smooth. Pass the puree through a fine-mesh strainer into a bowl and keep warm.

ASSEMBLE THE DISH

12. Warm the Venison Jus. Slice the venison. Divide the Kabocha Squash Puree among 4 warmed plates. Place the Venison Loins on top of the puree. Drizzle the Venison Jus around. Dot the plates with the remaining stuffing, scatter the Sage Chips around, sprinkle with flaky sea salt, and garnish with celery leaves.

Make It Faster *To make this into a more manageable, less restaurant-style meal, just cook the venison as-is (without stuffing it) and serve it with the stuffing on the side and the puree (if you like). It will taste equally delicious.*

The secret to success

BUTCHER'S CUTS

"A lot of people are turned off by offal because they haven't had many chances to eat it or they haven't had it prepared properly. I grew up eating offal, and I love it! My granddad used to fry up some kidneys for breakfast with some eggs, and my mom made the best liver and onions with stewy gravy. I think more people should eat offal. These neglected cuts can often be the most delicious!"

—APRIL BLOOMFIELD

SERVES 4 Most people drink beer in the summer when it's hot out; the cold beer cools them off. I'm the same way unless you're talking about a Guinness, which I start drinking when the weather turns decidedly cold. The deep caramel, malty flavors taste better in the fall and winter and are excellent complements to meaty stews and soups. When I was making this dish in the winter, I knew I needed a strong beer to stand up to the bold oxtail flavor. Guinness happened to be on hand and made its way into this dish.

FOR THE OXTAILS

7 pounds oxtails, cut into 2-inch pieces

8 sprigs fresh thyme

2 sprigs fresh rosemary

1 celery stalk

2 fresh or 1 dried bay leaves

1½ strips bacon

Canola oil

Kosher salt

Freshly ground black pepper

4 shallots, peeled and diced

3 medium carrots, cut into 1-inch pieces

1 medium onion, cut into eighths

10 garlic cloves, halved

10 whole black peppercorns, cracked

3 tablespoons tomato paste

3 tablespoons all-purpose flour

8 cups full-bodied dry red wine

4 cups ruby port

5 cups Veal Stock (see page 382) or store-bought

3 cups Chicken Stock (see page 382) or store-bought

½ cup granulated sugar

Freshly ground black pepper

FOR THE PARSNIP PUREE

2 cups heavy cream

4 parsnips, peeled and cut into ½-inch slices

Kosher salt

2 ounces (4 tablespoons) unsalted butter

FOR THE SPAETZLE

1¾ cups all-purpose flour

4 large eggs

½ cup whole milk

¼ cup Guinness or other stout beer

2 tablespoons Pierre Poivre spice mix (see Sources, page 403) or smoked paprika

1 tablespoon kosher salt, plus more as needed

Olive oil

2 ounces (4 tablespoons) unsalted butter

FOR THE BÉCHAMEL SAUCE

2 tablespoons minced garlic

2 ounces (4 tablespoons) unsalted butter

¼ cup all-purpose flour

1½ cups whole milk

½ cup shredded aged cheddar

¼ teaspoon freshly ground nutmeg

Kosher salt

TO ASSEMBLE THE DISH

1 cup chopped fresh chives

¼ cup minced shallots

Kosher salt

Shredded aged cheddar

MAKE THE OXTAILS

1. Pat the oxtails dry. Place 4 sprigs of thyme, rosemary, celery, 1 fresh or ½ dried bay leaf, and ½ strip of bacon on the remaining piece of bacon and wrap the bacon around them. Using a piece of kitchen twine, tie the bouquet garni tightly and set aside.

2. In a large stockpot or a Dutch oven set over medium-high heat, warm enough oil to cover the bottom of the pot until just before it starts to smoke. Season the oxtails with salt and pepper. Add the oxtails and brown on all sides, about 10 minutes. Transfer to a plate and set aside. Discard the oil.

3. Add more oil to the pot, followed by the shallots, carrots, onion, garlic, and peppercorns, and cook until the vegetables are light brown, 4 to 6 minutes. Stir in the tomato paste and cook for 2 minutes. Stir in the flour until well incorporated. Add 4 cups of the wine, 2 cups of the port, and the reserved bouquet garni. Bring to a simmer over medium heat, reduce the heat to low, and cook until the sauce has reduced to a third of its original volume.

4. While the sauce reduces, preheat the oven to 300°F; position the rack in the middle. Return the oxtails to the pot, and add the stocks. Raise the heat to medium-high and bring to a simmer. Place a piece of parchment paper over the pot, then place the lid on top of the parchment, and place the pot in the oven. Braise the meat for about 4 hours or until the oxtails are tender and the meat is falling off the bone. Taste and adjust the seasoning.

5. While the oxtails cook, make a port reduction: In a 4-quart pot, combine the sugar and the remaining 4 cups wine, 2 cups port, 4 sprigs thyme, 1 fresh or ½ dried bay leaf, and pepper and bring to a boil over high heat. Cook until the liquid has reduced to 2 cups, about 30 minutes. Remove from the heat and set aside.

6. Remove the oxtails and strain the sauce, discarding the vegetables. Pick the meat off the bones and set aside in a container large enough for the meat and sauce. Return the sauce to the stove over medium-high heat and cook, skimming off the fat as needed, until it has reduced to about 2 cups of sauce. Add the reserved port reduction and cook, skimming off the fat as needed, until the sauce has reduced to about 2 cups, about 30 minutes. Pour the sauce over the reserved oxtail meat, cover, and refrigerate overnight.

7. When ready to serve, in a saucepot, warm 1½ cups of the oxtail meat with 1½ cups of the oxtail wine sauce over medium heat, 10 to 15 minutes.

MAKE THE PARSNIP PUREE

8. In a medium pot, bring the cream, parsnips, and a couple of pinches of salt to a boil over medium-high heat. Reduce the heat to low and simmer until the parsnips are soft, about 10 minutes.

9. While the parsnips cook, in a medium sauté pan, heat the butter over medium heat until the solids are a rich brown and the butter smells nutty. Remove from the heat and keep warm.

10. Using a slotted spoon, transfer the parsnips to a blender; discard the cream or reserve it for another use. Add the reserved brown butter and blend until smooth. Transfer the puree to an ice bath and let cool completely.

MAKE THE SPAETZLE

11. While the oxtails cook, in a large bowl, whisk together the flour, eggs, milk, beer, ¼ cup of the Parsnip Puree, Pierre Poivre, and salt. Bring a large pot of salted water to a simmer, and using a perforated hotel pan or a large, wide colander, push the batter through the holes into the water. Wait for the spaetzle to float to the top and then count to 10. Using a slotted spoon, transfer the cooked spaetzle to an ice bath and let cool for 2 minutes. Drain and transfer the cooled spaetzle to another bowl and refrigerate until ready to use.

12. Right before serving, add enough oil to a large sauté pan to cover the bottom of the pan and set it over high heat. Just before it starts to smoke, add 2 cups of the spaetzle to the pan in an even layer (you may have to do this in batches). Cook until the spaetzle begins to brown, add the butter, and cook until the spaetzle is crispy. Transfer to a paper towel–lined tray.

MAKE THE BÉCHAMEL SAUCE

13. In a 4-quart pot set over medium heat, combine the garlic with 2 tablespoons of the butter, and heat until the garlic is roasted, about 2 minutes. Using a wooden spoon, stir in the remaining 2 tablespoons butter and the flour, and cook, stirring, for about 5 minutes or until the flour is cooked into the mixture. Whisk in the milk until incorporated. Bring to a boil. Reduce the heat to low and simmer until thickened, about 10 minutes. Whisk to make sure the bottom of the pot doesn't get scorched. Whisk in the cheddar and nutmeg, and season to taste with salt. Set aside and keep warm until ready to use. You will have 2 cups of béchamel, but will only need 1 cup for this recipe. Freeze the remaining sauce for later use. You can rewarm the frozen sauce over a hot water bath, but you may need to add more milk to loosen it up. Right before serving, warm 1 cup of the béchamel over low heat.

ASSEMBLE THE DISH

14. While the oxtails and sauce warm up, stir the Béchamel into the fried spaetzle. Remove from the heat and set aside. Once the oxtails and sauce are warm, stir in the fried spaetzle, 3 tablespoons of the chives, and the shallots. Taste and adjust the seasonings. Divide among 4 warmed ovenproof bowls. Sprinkle with the aged cheddar and set under the broiler until the cheese is bubbling and golden, 1 to 2 minutes. Sprinkle the remaining chives on top and serve.

VEAL CHEEKS + BONE MARROW + POTATOES + JIM BEARD SALAD

SERVES 4 James Beard was a great friend of my family and had a huge influence on my father's career—he and my father shared a vision for the way the American culinary scene needed to change. My younger brother, Bryan, actually named him Grandpa Yoda because of his prominent ears. In many ways, Jim was more than just my father's friend—Jim was also his mentor. It was Jim who came up with the name for his restaurant, An American Place, drawing inspiration from photographer Alfred Stieglitz's gallery for American artists under the same name. As my father was trying to bring back the glory of American ingredients and dishes, Jim thought it was an appropriate name and a tribute to a great American artist as well as a culinary tradition.

It should go without saying that Jim loved to eat, and this salad was one of his favorites: a generous helping of raw onion and flat-leaf parsley dressed with a bracing vinaigrette. It's as simple as salads get—and utterly delicious. Initially, I was inspired to put together a meal around this salad, and eventually the dish evolved into a collection of some of Jim's favorite things to eat.

FOR THE VEAL CHEEKS

8 veal cheeks

Kosher salt

8 sprigs fresh thyme

2 sprigs fresh rosemary

1 celery stalk

1 fresh or ½ dried bay leaf

1 bacon slice

Canola oil

2 ounces (4 tablespoons) unsalted butter

1½ garlic heads, halved

10 garlic cloves, halved

4 shallots, diced

1 medium carrot, cut into 1-inch pieces

1 medium onion, cut into eighths

10 whole black peppercorns, cracked

3 tablespoons tomato paste

3 tablespoons all-purpose flour

3 cups dry red wine, such as Cabernet Sauvignon

1½ cups ruby port

2½ cups Veal Stock (see page 382) or store-bought

1½ cups Chicken Stock (see page 382) or store-bought

¼ cup granulated sugar

Freshly ground black pepper

10 large fresh shiitake mushroom caps, diced

FOR THE MARROW-POTATO PUREE

3 pounds bone marrow bones, cut 2½-inch pieces

Kosher salt

Freshly ground black pepper

½ recipe Basic Potato Puree (see page 396), made with half the butter called for in the recipe

FOR THE PARSLEY-SHALLOT SALAD

1 cup fresh flat-leaf parsley leaves

1 shallot, thinly sliced

3 tablespoons sherry vinegar

2 tablespoons extra-virgin olive oil

Kosher salt

TO ASSEMBLE THE DISH

Flaky sea salt, such as Maldon

3 tablespoons chopped fresh curly parsley

1 recipe Garlic Butter (see page 228), melted

1. Pat the cheeks dry and season liberally with salt. Refrigerate, uncovered, overnight.

2. Remove the cheeks from the refrigerator and let sit at room temperature for 40 minutes before cooking. Preheat the oven to 300°F; position the rack in the middle. Place 6 sprigs of the thyme, the rosemary, celery, and ½ fresh or ¼ dried bay leaf over bacon and wrap the bacon around. Tie a piece of kitchen twine around the bouquet garni and set it aside.

3. In a large heavy-bottomed pot or a Dutch oven set over high heat, warm enough oil to cover the bottom of the pan. Just before it starts to smoke, add the bouquet garni and cook until the bacon fat is rendered. Add the butter and halved heads of garlic, and cook until the butter browns, 2 to 3 minutes. Remove half of the butter from the pot and discard it. Return the pot to the stovetop, add the shallots, carrots, onions, and peppercorns, and cook until the vegetables brown slightly, about 5 minutes. Stir in the tomato paste and cook for 2 minutes. Stir in the flour until incorporated. Add 1 cup of the wine and 1 cup of the port and cook until the sauce has reduced to a third of its original volume. Add the cheeks to the pot, and then add the stocks. Bring to a simmer. Place a piece of parchment paper over the pot, and cover tightly with foil. Transfer the pot to the oven and braise the cheeks for about 2 hours, or until the meat is tender.

4. While the cheeks cook, make a port reduction: In a 4-quart pot, combine the sugar and the remaining 2 cups wine, ½ cup port, 2 sprigs thyme, ½ fresh or ¼ dried bay leaf, and black pepper, and bring to a simmer over high heat. Cook until the liquid has reduced to about 1 cup, about 15 minutes. Remove from the heat and set aside.

5. Transfer the cheeks to a container large enough to hold the cheeks and sauce. Strain the sauce through a fine-mesh strainer into a pot. Return the sauce the stovetop over medium-high heat, add the port reduction, and cook, skimming off the fat as needed, until the liquid has reduced to about 2 cups, about 20 minutes. Pour the sauce over the cheeks, cover, and refrigerate overnight.

6. In a large sauté pan set over high heat, warm enough oil to cover the bottom of the pan until just before it starts to smoke. Add the shiitakes, reduce the heat to medium, and cook until the mushrooms are browned, 90 seconds to 2 minutes. Season to taste with salt and transfer to a parchment paper–lined plate. Set aside.

7. While you cure the veal cheeks, soak the bone marrow in a bowl of cold water in the refrigerator for at least 6 hours or up to 12, changing the water every 2 hours.

8. Preheat the oven to 450°F; position the rack in the middle. Take all but 4 of the marrow bones, pat them dry, and place them in a roasting pan. Season with salt and pepper, and roast for 1 hour or until the fat has rendered and begins to caramelize. It will look like rendered bacon fat. Reduce the oven temperature to 350°F.

9. Pour the rendered marrow fat into a saucepot, skimming off and discarding any big pieces that float in the oil using a slotted spoon. Set the marrow fat aside and let cool until semisolid.

10. Clean any meat off the remaining 4 marrow bones and place them in a roasting pan. Add enough water to come 1 inch up the sides of the pan and season the marrow bones with salt and pepper. Roast the bones for 15 minutes or until the marrow can be easily pierced with a needle. If the marrow bones need more time, cook them longer, but watch carefully—if it becomes too warm, the marrow will liquefy and leak out of the bones. Check on the bones every 5 minutes. Transfer to a cooling rack and let cool to room temperature.

11. Spoon the reserved, rendered marrow fat into the Basic Potato Puree and whisk until incorporated. Bear in mind that you cannot add hot liquid marrow fat to the puree or the puree will break, which is why the marrow fat needs sufficient time to cool and solidify. Set aside and keep warm until ready to serve. (You will have some extra marrow fat left over—save it and use it in place of bacon fat for frying eggs or potatoes.)

12. In a medium bowl, toss together the parsley and shallot. In a small bowl, whisk together the vinegar and oil. Right before serving, toss the salad and dressing together with a pinch of salt.

13. When ready to serve, preheat the oven to 350°F. Reheat the cheeks in the oven until warmed through. Set aside.

14. Preheat the broiler on high. Broil the 4 marrow bones for 2 minutes. Meanwhile, divide the Marrow-Potato Puree among 4 warmed plates. Spoon the warmed cheeks on top of the puree and sprinkle with flaky sea salt. Stir the reserved shiitakes and parsley into the remaining sauce. Spoon some of the sauce over the cheeks and drizzle them with some of the Garlic-Thyme Butter. Place a marrow bone on each plate and scatter the Parsley-Shallot Salad around the plate.

STOKES FARM

RON BINAGHI AND TOM MARGOTTA

Ron Binaghi remembers the very first farmers' market in New York on the Upper East Side in 1976, where he and his father sold out of everything in no time. "Is there a famine in the city?" his father wondered. The first of many greenmarkets to spring up all over the city, selling out of everything was a sign that people were hungry for fresh, local produce. Stokes Farm, which is pesticide-free and famed for their beautiful herbs as well as their tomatoes, has been a faithful presence at New York's greenmarkets ever since.

In a time when many people choose to move away from farms to cities to pursue advanced degrees and desk jobs, Ron Binaghi, a fifth-generation farmer who started working on the family farm in 1976 when he was just nineteen years old, finds farming to be incredibly mentally challenging. "If you want to put your mind to it, it is . . . intellectually stimulating. You have to be a plumber, an architect, a psychiatrist, a banker, a marketer, an irrigation specialist, a carpenter. You have to wear a lot of hats."

Farming has been in Ron's blood since he was a little kid. "When I got in trouble," he recalls, "I just wanted to be grounded like regular kids and be sent to my room. My father, on the other hand, had a different idea and would make me do chores on the farm. While all my friends wanted to come and work on the farm, I wanted to be grounded like all the other kids—to stay in my room and think about what I did. I *really* wanted to think about what I did! But it never happened."

Ron never felt that college was for him. Instead, he got married at nineteen and put all of his efforts into the family farm. "When you get married that early," he says, "it ramps up your ambition level—makes you grow up fast." But despite being what is now considered an adult, well past his teens with married

children of his own, Ron still refers to himself as "almost a grown-up." His conversation is often interrupted with his contagious chuckle. His son is now on board helping as well. Following in his grandfather's footsteps, Ron's son started at Rutgers on a scholarship singing, but after about a semester came back to work on the farm.

While Ron interacts with customers at Union Square, we are fortunate enough, to have his colleague Tom Margotta at the greenmarket in Tribeca, a block away from the restaurant. I first met Tom when I was working at BLT and was coming to the Union Square greenmarket to buy produce. In time we got to know each other better. Sometime after I moved to Tribeca and opened my own place I ran into Tom at the Stokes stand, at the greenmarket—he had also moved! Whenever I go to the greenmarket, it's always nice to see him and catch up while my chefs and I source some amazing produce.

SERVES 4 I know this might sound weird, but whenever I think of a BLT, I always hear Billy Crystal's voice from *The Princess Bride*, "Sonny, true love is the greatest thing in the world. Except for a nice MLT—a mutton, lettuce, and tomato sandwich, where the mutton is nice and lean and the tomato is ripe. They're so perky, I love that!" While ours is definitely a BLT (as opposed to an MLT), it's a more playful version of the traditional sandwich.

We use tomatoes from a wonderful New Jersey vendor, Stokes Farms. If you have a greenmarket near you, find a farmer who sells tomatoes that you like. It will make your summers, and your BLTs, much improved.

FOR THE PIG EARS

4 pig ears (ask your butcher)

3 sprigs fresh thyme

2 sprigs fresh flat-leaf parsley

2 fresh or 1 dried bay leaves

2 outer leek greens
or 1 celery stalk

2 cups dry white wine

½ cup diced carrots

½ cup diced celery

½ cup diced onions

1 tablespoon kosher salt,
plus more as needed

Canola oil

All-purpose flour

Kosher salt

FOR THE SMOKED ONION RÉMOULADE

1 recipe Smoked Onion Rémoulade (see page 390)

FOR THE BREAD CRACKERS

Extra-virgin olive oil

4 paper-thin slices
Pullman loaf

Kosher salt

Freshly ground black pepper

FOR THE TOMATO SALAD

2 pounds heirloom tomatoes, cut into assorted shapes and sizes

2 cups diced orange watermelon or regular watermelon

1 cup basil leaves

½ red onion, julienned

Kosher salt

Freshly ground black pepper

Extra-virgin olive oil

Sherry vinegar

TO ASSEMBLE THE DISH

Basil leaves

Flaky sea salt, such as Maldon

MAKE THE PIG EARS

1. Soak the pig ears in a bowl of cold water in the refrigerator for 6 hours, changing the water every 2 hours. Make a bouquet garni by sandwiching the thyme, parsley, and bay leaves between the leek greens or along the celery stalk. Tie with kitchen twine to secure and set aside.

2. Place the ears in a large stockpot, cover with water, and bring to a boil. Remove from the heat, drain, and return the ears to the pot. Return the pot to the stove, add the wine, carrots, celery, onions, salt, and 12 cups of water, and bring to a simmer over medium heat. Reduce the heat to low and maintain an active simmer for 3 hours or until the ears are fork-tender. Remove the pot from the heat and let cool slightly. Refrigerate overnight in the cooking liquid.

3. Remove the pig ears from the liquid and slice them at a slight angle to get the meat along with the cartilage. Set aside until ready to use.

4. When ready to serve, add 1½ inches of oil to a Dutch oven and warm the oil over medium-high heat until it registers 350°F on a deep-frying thermometer. Dredge the ears in flour until well coated. Gently lower the ears into the oil and fry the ears until crispy, about 2 minutes. Transfer to a paper towel–lined plate and season with salt.

MAKE THE SMOKED ONION RÉMOULADE

5. Prepare the Smoked Onion Rémoulade. Set aside.

MAKE THE BREAD CRACKERS

6. Preheat the oven to 300°F; position the rack in the middle. Drizzle olive oil over the bread and season with salt and pepper. Bake for 5 minutes or until dry. Transfer to a cooling rack and set aside.

MAKE THE TOMATO SALAD

7. In a large nonreactive bowl, toss together the tomatoes, watermelon, basil, onion, salt, and pepper. Set aside.

8. Right before serving, add the olive oil and sherry vinegar to the Tomato Salad and toss to combine.

ASSEMBLE THE DISH

9. Divide the Smoked Onion Rémoulade among 4 chilled plates and spoon some Tomato Salad on top. Lay the fried pig ears and Bread Crackers around, scatter some basil leaves on top, and sprinkle with flaky sea salt.

Make It Faster *Make the Smoked Onion Rémoulade and the Tomato Salad and serve them on toasted bread with your favorite cooked bacon.*

Vapor locks!

SERVES 4 This is a bar staple at the restaurant. We get whole ducks delivered to the restaurant from Joe Jurgielewicz & Son, and use the duck breast for dinner entrées. But then there's all this duck meat left over: the legs, the liver, and so on. So we came up with ways to use the whole animal. It was our way of not wasting anything but the beak and the feet. What was an experiment, became an instant hit and a permanent fixture at the restaurant. Now, it's one of the dishes that people come in for. They will sit at the bar and order these duck jars along with their drinks.

FOR THE DUCK LIVER MOUSSE

1 cup ruby port

7 sprigs fresh thyme

3 tablespoons granulated sugar

1 shallot, sliced, plus 2 tablespoons chopped shallots

1 garlic clove, chopped

1 fresh or ½ dried bay leaf

1 pound duck livers, patted dry

1 tablespoon pink curing salt

1 teaspoon kosher salt

Canola oil

3 tablespoons brandy

2 ounces foie gras terrine or unsalted butter, cut into 8 pieces

2 tablespoons heavy cream

2 tablespoons duck fat or 1 ounce (2 tablespoons) unsalted butter, cut into 4 pieces

1 ounce (2 tablespoons) unsalted butter, cut into 4 pieces

Extra-virgin olive oil

TO ASSEMBLE THE DISH

4 sprigs fresh thyme

Smoked salt

Pierre Poivre spice mix (see Sources, page 403) or black pepper

4 pieces filone or other country bread with a thick crust, toasted

1 recipe MF Pickles (see page 397)

MAKE THE DUCK LIVER MOUSSE

1. In a small nonreactive pot, combine the port, thyme, sugar, sliced shallot, garlic, and bay leaf, and simmer over medium-high heat until the liquid has reduced to about ¼ cup, 15 to 20 minutes. Strain the reduction through a fine-mesh strainer into a bowl and set aside.

2. Season the livers with the pink and kosher salts. Add enough canola oil to a large sauté pan to cover the bottom of the pan and set it over high heat. Just before it starts to smoke, add the livers to the pan in one even layer without overcrowding (you may need to do this in batches). Reduce the heat to medium and cook, without moving the livers, for 1 minute. Add the remaining chopped shallots and brandy, stir, and cook for 1 minute more—the livers should be medium-rare. Transfer the livers to a blender and add the reserved port reduction. Blend, and when the mixture is sufficiently uniform, with the blender running, add the terrine, heavy cream, duck fat, and butter, piece by piece. Blend the mousse on high speed for 1 minute. Taste and adjust the seasonings. Pass the mousse through a fine-mesh strainer over a bowl set in an ice bath and let cool. Once the mousse is cool, transfer it to a pastry bag fitted with a large plain tip and pipe it into 4 (4-ounce) glass jars. Drizzle some extra-virgin olive oil on top to prevent discoloration, and refrigerate until ready to use.

ASSEMBLE THE DISH

3. Pick the leaves off the thyme sprigs and sprinkle the leaves in the jars. Sprinkle smoked salt and Pierre Poivre over the mousse. Serve with the toasted bread and MF Pickles.

FOIE GRAS + APRICOT PRESERVES + PEPPERCORNS + SALTS + TOAST

SERVES 4 To me, foie gras is one of those perfect ingredients that doesn't need much assistance in order to taste absolutely delicious. This dish is as simple as it gets. I bring this home for a Christmas morning breakfast for my mom every year. Even though it's a little bit gluttonous, she loves it—and it's become a family tradition of sorts. Plus, Christmas morning deserves a little indulgence.

At the restaurant, we serve the foie gras accompanied by different salts so diners can season it as they like. It's a cool way to get people started on their meal.

FOR THE APRICOT CHUTNEY

2 cups diced dried apricots

2 cups granulated sugar

One (1-inch) piece
fresh ginger, halved

2 sprigs fresh mint

FOR THE FOIE GRAS

One (1¼-pound) lobe
foie gras, preferably
Hudson Valley

4 cups whole milk

3 teaspoons sea salt

½ teaspoon pink curing salt

½ teaspoon freshly
ground white pepper

½ teaspoon granulated sugar

TO ASSEMBLE THE DISH

12 (½-inch-thick) slices
country bread, lightly toasted

Smoked salt (see Sources,
page 403; optional)

Black volcanic salt (see
Sources, page 403; optional)

Vanilla salt (see Sources,
page 403; optional)

Flaky sea salt, such
as Maldon

Pierre Poivre spice mix
(see Sources, page 403)
or smoked paprika

Note *You need to go through the entire lobe of foie gras with a paring knife to carefully pick out and discard the veins, one by one. It is tedious work, but pretty necessary unless you like veins in your foie gras!*

MAKE THE APRICOT CHUTNEY

1. Sterilize 2 pint jars by placing them in a large stockpot filled with boiling water for 5 minutes. Using jar tongs, transfer the jars to a clean dish towel, facing down.

2. In a medium saucepan, combine the apricots, sugar, ginger, and mint with 3 cups of water and bring to a simmer over medium heat until the apricots get soft and the mixture is jamlike. Remove the chutney from the heat and keep warm. Transfer the chutney to the sterilized jars and let cool. Cover and refrigerate until ready to use.

MAKE THE FOIE GRAS

3. Clean and devein the foie gras (see Note). Place the foie gras and milk in a medium container or a resealable bag and refrigerate overnight.

4. Remove the foie gras from the milk, pat it dry, and season it with the sea salt, pink salt, white pepper, and sugar. Wrap the foie gras in plastic wrap and refrigerate overnight.

5. Preheat an immersion circulator filled with water to 100°F. Remove the plastic wrap from the foie gras, separate the foie gras into 4 logs, and using more plastic wrap, roll each log tightly into a cylinder, tightly securing both ends. Place the wrapped foie gras logs into a

vacuum-seal bag, seal it, and poach in the immersion circulator for 1 hour. (If you don't own an immersion circulator, please see the Note.) Transfer the sealed bag to an ice bath and chill for about 2 hours.

ASSEMBLE THE DISH

6. Slice the chilled foie gras logs into ½-inch-thick slices and divide them among 4 plates. Serve with the toasted bread, Apricot Chutney, various salts, and Pierre Poivre alongside.

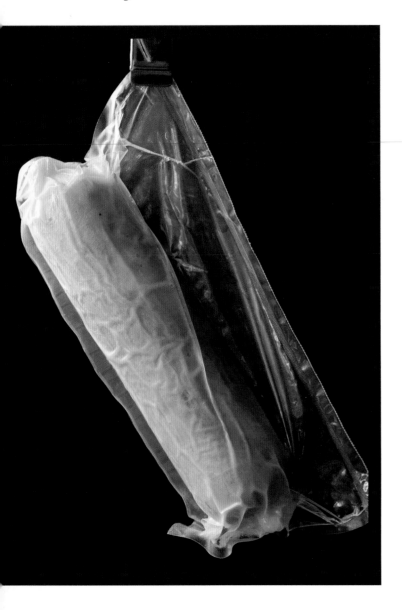

Note *If you don't have an immersion circulator, you can wrap the foie gras in cheesecloth instead of plastic wrap and poach it on the stovetop in rendered duck fat: In a medium pot over medium-low heat, bring 9 cups of rendered duck fat to 180°F. Add the foie and poach for 90 seconds, and immediately transfer it to the refrigerator to cool for 20 minutes. Take the foie out of the refrigerator and twist the cheesecloth it is wrapped in tighter. The foie will start coming out a bit on the sides. Wrap it in additional layers of cheesecloth, tighten the ends to form a tight log, and hang the foie log in the refrigerator for 6 hours more or up to 1 day. This will give you just the taste and texture you are used to when you order foie gras at a fine dining restaurant. Alternatively, you can purchase a premade foie gras terrine, available at fine foods shops and online, and just make the chutney. It allows for a nearly effortless appetizer to enjoy with your friends and family. Also, if you don't have a collection of fancy salts, don't worry about it. All you need is one quality finishing salt to get a good feel for the tasting notes in this dish. I like Maldon sea salt, and in the last few years, a lot more stores have been selling it.*

FOIE GRAS ELVIS PRESLEY + BACON + BANANA + PINE NUT BUTTER + SUMAC

SERVES 4 Most people probably don't know that Elvis Presley's favorite thing to eat was a peanut butter, banana, and bacon sandwich cooked in bacon grease. As soon as I found out about this, I knew I had to try it—and I absolutely loved it. After playing around with it a bit, this is what we came up with at the restaurant. The pine nuts replaced the peanut butter, the foie gras was added, and the banana turned into a banana puree. This dish would not be complete without Elvis Presley Whiskey, which we served at Cochon 555 (see page 376).

FOR THE PINE NUT BUTTER

1 cup toasted pine nuts

1 tablespoon mild honey

1 teaspoon kosher salt

Pinch of freshly ground black pepper

FOR THE BREAD CRACKERS

4 paper-thin slices Pullman loaf

Extra-virgin olive oil

Kosher salt

Freshly ground black pepper

DUCK SKIN CRUMBLE

¼ cup rolled oats

¼ cup packed light brown sugar

¼ cup all-purpose flour

1 tablespoon ground cinnamon

1 ounce (2 tablespoons) unsalted butter, melted

Duck skin from 2 duck breasts (see Note)

½ recipe Duck Glaze (see page 391)

FOR THE BANANA AND CELERY ROOT PUREE

1 cup sliced celery root

1 banana, sliced

1 cup heavy cream

1 cup Chicken Stock (see page 382) or store-bought

Kosher salt

2 ounces (4 tablespoons) unsalted butter

FOR THE FOIE GRAS

½ cup thinly sliced applewood-smoked bacon (about 2 thick strips)

4 slices frozen foie gras (see Sources, page 403)

Kosher salt

Canola oil

TO ASSEMBLE THE DISH

½ cup pine nuts

Micro celery (see Sources, page 403) or chiffonade of fresh celery leaves

Ground sumac

Smoked salt (see Sources, page 403)

MAKE THE PINE NUT BUTTER

1. In a medium dry skillet, toast the pine nuts over medium heat until slightly golden brown, about 3 minutes. Transfer to a bowl and let cool. Place the pine nuts, honey, salt, and pepper into a food processor fitted with a blade and process until smooth, about 2 minutes. If the mixture gets too sticky, you might need to add a bit of water. Transfer to a covered container and store at room temperature until ready to use.

MAKE THE BREAD CRACKERS

2. Preheat the oven to 300°F; position the rack in the middle. Set the bread in a shallow baking pan, drizzle with olive oil, and season with salt and pepper. Bake for 5 minutes or until crispy. Transfer to a cooling rack and set aside. Raise the oven temperature to 350°F.

MAKE THE DUCK SKIN CRUMBLE

3. In a medium bowl, stir together the oats, brown sugar, flour, cinnamon, and butter until combined. Spread out the crumble over a Silpat- or parchment paper–lined quarter-sheet pan and, using a silicone spatula, flatten it out. Bake the crumble for about 8 minutes or until it begins to crisp up. Transfer to a cooling rack and let cool to room temperature. Keep the oven on.

4. Place the duck skins over a Silpat- or parchment paper–lined shallow baking pan and stretch the skins out so they lie flat. Place another piece of Silpat or parchment paper over the skins and place another baking pan over

the parchment, so that the duck skins are sandwiched flat between the parchment and pans. Bake the duck skins for 45 minutes to 1 hour or until the skins are flat and crispy (the cooking time will vary depending on how fatty the skins are). Be careful removing the pan from the oven as there will be a lot of rendered duck fat between the baking pans. Remove the top baking pan. Allow the skin to cool slightly; pour off the rendered duck fat and reserve it. Brush the duck skins with the Duck Glaze and return the glazed skins to the oven. Bake for 5 minutes or until the glaze caramelizes. Transfer the pan to a cooling rack and let sit until the glazed skins are cool enough to handle. Cut the skins into ½-inch equilateral triangles, and let the triangles cool completely.

5. In a medium bowl, toss together the oat crumble, duck skin triangles, and 2 tablespoons of the reserved rendered duck fat until thoroughly combined.

MAKE THE BANANA AND CELERY ROOT PUREE

6. In a 2-quart saucepot, combine the celery root, banana, cream, stock, and a pinch of salt and bring to a simmer over medium heat. Reduce the heat to low and cook until the celery root is soft, 15 to 20 minutes. Strain through a fine-mesh strainer into a bowl, reserving the cooking liquid, and transfer the solids to a blender.

7. In a small sauté pan, cook the butter over medium heat until the solids turn a rich brown. Transfer the brown butter to the blender with the celery root mixture. Starting on low speed and gradually increasing to high, puree the mixture for about 1 minute or until smooth. You may need to add a bit of the reserved cooking liquid to get the blender to go. (The remaining cooking liquid makes an excellent base for a soup or a sauce.) Pass the puree through a fine-mesh strainer into a bowl and set aside in a warm place.

MAKE THE FOIE GRAS

8. Add the bacon to a sauté pan set over medium heat and cook until crispy, 5 to 7 minutes. Strain, reserving the bacon fat for another use. Set the bacon aside.

9. Using a paring knife, score the foie gras—this will help the salt penetrate. Season with salt and set aside.

10. Add enough oil to a large sauté pan to cover the bottom of the pan and set it over high heat. Just before it starts to smoke, add the foie gras and reduce the heat to medium. Cook the foie gras for 1 minute or until the bottom is nicely browned. Flip the foie gras over and baste it a few times in its own fat. Add the cooked bacon to the pan and baste for another 20 seconds. Transfer the foie gras to a warmed plate; transfer the pan juices and cooked bacon to a separate saucepot.

ASSEMBLE THE DISH

11. In a small dry skillet, toast the pine nuts over low heat until slightly golden brown, about 3 minutes. Transfer to a bowl and let cool.

12. Spoon a little Banana and Celery Root Puree onto each of 4 warmed plates and top with a slice of the foie gras. Spoon some of the Pine Nut Butter on the plates and sprinkle with the celery. Scatter the toasted pine nuts and sumac around. Spoon the reserved bacon and pan juices over the foie gras, and top with some of the Duck Skin Crumble. Finish the plates with a sprinkling of smoked salt. Serve with the Bread Crackers while Elvis plays in the background.

Note *The best, and easiest, way to remove duck skin from the breast is to grab the breast with one hand and pull the skin off with the other.*

MØSEFUND MANGALITSA

HEIDI NORMAND

When Heidi Normand speaks of Mangalitsa pigs, her voice sparkles and you can tell she is excited. She can tell you all about G. C. Andersen, a financier, who spent years traveling Europe and eating the great Old World cuisine and discovering Mangalitsa meat. She can tell you how Mangalitsa is a cross between a lard pig and a wild boar, making the meat extra fatty and extra flavorful. She can tell you how, when Andersen returned to the States and couldn't find Mangalitsa meat, he made it his mission to bring it to the United States and popularize it. Andersen did what any devoted food enthusiast with the means would do—

he started a farm, Møsefund, to try to grow the Mangalitsa population and increase knowledge about it among consumers. It was his firm belief that if the consumers got their hands on Mangalitsa pork, they would go crazy for it.

At the time when Møsefund was starting up, there was only one person, Heath Putnam, who was working to build a bigger distribution of Mangalitsa meat out of the West Coast. As Møsefund grew in scale, it made sense to merge their Mangalitsa populations with Putnam's, and in 2012, Anderson purchased Putnam's pig stock and combined it with his own.

Meanwhile, Andersen's personal chef, Michael Clampfner, a Culinary Institute of America graduate, had spent a number of years working for the Andersen family. Michael, who was passionate about quality ingredients, started to help with the business and eventually brought on Heidi to be the unofficial Mangalitsa Møsefund ambassador. She is, perhaps, the only purveyor we use who has more tattoos than me.

Before she came on board, Heidi happened to live twenty-five minutes away from Møsefund, and had earlier connected with Michael through Twitter while helping to source the meat for Charcutepalooza, a year-long home-cook meat-curing endeavor. One day, bored by her job at the time, she took to Twitter and asked the universe for a job in the food industry. Twenty minutes later, Michael tweeted her back—and Heidi had a job. She came on board focused on spreading the Mangalitsa enthusiasm to anyone who would listen. This is the job she was born to do.

As Møsefund grows in popularity, the team is working to clean up the breed and continue to improve the quality of the meat. With four hundred to seven hundred pigs at any given time, the farm supplies both restaurants and Mangalitsa-loving individuals with delicious pork.

HEIDI NORMAND of Møsefund Mangalitsa Farm

MANGALITSA PIG CHEEK CROSTINI + LARDO + HEART + GAZPACHO + FAIRY TALE EGGPLANT

SERVES 4 The Mangalitsa breed is extra fatty and flavorful, and was bred, in the past, as a lard hog. Mangalitsas, aptly nicknamed "curly haired hogs," have slightly curly hair, a reminder of the breed's wilder ancestry, and a somewhat grumpy demeanor (again, thanks to its wilder ancestry). Because they produce so little lean meat, until recently, it was impossible to find them in the United States, and so Mangalitsas remain a bit of a novelty here. But with the resurgence of charcuterie, homemade bacon, and such, Mangalitsas are now being bred by small-scale farmers in America. We get our Mangalitsa pork from a wonderful producer called Møsefund Farm. I highly recommend that you give Mangalitsa a try—it will change you.

FOR THE MANGALITSA LARDO

3 tablespoons Ararat spice mix (see Sources, page 403)

3 tablespoons kosher salt

2 tablespoons pink curing salt

One (10-ounce) piece Mangalitsa fat, cut into a 1-inch-tall block

FOR THE PIG CHEEKS

1 tablespoon whole black peppercorns

1 tablespoon coriander seeds

1 tablespoon fennel seeds

1 cup kosher salt

½ cup packed dark brown sugar

2 tablespoons pink curing salt

1 fresh rosemary sprig

1 fresh thyme sprig

1 fresh or ½ dried bay leaf, crushed

4 Mangalitsa pig cheeks, fat removed

4 cups rendered Mangalitsa lard or regular lard

4 heirloom cherry tomatoes, halved

4 slices Pullman loaf

2 tablespoons chopped fresh curly parsley

FOR THE PIG HEART

1 pig heart

2 cups white wine vinegar

1 tablespoon mustard seeds

1 teaspoon kosher salt, plus more as needed

½ cup extra-virgin olive oil

3 tablespoons chopped fresh curly parsley

1 tablespoon chopped fresh rosemary

1 tablespoon chopped fresh thyme

1 teaspoon crushed pink peppercorns

1 garlic clove, chopped

FOR THE GAZPACHO

1 Italian eggplant, cut lengthwise into ¼-inch-thick slices

1 zucchini, cut lengthwise into ¼-inch-thick slices

1 summer squash, cut lengthwise into ¼-inch-thick slices

1 red onion, sliced ¼ inch thick

Extra-virgin olive oil

Kosher salt

Freshly ground black pepper

2 Brandywine tomatoes or other large heirloom beefsteak tomatoes, quartered

2 Kirby cucumbers

1 cup quality bottled tomato juice, plus more as needed

¼ cup sherry vinegar, plus more as needed

3 tablespoons mustard oil (see Sources, page 403), plus more as needed

FOR THE LIME SOUR CREAM

¼ cup sour cream

Finely grated zest of 1 lime

Fine sea salt

TO ASSEMBLE THE DISH

4 Fairy Tale eggplants

Mustard oil (see Sources, page 403)

1. In a small bowl, combine the Ararat and kosher and pink salts, and rub the mixture all over the Mangalitsa fat. Transfer to a vacuum-seal bag and seal. Refrigerate the lardo for at least 3 weeks. Alternatively, you can wrap the fat tightly in plastic wrap and refrigerate for 5 to 6 weeks—it takes longer to cure without a vacuum seal.

MAKE THE PIG CHEEKS

2. In a small, dry skillet, toast the peppercorns, coriander, and fennel over low heat, shaking the pan frequently, until fragrant, 2 to 3 minutes. Transfer the toasted spices to a small bowl and set aside to cool.

3. Add the cooled spices to a medium bowl and combine with the kosher salt, brown sugar, pink salt, rosemary, thyme, and bay leaf. Pat the pig cheeks dry and rub the spice cure all over the meat. Refrigerate, uncovered, overnight.

4. The next day, preheat the oven to 200°F; position the rack in the middle. Place the lard in a 2-quart pot, and over medium heat, warm the lard until the temperature reaches 200°F on a deep-frying thermometer. Meanwhile, rinse the cheeks under cold running water and place them in a baking dish. Pour the lard over the cheeks, cover the dish with parchment paper and then in foil, and bake the cheeks for 12 hours. Transfer to a cooling rack or a refrigerator and let cool, in the lard, until ready to use. If making ahead, cover and refrigerate until needed.

5. When ready to serve, return the pig cheeks to the stove, and over medium-low heat, warm the meat until it softens a bit. Remove the pan from the heat, and using two forks, shred the meat and set it aside. Quarter the cherry tomatoes.

6. When ready to serve, light a grill or preheat a grill pan. Grill the bread slices on both sides until slightly charred, but still soft inside. Alternatively, broil the bread on high for 1 minute or until one side of the bread is slightly charred. Spread the cheek mixture in a thin, even layer over the grilled bread. Arrange 2 cherry tomato halves on each slice and sprinkle with parsley. Top with a thin slice of the Mangalitsa Lardo (sliced on a mandoline on the thinnest setting). Grill or broil the crostini until the lardo melts, about 1 minute. Remove the crostini from the heat.

MAKE THE PIG HEART

7. Preheat the oven to 300°F; position the rack in the middle. Place the heart in a 4-quart Dutch oven or an ovenproof pot. In a nonreactive saucepan, combine the vinegar, mustard seeds, and salt with 2 cups of water, and bring to a boil. Pour the marinade over the heart, cover the pot, and transfer to the oven. Cook the heart for 3 to 4 hours or until fork-tender. Transfer the pot to a cooling rack, and once the heart has cooled, slice it, against the grain, into 4 slices. Place the heart slices in a bowl and pour over the braising liquid. Set aside.

8. In a separate bowl, stir together the olive oil, parsley, rosemary, thyme, pink peppercorns, and garlic. Set the olive oil–herb marinade aside until ready to grill the pig heart.

9. When ready to serve, light a grill or preheat a grill pan. Remove the heart slices from the braising liquid, season with additional salt, and brush with the olive oil–herb marinade. Grill over high heat, turning occasionally, until slightly charred, 5 to 8 minutes. Maintain the grill heat for the gazpacho. Alternatively, place the heart on a shallow baking pan and cook under a broiler for about 2 minutes per side or until slightly charred. Remove from the heat and set aside.

MAKE THE GAZPACHO

10. Place the Italian eggplant, zucchini, summer squash, and onion in a bowl, season with enough olive oil to coat, and add salt and pepper to taste. Grill the vegetables over high heat, turning occasionally, until charred, 3 to 5 minutes. Maintain the grill heat for assembling the dish. Alternatively, place the vegetables on a baking pan and cook under a broiler for about 1 minute each side or until charred. Transfer to a cooling rack and let cool. Pass the grilled vegetables, tomatoes, and 1 cucumber through a food mill fitted with medium holes into a bowl.

11. Brunoise (see page 48) the remaining cucumber and add it to the puree. Add the tomato juice, vinegar, and mustard oil, and season to taste with salt. Keep in mind that vegetables vary in flavor, acidity, and water content, so the amount of tomato juice, vinegar, oil, or salt might vary. Taste, and adjust the gazpacho seasonings to your preference.

MAKE THE LIME SOUR CREAM

12. In a small bowl, combine the sour cream with lime zest and sea salt, and mix to incorporate. Cover and refrigerate until needed.

ASSEMBLE THE DISH

13. When ready to serve, grill the Fairy Tale Eggplants over high heat, 5 to 8 minutes or until slightly charred. Alternatively, place the eggplant on a shallow baking pan and cook under a broiler for about 2 minutes per side or until slightly charred. Remove from the heat and set aside.

14. Divide the gazpacho among 4 chilled bowls, and spoon the Lime Sour Cream in the center. Place the pig cheek–lardo crostini on top, and drizzle with the mustard oil. Serve each bowl with a grilled eggplant and a slice of the grilled pig heart.

Make It Faster *If you want to make this, but simply don't have the time to get all the components done, the pig cheeks and gazpacho along with the Lime Sour Cream make a superb summer Sunday lunch. You can skip the overnight cure, and just slow cook the cheeks in the oven. Whip up the gazpacho, and serve it along with the cheeks.*

Yuri and John, working hard as ususal

JOE JURGIELEWICZ DUCK HAM + MOUSSE + LARD + HONEYCRISP APPLES

SERVES 4 I can't even remember when I met Joe, but one day he just showed up at the restaurant and brought me some duck to try. I did a literal blind taste test of the duck we were using at the time alongside his duck, and I actually got really pissed off at myself that I hadn't been serving this before.

You can make all the components in advance (in fact, the mousse tastes better if it's made the night before), and serve it at room temperature when company shows up. It's a cool way to enjoy some wine and extraordinary snacks with your friends.

FOR THE DUCK MOUSSE

1 pound mixed duck livers, hearts, and kidneys

1 cup ruby port

3 tablespoons granulated sugar

1 shallot, sliced, plus 2 tablespoons chopped shallots

1 garlic clove, chopped

7 sprigs fresh thyme

1 fresh or ½ dried bay leaf

Canola oil

1 tablespoon pink curing salt

1 teaspoon kosher salt

3 tablespoons brandy

2 ounces foie gras terrine or unsalted butter, cut into 8 pieces

2 tablespoons heavy cream

2 tablespoons duck fat or 1 ounce (2 tablespoons) unsalted butter, cut into 4 pieces

1 ounce (2 tablespoons) unsalted butter, cut into 4 pieces

FOR THE DUCK HAM

6 boneless, skinless duck thighs

3 grams kosher salt

2 grams pink curing salt

1 gram Pierre Poivre spice mix (see Sources, page 403)

5 grams Activa (see Sources, page 403; optional)

Extra-virgin olive oil

FOR THE DUCK LARD

1 pound duck fat

1 teaspoon black truffle oil

1 tablespoon chopped black truffles

FOR THE PICKLED APPLES

1 teaspoon coriander seeds

1 teaspoon cumin seeds

1 teaspoon white peppercorns

1 teaspoon black peppercorns

1 sprig fresh thyme

1 fresh or ½ dried bay leaf

1 cup apple cider vinegar

3 tablespoons granulated sugar

¼ jalapeño, sliced

1 teaspoon kosher salt

1 teaspoon ground turmeric

1 firm, tart apple (preferably Honeycrisp), quartered

TO ASSEMBLE THE DISH

Canola oil

Fresh flat-leaf parsley leaves

Black truffle oil or extra-virgin olive oil

Mustard oil (see Sources page 403)

Flaky sea salt, such as Maldon

Pierre Poivre spice mix (see Sources page 403) or smoked paprika

+ Unfortunately, to get the right texture on the duck thighs, there is no alternative to sous-vide cooking with this recipe. While you can make a homemade version of sous-vide poaching while standing over a pot and adding ice cubes to maintain a steady temperature, you probably don't want to do so for 6 hours. Instead, try to find smoked duck breast or duck ham that is often sold at fine foods stores.

291

MAKE THE DUCK MOUSSE

1. Pat the duck organs dry with paper towels. Set aside.

2. In a small saucepot, combine the port, sugar, sliced shallot, garlic, thyme, and bay leaf and cook over medium heat until the port has reduced to about ¼ cup. Strain the reduction into a small bowl and set aside.

3. In a large sauté pan set over high heat, add enough oil to cover the bottom of the pan. Just before it starts to smoke, season the organs with the pink and kosher salts and add the organs to the pan in one even layer. Reduce the heat to medium and cook the organs, without stirring, for 2 minutes. Add the chopped shallots and brandy, and stand back—the brandy could flame up. Stir the organs, and cook for 1 minute more for medium-rare. Transfer the organs to a blender and add the reserved port reduction. Starting with the blender on low and gradually increasing the speed, add the terrine, heavy cream, duck fat, and butter, piece by piece. Blend on high for 1 minute. Taste and adjust the seasonings if needed. If the mousse is not completely smooth, pass it through a fine-mesh strainer into a medium bowl. Set the bowl over an ice bath or refrigerate until cold. Cover and refrigerate overnight.

MAKE THE DUCK HAM

4. Pat the duck thighs dry, and season with the kosher and pink salts and the Pierre Poivre. In a small bowl, combine the Activa with 2 tablespoons warm water and whisk until smooth. Brush the Activa mixture all over the duck thighs. Lay out a large piece of plastic wrap on a counter and place 3 of the thighs on the plastic wrap, with the side where the skin used to be face down. Place the remaining 3 thighs on top of the other thighs, "skin" side up. Roll the thighs into a tight cylinder in the plastic wrap and twist off the ends to secure. Place the cylinder into a vacuum-seal bag and seal the bag. Drizzle some extra-virgin olive oil on top to prevent discoloration. Refrigerate overnight.

5. The next day, fill an immersion circulator with water and preheat to 156°F. Poach the duck for 6 hours. Transfer the bag to an ice bath and cool for about 10 minutes. Remove from ice, remove the duck ham from the bag, and slice the ham into ¼-inch-thick slices.

MAKE THE DUCK LARD

6. Set a large dry sauté pan over high heat and add the duck fat—you will hear it sizzle. Reduce the heat to low and let the fat render for about 1 hour. Strain the fat through a fine-mesh strainer into a medium bowl. Set the bowl over an ice bath and whisk until cool. Once the fat begins to set, transfer it to a container, cover, and refrigerate overnight.

7. The following day, transfer the rendered fat to a food processor, add the truffle oil, and process for 10 to 15 seconds or until the fat looks light and airy. Fold in the truffles and transfer to a pastry bag or a resealable plastic bag with one corner snipped to form a quarter-size hole. Pipe the mixture onto plastic wrap and roll it into a tight cylinder, about 1½ inches in diameter, twisting both ends to secure (it will look like a log of butter). Transfer to the freezer and let sit at least 3 hours before using.

MAKE THE PICKLED APPLES

8. In a small dry skillet, toast the coriander, cumin, and both kinds of peppercorns, over medium-low heat until toasted and fragrant. Transfer the spices to a small dish and set aside to cool. Once cool, transfer the spices to a piece of cheesecloth and add the thyme and bay leaf. Tie the corners of the cheesecloth together to form a sachet.

9. In a small, nonreactive saucepot set over high heat, combine the sachet, vinegar, sugar, jalapeño, salt, and turmeric with 1 cup of water and bring to a boil. Meanwhile, slice the apples into ⅛-inch-thick half-moons and transfer to a nonreactive bowl. Once the marinade comes to a boil, pour it over the apple slices and allow to stand for 4 hours, at room temperature, before serving. If making this in advance, refrigerate until ready to use.

ASSEMBLE THE DISH

10. Add enough oil to a skillet to come ½ inch up the sides of the skillet and warm the oil over medium heat. Fry the parsley leaves until crispy, about 30 seconds, and transfer to a paper towel–lined plate. Let cool.

The last photo for the book!

11. Slice the Duck Lard into four ½-inch-thick slices and divide among 4 buttered ramekins. Drizzle the lard with some truffle oil and sprinkle some flaky sea salt on top. Slice the Duck Ham into four ½-inch-thick slices. Divide the Duck Ham among 4 small plates, drizzle with mustard oil, and top with flaky sea salt. Place a small scoop of the Duck Mousse on the side of the ham, and add a pinch of Pierre Poivre and flaky sea salt. Serve with the Duck Lard and Pickled Apples on the side, along with whatever greens happen to be in season.

Make It Faster *If you want to use every scrap of duck you have but don't want to make every single component of this dish, just make one or two components at a time, and serve them with either Pickled Apples, which play nicely off the fattiness of the duck, or whatever pickles you happen to have on hand.*

MARC FORGIONE

OXTAIL AND BONE MARROW WELLINGTON + PORCINI MUSHROOMS

SERVES 4 Beef Wellington started out as a lavish and fashionable dish served at fancy dinner parties and banquets many decades ago. Some stories suggest that the dish was named after Arthur Wellesley, 1st Duke of Wellington, while others claim that the dish was invented in Wellington, New Zealand. Whatever its origins, it is decadent, delicious, and hearty. For whatever reason, however, Beef Wellington has been made poorly so many times that it developed a bad reputation and has since fallen out of fashion. We decided to bring back its former glory days by making it the right way—and then some.

Our version of Beef Wellington is even a bit more decadent than its traditional ancestor. We threw in some bone marrow and used braised oxtail meat in place of the tenderloin. There's a lot of prep involved, but trust me, it's well worth the time and effort. Once you have all the components, it takes just minutes to come together and cook.

FOR THE BONE MARROW

4 (6-inch) marrow bones, split in half

Kosher salt

Freshly ground black pepper

3 sprigs fresh thyme

1 fresh or ½ dried bay leaf

FOR THE OXTAILS

4 sprigs fresh thyme

1 sprig fresh rosemary

½ celery stalk

1 fresh or ½ dried bay leaf

1 strip bacon

Canola oil

3½ pounds oxtails, cut into 2-inch pieces

Kosher salt

Freshly ground black pepper

2 shallots, diced

2 medium carrots, cut into 1-inch pieces

½ medium onion, cut into eighths

5 garlic cloves, halved

5 whole black peppercorns, cracked

1½ tablespoons tomato paste

1½ tablespoons all-purpose flour

6 cups full-bodied dry red wine

2 cups ruby port

2½ cups Veal Stock (see page 382) or store-bought

1½ cups Chicken Stock (see page 382) or store-bought

¼ cup granulated sugar

Freshly ground black pepper

FOR THE DUCK LIVER MOUSSE

1 recipe Duck Liver Mousse (see page 345)

FOR THE MUSHROOM DUXELLES

1 recipe Mushroom Duxelles (see page 396)

FOR THE SHALLOT MARMALADE

1 cup ruby port

2 shallots, thinly sliced

2 tablespoons granulated sugar

1 tablespoon cracked black peppercorns

1 sprig fresh thyme

1 fresh or ½ dried bay leaf

FOR THE WELLINGTON

All-purpose flour, for dusting

2 (11 x 11 x ¼-inch) sheets puff pastry

1 large egg, lightly beaten

Flaky sea salt, such as Maldon

Pierre Poivre spice mix (see Sources, page 403) or smoked paprika

16 leaves fresh flat-leaf parsley, plus more for garnish

3 large egg yolks, beaten

Canola oil

1 small white button mushroom

1 (¾-ounce) black truffle (optional)

MAKE THE BONE MARROW

1. Soak the bones in a bowl of water in the refrigerator for 12 hours, changing the water every 3 hours.

2. Preheat the oven to 350°F; position the rack in the middle. Place the soaked bones in a roasting pan, bone side down, and season with salt and pepper. Add enough water to cover the bottom of the pan, and add the thyme and bay leaf. Cover the pan with foil and bake for 10 minutes or until you can easily stick a needle into the marrow and pull it out. If the marrow needs more time, cook for 5 minutes more and then check for doneness. Watch the marrow carefully; if the marrow overcooks, it will liquefy and seep out onto the roasting pan. Transfer the pan to a cooling rack and let the marrow bones sit at room temperature, covered, for 20 minutes. Remove the foil and set aside to cool.

MAKE THE OXTAILS

3. While the marrow bones are soaking, place 2 sprigs of the thyme, ½ of the rosemary sprig, celery, and ½ fresh or ¼ dried bay leaf on the strip of bacon and wrap the bacon around. Using a piece of kitchen twine, tie the bouquet garni tightly and set aside.

4. Add enough oil to a large stockpot or a Dutch oven to cover the bottom of the pot and set it over medium-high heat. Season the oxtails with salt and pepper. Just before the oil starts to smoke, add the oxtails and brown on all sides, 8 to 10 minutes. Transfer the oxtails to a plate and set aside. Discard the oil.

5. Add more oil to the pan and add the shallots, carrots, onion, garlic, and peppercorns, and cook until light brown, 4 to 6 minutes. Stir in the tomato paste and cook for 2 minutes. Stir in the flour until well incorporated, and add 2 cups of the wine, 1 cup of the port, and the bouquet garni. Bring to a simmer over high heat, reduce the heat to low, and cook until the mixture has reduced to one-third of its original volume.

6. Meanwhile, preheat the oven to 300°F; position the rack in the middle. Return the oxtails to the pot with the vegetables and add the stocks. Raise the heat to medium-high and bring to a simmer. Cover the pot, transfer to the oven, and bake for about 4 hours.

7. While the oxtails cook, make the port reduction: In a nonreactive 4-quart pot, combine the sugar with the remaining 4 cups wine, 1 cup port, the remaining 2 sprigs thyme, ½ fresh or ¼ dried bay leaf, and black pepper to taste, and bring to a boil. Cook until the liquid has reduced to 2 cups, about 30 minutes. Remove from the heat and set aside.

8. Remove the oxtails and strain the stock through a fine-mesh strainer, discarding the vegetables. Pick the meat off the bones and set aside in a large container. Return the pot with the stock to the stove over medium heat, and cook, skimming off the fat as needed, until the liquid has reduced to 2 cups of sauce. Add the reserved port reduction, raise the heat to medium-high, and cook, skimming off the fat as needed, until the sauce has reduced to about 2 cups and has a thick consistency. Pour the finished sauce over the reserved oxtail meat, cover, and refrigerate overnight.

MAKE THE DUCK LIVER MOUSSE

9. Prepare the Duck Liver Mousse.

MAKE THE MUSHROOM DUXELLES

10. Prepare the Mushroom Duxelles.

MAKE THE SHALLOT MARMALADE

11. In a small saucepot, combine the port, shallots, sugar, peppercorns, thyme, and bay leaf, and set over medium heat. Cook, stirring from time to time, until the port has the consistency of thick syrup and the mixture looks like loose jam, about 20 minutes. Discard the thyme and bay leaf and set aside.

MAKE THE WELLINGTON

12. Preheat the oven to 350°F; position the rack in the middle. Lightly flour a work surface and lay the puff pastry on top. Cut the pastry into 4 x 6-inch pieces; they should be large enough so that there is 2 inches of space from the top of the bone marrow and you can fold the pastry over with 1 inch of overlap. Brush half of 1 pastry piece with the beaten egg and place a piece of the bone marrow in the center. Spread a layer of oxtails on top of the marrow with the bone, top with Duck Liver Mousse, and finish with a layer of Mushroom Duxelles. Spread

Shallot Marmalade over the top, and sprinkle with flaky sea salt and Pierre Poivre. Arrange 4 of the parsley leaves in a straight line over the marmalade. Fold the pastry over and seal on the side where the bone is. Brush the top of the pastry with the beaten egg yolks and sprinkle some more flaky sea salt on top. Repeat to fill the other puff pastry pieces. Transfer the filled pastry to a Silpat- or parchment paper–lined shallow baking pan and bake for 12 minutes or until the pastry is golden brown and puffy. While the Wellingtons bake, lay out two pieces of parchment paper and very lightly brush both pieces with oil. Lay out the parsley leaves for the garnish over one piece of the parchment paper so that the leaves are flat against the paper. Place the second piece of parchment paper, oiled side down, over the leaves, and transfer to the microwave. Microwave the leaves in 30-second intervals for a total of about 90 seconds to 2 minutes or until the leaves are crisp. Check on the leaves after each interval to see if they are crisp. Once done, remove the leaves from the parchment paper and set them aside.

13. Transfer the Wellingtons to a cooling rack and slice the white button mushroom on top. Serve the Wellingtons with the remaining sauce from the oxtails and remaining Shallot Marmalade. Finish with black truffle shavings, if using, and the parsley.

Make It Faster *You can make the dish a little bit faster by using a quality premade foie gras terrine. You can also double a batch of the Short Ribs (see page 228) and freeze the other half until you're ready to make this recipe.*

FORAGED AND FOUND EDIBLES

AARON SCHAAL

I am always amazed by how diverse wild edibles are and love using them at the restaurant. Thanks to Foraged and Found Edibles, founded in 2001 by Jeremy Faber, I can do it more easily.

Jeremy grew up loving to wander in the forests surrounded by the wilderness. So a forestry major in college seemed a logical choice, but somewhere along the way Jeremy had a change of heart, decided to pursue cooking instead, and departed for the CIA. Upon graduating, Jeremy realized he wanted to live closer to the woods and moved to Seattle. It was while cooking at various restaurants that Jeremy started foraging for wild foods and including them on his menus.

From that love of foraging, and a particularly fruitful morel season in the Washington Cascades, a full-time foraging career emerged, and Foraged and Found was born. Jeremy's company works strictly in accordance with what the season's and nature's offerings might be at any given time: fiddlehead ferns and morels in the spring; berries and chanterelles in the summer; mushrooms in the fall, just to name a few.

While still a small company at its core, Jeremy and his colleagues work with dozens of foragers to gather produce for the greenmarkets and purveyors across the country and ship them as quickly as possible to their clients. They have been amazing in working with my restaurant, eager and enthusiastic about their foraged ingredients, and it is their passion and hard work that has allowed us to have more wild ingredients on our menus than ever before.

LAMB NECK + VADOUVAN CURRY + YOUNG SPRING VEGETABLES + CARROT PUREE

SERVES 4 This was a dish we served on our first spring menu, to much acclaim. During winters the greenmarket doesn't have much to offer, and seeing the first-of-the-spring produce makes me want to rush back into the kitchen and cook new dishes.

This meal is very flexible when it comes to your spring vegetables. Whatever you have on hand, whatever looks the best at the farmers' market, or if you like to forage for your food, whatever is in season in the woods, can be used in place of any of the vegetables here. Enjoy discovering your favorite combination. You can prepare most of the components for the dish while the lamb necks are cooking as they take a bit of time.

FOR THE LAMB NECKS

3 strips bacon

12 sprigs fresh thyme

4 sprigs fresh rosemary

2 celery stalks

3 fresh or 1½ dried bay leaves

3 lamb necks

1¾ cups Vadouvan curry powder (see Sources, page 403), plus more as needed

Extra-virgin olive oil

Kosher salt

Freshly ground black pepper

10 garlic cloves, halved

4 shallots, diced

3 carrots, cut into 1-inch pieces

1 medium onion, cut into eighths

10 whole black peppercorns, cracked

¼ cup tomato paste

¼ cup all-purpose flour

6 cups dry white wine

3 cups white port

5 cups Veal Stock (see page 382) or store-bought

3 cups Chicken Stock (see page 382) or store-bought

FOR THE GARLIC CHIPS

2 cups extra-virgin olive oil

6 garlic cloves, sliced paper-thin

FOR THE YOUNG SPRING VEGETABLES

1 cup fiddlehead ferns

1 cup green peas

8 young white asparagus stalks (substitute green if white is unavailable)

12 baby carrots

8 young green asparagus stalks

Olive oil

1 cup spring onions, julienned

1 ounce (2 tablespoons) unsalted butter

⅓ cup chiffonade of fresh mint

¼ cup chopped fresh curly parsley

Kosher salt

FOR THE CARROT PUREE

3 sprigs fresh mint

1 pound carrots, chopped

3 cups heavy cream

8 ounces (16 tablespoons) unsalted butter

Kosher salt

TO ASSEMBLE THE DISH

Pea shoots

Flaky sea salt, such as Maldon

MAKE THE LAMB NECKS

1. On a cutting board, arrange the bacon strips so their long edges overlap slightly. Place 8 sprigs of the thyme, the rosemary, celery, and 2 fresh or 1 dried bay leaves on overlapping pieces of bacon and wrap the bacon around. Using a piece of kitchen twine, tie the bouquet garni tightly and set aside.

2. Pat the necks dry and place them in either a large bowl or a resealable bag. Season the necks with 1½ cups of the curry powder, enough olive oil to coat, salt, and pepper. Cover and refrigerate overnight.

3. Preheat the oven to 425°F; position the rack in the middle. Place the necks in a roasting pan fitted with a roasting rack, transfer to the oven, and roast for 25 to

30 minutes or until browned on all sides. Transfer the necks to a cooling rack and set aside.

4. Reduce the oven temperature to 300°F. Pour off most of the fat that has rendered from the lamb into a large ovenproof saucepot set over medium heat. Reserve the cooking juices that have collected at the bottom of the roasting pan. Add the bouquet garni and cook until the bacon has rendered. Add the garlic, shallots, carrots, onion, peppercorns, and 3 tablespoons of the curry powder to the saucepot and cook until the vegetables are light brown, about 10 minutes. Stir in the tomato paste and cook for 2 minutes. Stir in the flour, add the wine and port, and cook until the liquid has reduced to about one-third of its original volume, about 30 minutes. Add the necks and the reserved pan juices to the saucepot and add the stocks. Bring to a simmer and remove from the heat. Place a piece of parchment paper over the pot, and cover tightly with foil. Transfer the pot to the oven and cook for 2½ to 3 hours or until the necks are tender.

5. Remove the lamb necks from the pot and set aside in a container large enough to hold the necks and the sauce. Strain the sauce through a fine-mesh strainer, return it to the stovetop over medium heat, and simmer the sauce, skimming off fat as needed, until it has reduced to about 2 cups, about 20 minutes. Add the reduced sauce to the container with the lamb necks, cover, and refrigerate overnight.

6. When ready to serve, preheat the oven to 350°F; position the rack in the middle. Reheat the necks in the oven, covered, for 20 to 30 minutes; uncover and cook for 20 minutes more or until the meat is soft and warmed through.

7. In a small, dry skillet set over medium heat, toast the remaining 1 tablespoon curry powder, stirring, for 2 to 3 minutes or until fragrant. Add the toasted curry to the pot with the lamb necks and stir to incorporate. Taste and add more curry, if needed.

MAKE THE GARLIC CHIPS

8. While the lamb necks are reheating, warm the oil in a skillet over medium-high heat until it registers 300°F on a deep-frying thermometer. Add the garlic slices and fry until crispy, 20 to 30 seconds. Using a slotted spoon, transfer the garlic chips to a paper towel–lined tray and set aside.

MAKE THE YOUNG SPRING VEGETABLES

9. Bring a pot of salted water to a boil. Preheat the oven to 425°F; position the rack in the middle. Blanch the fiddlehead ferns in the boiling water for 1 minute, and using a slotted spoon, transfer them to an ice bath. Repeat the blanching process with the peas and white asparagus. Drain and set the blanched vegetables aside.

10. Toss the carrots and green asparagus in olive oil and place on a shallow baking pan. Roast for 10 to 15 minutes, or until the green asparagus is tender. Remove from the heat and set aside.

11. Add enough oil to a large sauté pan to cover the bottom of the pan and set it over high heat. Just before it starts to smoke, add the onions, reduce the heat to medium, and cook, stirring occasionally, until the onions are soft. Set aside.

12. When ready to serve, while the necks reheat (toward the end of reheating), in a large sauté pan, melt the butter over medium heat and add the fiddleheads, peas, white and green asparagus, onions, and carrots, and cook until warmed through, about 3 minutes. Stir in the mint and parsley and season to taste with salt. Remove from the heat.

MAKE THE CARROT PUREE

13. While the lamb necks are reheating, tie the mint into a bundle with kitchen twine. In a saucepot, combine the mint bundle, carrots, cream, butter, and a few pinches of salt, and simmer over medium heat until the carrots are soft, 8 to 10 minutes. Transfer the carrots to a blender and squeeze the liquid from the mint bundle over the carrots. Puree the carrots on high for 90 seconds, adding a bit of the cooking liquid if needed. Set aside and keep warm until ready to serve. Discard the remaining cooking liquid.

ASSEMBLE THE DISH

14. Divide the Carrot Puree among 4 warmed plates. Place the lamb necks on top of the puree and scatter the Garlic Chips over the meat. Add the Young Spring Vegetables on the side, garnish with the pea shoots, and sprinkle with flaky sea salt.

KOPPERT CRESS USA

NICOLAS MAZARD

To anyone who thinks micro greens are just a pretentious way to make food look restaurant-pretty, Nicolas Mazard will tell you that they are "living condiments." But first, he'll probably offer you some micro greens to try. Some will taste faintly of the sea and oysters, some of sambuca, and others of a forest after the rain.

Upon trying his micro greens for the first time, the response he hears most often is, "Holy shit, what did you do to the plant?"

The experience with micro greens in the United States, prior to Koppert Cress, that is, had been a disappointment. More often than not, the micro greens looked lackluster, offering little in the taste department. They were purely cosmetic, a finishing touch before the food went out to the table. Koppert Cress, on the other hand, offers intensely flavored micro greens that transform the final taste of the dish rather than just acting as decoration.

Raised in Paris and the French countryside by his farmer mother, Mazard was fascinated with farming and agriculture from an early age and studied agriculture and business in college.

At some point he and his brother had plans to open a garden center in France—something like Home Depot in the United States, but focused entirely on plants and gardens. But plans changed and Nicolas found himself taking a job as a marketing specialist with Koppert Cress in 2001. "I wanted to work with something unique and amazing. I was fascinated with things like vanilla, which is an orchid, and its value and versatility in cooking," Mazard recalls.

He found that "unique and amazing" in Koppert Cress, a Dutch company that grows unique heirloom and forgotten rare varieties of herbs, and reintroduces them to chefs at fine restaurants.

The Szechuan button, for example, has been used in African cooking and medicine for hundreds of years. When placed on the tongue, people experience a tingling sensation, "like nature's Pop Rocks." In modern cuisine, it's been used to infuse drinks and sorbets, but at our restaurant, it is served alongside the Hiramasa Tartare (see page 61), one of our signature dishes.

When Mazard was hired, he was the first marketing professional to join the tiny company. Seeing an opportunity, Mazard quickly built out the European business and eventually expanded the business in the United States.

With over twenty-eight employees today, the company has a one-acre greenhouse on Long Island with plans to add another in the near future. The operation allows Mazard to provide micro greens to restaurants all over the East Coast and out to the Midwest. Looking to the future, Mazard plans to eventually expand to the West Coast, as well as to bring micro greens to finer stores across the United States for home cooks who want to elevate their dishes to a more sophisticated level of flavor.

HAMPSHIRE PORK TENDERLOIN AND BELLY + SUCKLING PIG HEAD + OLDE SALT CLAMS + MATSUTAKE MUSHROOMS + BLACK GARLIC JUS

SERVES 4 I came up with snout-to-tail displays while at Charlie Palmer's Pigs and Pinot food festival in 2011. We had an *Iron Chef*–style battle against the Voltaggio brothers and this was one of the dishes I created. I like using a lot of different heritage pig breeds, but the Hampshire breed is one of my favorites and wound up working great for the dish. I never cease to marvel at what a utilitarian animal a pig is—you really can use almost any part of the animal and make something delicious with it.

The Hampshire breed, muscled and fast-growing, is one of the oldest and most popular American heritage breeds of hogs. Imported from Hampshire, England, in the early 1830s, the Hampshire quickly assumed its prominent place in the American animal-farming landscape as a sturdy and utilitarian animal with a reputation of being one of the leanest of the North American breeds. Its meat is a perfect match for this dish.

FOR THE CURE

2 cups kosher salt

½ cup packed dark brown sugar

¼ cup whole black peppercorns

¼ cup red pepper flakes

Leaves from 2 sprigs fresh rosemary

Leaves from 2 sprigs fresh thyme

1 fresh or ½ dried bay leaf, crushed

FOR THE PIG HEAD PORK CAKES

1 suckling pig head from an 18-pound pig, split

3 tablespoons whole black peppercorns

2 tablespoons fennel seeds

2 sprigs fresh thyme

1 sprig fresh rosemary

1 fresh or ½ dried bay leaf

1 medium yellow onion, halved

8 cups canola oil, plus more as needed

1 carrot

1 cup grainy mustard

¼ cup red pepper flakes

3 tablespoons chopped fresh tarragon

3 tablespoons chopped fresh chives

2 heads garlic, halved

2 shallots, minced

3 cups all-purpose flour

1 teaspoon kosher salt, plus more as needed

4 large eggs

1 recipe Bacon Bread Crumbs (see page 381) or regular bread crumbs

FOR THE PORK BELLY

5 pounds pork belly, preferably from a Hampshire pig

8 cups canola oil

3 tablespoons whole black peppercorns

2 tablespoons fennel seeds

2 sprigs fresh thyme

1 sprig fresh rosemary

1 fresh or ½ dried bay leaf

2 heads garlic, halved

1 carrot

1 recipe Onion Brûlé (see page 393)

FOR THE TENDERLOIN

16 pieces thinly sliced speck

¼ cup chopped fresh curly parsley

4 (4-ounce) Hampshire pork tenderloins

Canola oil

2 ounces (4 tablespoons) unsalted butter

4 sprigs fresh thyme

FOR THE BLACK GARLIC JUS

1 head black garlic

2 pounds Olde Salt littleneck clams, rinsed

2 cups Chicken Stock (see page 382) or store-bought

1 cup dry white wine

1 strip thick-cut bacon

3 sprigs fresh thyme

1 fresh or ½ dried bay leaf

TO ASSEMBLE THE DISH

Mustard oil (see Sources, page 403)

Affilia pea shoots (see Sources, page 403; optional)

4 medium matsutake mushrooms

MAKE THE CURE

1. In a large bowl, combine the salt, sugar, peppercorns, pepper flakes, rosemary, thyme, and bay leaf. Divide the mixture evenly into 2 separate bowls.

MAKE THE PIG HEAD PORK CAKES

2. Pat the pig head dry and rub 1 bowl of the cure all over. Refrigerate, uncovered, overnight.

3. Preheat the oven to 275°F; position the rack in the middle. Rinse the pig head under cold running water, pat dry, and set aside in a roasting pan. Place the peppercorns, fennel, thyme, rosemary, and bay leaf on a piece of cheesecloth and tie the ends together to form a sachet. Warm a dry skillet over high heat. Add the onion halves, cut side down, and sear until blackened. Remove the onion from heat. Place the sachet, oil, carrot, and blackened onion into a 4-quart pot set over medium-high heat. Warm the oil until the temperature registers 200°F on a deep-frying thermometer. Pour the warm oil mixture over the pig head, cover the roasting pan with parchment paper, and then cover with foil. Bake for 3 hours or until the head is fork-tender. Refrigerate, covered and in the oil, overnight.

4. Return the roasting pan to the stovetop, and warm the oil over medium heat, until you can easily pull out the head halves. Remove the pan from the heat and set aside. Pull all the meat from the head, making sure to get into every little crevice. Run your knife through the strands, so that the meat is no longer than 1 inch. Peel and chop the tongue and brains. Very finely dice the ears, skin, and fat. Basically, the only "garbage" should be the bones, teeth, eyes, and end of the snout. The rest gets used in this dish. You should wind up with about 8 cups of meat. In a large bowl, combine the meat with the mustard, red pepper flakes, tarragon, chives, garlic, and shallots. Set aside while you prepare the breading station for the patties.

5. In a shallow bowl combine the flour and salt and set aside. In a medium bowl lightly beat the eggs and set aside. Place the Bacon Bread crumbs nearby in a shallow, wide bowl.

6. Slightly moisten your hands and shape the pig head meat into 3-inch-wide and ½-inch-thick round, pork patties—you should wind up with 10 to 15 patties.

7. Dip each patty in the flour mixture, then in the beaten eggs, and finally in the bread crumbs. Set aside 4 patties and freeze the remaining patties for another use (they are excellent for a Sunday brunch, with a fried egg on top). Transfer the reserved breaded patties to the refrigerator until ready to assemble the dish.

8. When ready to serve, add 2 inches of oil to a Dutch oven or a skillet with tall sides. Heat the oil over medium-high heat until it registers 350°F on a deep-frying thermometer. Carefully slide the pork cakes into the hot oil and fry them for 40 seconds or until the outside is golden and crispy. Transfer the cakes to a paper towel–lined tray and season with salt.

MAKE THE PORK BELLY

9. While the pig head rests overnight, make the pork belly, as it too will need an overnight rest. Rub the remaining bowl of The Cure all over the pork belly pieces, and refrigerate, uncovered, overnight.

10. Preheat the oven to 300°F; position the rack in the middle. Add the oil to a large Dutch oven and set it on the stovetop over medium-high heat. Warm the oil until the temperature registers 180°F on a deep-frying thermometer. While waiting on the oil, place the peppercorns, fennel, thyme, rosemary, and bay leaf into a piece of cheesecloth and tie the ends together to form a sachet.

11. Rinse the belly under cold, running water, and thoroughly pat dry. Place the belly, spice sachet, garlic, carrot, and Onion Brûlé in the oil, cover the pot, and transfer it to the oven. Cook the belly for 3 hours. Transfer to a cooling rack and let cool slightly before refrigerating overnight.

12. Remove the belly from the fat and wipe off any excess fat from the meat. Cut the belly into 3 even squares and freeze until solid, 4 to 6 hours. Once solid, cut the belly into 16 (⅛-inch-thick) slices. Set aside the slices on a piece of parchment paper.

13. Separate the speck slices into groups of 4, each piece with a group laid out to slightly overlap the other. Sprinkle each speck "block" with 1 tablespoon of the parsley. Place the tenderloins at the bottom of each speck "block" and roll them into cylinders. Lay out 4 pieces of plastic wrap on the counter and transfer each tenderloin cylinder onto its own piece of wrap. Wrap the meat as tightly as possible, twisting at both ends.

14. SOUS-VIDE COOKING INSTRUCTIONS (see step 15 for Sous-Vide Alternative Instructions): Preheat an immersion circulator filled with water to 140°F. Place each tenderloin cylinder in a small vacuum-seal bag and seal the bags. Poach the tenderloins for 2 hours. Remove the tenderloins from the bags and set aside until ready to assemble the dish.

15. SOUS-VIDE ALTERNATIVE INSTRUCTIONS: Preheat the oven to 400°F; position the rack in the middle. Add enough oil to a large ovenproof sauté pan to cover the bottom of the pan and set it over high heat. Just before the oil starts to smoke, remove the plastic wrap from the tenderloins and add them to the pan, seam side down, and reduce the heat to medium (you may need to do this in batches). Cook the tenderloins until browned on the bottom, 3 to 5 minutes. Flip the tenderloins over, transfer the pan to the oven, and cook until medium, 5 to 10 minutes or until the internal temperature of the loins registers between 140°F and 145°F on a meat thermometer. Set aside until ready to serve.

16. When ready to serve, add enough oil to a large sauté pan to cover the bottom of the pan and set it over high heat. Just before the oil starts to smoke, add the speck-wrapped tenderloins to the pan, and reduce the heat to medium. Cook the tenderloins until browned on the bottom, 3 to 5 minutes. Add the butter and thyme and baste the meat for 1 minute. Flip the tenderloins over and baste for 1 minute more. Transfer to a plate and let sit for 5 minutes. (If you cooked the tenderloin in the oven, return the meat to the stovetop, and over medium-high heat, add the butter and thyme and baste for 1 to 2 minutes. Let the meat rest 5 minutes before slicing.)

17. Fill a small bowl with hot water and soak the black garlic for about 10 minutes. Peel the garlic (the skins should pop right off) and set aside. In a large saucepot, combine the clams, stock, wine, bacon, thyme, and bay leaf and cook over medium heat. As soon as the clams begin to open, remove the pot from the heat. Strain the jus through a fine-mesh strainer into a bowl and discard the bacon and herbs. Add the black garlic to the jus, and using an immersion blender or a stand blender, puree the liquid until smooth. Keep both the clams and the jus warm. Right before serving, reheat the jus until almost simmering and transfer to a gravy boat.

18. Slice each pork tenderloin into 3 pieces and divide the tenderloins among 4 warmed plates. Divide the pork belly slices and pork cakes among the plates, placing them around the tenderloins. Spoon the reserved clams around and drizzle everything with a little mustard oil. Scatter the pea shoots around, if using. Thinly shave the matsutake mushrooms over the dish. Serve with the Black Garlic Jus alongside at the table.

Make It Faster *It's funny, but when you order this dish at the restaurant and it arrives, it looks like the simplest, easiest thing in the world. But looks can be deceiving: This dish, in its entirety, is very time-consuming and demanding. If you want to challenge your inner butcher or charcuterie-artisan, go ahead—in the end you will feel incredibly empowered. But if you're trying to just get a feel for this dish and how much fun nose-to-tail cooking can be, just try making the Pig Head Pork Cakes the first time around. And maybe play around with various components separately. It's amazing how much of the animal we can really use and how little goes to waste if you know what you're doing.*

SUCKLING PIG FACE + MUSTARD + TOAST + MF PICKLES + TAHOON

SERVES 4 One night a few years ago, my brother came over to the restaurant for dinner. At the time he was a chef at this barbecue spot on Long Island, and was constantly around pork. I wanted to give him something he might not have had before: half a pig's head with toast and MF Pickles, which were inspired by an English take on an Indian pickle. Now at the restaurant, Thursday nights are pig face nights, and people call weeks ahead to get a table.

6 whole cloves

1 recipe Onion Brûlée (see page 393)

1 recipe The Cure (see page 391)

One suckling pig head, split

3 tablespoons black peppercorns

2 tablespoons fennel seeds

3 sprigs fresh thyme

3 sprigs fresh rosemary

1 fresh or ½ dried bay leaf

8 cups canola oil

2 heads garlic, halved

1 medium carrot, peeled

1 cup Tahoon cress (see Sources, page 403) or chiffonade of watercress

1 recipe MF Pickles (see page 397)

8 thick slices crusty bread, toasted

1 cup grainy mustard

1. Stick the cloves into the Onion Brûlé and set aside.

2. Rub The Cure over the pig head, making sure it is evenly distributed. Refrigerate, uncovered, overnight.

3. Preheat the oven to 275°F; position the rack in the middle. Rinse the pig head under cold water, pat dry, place in a roasting pan, and let the head come to room temperature.

4. Place the peppercorns, fennel seeds, thyme, rosemary, and bay leaf in a 2-ply piece of cheesecloth and tie the ends together to form a sachet; set aside. In a large stockpot set over medium-high heat, combine the Onion Brûlé, oil, garlic, carrot, and sachet. Heat the oil over medium heat until it registers 200°F on a deep-frying thermometer. Pour the warm oil and contents of the pot over the pig head. Cover everything with parchment paper, then wrap tightly in foil. Roast the pig head for 3 hours. Transfer to a rack and let cool in the oil at room temperature for 2 hours before refrigerating overnight.

5. When ready to serve, preheat the oven to 400°F; position the rack in the middle. Set the roasting pan over 2 burners on low heat until you can easily pull the head out of the oil. Transfer the pig head halves to another baking pan and warm them in the oven for about 15 minutes or until the skin is crispy and shiny (the skin should look lacquered). Remove the head from the oven and transfer to a platter. Sprinkle some cress around and serve, immediately, with the MF Pickles, toasted bread, and mustard.

DESSERT

"Desserts are last, but don't let them be least. A dessert is almost like the gift at the end of the meal, a bonus. To me, a perfect dessert is one that has focus, great textures, a balance of flavors, some contrast, and most important, is just damn delicious, leaving you wishing for one more bite."

—JOHNNY IUZZINI

LEMON CHEESECAKE BITES + STRAWBERRY CONSOMMÉ + STRAWBERRY SORBET + CANDIED LEMON VERBENA

MAKES ABOUT 12 (1½-INCH) SQUARES I love being inspired by a dish I have eaten somewhere else. I had this beautiful strawberry consommé during the dessert course at Michel Trauma's restaurant in France. The servers just keep filling your glass whenever you finished it. At the time I had never tasted anything like it. It was the most intense strawberry flavor, but not at all cloying. When we started to put the lemon cheesecake bites together at our restaurant, I instantly thought of what a perfect fit the strawberry consommé would be. The combination of lemon, strawberries, and lemon verbena is absolutely incredible. We serve it with a scoop of strawberry sorbet garnished with a candied lemon verbena leaf.

FOR THE STRAWBERRY SORBET

4 cups (about 1 pound) strawberries, hulled and halved

6 tablespoons granulated sugar

2 cups Simple Syrup (see page 394)

FOR THE GRAHAM CRACKER CRUST

1½ cups graham cracker crumbs (from 10 whole graham crackers)

¼ cup granulated sugar

3 ounces (6 tablespoons) unsalted butter, melted

FOR THE LEMON CHEESECAKE BITES

1½ pounds cream cheese, softened

1¼ cups granulated sugar

3 large eggs, room temperature

5 teaspoons cornstarch

1½ teaspoons pure vanilla extract

1 teaspoon finely grated

lemon zest

1½ teaspoons kosher salt

3 large egg yolks

6 tablespoons heavy cream

¼ cup whole milk

¼ cup fresh lemon juice

FOR THE STRAWBERRY CONSOMMÉ

2 cups strawberries, preferably local, hulled and sliced crosswise

1 cup granulated sugar

1 sprig fresh mint

1 sprig fresh lemon verbena

2 turns freshly ground black pepper

FOR THE CANDIED LEMON VERBENA LEAVES

12 fresh lemon verbena leaves, washed and dried

1 large egg white

½ cup granulated sugar

TO ASSEMBLE THE DISH

1 recipe Whipped Cream (see page 325)

MAKE THE STRAWBERRY SORBET

1. In a saucepot, combine the strawberries and sugar with 1 cup of water, and bring to a boil over medium heat. Reduce the heat to medium and cook at a lively simmer for 15 to 20 minutes. Transfer the strawberries and syrup to a blender and puree until smooth. Strain the liquid through a fine-mesh strainer into a bowl and stir in the Simple Syrup. Refrigerate for at least 2 hours or until completely cold.

2. Transfer the mixture to an ice cream machine and process according to the manufacturer's instructions. Remove the sorbet from the machine, transfer to a container, cover, and freeze for at least 2 hours, or until firm.

MAKE THE GRAHAM CRACKER CRUST

3. Preheat the oven to 350°F; position the rack in the middle. In a medium bowl, combine the crumbs with the sugar until blended. Add the melted butter and, using your hands, work the mixture until the crumbs are all moist and coated with butter. Transfer the crumbs into a 9 x 13-inch pan and press them into an even layer on the bottom of the pan. Bake the crust for about 10 minutes or until toasted. Remove the pan from the oven and let the crust cool completely.

4. In the bowl of a stand mixer fitted with the paddle attachment, combine the cream cheese, sugar, eggs, cornstarch, vanilla, lemon zest, and salt and beat on medium speed until the mixture is light and fluffy and no chunks of cream cheese remain, 3 to 4 minutes. Stop the mixer and scrape the sides of the bowl with a rubber spatula and mix again until thoroughly combined.

5. Add the egg yolks, one at a time, with the mixer on medium-low speed, stopping the mixer to scrape down the sides after each addition. With the mixer on low speed, gradually add the heavy cream, milk, and lemon juice. At this point, the batter should be smooth and free of any lumps.

6. Pour the batter into the prepared crust. Place the pan into a larger pan and fill the larger pan with enough water to come halfway up the sides of the smaller

pan. Bake the batter for 40 to 45 minutes or until the cheesecake is firm to the touch and the center is no longer jiggly. Carefully remove the smaller pan from the water bath and let it cool. Using a knife dipped in hot water, carefully cut the cheesecake into twelve 1½-inch individual squares. Wipe the knife, dip it back into the hot water, and wipe it dry between cuts.

MAKE THE STRAWBERRY CONSOMMÉ

7. In a saucepot, combine the strawberries, sugar, mint, verbena, and pepper with 1½ cups of water and bring to a simmer over medium-low heat. Cook, uncovered, for about 40 minutes or until the mixture has a thickish, jamlike consistency and the strawberries are beginning to disintegrate. Strain the mixture through a fine-mesh strainer into a bowl; reserve the fruit and discard the mint and verbena sprigs. Place the bowl of strawberry consommé over an ice bath and cool the liquid until ice cold. Refrigerate the consommé and strawberries, separately, until needed.

MAKE THE CANDIED VERBENA LEAVES

8. Line a baking sheet with parchment paper. Dip the leaves in the egg white, then in the sugar until evenly coated. Transfer the leaves to the lined baking sheet and let stand in a dry place for about 2 hours.

ASSEMBLE THE DISH

9. For each serving, arrange 3 pieces of cheesecake on a plate. Spoon some Strawberry Consommé around the cheesecake and top one piece with a quenelle of Strawberry Sorbet. Scatter the reserved macerated strawberries around, top another cheesecake piece with a dollop of the Whipped Cream, and garnish with a Candied Lemon Verbena Leaf.

APPLE PIE SOUFFLÉ + SALTED CARAMEL

MAKES 4 TO 6 (6-OUNCE) SOUFFLÉS This dessert was originally created during an *Iron Chef America* episode for a familiar-to-me themed battle—Thanksgiving—except this was round two, and I was paired with Jose Garces, an Iron Chef, against two other Iron Chefs: Michael Symon and Bobby Flay. Since I was going up against some very stiff competition, I knew I had to dig deep into my bag of tricks and pull out something that would truly wow the judges. The soufflé didn't disappoint, and Henry Winkler, a.k.a. "the Fonz," who was one of the judges, said it was the best soufflé he'd ever had.

The recipe here makes six dessert-size soufflés, but if you happen to be making dinner for four people, stick with these proportions (3 cups apple puree to 1½ cups whipped egg whites) to get a perfect soufflé every time. No one has ever complained about having an extra soufflé lying around.

FOR THE SALTED CARAMEL

1 cup granulated sugar

2 tablespoons light corn syrup

¾ cup heavy cream

2 ounces (4 tablespoons) unsalted butter, cubed

1½ teaspoons fine sea salt, plus additional to taste

FOR THE APPLE PIE SOUFFLÉ

¾ ounce (1½ tablespoons) unsalted butter, cubed, plus additional for buttering the ramekins

1 cup plus 1 tablespoon granulated sugar, plus additional for dusting the ramekins

1 teaspoon ground cinnamon, plus additional for dusting the ramekins

6 large Granny Smith or Honeycrisp apples, cored and sliced

1 teaspoon ground ginger

1 teaspoon ground cloves

1 cup egg whites (from about 6 large eggs), room temperature

Pinch of kosher salt

Pinch of cream of tartar

Confectioners' sugar, for dusting the soufflés

MAKE THE SALTED CARAMEL

1. Combine the sugar, corn syrup, and ¼ cup of water in a very clean saucepot and bring to a boil over medium-high heat. Continue to cook the caramel until it becomes a medium amber color (or the color of an Irish setter)—watch carefully and do not let the caramel burn. While the caramel cooks, do not stir it with a spoon, but gently swirl the caramel around the pot. Use a clean, moist pastry brush to remove any sugar crystals that form on the sides of the pot. As soon as the caramel is ready, remove it from the heat and gently whisk in the heavy cream and butter. Be careful: The caramel will bubble and sputter, so stand back. Whisk in the salt. Taste and add more salt if you like. Transfer the caramel to a bowl; you will have about 2 cups salted caramel. Refrigerate the sauce until needed. The sauce will keep, covered, for up to 2 weeks in the refrigerator.

PREPARE THE APPLE PIE SOUFFLÉ

2. Preheat the oven to 350°F; position the rack in the middle. Generously butter 4 to 6 (6-ounce) ramekins and dust the inside of the ramekins with sugar and cinnamon. Set the ramekins aside.

3. Toss the apples with the butter, 1 cup of the sugar, the cinnamon, ginger, and cloves and transfer the mixture to an ovenproof roasting pan. Bake the apples for about 30 minutes or until they are soft and falling apart.

4. Transfer the cooked apples, without their cooking liquid, to a blender and puree until they are completely smooth; the texture should be smoother and finer than regular applesauce. (At the restaurant, we use a Vitamix to get our apple puree to the right consistency, but at home you can use a regular blender and then strain your puree through a fine-mesh strainer or a chinois to get any remaining lumps out.) Transfer the apple puree to a bowl and let cool to room temperature. You should have about 4 cups apple puree.

5. Place the egg whites and salt in the bowl of a stand mixer fitted with the whisk attachment. Beat the egg whites on medium speed and slowly add the remaining 1 tablespoon sugar and cream of tartar. Continue beating until the egg whites become foamy. Raise the mixer speed to high and beat until stiff peaks form (when the whisk is lifted from the mixture, there should be a standing peak in the area where it was lifted).

6. Measure 3 cups of the apple puree into a separate bowl, and use a rubber spatula to gently fold in 1½ cups of the whipped egg whites.

7. Fill the ramekins to the top with the batter, and smooth out the tops with an offset spatula. Place a kitchen towel on the counter and gently tap the ramekins on the towel to release any trapped air bubbles. Transfer the ramekins to a baking sheet and bake for about 8 minutes or until the soufflés have risen and are firm when lightly tapped. While the soufflés bake, do not open the door to the oven.

8. While the soufflés bake, gently reheat the Salted Caramel in a small saucepan over low heat until warm and easily pourable.

9. Remove the soufflés and sprinkle them with confectioners' sugar. Poke a small hole in the middle of each soufflé and drizzle warmed Salted Caramel into it. Serve the soufflés immediately, with the remaining salted caramel sauce on the side.

MINI MEYER LEMON PIES

MAKES 15 TO 16 MINI PIES There are a few things I like the taste of but don't necessarily eat because of the ingredients that go into making them. One of the things I don't like to admit is that I actually like McDonald's breakfast offerings—and I love their apple pie. This dessert was inspired by those crispy, deep-fried apple hand pies. You can use any fruit filling you want, but here, I really love to use fragrant, tart Meyer lemon curd. These are particularly great in the winter when Meyer lemons are in season and there's not much available in the way of fruit but citrus.

4 large egg yolks, room temperature

6 tablespoons fresh Meyer lemon juice or other fresh citrus juice

6 tablespoons granulated sugar

2 ounces (4 tablespoons) unsalted butter, cubed

1 egg, lightly beaten

All-purpose flour

1 (11 x 16-inch) store-bought puff pastry sheet (see Sources, page 403)

4 cups canola oil, for frying

Confectioners' sugar, for dusting

1. In a medium nonreactive bowl, whisk the egg yolks until combined.

2. In a medium nonreactive saucepan, combine the lemon juice, sugar, and butter and place over medium heat, whisking to completely dissolve the sugar. Make sure the sugar is fully dissolved and the butter is melted. Bring the liquid to a boil, then remove from the heat. Slowly pour one-third of the hot lemon mixture into the egg yolks while whisking vigorously to temper the eggs. After the first third of the lemon mixture has been incorporated, slowly pour in the remaining mixture, whisking constantly until well combined.

3. Return the mixture to the saucepan and place the pan over low heat. Do not let the curd come to a boil. Whisk constantly, until the curd thickens and coats the back of a spoon, 5 to 7 minutes. Remove the curd from the heat and transfer it to a clean, nonreactive bowl; you will have about ¾ cup lemon curd. Cover the bowl and let the curd cool completely.

4. Line a baking sheet with parchment paper. Whisk the egg with 1 tablespoon of water until combined. On a lightly floured surface, roll out the puff pastry until it is a roughly 12 x 19-inch rectangle. Using a 3½-inch ring cutter, cut out discs of the puff pastry—you should be able to cut out about 15 discs. Using a pastry brush, brush the top half of each puff pastry disc with the egg wash. Add 2 to 3 tablespoons of the Meyer lemon curd and fold the puff pastry over to make a small half-moon shaped pie. Press or crimp the edges to seal. Repeat with the remaining dough discs and lemon curd. Transfer the filled pies to the lined baking sheet and freeze for 1 hour or until frozen through.

5. Place the oil in a large, high-sided pan set over medium-high heat, and heat until the oil registers 350°F on a deep-frying thermometer. Line a tray or large plate with paper towels. Gently slide up to 8 pies into the oil (do not crowd the pan or the temperature will drop) and fry until the pies are golden brown and crispy, 2 to 3 minutes. Be careful when frying—the oil may spatter, so stand back and wear protective clothing. Using a slotted spoon, remove the pies from the oil and transfer to the paper towel–lined tray. Repeat with the remaining pies. Dust the pies with confectioners' sugar and serve warm.

Note *If you're making these hand pies for a crowd, this recipe can be easily doubled or tripled.*

PINEAPPLE UPSIDE-DOWN CAKE SUNDAE

SERVES 10 At the restaurant we always do a seasonal sundae—and this is a great one to do in the winter when there aren't many in-season fruits other than tropical ones. It's a fun way to take something familiar like an upside-down cake and make it a bit more festive. When ice creams and sorbets pool at the bottom and some of the cake soaks them up, the combination is absolutely delicious.

FOR THE TOASTED ALMOND ICE CREAM

1½ cups chopped almonds

1⅓ cups whole milk

1⅓ cups cream

⅔ cup granulated sugar

3 large egg yolks, room temperature

1 teaspoon pure almond extract (optional)

FOR THE PINEAPPLE SORBET

2 cups granulated sugar

2 cups pineapple juice, preferably fresh

FOR THE COCONUT ICE CREAM

1⅓ cups coconut milk

1⅓ cups heavy cream

⅔ cup granulated sugar

3 large egg yolks

FOR THE ALMOND CAKE

8 ounces (16 tablespoons) unsalted butter, softened, plus additional for greasing the pan

1¼ cups granulated sugar

4 large eggs, room temperature

1 teaspoon almond extract

1½ cups all-purpose flour

6 tablespoons almond flour

¾ teaspoon baking powder

¼ teaspoon salt

¾ cup sour cream

FOR THE ALMOND CRUMBLE

1½ cups packed dark brown sugar

1 cup almond flour

1 cup chopped or sliced almonds

½ cup all-purpose flour

2 ounces (4 tablespoons) unsalted butter, cut into small pieces

FOR THE PINEAPPLE CHUTNEY

1 pineapple, peeled, cored, and chopped into ½-inch pieces

1 cup packed dark brown sugar

½ cup pineapple juice, preferably fresh

2 ounces (4 tablespoons) unsalted butter

TO ASSEMBLE THE DISH

30 (½-inch-thick) slices fresh pineapple

2 tablespoons granulated sugar

3 tablespoons mild honey

Finely grated zest of 1 lime

2 cups heavy cream

¼ cup packed dark brown sugar

MAKE THE TOASTED ALMOND ICE CREAM

1. Preheat the oven to 300°F; position the rack in the middle. Toast the almonds in a shallow baking pan for 5 to 7 minutes or until golden and fragrant. Watch carefully to be sure they don't burn. Transfer the almonds to a bowl and set aside to cool.

2. In a saucepan, combine the milk, cream, sugar, and toasted almonds, and bring to a simmer over medium heat, stirring to dissolve the sugar. Remove the mixture from the heat.

3. In a medium bowl, whisk together the egg yolks. Slowly drizzle one-third of the hot milk-cream mixture into the egg yolks while stirring constantly with a whisk (but not whisking) to temper the eggs. Pour the tempered egg yolk mixture slowly into the remaining milk-cream mixture in the pan, whisking constantly. Return the saucepan to the stovetop over low heat, and cook, stirring, until the custard is thick enough to coat the back of a spoon, 5 to 8 minutes. Taste the custard; if you want even more almond flavor, add the almond extract. Pass the mixture through a fine-mesh strainer into a bowl, cover, and refrigerate for at least 2 hours and preferably overnight. Discard the almonds. Transfer the chilled custard to an ice cream machine and process according to the manufacturer's instructions. Remove the ice cream from the machine, transfer to a container, and freeze until ready to use, at least 2 hours.

MAKE THE PINEAPPLE SORBET

4. In a nonreactive saucepan, combine the sugar with 2 cups of water and bring the liquid to a simmer over medium heat, stirring until all the sugar has dissolved. Add the pineapple juice and stir to combine. Transfer

the liquid to a nonreactive bowl and refrigerate for at least 2 hours and preferably overnight. Transfer the mixture to an ice cream machine and process according to the manufacturer's instructions. Remove the sorbet, transfer to a container, and freeze until ready to use, at least 2 hours.

MAKE THE COCONUT ICE CREAM

5. In a saucepan, combine the coconut milk, heavy cream, and sugar and bring the mixture to a simmer over medium heat, stirring to dissolve the sugar. Remove the mixture from the heat.

6. In a medium bowl, whisk together the egg yolks. Slowly drizzle one-third of the coconut milk mixture into the egg yolks while stirring constantly with a whisk (not whisking) to temper the eggs. Pour the tempered egg yolk mixture slowly into the remaining coconut milk mixture in the pan, whisking constantly. Return the saucepan to the stovetop over low heat, and cook, stirring, until the custard is thick enough to coat the back of a spoon, 5 to 8 minutes. Pass the mixture through a fine-mesh strainer into a bowl and refrigerate it for at least 2 hours and preferably overnight. Transfer the custard to an ice cream machine, and process according to the manufacturer's instructions. Remove the ice cream from the machine, transfer to a container, and freeze until ready to use, at least 2 hours.

MAKE THE ALMOND CAKE

7. While the ice cream custards rest in the refrigerator, make the cake. Preheat the oven to 350°F; position the rack in the middle. Butter a 9 x 9-inch pan and set aside. In the bowl of a stand mixer, cream together the butter and sugar on medium speed until light and fluffy, 8 to 10 minutes. Add the eggs, one at a time, stopping the mixer and scraping down the sides of the bowl after each addition. Add the almond extract and beat until combined.

8. In a medium bowl, combine the all-purpose flour, almond flour, baking powder, and salt. Whisk to incorporate the ingredients.

9. With the mixer on medium speed, add half of the sour cream to the creamed butter, alternating it with the flour mixture, until well combined, stopping the mixer and scraping down the sides and bottom of the bowl after each addition.

10. Pour the batter into the greased pan. Bake for 25 to 30 minutes, rotating the pan every 10 minutes, until the top is golden brown and a cake tester comes out clean when inserted into the cake. Leave the oven on. Transfer the cake to a rack to cook. Let the cake cool completely.

MAKE THE ALMOND CRUMBLE

11. Line a baking sheet with parchment paper. In a large bowl, combine the sugar, almond flour, almonds, all-purpose flour, and butter. Work the butter in with your hands until it resembles a coarse meal. All butter should be mixed in; there should be no visible large pieces.

12. Form a couple of large balls with your hand and crumble the balls onto the lined baking sheet. Bake for 5 to 10 minutes or until the crumble is golden brown, checking after the first 5 minutes and continuing to bake in 5 minute increments if it does not appear golden brown. Break the crumble into small pieces with a metal spatula and transfer the pan to a cooling rack to cool completely. If some of the crumble pieces are too large, you can break them up by pulsing them in a food processor fitted with a metal blade. Set the crumble aside until ready to use.

MAKE THE PINEAPPLE CHUTNEY

13. In a nonreactive saucepan, combine the pineapple, sugar, pineapple juice, and butter and bring the mixture to a boil over medium-high heat. Reduce the heat to low and simmer until the mixture becomes syrupy, 15 to 20 minutes. Remove from the heat and set aside.

TOASTED ALMOND ICE CREAM AND PINEAPPLE SORBET

14. Remove the Toasted Almond Ice Cream and Pineapple Sorbet from the freezer and set aside to soften until pliable, about 10 minutes. When pliable, combine equal parts ice cream and sorbet together in a large bowl and mix with a spoon to make a swirled effect. Return the swirled ice cream/sorbet to the freezer.

15. Place a large metal bowl in the freezer to chill. Place the pineapple slices on a tray and sprinkle them evenly with the sugar, drizzle with honey, and top with the lime zest. Transfer the pineapple slices to a vacuum-seal bag and seal the bag. Refrigerate for 2 hours.

16. In the chilled bowl, combine the cream and sugar and, using either a stand mixer or hand-held mixer, whip the cream on high speed until stiff peaks form.

17. For each serving, line the sides of a 12-ounce sundae glass with 3 of the fresh macerated pineapple slices. Crumble some of the Almond Cake in a thin layer in the bottom of the glass. Top with 2 scoops of the Almond Ice Cream–Pineapple Sorbet swirl and 1 scoop of the Coconut Ice Cream. Drizzle the Pineapple Chutney on top and add a small handful of the Almond Crumble. Spoon a dollop of whipped cream on top and serve.

Vanna, listening to reason

PECAN PIE BREAD PUDDING + BOURBON VANILLA ICE CREAM

SERVES 8 I asked Ashton, my pastry chef, to do something fun and interesting with pecan pie, and this is her spin. Pecan pie is rich on its own, but served with bread pudding, it's even more decadent. The dessert was a hit with our patrons—and we return to the recipe time and time again. It's even better when paired with Banana Jameson (see page 376), or with the addition of banana to the bread pudding (see variation, page 322).

FOR THE BOURBON VANILLA ICE CREAM

1⅓ cups heavy cream

1⅓ cups whole milk

⅔ cup granulated sugar

3 large egg yolks

1 vanilla bean, split and seeds scraped out

1 tablespoon bourbon

FOR THE BROWN SUGAR CRUMBLE

1 cup finely chopped pecans

3 cups packed dark brown sugar

2 ounces (4 tablespoons) unsalted butter, melted

FOR THE BREAD PUDDING

1 cup whole milk

1 cup heavy cream

1 cup granulated sugar

5 large eggs, room temperature

6 tablespoons dark corn syrup

12 (1-inch-thick) bread or brioche slices

Unsalted butter, for the ramekins

FOR THE PECAN CARAMEL

1 cup finely chopped pecans

1½ cups packed dark brown sugar

1½ cups dark corn syrup

2½ ounces (5 tablespoons) unsalted butter, cut into tablespoon-size pieces

MAKE THE BOURBON VANILLA ICE CREAM

1. In a saucepot, combine the heavy cream, milk, and sugar, and bring to a simmer over medium-high heat, stirring constantly (to prevent scorching on the bottom). Remove the mixture from the heat.

2. In a heatproof bowl, whisk the egg yolks until smooth. Slowly drizzle one-third of the milk mixture into the egg yolks, whisking constantly, to temper the eggs. Pour the tempered egg yolks into the saucepan with the remaining milk mixture, whisking constantly and being careful not to curdle the eggs. Add the vanilla bean and seeds to the mixture and whisk until combined.

3. Return the pot to the stovetop over low heat, and stir the custard with a wooden spoon until the mixture thickens slightly and coats the back of the spoon, 7 to 8 minutes. Immediately remove the custard from the heat and stir in the bourbon. Strain the mixture through a fine-mesh strainer into a bowl and refrigerate for at least 2 hours, and preferably overnight. Transfer the chilled custard to an ice cream maker and process according to manufacturer's instructions. Remove the ice cream from the machine, transfer to a container, and freeze for at least 2 hours or until firm.

MAKE THE BROWN SUGAR CRUMBLE

4. Preheat the oven to 300°F; position a rack in the middle. Toast the pecans in the oven in a shallow baking dish for 5 to 7 minutes or until fragrant. Transfer the pecans to a bowl and let cool completely—maintain

the oven temperature. Once the pecans are cool, add the brown sugar and melted butter and mix with your hands, until the mixture resembles a crumble topping when sprinkled.

MAKE THE BREAD PUDDING

5. In a large bowl, whisk together the milk, heavy cream, sugar, eggs, and corn syrup until fully combined.

6. Cut the bread into cubes and add them to the milk mixture. Gently fold the cubes into the batter until they are fully coated. Allow the bread to soak at room temperature for at least 30 minutes. (Note: If you can, do this in advance and soak the bread for 2 days, refrigerated, to get the maximum flavor.)

7. Preheat the oven to 375°F; position the rack in the middle. Butter 8 (6-ounce) ramekins. Spoon the bread mixture into the ramekins and sprinkle the Brown Sugar Crumble on top of the bread. Place the ramekins on a baking sheet and bake for 35 to 40 minutes or until the bread pudding is golden brown and bubbling.

MAKE THE PECAN CARAMEL

8. Toast the pecans in the 300°F oven in a shallow baking pan for about 5 minutes or until fragrant. Transfer the pecans to a small bowl and let cool completely.

9. In a medium saucepan, combine the brown sugar and dark corn syrup. Bring the mixture to a boil over medium heat, whisking until the sugar is dissolved. Remove the saucepan from the heat and whisk in the butter, 1 tablespoon at a time. Stir the pecans into the caramel and keep warm.

ASSEMBLE THE DISH

10. Drizzle the Pecan Caramel over the bread puddings. Top each bread pudding with a scoop of the Bourbon Vanilla Ice Cream and serve.

Banana Bread Pudding Variation

1. Follow the recipe through step 4. In a large bowl, whisk together the milk, heavy cream, sugar, and eggs until fully combined. Measure out 1 cup of the mixture and transfer it to a blender.

2. Peel 3 large (or 4 small) bananas and place them in the blender with the reserved milk mixture. Puree the mixture until smooth and uniform. Whisk the banana puree into the bowl of milk mixture. Proceed with step 6 and follow the rest of the recipe as written.

Why are 86ing that so early?!

WEAK-IN-THE-KNEES BROWNIES + COCOA MARSHMALLOWS + COFFEE NUTELLA ICE CREAM

MAKES 16 (2-INCH SQUARE) BROWNIES; MAKES 150 (1-INCH) MARSHMALLOWS The name says it all: The first time I tasted these brownies, I got weak in the knees.

FOR THE COCOA MARSHMALLOWS

4 teaspoons (½ ounce) powdered gelatin

1 cup granulated sugar

2 large egg whites, room temperature

2 tablespoons light corn syrup

½ cup plus 2 tablespoons unsweetened cocoa powder (see Sources, page 403), plus additional for dusting the pan

1 cup confectioners' sugar, plus more for dusting the pan and coating marshmallows

FOR THE COFFEE NUTELLA ICE CREAM

1⅓ cups heavy cream

1⅓ cups whole milk

⅔ cup granulated sugar

½ cup Nutella or other hazelnut-chocolate spread

2 tablespoons espresso powder

3 large egg yolks

FOR THE CANDIED HAZELNUTS

1 cup hazelnuts

1 cup granulated sugar

2 teaspoons espresso powder

2 teaspoons cocoa powder

FOR THE NUTELLA SAUCE

1½ cups Nutella or other hazelnut-chocolate spread

1 cup heavy cream

FOR THE BROWNIES

4 ounces milk chocolate, chopped

4 ounces dark chocolate (71 percent cacao), chopped

8 ounces (16 tablespoons) unsalted butter, cubed

1¾ cups granulated sugar

1½ cups packed dark brown sugar

4 large eggs, room temperature

1 cup all-purpose flour

MAKE THE COCOA MARSHMALLOWS

1. Place 6 tablespoons of cold water in a small bowl. Sprinkle the gelatin over water, stir, and set aside.

2. Place 1 cup of water in a pot wide enough for the bottom of a stand mixer bowl to fit snugly on top. Bring the water to a boil, then reduce the heat to maintain a gentle simmer. In a bowl of a stand mixer, combine the sugar, egg whites, corn syrup, and 2 tablespoons of the cocoa powder with 2 tablespoons of water. Place the mixer bowl over the pot of simmering water and whisk continuously until all the sugar is dissolved and the mixture is hot to the touch. Remove the bowl from the heat and stir in the bloomed gelatin (the gelatin should have doubled in size and will not be in powdered form).

3. Affix the mixer bowl to a stand mixer fitted with the whisk attachment. Mix the batter on medium speed until the mixture is thick and glossy, 5 to 8 minutes. The mixture should be thick and light in color, and when you remove the whisk, it should feel elastic and the batter will cling to the whisk. Immediately transfer the batter to a pastry bag fitted with a ½-inch tip or a resealable plastic bag with one corner snipped to make a ½-inch-wide opening (see Note).

4. Combine the remaining ½ cup cocoa powder with 1 cup of confectioners' sugar and lightly coat a baking sheet with half of the cocoa–confectioners' sugar mixture. Pipe long strands of the marshmallow mixture onto the sheet tray. If, when you start to pipe the marshmallows, the batter is too runny, let it sit in the bag for 1 to 2 minutes, and then try again. Sift more of the cocoa–confectioners' sugar mixture over the strands until totally covered. Allow the marshmallows to come to room temperature. When firm, cut the marshmallows into 1-inch pieces and toss them in the remaining confectioners' sugar.

5. In a saucepot, bring the cream, milk, sugar, Nutella, and espresso powder to a simmer over medium heat, stirring periodically to prevent the liquid from burning on the bottom. Remove from the heat.

6. In a medium bowl, whisk together the egg yolks. Slowly drizzle one-third of the warm mixture into the egg yolks, whisking constantly, to temper the eggs. Pour the tempered egg yolk mixture into the pot with the remaining milk mixture, whisking constantly. Return the saucepot to the stovetop over low heat. Stir the mixture constantly until it is thickened and coats the back of the spoon, 2 to 3 minutes. Remove the custard from the heat and strain it through a fine-mesh strainer into a bowl. Set the bowl over an ice bath and stir until cool, 5 to 10 minutes. Refrigerate the custard until cold, at least 2 hours and preferably overnight. When completely cold, transfer the custard to the ice cream maker and freeze according to manufacturer's specifications. Transfer the ice cream to a container, cover, and freeze for at least 2 hours or until firm.

MAKE THE CANDIED HAZELNUTS

7. Preheat the oven to 300°F; position the rack in the middle. Toast the hazelnuts in a shallow baking pan for 7 to 9 minutes or until fragrant. Transfer the nuts to a bowl and allow them to cool.

8. In a saucepot set over medium-high heat, combine the sugar, espresso powder, and cocoa powder with ¼ cup water and bring the syrup to a boil. Cook the syrup until it reaches a hard-crack stage (between 300°F and 320°F) on a candy thermometer. (If you dip a spoon into the syrup and plunge it into cold water and the sugar becomes hard instantly, the sugar has reached the hard-crack stage). Remove the pot from the heat, add the reserved hazelnuts and stir until the hazelnuts are coated in the thick syrup. Keep stirring until the nuts lighten in color and look almost "sandy"; this is when they are crystallizing and hardening. Immediately transfer the nuts to a wax paper–lined tray set over a cooling rack, and evenly spread out the mixture. Let the candied nuts cool to room temperature. Transfer the nuts to a food processor and pulse into coarse crumbs.

MAKE THE NUTELLA SAUCE

9. Place the Nutella in a large bowl. In a saucepot, bring the heavy cream to a boil over medium-high heat and pour over the Nutella. Let the mixture sit for 1 minute before whisking it together until smooth and shiny. Set aside.

MAKE THE BROWNIES

10. Preheat the oven to 350°F; position the rack in the middle. Place a metal bowl over a medium saucepan of 2 inches of simmering water. Do not let the bottom of the bowl touch the water. Combine the milk and dark chocolates and butter in the metal bowl and stir until the chocolate is completely melted and the mixture is smooth and homogeneous.

11. In a large bowl, whisk together the sugars and the eggs until well combined. Add the melted chocolate to the sugar-egg mixture, and mix until well combined. Add the flour and stir until the batter is free of any lumps. Pour the batter into a (8 x 8-inch) baking pan and bake for 25 to 30 minutes or until a tester inserted into the center of the cake comes out clean. Transfer the pan to a cooling rack and allow it to cool completely before cutting into 16 individual squares. The brownies should keep for 3 days, tightly wrapped, at room temperature.

TO ASSEMBLE THE DISH

12. Serve the Brownies with a scoop of the Coffee Nutella Ice Cream drizzled with Nutella Sauce and topped with Candied Hazelnuts. Place a Cocoa Marshmallow on the side.

Note *If you don't own a pastry bag or don't want to pipe your marshmallows, spread the mixture onto a 9 x 9-inch cake pan using a rubber spatula. Smooth out the top and sift the cocoa–confectioners' sugar mixture over the marshmallows and let set at room temperature. When the marshmallows are firm, cut them into 1-inch pieces and toss them in more of the cocoa–confectioners' sugar mixture.*

Variations *For Espresso Marshmallows, add 1 tablespoon of instant espresso instead of the cocoa powder when combining all the ingredients.*

For plain marshmallows, omit the cocoa powder altogether.

LADY ASHTON'S CHOCOLATE CAKE + CHOCOLATE BUTTERCREAM + WHIPPED CREAM

MAKES 1 (8-INCH) DOUBLE-LAYER CAKE This chocolate cake got Ashton, who was our hostess at the time, from the front of the house to the back of the house and into the kitchen as a pastry chef. At the time, I was doing our pastries myself, trying to save a little extra money for the restaurant. I was having a hard time with it, given that I was also cooking on the line and trying to run the restaurant. One day, Ashton came up to me. "Chef, is it okay if I make you a chocolate cake?" Who says no to an offer like that? Certainly not me. So, I said, "Sure, I'd love a chocolate cake!" Ashton's cake was incredible— I absolutely loved it and wanted to put it on the menu immediately. About three weeks later, we started to discuss her helping out with pastries. Things kind of went from there and, as they say, the rest is history.

FOR THE CAKE

Unsalted butter or cooking spray for the pan

4 ounces unsweetened chocolate, chopped

1 cup boiling water

2 large eggs, room temperature

½ cup sour cream

½ cup vegetable oil

½ teaspoon pure vanilla extract

2¼ cups granulated sugar

1½ cups all-purpose flour

¾ teaspoon baking powder

½ teaspoon kosher salt

FOR THE CHOCOLATE BUTTERCREAM

8 large egg whites

2¼ cups granulated sugar

24 ounces (48 tablespoons) unsalted butter, chopped into 1-inch cubes

1 cup confectioners' sugar

2 teaspoons pure vanilla extract or 1 vanilla bean, split open and seeds scraped out (see Note)

1 cup unsweetened Dutch-process cocoa powder (see Sources, page 403)

FOR THE WHIPPED CREAM

2 cups heavy cream

⅓ cup granulated sugar

MAKE THE CAKE

1. Preheat the oven to 350°F; position the rack in the middle. Generously butter or spray 2 (8-inch) round cake pans and line the bottoms with rounds of parchment paper. Place the chocolate in a bowl and pour hot water over it. Whisk the chocolate and water together until the chocolate is fully melted, and set aside to cool.

2. In a large bowl, whisk together the eggs, sour cream, oil, and vanilla extract or vanilla seeds, whisking thoroughly after each addition. Add the chocolate mixture to the egg mixture and whisk until smooth.

3. In a medium bowl, whisk together the sugar, flour, baking powder, and salt until well combined. Add the dry ingredients to the egg mixture in 4 additions, whisking after each addition until fully combined.

4. Evenly divide the cake batter between the cake pans and smooth out the tops with a spatula. Bake the cakes for 30 to 35 minutes or until a cake tester inserted into the center of the cake comes out clean. Be sure to turn the cakes every 10 minutes or so to ensure even baking. Transfer the cakes to cooling racks and let sit for 5 minutes before inverting the cakes onto the racks. Let the cakes cool completely before icing.

MAKE THE CHOCOLATE BUTTERCREAM

5. In a saucepot, bring 1 inch of water to a simmer over low heat. In the clean, dry bowl of a stand mixer, whisk together the egg whites and sugar. Place the bowl over the pot of simmering water (do not let the bottom of the bowl touch the water) and whisk until the egg white mixture is warm to the touch and the sugar granules are fully dissolved. Remove from the heat and affix the bowl to the stand mixer fitted with the whisk attachment. Whisk the warmed egg whites on medium speed until the bowl is cool to the touch. With the mixer on low, add the cubes of butter one at a time. When all the butter has been added, raise the mixer speed to medium. The mixture will go through a phase where it resembles cottage cheese—anticipate this and do not be discouraged. Continue beating the mixture until it is uniform and smooth, 2 to 3 minutes. Add the confectioners' sugar and vanilla extract or seeds and mix to fully incorporate.

6. With the mixer on low speed, whisk the cocoa powder, ¼ cup at a time, until the cocoa is fully incorporated and the buttercream is smooth. Stop the mixer and scrape down the sides of the bowl before each cocoa addition.

ASSEMBLE THE CAKE

7. Using a serrated knife, trim the tops of the cakes so they are straight and even. Center one of the cakes, trimmed side up, on a rotating cake stand. Place ½ to ¾ cup of the buttercream on the center of the cake layer. Using an offset spatula, spread the frosting evenly over the layer until it reaches the edges.

8. Carefully place the second cake layer, trimmed side down, over the first layer; this will ensure that the cake will have a smooth top and will be easier to frost.

9. Place 1 cup of the buttercream on the center of the cake; this will be your crumb coat (see Sidebar). Spread the buttercream in a thin layer all over the cake, starting with the top and working your way down and over the sides. The crumb coat will trap any crumbs so that the cake does not have any crumbs in the second coating of buttercream. Be sure to also fill any gaps between the cake layers with the crumb coat, smoothing out (to the best of your ability) the frosting. Refrigerate the cake on the stand for at least 30 minutes and up to 1 hour.

10. Return the cake stand to the counter and place about 1 cup of the buttercream on top. Using an offset spatula, frost the cake evenly from the top down, adding more buttercream as needed. Frost the sides of the cake as well. To smooth out the top, using the back side of your spatula, sweep across the cake from edge to edge in one direction in one smooth motion. Wipe the spatula clean. Smooth out the sides of the cake by placing the back side of the spatula against the buttercream and applying gentle pressure as you slowly turn the cake stand. You can also choose to pipe the second coat of frosting (as shown in picture) using a #21 cake tip.

MAKE THE WHIPPED CREAM

11. When ready to serve, in the chilled bowl of a stand mixer fitted with the whisk attachment (or using a hand-held mixer), whip the cream and sugar on high speed until stiff peaks form, 2 minutes.

12. To serve, slice the cake and serve each slice with a dollop of whipped cream on top or just dust with confectioners' sugar.

Note *Don't discard that scraped vanilla bean—they are expensive—so try to get the most use out of them. Let the vanilla bean pod dry, and use it to infuse the dairy base for ice cream, or place it in a jar of sugar to make vanilla sugar. You can also add it to a bottle of your favorite spirit to give it amazing vanilla flavor.*

+ A crumb coat is essential to getting that beautiful, perfectly applied frosting. By applying the crumb coat and chilling the cake before applying more frosting, you are trapping all the loose crumbs in the first coat. When you finish frosting the cake, the result will be a beautiful, crumb-free frosting and a cake that is stunning in looks as well as in taste.

TEN-MINUTE COOKIES AND MILK

MAKES 16 (3-INCH) COOKIES It's hard to beat a freshly baked cookie right out of the oven, especially when it's accompanied by a glass of very cold milk. I remember when I was a kid, my mom would bake cookies and set them on the counter to cool. I always tried to grab a cookie without her noticing, but she always saw me coming, and would gently tap my hand, telling me that the cookies needed to rest a little bit before I could eat them. She probably didn't want me to burn the roof of my mouth, but all I wanted was a hot cookie, with warm melted chocolate, right out of the oven. And that's how we serve them to our guests at the restaurant: baked to order and hot from the oven, accompanied by a glass of cold milk, of course.

8 ounces (16 tablespoons) unsalted butter, cubed and softened

¾ cup packed dark brown sugar

½ cup granulated sugar

1 large egg, room temperature

1 teaspoon pure vanilla extract

2 cups all-purpose flour

¾ teaspoon baking soda

¾ teaspoon kosher salt

½ teaspoon baking powder

1 cup semi-sweet chocolate chips

Whole milk, for serving, preferably unhomogenized

1. Preheat the oven to 350°F; position the rack in the middle. Line a baking sheet with parchment paper or a Silpat. In the bowl of a stand mixer fitted with the paddle attachment, combine the butter with the sugars and beat on medium-high speed until the mixture is light and fluffy, 8 to 10 minutes. Add the egg and beat until fully incorporated. Add the vanilla extract and beat until fully incorporated.

2. In a large bowl, whisk together the flour, baking soda, salt, and baking powder. With the mixer on low speed, add the dry ingredients to the butter mixture, 1 cup at a time, beating until fully incorporated. Either fold in the chocolate chips by hand or mix them in on low speed. The dough will be slightly sticky. You can use the dough right away or cover the bowl in plastic wrap and refrigerate for up to 2 days to make it easier to work with.

3. Using a 1½- to 2-inch diameter cookie scoop, spoon balls of the cookie dough onto the lined baking sheet. Lightly press the dough balls to 2 to 3 inches in diameter, leaving 2 inches of space between the cookies. Bake the cookies for 10 minutes, rotating the pan after 5 minutes or until edges are golden brown. (Note: It's better to slightly underbake the cookies to maintain a soft, gooey center and a chewy, toothsome edge, but if you prefer a crispier cookie, flatten the dough balls more and bake for 1 to 2 minutes longer.) Serve warm, with a glass of very cold milk.

OLIVE OIL–RUM TORTA + BLOOD ORANGE SYRUP + CRÈME FRAÎCHE ICE CREAM

MAKES 1 (8X12-INCH) CAKE; SERVES 8 This is a dessert I made for my fiancée's birthday, before I opened my restaurant, when we had first started dating. Kristin loves anything blood orange, so I set out to create a dessert that would impress. I was basically homeless at the time, between apartments, and made her dessert at her place. I have always loved a simple Italian-style olive oil cake, and thought that the blood orange flavor, with its bitter and sweet notes, would play well against the herbal notes of the olive oil. Kristin loved the cake, and it was the very first thing to go on our dessert menu.

FOR THE CRÈME FRAÎCHE ICE CREAM

1⅓ cups heavy cream

1⅓ cups whole milk

⅔ cup granulated sugar

½ cup crème fraîche

3 large egg yolks

FOR THE OLIVE OIL TORTA

1½ cups extra-virgin olive oil, plus more for the pan

3 large eggs, room temperature

Finely grated zest of 1 large orange (about 1 tablespoon), plus more for garnish

2½ cups granulated sugar

1½ cups whole milk

½ teaspoon baking powder

½ teaspoon baking soda

½ teaspoon kosher salt

2½ cups all-purpose flour

FOR THE RUM SIMPLE SYRUP

1 cup granulated sugar

¼ cup light rum

FOR THE BLOOD ORANGE SYRUP

1 cup fresh blood orange juice

1 cup granulated sugar

TO ASSEMBLE THE DISH

Confectioners' sugar, for dusting

Orange zest

MAKE THE CRÈME FRAÎCHE ICE CREAM

1. In a saucepot, combine the cream, milk, sugar, and crème fraîche and bring to a simmer over medium heat, stirring with a whisk (but not whisking) to prevent the liquid from burning on the bottom. Remove from the heat.

2. In a medium bowl, whisk together the egg yolks. Slowly drizzle about one-third of the warm milk mixture into the egg yolks, whisking constantly, to temper them. Return the tempered egg yolks to the pot with the remaining warm milk mixture, whisking vigorously. Return the pot to the stovetop, set it over low heat, and whisk the custard, as it warms, until it thickens and coats the back of a spoon, 5 to 8 minutes. Remove the custard from the heat and strain it through a fine-mesh strainer into a bowl. Place the bowl over an ice bath and stir the custard until it is cool to the touch. Cover and refrigerate the custard for at least 2 hours and preferably overnight. Transfer the custard to an ice cream maker and process according to the manufacturer's instructions. Transfer the ice cream to a covered container and freeze for at least 2 hours or until firm.

MAKE THE OLIVE OIL TORTA

3. Preheat the oven to 350°F; position the rack in the middle. Oil an 8 x 12-inch rectangular cake pan and line the bottom with parchment paper cut to fit. In a large bowl, whisk together the eggs with the orange zest until well

combined. Add the sugar, oil, and milk, whisking after each addition until fully incorporated. Whisk in the baking powder, baking soda, and salt.

4. Mix the flour into the batter until no lumps remain. Pour the batter into the prepared cake pan and smooth out the top using a spatula. Bake the cake for 30 to 40 minutes or until a cake tester inserted into the center of the cake comes out clean. Be sure to rotate the cake every 10 minutes for even baking (it will also tell you exactly when the cake is done—the top of the cake will get golden brown and the edges of the cake will begin to pull away from the sides of the pan). Transfer the cake to a cooling rack and let cool in the pan for 5 minutes before inverting the cake onto the rack. Let cool completely.

MAKE THE RUM SIMPLE SYRUP

5. In a saucepan, combine the sugar with 1 cup of water and bring to a boil over medium-high heat, stirring until the sugar is fully dissolved. Remove from the heat and allow the syrup to come to room temperature. Stir in the rum.

MAKE THE BLOOD ORANGE SYRUP

6. In a small nonreactive pot, combine the orange juice and sugar with ½ cup of water and bring to a boil over high heat. Transfer the syrup to a nonreactive container, cover, and refrigerate until needed; it will keep for up to 3 days.

ASSEMBLE THE DISH

7. Make a few small slits in the top of the cake. Drizzle some of the Rum Simple Syrup over the cake and allow the cake to absorb the syrup before slicing it into 8 (4 x 3-inch) pieces. Serve the cake with a drizzle of the Blood Orange Syrup and a scoop of the Crème Fraîche Ice Cream. Dust the cake with some confectioners' sugar and sprinkle with a little orange zest.

At the restaurant, we serve only Bob Marcelli's cheeses, and even aside from our personal connection (he worked for my dad at An American Place), Bob's cheeses are some of the best I've ever had. But the story of how these cheeses came to be available in the United States is something of a happy accident.

A chef by training, Bob Marcelli stumbled into cheese making after he took a family trip to visit a village in Abruzzo, where his grandfather grew up. To escape the lack of opportunity, Bob's grandfather left his beautiful little village when he was about sixteen years old for the promise of a better life in the United States, and never looked back.

The original plan was to stay in Bob's grandfather's village for three days. "What are we going to do there for three whole days?" Bob thought at the time, expecting to be bored day one.

But in a surprising turn of events, Bob fell in love with the village and its landscape. He met his cousin Nunzio and the communication between the two proved amusing, as Bob didn't speak any Italian and Nunzio spoke only snippets of broken English. Bob quickly learned of the family business, the farm they started in the 1970s to preserve the way of life that has existed in Italy for centuries. On the farm, the family raised sheep and made cheese the old-fashioned way, which happened to coincide with the rising interest in authentic food products in the United States.

When Bob tasted the cheese, he was blown away. Never in his life had he ever tasted anything like it. Being a chef, Bob was used to working with great ingredients, but what he had just tasted was so extraordinary and so off the charts that he and his father decided they should do something for their

Italian cousins. Over the next couple of years, they went back and forth visiting one another, and finally Bob decided to bring some of the cheese to the States, knowing there would be demand for it. At first, Nunzio was resistant to the idea—he didn't want his way of life to be altered. But eventually he agreed to start exporting the cheeses, and he and Bob spent the year that followed trying to figure out the labyrinthine rules of exporting and importing a food product from Italy to the United States. Finally, the cheese made it to U.S. soil, and Bob and his family started doing cheese tastings for some chefs—one of whom was my dad, who loved the cheeses and encouraged me to try them.

At that time, I was in the process of opening my restaurant. I had grown up with Bob's kids and knew his family very well. Two of Bob's kids went to the Culinary Institute of America and were on my opening restaurant staff. It was a nice little family circle.

The first time I tasted one of Marcelli's cheeses—the Gregoriano, I think—I closed my eyes and could almost see the sheep grazing on the hills at the farm and smell the Abruzzo air. In the end, I wound up being Bob's first customer—something I'm very proud of.

A few bites of Marcelli's cheeses is the perfect way to end an evening of good food and wine. We serve the cheeses with Abruzzo honey, but at home, you can serve the cheese with your finest honey, some toast, and if you like, Candied Hazelnuts (see page 323).

BOB & ANDY MARCELLI of Marcelli Cheeses

BRUNCH

"I hate brunch, I really do, so many horrible brunches, nightmares. I was traumatized as a young cook—bad Canadian bacon, frozen English muffins, hollandaise sauce dripping off of my face mixed with sweat. I vowed as a cook to do brunch differently, to treat it as another important service, with attention to the choice of ingredients and how the menu was written. I wanted to approach brunch without the obligatory notion that it was merely a hangover remedy."

—MARC MEYER, COOKSHOP

MAKES 1 DRINK AND ENOUGH GARNISH FOR 10 DRINKS My general manager, Matthew Conway, used to do this Bloody at his mother's restaurant, where they garnished it with pickled shrimp and Havarti cheese with dill. When he first offered to make me one, I told him "No way!" Matthew being Matthew, of course, he made it for me anyway and I couldn't believe how much I enjoyed it. I am not being biased, but it really is the best Bloody you will ever have.

We now make our own proprietary Bloody mix called Batch 22. It took us a while to develop and make just right, and it's perhaps the only restaurant recipe that I won't be sharing with you here. However, Batch 22 should be widely available. I like our mix so much that I actually have a hard time drinking Bloodys made without Batch 22.

At the restaurant, the vegetable garnishes change according to the season. Some of our favorites appear during the spring—beautiful green beans or haricots verts. It makes for a beautiful presentation to have the beans sticking out of the Bloody. We garnish it with a block of Havarti cheese with dill, a green olive, a pickled shrimp, depending on the season, whatever pickled vegetables we have on hand, and lemon and lime wedges.

FOR THE PICKLED SHRIMP

10 medium tail-on shrimp

½ cup white wine vinegar

1 tablespoon granulated sugar

1 teaspoon kosher salt

½ teaspoon black peppercorns

¼ teaspoon ground turmeric

1 fresh or ½ dried bay leaf

Pinch of red pepper flakes

FOR THE PICKLED VEGETABLES

15 to 20 green beans or haricots verts

1 cup white wine vinegar

1 tablespoon granulated sugar

1 teaspoon kosher salt

½ teaspoon black peppercorns

1 fresh or ½ dried bay leaf

Pinch of red pepper flakes

FOR THE BLOODY

2 ounces Batch 22 Marc Forgione Bloody mix (see Sources, page 403)

1 ounce of your favorite vodka

1 green olive

1 cube Havarti cheese with dill

1 lemon wedge

1 lime wedge

Micro horseradish greens (see Sources, page 403; optional)

MAKE THE PICKLED SHRIMP

1. Place the shrimp in a nonreactive 3-cup bowl or jar. In a nonreactive saucepot, combine the vinegar, sugar, salt, peppercorns, turmeric, bay leaf, and pepper flakes with ½ cup of water and bring to a boil over high heat. Pour the liquid over the shrimp and stir to combine. Cover and refrigerate for 24 hours. The pickled shrimp will keep in an airtight container in the refrigerator for up to 1 week.

MAKE THE PICKLED VEGETABLES

2. Trim the beans and place them in a nonreactive 3-cup bowl or jar. In a nonreactive saucepot, combine the vinegar, sugar, salt, peppercorns, bay leaf, and pepper flakes with 1 cup of water and bring to a boil over high heat. Pour the liquid over the vegetables and stir to combine. Cover and refrigerate for 24 hours. The pickled vegetables will keep in an airtight container in the refrigerator for up to 1 month.

3. In a tall glass filled with ice, combine the Bloody Mary mix with the vodka and stir once. Garnish with an olive, a cube of Havarti, a pickled shrimp, and a pickled vegetable. Add the citrus wedges and a pinch of micro horseradish, if using, and serve.

SCRAMBLED EGGS + WILD KING SALMON + OSETRA CAVIAR

SERVES 4   I was shown this style of scrambled eggs while working in France. When I first tasted it, I could not believe I was eating scrambled eggs—they tasted so delicate and smooth, almost like an egg puree. Once you add a little smoked salmon and caviar, it becomes a very elegant amuse-bouche. We serve this in the eggshell, which makes for a stunning and sophisticated presentation.

SPECIAL EQUIPMENT

Cold Smoker

FOR THE SALMON

1 (12-ounce) center fillet of wild salmon, skin off

2 cups kosher salt

1 cup light brown sugar

2 tablespoons chopped fresh dill

1 tablespoon fennel seeds

1 tablespoon coriander seeds

1 tablespoon cracked white peppercorns

2 medium red onions, thinly sliced

½ cup fresh lime juice

FOR THE EGGS

8 large eggs, preferably farm-fresh (we use Feather Ridge Farm)

½ cup heavy cream

4 ounces (8 tablespoons) unsalted butter, diced

Kosher salt

4 teaspoons chopped fresh chives

3 tablespoons plus 2 teaspoons caviar (preferably osetra)

FOR THE BRIOCHE

4 (½-inch-thick) slices brioche

1 ounce (2 tablespoons) Clarified Butter (see page 390), melted

4 teaspoons cracked black peppercorns

Kosher salt

TO ASSEMBLE THE DISH

Extra-virgin olive oil

Chive blossoms (optional)

MAKE THE SALMON

1. Pick the remaining bones out of the salmon and thoroughly dry the salmon with paper towels. Place the salmon on a large piece of plastic wrap. In a bowl, mix together the salt, sugar, dill, fennel, coriander, and peppercorns.

2. In medium nonreactive bowl, toss the onions with the lime juice. Pack the onions around the salmon and season generously with the curing spices. Wrap the coated salmon in the plastic wrap. Place the wrapped salmon into a dish that is deep enough to hold any liquid that might leak out. Refrigerate for 12 hours. Remove the plastic wrap and discard it; reserve the onions. Rinse the salmon under cold water and pat dry.

3. Using a cold smoker, place the salmon and the onion on separate trays and smoke them for 25 minutes. Refrigerate the smoked salmon until cold, then slice it into paper-thin slices, cover, and refrigerate until needed. If you don't have a cold smoker, refrigerate the salmon for 24 hours—you will have delicious gravlax instead.

MAKE THE EGGS

4. Using an egg topper, gently crack the eggs and remove the top of the shell. Reserving the eggshells, gently transfer the eggs into a medium bowl. Add the cream and whisk together until smooth. Add 6 tablespoons of the butter, cover, and refrigerate.

5. Rinse the inside of the eggshells with warm water and, using the tip of your finger, gently pull out any membranes that remain in the shell. Set the eggshells upside down on a paper towel and dry thoroughly. Reserve 4 eggshells.

6. Melt the remaining 2 tablespoons of butter in a chilled 2-quart pot set over medium heat. Pour the reserved egg mixture into the pot, season with salt, and whisk constantly until the eggs just begin to set, about 5 minutes. Fold in the chives and fill the reserved eggshells with the egg mixture. Top each egg with some of the caviar.

MAKE THE BRIOCHE

7. Preheat the oven to 350°F; position a rack in the middle. Ten minutes before serving, place the brioche on a shallow baking sheet and brush the pieces with some of the Clarified Butter. Season with pepper and salt. Toast the buttered brioche slices in the oven for about 5 minutes or until toasted. Transfer the slices to a cutting board and remove the crusts. Cut each brioche slice into 3 pieces. Set aside.

ASSEMBLE THE DISH

8. Lay the salmon slices over the warm brioche slices. Serve the salmon-topped brioche toasts alongside the eggs. Drizzle the toasts with some olive oil and sprinkle with chive blossoms, if using. If any leftover eggs remain, serve them on the side with some toast.

Make It Faster *If you can get your hands on some good prepared gravlax or smoked salmon, you can make this dish last-minute without having to cure your own salmon. Sometimes breakfasts and brunches come together without much planning or foresight, and having a quality premade gravlax on hand allows for some spontaneity.*

FEATHER RIDGE FARM

KATIE BOGDANFFY

Feather Ridge Farm, a three-generation family-run poultry farm established in 1938, is one of the few poultry-only farms remaining in New York State. Chicken-farming know-how spanning several generations is what gives Feather Ridge Farm the ability to produce some of the best-tasting eggs I've ever had. The Bogdanffy family sold eggs to my father back in the day, which is how I came to know the farm.

Today the farm is run by the Bogdanffy siblings: Katie, Hallie, and Stephen, with their father and grandparents assisting as well, making the farm a family affair. Together, they care for ten thousand chickens (actually classifying Feather Ridge as a small operation).

Katie and her family raise Rhode Island Red chickens—classic laying hens, docile and sweet, and good egg producers. Katie and her family use all-natural practices to raise their chickens, never any hormones or drugs. In fact, to feed their chickens, the Bogdanffys mill their own food using a mill that Katie's father, a Cornell graduate, designed and built himself. And because they grind their own food, they are able to source all the feed ingredients, supporting their local farms and economy. Thus, the chickens eat a varied diet without any additives or fillers, something that's evident when you crack open one of their eggs. The yolk is large, thick, and bright orange.

Because the farm produces eggs year-round, the chickens remain indoors in old, spacious barns where they run around, perch, and lay eggs in nests. Keeping the chickens indoors keeps them cleaner and healthier, Katie explains, eliminating the need for antibiotics, which keeps in line with their no-drug philosophy. The eggs are hand-gathered several times a day to ensure freshness, and are thoroughly washed.

Busy as they are, the Bogdanffys still think of ways to improve their farm, and plan to go green in the near future, hoping to install solar panels to power about two-thirds of the farm. There are also plans to raise pigs sometime in the near future.

"I want to [be able to] say that we have green eggs and ham," Katie shared. Soon enough—she will.

FEATHER RIDGE FARM EGGS IN A JAR + WHITE ALBA TRUFFLES + PARMIGIANO-REGGIANO CROSTINI

SERVES 4 This is a very special breakfast; however, if you don't have truffles, just add a couple of drops of truffle oil, and it will still be delicious. I made this for breakfast one morning during truffle season, and it was so good that I wanted the rest of the world to taste it. When you open the top of the jar, the aroma that comes out is beyond words, something everyone should experience at least once.

Try to get your hands on the freshest eggs available—if you live near a greenmarket, chances are one of the farmers sells eggs. Freshly laid eggs will always be more delicious than anything you can get at the store. At the restaurant, we get our eggs from Feather Ridge Farm out of upstate New York—their eggs are delicious, with rich, orange yolks that have unparalleled flavor.

SPECIAL EQUIPMENT

4 clean pint glass jars with hermetic flip lids

FOR THE EGGS IN JARS

1 cup Red Wine Sauce (see page 392)

1 cup shaved Brussels sprouts

1 cup diced Butternut Squash Confit (see page 73)

1 cup finely grated Parmigiano-Reggiano

8 large eggs, preferably farm-fresh

¼ cup chopped fresh chives

¼ cup Pierre Poivre spice mix (see Sources, page 403)

Flaky sea salt, such as Maldon

1 (¾-ounce) white truffle

TO ASSEMBLE THE DISH

Toasted bread slices

White Alba truffle

Grated Parmigiano-Reggiano

MAKE THE EGGS IN JARS

1. Preheat the oven to 325°F; position a rack in the middle. In a small saucepot, heat the Red Wine Sauce over medium heat until it is warm to the touch. Divide the sauce evenly among the jars. Divide the Brussels sprouts, Butternut Squash Confit, and Parmigiano-Reggiano evenly among the jars. Crack 2 eggs directly into each jar and top each with a sprinkle of the chives, the Pierre Poivre, and some flaky sea salt. Shave some truffle on top and seal the jars. Transfer the jars to a large casserole dish and fill it with enough warm water to come halfway up the sides of the jars. Transfer to the oven and bake for 25 minutes for runny eggs. Remove the jars from the water bath and wipe the outside dry. Let cool slightly until easy to handle.

ASSEMBLE THE DISH

2. Bring the jars to the table, and let everyone open their own jar (let them know to take care with the hot steam inside). Serve with toasted bread and additional shaved truffle and Parmigiano-Reggiano. Dip the toast into the jars and enjoy.

SERVES 4 The year we put this steak on the menu, it was a cold winter, and I was kind of playing with the idea of steak and eggs for a brunch dish. Steak and eggs is a cool way to do dinner for breakfast, a hearty meal that sticks to your ribs and keeps you full and warm. The dish wound up being one of our first cold-weather steak dishes at the restaurant, and it was so successful that it eventually became a fixture on our dinner menu. I think the foie gras mousse, served with the steak in all its decadent glory, is what seals the deal here.

FOR THE RED WINE SAUCE

3 tablespoons canola oil

¾ cup chopped button mushrooms

3 shallots, sliced

1 garlic clove, chopped

2 tablespoons black peppercorns

1 tablespoon granulated sugar

½ cup red wine vinegar, plus more as needed

4 cups dry red wine

1 cup ruby port

1 sprig fresh thyme

1 fresh or ½ dried bay leaf

4 cups Veal Stock (see page 382) or store-bought

1 cup Chicken Stock (see page 382) or store-bought

Kosher salt

FOR THE DUCK LIVER MOUSSE

1 cup ruby port

7 sprigs fresh thyme

3 tablespoons granulated sugar

1 shallot, sliced

1 garlic clove, chopped

1 fresh or ½ dried bay leaf

1 pound duck livers, patted dry

1 tablespoon pink curing salt

1 teaspoon kosher salt

Canola oil

3 tablespoons brandy

2 tablespoons chopped shallots

2 ounces foie gras terrine or unsalted butter, cut into 8 pieces

2 tablespoons heavy cream

2 tablespoons duck fat or 1 ounce (2 tablespoons) unsalted butter, cut into 4 pieces

1 ounce (2 tablespoons) unsalted butter, cut into 4 pieces

FOR THE COFFEE-RUBBED FLATIRON STEAK

3 tablespoons cumin seeds

½ cup freshly ground coffee

3 tablespoons freshly ground black pepper

3 tablespoons chili powder

2 tablespoons kosher salt

1 tablespoon ground cinnamon

4 (8-ounce) flatiron steaks

Canola oil

FOR THE EGGS

4 slices thick-cut, applewood-smoked bacon

Canola oil

1 cup Caramelized Onions (see page 398)

1 cup Mustard Greens (see page 259)

4 large eggs

4 thick pieces filone or baguette (see Sources, page 403), toasted

Flaky sea salt, such as Maldon

Cracked black pepper

MAKE THE RED WINE SAUCE

1. Add the oil to a 3-quart pot set over medium heat. Add the mushrooms, shallots, and garlic, and cook, stirring, until the shallots are translucent, 3 to 5 minutes. Add the peppercorns and cook, stirring, for 1 minute more. Add the sugar and cook, stirring, for 1 minute more. Add the vinegar and deglaze the pan, scraping the bottom of the pan with a wooden spoon. Cook until the pan is dry. Add the wine, port, thyme, and bay leaf and raise the heat to medium-high. Cook until the liquid has reduced by half, about 20 minutes. Add the stocks and cook until the liquid has reduced by half, about 20 minutes. Strain the liquid through a fine-mesh strainer and return to the pan. Set the pan over medium heat

and skim off any excess fat, tilting the pot slightly to make it easier to skim. Season to taste with salt and more red wine vinegar, if you like. Strain the sauce again and set aside. You should have about 3 cups of the finished sauce. Reserve 1 cup for this recipe and freeze the remainder for later use.

MAKE THE DUCK LIVER MOUSSE

2. In a small nonreactive pot, combine the port, thyme, sugar, shallot, garlic, and bay leaf, and simmer over medium-high heat until the liquid has reduced to about ¼ cup, 15 to 20 minutes. Strain the reduction through a fine-mesh strainer into a bowl and set aside.

3. Season the livers with the pink and kosher salts. Add enough oil to a large sauté pan to cover the bottom of the pan and set it over high heat. Just before it starts to smoke, add the livers to the pan in one even layer without overcrowding (you may need to do this in batches). Reduce the heat to medium and cook, without moving the livers, for 1 minute. Add the brandy and shallots, stir, and cook for 1 minute more—the livers should be medium-rare. Transfer the livers to a blender and add the reserved port reduction. Blend, and when the mixture is sufficiently uniform, with the blender running, add the terrine, heavy cream, duck fat, and butter, piece by piece. Blend the mousse on high speed for 1 minute. Taste and adjust the seasonings. Pass the mousse through a fine-mesh strainer over a bowl set in an ice bath and let cool. Refrigerate the mousse until ready to use.

MAKE THE COFFEE-RUBBED FLATIRON STEAK

4. In a small dry skillet, toast the cumin seeds over low heat until fragrant, about 2 minutes, making sure to shake the pan frequently. Transfer the cumin to a spice grinder and finely grind. (To toast preground cumin, just warm it up in a dry skillet over medium heat, stirring, until it smells fragrant.) Place the toasted cumin, coffee, pepper, chili powder, salt, and cinnamon in the spice grinder and grind everything together until combined.

5. Pat the steaks dry. Brush the meat with a little oil. Spread the coffee rub out on a tray and roll the steaks in the mixture to coat. Cover and refrigerate for 1 hour but no longer; otherwise, the meat will begin to cure.

6. Preheat the oven to 400°F; position the rack in the middle. Add enough oil to a large sauté pan to cover the bottom of the pan and set it over high heat. Just before the oil starts to smoke, add 2 of the steaks and sear on each side until browned, 3 minutes per side. Transfer the seared steaks to a baking sheet, and repeat with the remaining 2 steaks. Let the seared steaks sit for 5 minutes, then transfer them to the oven and cook for 3 to 5 minutes. Return the steaks to the sauté pan over medium-high heat; reduce the oven temperature to 375°F. Baste the steaks with their juices for 1 minute. Transfer the steaks to a carving board and let rest for 15 minutes before slicing.

MAKE THE EGGS

7. Place the bacon on a rack set on top of a baking sheet, and bake for 12 to 15 minutes or until crispy. Set the cooked bacon aside.

8. Shortly before serving, add enough oil to a medium skillet to cover the bottom of the pan and set it over medium heat. Add the Caramelized Onions and Mustard Greens and cook until warm. Remove from the heat and set aside.

9. When ready to serve, add enough oil to a large sauté pan to cover the bottom of the pan and set it over high heat. Add the eggs and as soon as the whites are set, reduce the heat to low. Cook the eggs, sunny-side up, for about 3 minutes. While the eggs cook, cut the filone or baguette toasts in half and spread the Duck Liver Mousse over the bread. Divide the toasts among 4 warmed plates. Slice the steaks on a 45-degree angle, fan out the slices and plate the meat on top of the toast slices. Spoon some Red Wine Sauce around the steak. Remove the eggs from the heat and add an egg on top of each plate. Season the eggs with some flaky sea salt and cracked black pepper, and garnish with the cooked bacon. Serve with the Caramelized Onions and Mustard Greens on the side.

Make It Faster   *Make the Coffee-Rubbed Flatiron Steak and serve it with fried eggs. Instead of making the mousse, purchase a foie gras terrine at a fine foods shop, and serve it on the side for a decadent Sunday brunch.*

EGGS BENNY + LA QUERCIA PROSCIUTTO

SERVES 4 This is our version of the classic brunch favorite, eggs Benedict. While it can never replace the original, it has the same spirit but with our own twist. Instead of ham, we use prosciutto; instead of an English muffin, we swap in potatoes that are crushed with squash, green garlic, or corn, depending on what's in season. It's always a crowd pleaser and the crushed potatoes, when combined with the oozing egg yolk, are no joke.

FOR THE PROSCIUTTO

4 thin slices prosciutto, preferably La Quercia

FOR THE HOLLANDAISE

5 large egg yolks, room temperature

1 cup melted Clarified Butter (see page 390)

Kosher salt

½ teaspoon cayenne pepper

Juice of 1 lemon

1 tablespoon chopped Preserved Meyer Lemons (see page 391) or store-bought

FOR THE POTATOES

5 large Yukon Gold potatoes (2½ to 3 pounds)

1 garlic head, halved

1 sprig fresh thyme

Kosher salt

2 heads green garlic (or use whatever is in season: mushrooms, corn, squash, etc.)

4 ounces (8 tablespoons) unsalted butter

Freshly ground black pepper

1 tablespoon chopped fresh curly parsley

2 teaspoons chopped fresh tarragon

FOR THE EGGS

8 large eggs, farm-fresh preferably

Distilled vinegar, for poaching eggs (optional)

TO ASSEMBLE THE DISH

Pea shoots

Flaky sea salt, such as Maldon

Crushed black pepper

Cayenne pepper

MAKE THE PROSCIUTTO

1. Preheat the oven to 350°F; position the rack in the middle. Place the prosciutto on a parchment paper– or Silpat-lined baking sheet, cover it with more parchment paper or another Silpat, and stack another baking sheet on top. Bake for about 12 minutes or until the prosciutto is completely crispy. Remove the top baking sheet and transfer the bottom sheet with the prosciutto to a cooling rack. Let cool for about 1 hour.

MAKE THE HOLLANDAISE

2. Bring 1 inch of water to a boil in a saucepot. Place a kitchen towel over the simmering water, and place a bowl over the towel. The towel is used to protect the bottom of the bowl from getting hit with the direct steam. Add the egg yolks to the bowl and whisk vigorously for about 5 minutes or until the egg yolks have turned white and are about as thick as mayonnaise.

3. Remove the bowl from the heat and whisk in the Clarified Butter in a slow and steady stream until completely emulsified. Season to taste with salt, and add the cayenne pepper and lemon juice. Fold in the Preserved Meyer Lemons and set the hollandaise aside; keep warm.

MAKE THE POTATOES

4. In a pot filled halfway with cold water, place the potatoes, garlic, thyme, and enough salt so that the water tastes like sea water. Cover the pot and bring the water to a boil. Turn down the heat and simmer until the potatoes are fork-tender, 25 to 30 minutes.

5. While the potatoes are cooking, slice the green garlic bulbs into ¼-inch-thick rings. Prepare an ice bath in a medium bowl. Bring a small pot of salted water to a boil and blanch the sliced green garlic in the boiling water for about 2 minutes. Immediately transfer the blanched green garlic to an ice bath.

6. Drain the potatoes and, using the back of a large spoon or a fork, smash them.

7. In a large sauté pan, warm the butter over medium heat just until it begins to brown and smell nutty. Add the blanched green garlic and potatoes, and crush them together. Season to taste with salt and pepper, and stir in the parsley and tarragon. Cook for 1 minute, remove from the heat, and set aside.

8. Press the potato–green garlic mixture into 8 (2½-inch) ring molds large enough to hold an egg on top. Set aside.

MAKE THE EGGS

9. IMMERSION CIRCULATOR POACHING: Preheat an immersion circulator filled with water to 145°F. Place the eggs (still in their shells) in the water and poach the eggs for 40 minutes. Remove the eggs from the water and set aside.

10. TRADITIONAL POACHING METHOD: Fill a pot with enough water to come at least 3 inches up the sides. Add 1 teaspoon of vinegar, if using, for each cup of water you use. Bring the water to a simmer. Crack an egg into a small bowl, and gently slide it into the simmering water; repeat with the remaining eggs, one by one (you may need to do this in batches). You might use two large spoons to contain the whites from bleeding around the water, but some of the fraying will happen no matter what. Simmer the eggs until the whites have grown more or less opaque, 3 to 4 minutes. Using a slotted spoon, gently remove the eggs from the water and transfer them to a cutting board. Trim the frayed edges off the whites. Set the eggs aside.

ASSEMBLE THE DISH

11. If you have cooked your egg using the immersion circulator, while the eggs are poaching, preheat the oven to 350°F; position the rack in the middle. As soon as the eggs are done, warm the potatoes in the oven for about 5 minutes or until heated through. Remove the ring molds and divide the potatoes equally among 4 warmed plates. If you have poached your eggs the traditional way, see "Make It Faster," below.

12. Using the back of a ladle, make an indent in the potatoes that looks like a "nest." Gently place an egg into each potato nest. Spoon hollandaise over each egg until covered by the sauce. Top the eggs with a prosciutto chip and some pea shoots, and sprinkle with some flaky sea salt, crushed black pepper, and cayenne pepper.

Make It Faster *If, like most people, you don't own an immersion circulator, you will opt to cook your eggs via the traditional poaching method, which will take you about 4 minutes. While you cook the potatoes, put the acidulated water on the stovetop and bring it to a simmer. As soon as your potatoes are done and plated, you can poach the eggs and place them on top of the potatoes. Top with the Hollandaise and prosciutto chip, and brunch is ready.*

BLACK PIG MEAT CO.

CHEF DUSKIE ESTES

I had previously mentioned that I made some lasting friendships while filming *Next Iron Chef* (see page 20), and here is a perfect example. Even though Chef Duskie Estes was technically my competitor when I met her, we became good friends in no time.

Duskie and her husband, Chef John Stewart, are raising heritage pigs, own a meat company, and cook at their award-winning restaurant, Zazu, in the heart of Sonoma Valley. They are as farm-to-table as it gets, and they make the finest bacon I've ever tasted. In fact, Duskie and her husband know good pork so well that they were crowned the King & Queen of Pork in 2011 in the final round of Cochon 555.

Most bacon is wet-cured and injected with liquid smoke—a process that takes less than a day. What you taste in the end is usually the salt and the artificial smoke flavoring. In contrast, the Black Pig Meat Co. takes twenty-one days to dry-cure the bacon and then finishes it with applewood smoke for about twelve hours, resulting in bacon that has a perfect balance of salt, brown sugar, and smoke—the kind of bacon where you can really taste the quality of pork.

Duskie's path to raising pigs and making charcuterie is rather unusual, since she spent more than half of her life as a vegetarian. Her philosophy was simple: If she couldn't take a life, she didn't deserve to eat meat. After working in a number of restaurants all over the West Coast, Duskie landed at the lauded Palace Kitchen in Seattle, where she met her husband. Every night, animals were being grilled on the spit, and cooking the meat and not tasting it was proving to be difficult for Duskie. She decided that if she was going to eat meat, then she would only raise meat that was humanely and ethically raised, and hopefully one day, she could raise her own farm animals.

When Duskie and John opened Zazu in 2001, they also decided to start curing their own meat as well as raising their own pigs. John studied salumi making with Mario Batali and his meat curer before he started making his own cured meats. After John's first successful batch of prosciutto, he got a tattoo on his forearm of the pig logo of Armandino Batali's salumi shop in Seattle. Then, John and Duskie started to purchase piglets and raise them to adulthood. And in 2012, they started mating their pigs and breeding piglets.

In their approach on how to raise their pigs, Duskie and John, outspoken advocates for animal welfare, decided against using any CAFO (Confined Animal Feeding Operation) practices. They wanted their pigs to have "a great life and one bad day," as Duskie put it, and believe the life of the animal should be respected.

The company name, Black Pig Meat Co., came from the very first pig they had, a Berkshire pig, a breed that happens to be black. Today, they use seven different breeds, not all of them black: Berkshire, Mangalitsa, Mule Foot, Duroc, Red Wattle (the breed for which they won King & Queen of Pork), Chester White, and Yorkshire. While the pigs are mixed colors, they have something in common: All are heritage breeds that are pasture raised and hormone-free.

SERVES 4 I grew up on Long Island, and a bacon, egg, and cheese sandwich with hot sauce from your local deli is as classic as it gets. My mom made a pretty mean BEC sandwich, too, and wrapped it in foil for me to grab as I was rushing out the door late for school. I came up with this version while I was at BLT Steak one morning after a few too many cocktails. There were always extra popovers lying around the kitchen, and sriracha was the go-to condiment at our family meals.

SPECIAL EQUIPMENT

2 popover tins with
6 wells each

FOR THE BACON

4 (¼-inch) thick-cut slices
Black Pig Meat Co. bacon
or other applewood-
smoked bacon

FOR THE POPOVERS

1 sprig fresh rosemary

1 sprig fresh thyme

1 fresh or ½ dried bay leaf

4 cups whole milk

8 large eggs, room
temperature

2 tablespoons kosher salt

Cooking spray

4 cups all-purpose flour

2¼ cups (10 ounces) grated
Parmigiano-Reggiano

FOR THE EGGS

12 large eggs, preferably
farm-fresh

½ cup julienned Marinated
Tomatoes (see page 398)

¼ cup finely grated
Parmigiano-Reggiano

Kosher salt

Freshly ground black pepper

1 ounce (2 tablespoons)
unsalted butter

1 tablespoon canola oil

1 tablespoon chopped
fresh chives

2 teaspoons chopped
fresh curly parsley

2 teaspoons red
pepper flakes

ASSEMBLE THE DISH

Finely grated Parmigiano-
Reggiano

Chopped fresh curly parsley

Red pepper flakes

Sriracha sauce

MAKE THE BACON

1. Preheat the oven to 350°F; position the rack in the middle. Lay the bacon out on a rack set on top of a shallow baking pan. Bake for 12 minutes or until the bacon is crispy. Set aside to cool. Leave the oven on.

MAKE THE POPOVERS

2. Place the rosemary, thyme, and bay leaf on a piece of cheesecloth and tie the ends together to form a sachet. Place the sachet and milk into a medium saucepot set over medium heat.

3. While the milk is warming up, place the eggs in the bowl of a stand mixer fitted with the whisk attachment, add the salt, and whisk the eggs on medium speed. Keep the mixer running while the milk warms up— the time it takes for the eggs and salt to be properly whisked is the time it takes for the milk to warm.

4. Spray the popover tins with nonstick cooking spray and place them on baking sheets. Place the baking sheets and popover tins in the oven to warm up.

5. As soon as the milk has small bubbles forming around the edge of the pot, remove the pot from the heat and discard the herb sachet. With the mixer motor still running, slowly whisk one-third of the infused milk into the eggs to temper them; add the milk slowly so as not to curdle the eggs. Gradually add another third of the milk, and then the final third. With the motor still running, whisk in the flour, 1 cup at a time, until fully incorporated, being careful not to overwhisk. Remove

the hot tins from the oven and pour the popover batter all the way to the top of each well. Sprinkle with Parmigiano-Reggiano and return the tins to the oven. Bake for about 20 minutes or until the popovers rise by half. Rotate the pan so the popovers cook evenly, and bake for another 20 minutes or until the popovers are golden brown and very puffy. Transfer the tins to a rack and let cool slightly.

MAKE THE EGGS

6. In a large bowl, whisk together the eggs, Marinated Tomatoes, and cheese, and season with salt and pepper.

7. In a large sauté pan, melt the butter with the oil over medium heat. As soon as the butter starts to brown and smell nutty, pour in the egg mixture (you may need to do this in batches, and if you do, ration your butter accordingly), reduce the heat to medium-low, and stir constantly with a wooden spoon until the eggs are scrambled to your liking. In the last minute of cooking, fold in the chives, parsley, and red pepper flakes.

ASSEMBLE THE DISH

8. Cut 4 popovers in half horizontally; reserve the remaining popovers for later use (see Note). Top the bottom half of each popover with scrambled eggs. Add a slice of bacon to each sandwich and close with the popover top. Sprinkle some cheese, parsley, and red pepper flakes on top. Serve with sriracha on the side.

Note   *The extra popovers are delicious on their own, or served alongside egg sandwiches, topped with butter and jam.*

More butter, please

FRIED QUAIL AND WAFFLES

SERVES 4 A couple of years ago when I was in Vegas, I had fried chicken and waffles at some diner and fell in love with the pairing. The crunchy, savory bites from the chicken balanced perfectly with the sweetness from the maple syrup and waffles. The pitfall of the recipe is that often, by the time you get your chicken and waffles, parts of the waffles are soggy. There are only a handful of places that can execute a perfect non-soggy waffle. For the amazing waffle recipe here, I tapped my good friend, master chef Laurent Tourondel. His waffles are light, crispy, and complex-tasting. And, to make it a bit more interesting, I swapped out chicken for quail. The result—something familiar and something new.

FOR THE MAÎTRE D' BUTTER

8 ounces (16 tablespoons) unsalted butter, softened

1 tablespoon finely chopped fresh curly parsley

1½ teaspoons chopped fresh chives

1 tablespoon finely chopped shallots

½ garlic clove, minced

Kosher salt

Freshly ground black pepper

FOR THE QUAIL

4 semi-boneless quail

2 cups buttermilk

Canola oil

2 cups all-purpose flour

1 tablespoon Ararat spice mix (see Sources, page 403)

2 teaspoons kosher salt

FOR THE WAFFLES

1½ tablespoons fresh yeast

2¼ cups whole milk

12 ounces (24 tablespoons) unsalted butter, melted

5 large eggs

2 vanilla beans, split open and seeds scraped out

3¼ cups all-purpose flour

1 tablespoon granulated sugar

1 teaspoon kosher salt

FOR THE ROSEMARY-INFUSED HONEY

1 cup mild honey

1 sprig fresh rosemary

1 (1-inch) piece fresh ginger

1 tablespoon crushed pink peppercorns

TO ASSEMBLE THE DISH

Ararat spice mix (see Sources, page 403)

Flaky sea salt, such as Maldon

MAKE THE MAÎTRE D' BUTTER

1. In the bowl of a stand mixer fitted with the paddle attachment, combine the butter, parsley, shallots, chives, garlic, and salt and pepper to taste. Beat on medium-high speed until all the ingredients are incorporated. Divide the butter among several large rectangles of plastic wrap. Using the plastic wrap to help smooth and mold the butter, roll the butter into tight 5- to 6-inch logs about the diameter of a silver dollar. Wrap the plastic wrap around the butter logs and refrigerate until needed.

MAKE THE QUAIL

2. In a large nonreactive bowl, soak the quail in the buttermilk overnight in the refrigerator.

3. When ready to assemble the dish, heat your deep fryer to 350°F, or fill a wide Dutch oven with at least 3 inches of oil and heat over medium heat until the temperature registers 350°F on the deep-frying thermometer. Remove the quail from the buttermilk and pat them dry. In a large wide bowl, whisk together the flour, Ararat, and salt. Coat the quail in the flour mixture, shaking off excess.

4. Fry the quail until golden brown and crispy, 4 to 6 minutes. Set the quail aside on a cooling rack set over paper towels as you finish them and let cool while you prepare the waffles.

MAKE THE WAFFLES

5. Dissolve the yeast in 2 cups of warm water. Let stand for 5 minutes, checking that no lumps remain in the water. If there are lumps, whisk gently to break up.

6. In a large bowl, whisk together the warm water with the yeast, milk, butter, eggs, and vanilla seeds. In a separate bowl, whisk together the flour, sugar, and salt. Whisk the dry ingredients into the wet ingredients and mix until combined. Once the ingredients are incorporated, let the batter sit at room temperature until it doubles in size, about 40 minutes. Stir the batter, and either use it immediately or cover and refrigerate it at least 3 hours or overnight (or for up to 2 days).

7. When ready to assemble the dish, cook the waffles in your waffle iron according to the manufacturer's instructions until golden brown.

MAKE THE ROSEMARY-INFUSED HONEY

8. In small saucepot, combine the honey, rosemary, and ginger with 1 tablespoon of water and bring to a boil over medium heat. Set the mixture aside in a warm place to infuse for about 1 hour. Remove and discard the ginger and rosemary and fold in the peppercorns. Keep the infused honey warm until ready to use.

ASSEMBLE THE DISH

9. For each serving, cut a waffle into 4 pieces and place a small pat of butter on each piece, then stack the waffle pieces on top of one another. Place a quail next to the stack. Sprinkle some Ararat and flaky sea salt over the quail and drizzle with the infused honey.

SUCK YOU SLIDERS

SERVES 4, MAKES 12 SLIDERS What happens when a patron, with a mouthful of slider, beckons you over and says, "These are the best sucking sliders I've ever had!"? You adopt the name, of course! We always have suckling pig in the restaurant in some shape or form, so to do sliders for brunch just seemed like the next logical step. We serve them with the hot cooking liquid on the side so you can dip the sliders in it. As for them being the "best sucking sliders," we'll let you judge for yourself.

FOR THE SUCKLING PIG

1 recipe The Cure
(see page 391)

1 leg (about 4 pounds)
suckling pig

6 sprigs fresh thyme

1 fresh or ½ dried bay leaf

2 thick strips applewood-
smoked bacon

4 cups pale ale, such
as Porkslap

2 cups Clarified Butter
(see page 390), melted

2 tablespoons chopped
fresh curly parsley

1 tablespoon grainy mustard

2 teaspoons red
pepper flakes

FOR THE SLAW

¼ head green cabbage
(about 1 pound)

1 tablespoon plus
1 teaspoon kosher salt

1 carrot, coarsely shredded

¼ medium red
onion, julienned

1 cup apple cider vinegar

1 tablespoon
granulated sugar

1 tablespoon mustard oil
(see Sources, page 403)

2 teaspoons chopped
fresh curly parsley

TO ASSEMBLE THE DISH

12 Potato Rolls (see page 37)

Whole-grain mustard

MAKE THE SUCKLING PIG

1. Rub The Cure all over the leg and refrigerate, uncovered, overnight. The following morning, rinse the leg under cold running water and pat the meat dry.

2. Preheat the oven to 300°F; position the rack in the middle. Wrap the thyme and bay leaf in the bacon and secure the bacon with butcher's twine.

3. Add the bacon bundle, ale, and Clarified Butter to a saucepot and bring to a boil. Transfer the leg to a large casserole and pour the butter mixture over the leg. Cover the pot with parchment paper, then a layer of foil, and finally the lid. Bake for 4 to 6 hours or until the leg meat is perfectly tender and falling apart. Refrigerate the cooked leg overnight, in the cooking liquid, so that the flavors fully develop.

4. The following day, preheat the oven to 350°F; position the rack in the middle. Remove the skin from the leg and lay it flat on a cutting board. Using the back of a paring knife, scrape off any excess fat. Lay the skin out on a Silpat- or parchment paper–lined shallow baking pan, place another Silpat or piece of parchment paper over the skin, and top with another shallow baking pan. Bake for 30 to 45 minutes or until the skin is brittle and looks like glass. Start checking on the skin after 20 minutes. Transfer the skin to a cooling rack and let cool completely.

5. Preheat the oven to 350°F; position the rack in the middle. Reheat the meat for about 10 minutes (do not turn the oven off). Transfer the casserole dish to a cutting

Pre-shift tasting and discussion

board, remove the leg from the liquid, and place the meat in a large bowl. Using two forks, shred the meat. Strain the cooking liquid through a fine-mesh strainer into a bowl and set aside. Add a couple of tablespoons of the cooking liquid, the parsley, the mustard, and the red pepper flakes to the bowl with the leg meat, and mix to combine.

MAKE THE SLAW

6. Place the cabbage in a colander or a perforated pan set over a dish or a tray. Season the cabbage with 1 tablespoon of the salt. Cover and refrigerate overnight. Squeeze the excess liquid from the cabbage and transfer the cabbage to a medium, nonreactive bowl. Discard the liquid. Add the carrot and onion, and toss to combine.

7. In a small nonreactive saucepot, combine the vinegar, sugar, and remaining 1 teaspoon salt with ½ cup of water, and bring to a boil over high heat. Pour the liquid over the cabbage mixture, and allow the mixture to come to room temperature. Stir in the mustard oil and parsley, and set aside.

ASSEMBLE THE DISH

8. Cut the Potato Rolls in half. Using the oven or a toaster, toast the buns to your liking and make sandwiches with the pork, slaw, and mustard. In a small saucepan, warm up some of the reserved pork leg cooking liquid and serve it on the side. Dip the sandwiches into the liquid, like a French dip.

FRENCH TOAST + CARAMELIZED BANANAS + WHIPPED CREAM

SERVES 4   Every chef has a French toast recipe in their arsenal, and this is ours. We didn't do anything crazy here, just good-quality ingredients done the right way. We don't serve dessert at brunch, but this usually does the trick if you're looking for something sweet. Our patrons love how thick our toast is cut; it helps with the presentation and also keeps the bread very moist.

FOR THE TOASTED WALNUTS

½ cup shelled walnuts

FOR THE FRENCH TOAST

5 large eggs

1 (15-ounce) can coconut milk

½ cup confectioners' sugar

1 shot espresso (about ¼ cup)

2½ tablespoons vanilla extract

2 tablespoons ground cinnamon

¼ teaspoon freshly ground nutmeg

1 teaspoon kosher salt

2 ounces (4 tablespoons) unsalted butter

4 (1½-inch-thick) slices good-quality brioche (we use Amy's Bread), air-dried overnight

FOR THE CARAMELIZED BANANAS

½ ounce (1 tablespoon) unsalted butter

2 bananas, peeled and sliced crosswise into ¼-inch-thick slices

1 tablespoon light brown sugar

FOR THE WHIPPED CREAM

1 cup heavy cream

1 tablespoon granulated sugar

½ teaspoon vanilla extract

TO ASSEMBLE THE DISH

Maple syrup, warmed

MAKE THE TOASTED WALNUTS

1. Preheat the oven to 300°F; position the rack in the middle. Toast the walnuts in a shallow baking pan for 10 minutes or until fragrant. Transfer to a bowl and let cool completely. Gently crack the walnut pieces and set them aside in a dry place until needed. Raise the oven temperature to 350°F.

MAKE THE FRENCH TOAST

2. In a large bowl, whisk together the eggs, coconut milk, confectioners' sugar, espresso, vanilla extract, cinnamon, nutmeg, and salt until well combined.

3. In a large ovenproof skillet, melt the butter over medium heat until foaming. Dip the brioche slices into the egg mixture until they are well saturated but not soaked all the way through. Add the brioche slices to the pan and cook until they are golden brown on each side, about 2 minutes per side. Transfer the bread slices to a baking sheet and bake until the toast is heated through, 5 to 10 minutes.

MAKE THE CARAMELIZED BANANAS

4. In a medium skillet, melt the butter over medium heat. Just before it browns and begins to smell nutty, add the bananas. Sprinkle with the brown sugar and toss in the pan over the heat for 1 minute, to coat. Remove from the heat and set aside.

MAKE THE WHIPPED CREAM

5. Right before serving, add the cream, sugar, and vanilla extract to a chilled bowl. Using a whisk or a handheld mixer, whip the cream until it is thick and holds stiff peaks.

ASSEMBLE THE DISH

6. Divide the French toast among 4 warmed plates. Spoon some Caramelized Bananas and Whipped Cream over the toast, and top with the reserved walnuts. Drizzle everything with warm maple syrup and serve.

CHILI LOBSTER + SCRAMBLED EGGS + TEXAS TOAST

SERVES 4 Chili Lobster (see page 161) is so popular that it's part of our tasting menu at the restaurant. The reason we originally put this on our brunch menu was because we had a recession-friendly Sunday supper prix-fixe, and for whatever reason, people were more willing to pay for it as a brunch item than a Sunday supper item. The Sunday supper days are gone, but the Chili Lobster has become a brunch staple and superstar. Sometimes, people even ask for it with a Tomahawk Chop (see page 242), which becomes the sickest, most decadent steak and eggs I've ever seen.

2 tablespoons sliced scallion, white parts and green parts separated, plus thinly sliced scallion greens, for garnish

1 recipe Chili Lobster (see page 137)

8 large eggs, preferably farm-fresh

Kosher salt

4 thick slices brioche or sourdough bread

3 ounces (6 tablespoons) unsalted butter

Freshly ground black pepper

1 tablespoon canola oil

1. In a small bowl filled with ice water, soak the scallion greens meant for garnish for 1 hour, then drain them and set aside.

2. As soon as the Chili Lobster is done, in a large bowl, whisk together the eggs with 2 pinches of salt. Fold in the 2 tablespoons of sliced scallions. Butter each bread slice with 1 tablespoon of the butter and season with salt and pepper. Cut each bread slice diagonally—you should wind up with 8 triangular slices. Toast the bread in a toaster oven until toasted and golden brown.

3. In a large sauté pan, melt the remaining 2 tablespoons butter with the oil over medium heat and cook just until the butter begins to brown and smell nutty. Pour the egg mixture into the pan and cook, stirring constantly, until just cooked through.

4. Divide the scrambled eggs among 4 warmed plates. Spoon some Chili Lobster and its sauce around the eggs on each plate and garnish with the scallion greens. Serve with the buttered toast and the additional lobster sauce on the side.

AN AMERICAN PLACE CHEDDAR-CHIVE BISCUITS

MAKES 24 BISCUITS These biscuits are a recipe from An American Place, and they remain the best I've ever had, which is why when I opened my restaurant, I brought the recipe with me. We serve them in lieu of the traditional Potato Rolls (see page 37) that we serve during our dinner service. They're brought to the table when guests just sit down for brunch, before they even have a chance to order a drink. We glaze them with maple syrup and serve them with lightly salted butter. We think it's the perfect way to kick off brunch.

3 cups all-purpose flour, plus more for the work surface

1 tablespoon plus 1 teaspoon baking powder

1 tablespoon granulated sugar

2¼ teaspoons kosher salt

½ cup grated cheddar cheese

1 bunch fresh chives, chopped

2½ cups heavy cream

Warm honey or maple syrup, for serving (optional)

Lightly salted butter (optional)

1. Preheat the oven to 350°F; position the rack in the middle. Line a baking sheet with parchment paper or Silpat. In a large bowl, whisk together the flour, baking powder, sugar, and salt until thoroughly combined. Stir in the cheese and chives. Add the heavy cream and mix or knead until a loose dough forms (5 or 6 times). Do not overknead.

2. Break off 1½-ounce pieces of dough and place them on the baking sheet with about 1½ inches of space between each. There's no need to shape the pieces of dough as they will bake into a rustic shape. Bake the biscuits for about 20 minutes or until golden brown. Serve warm, with a drizzle of honey or maple syrup and some lightly salted butter on the side if desired.

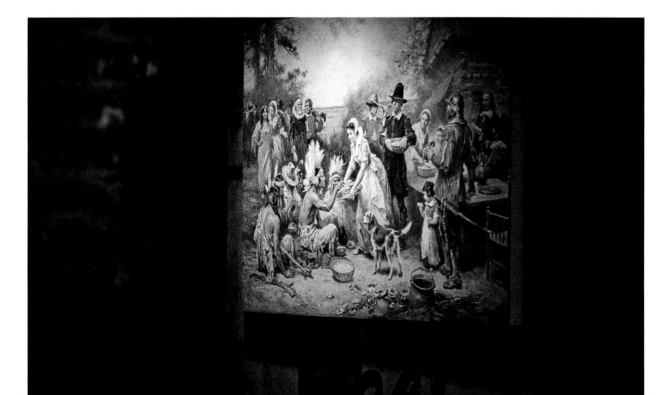

COCKTAILS

"Bartenders have gone back to their roots, and they are making all of their own bitters, liqueurs, shrubs, syrups, infusions, tinctures, and the like. They have researched the old ways, and have embraced them. They have practiced the techniques, and learned them well, even improved many of them. They have studied the classic cocktail recipes, and their craft is anchored in these classics, but today bartenders may be even more like chefs, creating original recipes that are balanced and textured and full of flavor. Seasonality is key to us, and we shop in the farmers' market for local produce, as well as for inspiration. Choices of herbs, spices, fruits, and vegetables used in cocktails are influenced by local fresh availability as much as they are by the food menu of the establishment."

—STEVE OLSON

BLACK CHERRY INFUSED TEQUILA

MAKES 1 (750 ML) BOTTLE

1 (750-ml) bottle Alma de Agave reposado tequila

1 pound black cherries, pitted

In a sterilized 2- or 3-quart jar, combine the tequila and cherries, cover, and let stand at room temperature for 2 to 3 days. Strain through a fine-mesh strainer into a bowl, pressing on the solids to extract their liquid. Discard the solids and transfer the infused tequila to an airtight container. Use within 1 month for best quality, but the infusion will keep indefinitely.

HONEYCRISP APPLE AND ROSEMARY INFUSED VODKA

MAKES 1 (750-ML) BOTTLE

1 (750-ml) bottle vodka, preferably Wódka

1 Honeycrisp apple, cored, quartered, and sliced thin

In a sterilized 2- or 3-quart jar, combine the vodka and apples, cover, and let stand at room temperature for 2 to 3 days. Strain through a fine-mesh strainer into a bowl, pressing on the solids to extract their liquid. Discard the solids and transfer the infused vodka to an airtight container. Use within 1 month for best quality, but the infusion will keep indefinitely.

FALL APPLE-ROSEMARY VODKA

MAKES 1 COCKTAIL My favorite apples to use in the restaurant are Honeycrisps. I think they are excellent fall apples: crisp, juicy, and with a perfect balance of sweet and tart. Last fall, as I was scooping out apple balls from a bunch of Honeycrisps to use in a sous-vide dish, I noticed how much juice had collected in the bowl. It was way too good to throw away, so I brought the juice to the bar for Cary, our bar manager, to use in a cocktail. The result is here for you—the best vodka cocktail ever made at Marc Forgione.

2½ ounces Honeycrisp Apple and Rosemary Infused Vodka (see page 364)

1 ounce Dolin Blanc Vermouth

½ ounce fresh lemon juice

½ ounce Apple-Rosemary Simple Syrup (recipe follows)

3 drops Brooklyn Hemispherical Apple Bitters

1 Honeycrisp apple, halved

1 rosemary sprig

In a cocktail shaker, stir together the infused vodka, vermouth, lemon juice, and Apple-Rosemary Simple Syrup. Pour into a double rocks glass filled with (1 x 1-inch) ice cubes. Using a melon baller, scoop out one apple ball. Pick the leaves off the rosemary sprig. Pierce the apple ball with the sprig, garnish the cocktail with it, and serve immediately.

APPLE-ROSEMARY SIMPLE SYRUP

MAKES ABOUT 2½ CUPS

2 cups apple juice, preferably fresh

1 cup granulated sugar

1 fresh rosemary sprig

In a medium nonreactive saucepan, combine the apple juice, sugar, and rosemary with 1 cup of water and bring to a boil over high heat. Strain through a fine-mesh strainer into a bowl and let cool. Discard the rosemary sprig. Transfer the apple-rosemary syrup to an airtight container and refrigerate until needed; it will keep for up to 1 week.

SPRING GIN RHUBARB

MAKES 1 COCKTAIL Spring is one of our favorite seasons here, especially behind the bar. After a long citrus-dominated winter, we cannot wait to start using the local ingredients that begin to arrive with the sunshine. The first thing to come out of the ground is rhubarb. In its raw form it is bitter and tart, but with a little sugar and some love, this is a very tasty plant with exceptional aromatics, but best of all . . . amazing color! We have done many rhubarb cocktails, but this is our favorite.

2 ounces Bulldog gin or other citrus-based gin

2 ounces Rhubarb Simple Syrup (recipe follows)

1 ounce fresh lime juice

½ ounce St. Germain elderflower liqueur

2 shakes Fee Bros. Rhubarb Bitters

Finely grated lime zest, for garnish

In a cocktail shaker filled with ice, combine the gin, Rhubarb Simple Syrup, lime juice, St. Germain, and bitters. Stir well and strain into a chilled martini glass. Garnish with a pinch of lime zest and serve.

RHUBARB SIMPLE SYRUP

MAKES 5 CUPS

2 cups granulated sugar

3 rhubarb stalks, chopped into ½-inch pieces

2 fresh mint sprigs, tied together

In a small nonreactive pot, combine the sugar and rhubarb with 4 cups of water and bring to a boil over high heat. Add the mint sprigs and remove them after 30 seconds, then strain the liquid through a fine-mesh strainer into a bowl and allow to cool. Discard the solids. Refrigerate the syrup in an airtight container until needed; it will keep for about 1 week.

SUMMER BLACK CHERRY TEQUILA

MAKES 1 COCKTAIL   Summer brings a variety of fruits we love to work with, like strawberries, peaches, and huckleberries, but our very favorite is cherries! Cherries and aged tequila are a match made in heaven. It's a bit of a pain to pit all the cherries needed to infuse the tequila, but the results are very much worth it. Another trick we keep up our sleeves is that rather than using straight fresh lime juice, we use a blend of fresh citrus juices instead. The citrus blend adds a complexity that brings out the diverse flavors in this refreshing and addictive cocktail.

2½ ounces Black Cherry Infused Tequila (see page 364)

1 ounce Citrus Blend (recipe follows)

½ ounce Cointreau

½ ounce Lemon Verbena Simple Syrup (recipe follows)

Fresh lemon verbena leaf

1 white cherry, pitted

In a cocktail shaker, stir together the infused tequila, Citrus Blend, Cointreau, and Lemon Verbena Simple Syrup. Pour the cocktail into a double rocks glass filled with (1 x 1-inch) ice cubes. Garnish with the lemon verbena leaf and white cherry.

CITRUS BLEND

MAKES ABOUT 1 CUP

Juice of 3 lemons

Juice of 3 limes

Juice of 2 oranges

Juice of 1 grapefruit

Combine the lemon, lime, orange, and grapefruit juices together in a jar or other airtight container. Refrigerate the citrus blend until needed; it will keep for 1 week.

LEMON VERBENA SIMPLE SYRUP

MAKES ABOUT 1¼ CUPS

1 cup granulated sugar

½ bunch fresh lemon verbena

In a medium pot, combine the sugar and lemon verbena with 1 cup of water and bring to a boil over high heat. Stir from time to time until the sugar dissolves. Strain the liquid through a fine-mesh strainer into a bowl and let cool. Transfer the syrup to an airtight container and refrigerate until needed; it will keep for about 1 week.

WINTER BLOOD ORANGE SAZERAC

MAKES 1 COCKTAIL As we mentioned earlier, the winter citrus season is long and tangy. There's no shortage of citrus at the restaurant, and our favorite winter fruit is the blood orange. The secret to this cocktail is technique and execution. It involves just the right amount of absinthe and Peychaud's, and a blood orange simple syrup that packs a lot of flavor but goes easy on the sugar. It is our belief that the original, and best, Sazerac uses a flamed orange peel, which is then discarded. We feel discarding the rind creates the best cocktail; otherwise, the peel releases too many oils and muddles the taste of rye and bitters.

Lucid Absinthe, to coat the glass

3 ounces Old Overholt rye or other rye

1 ounce Blood Orange Simple Syrup (recipe follows)

8 shakes Peychaud's Bitters

1 strip orange peel, pith removed

1. Mist the inside of a clean, chilled double rocks glass with absinthe. (A small spray bottle works nicely.)

2. In a cocktail shaker filled with ice, combine the rye, Blood Orange Simple Syrup, and bitters. Stir and pour the cocktail into the absinthe-coated glass.

3. Hold a lit kitchen lighter to the orange peel until it flames, then immediately put the flame out. Rub the smoking peel around the rim of the glass and discard the peel. Serve immediately.

BLOOD ORANGE SIMPLE SYRUP

MAKES 2½ CUPS

2 cups fresh blood orange juice

1 cup granulated sugar

In a small nonreactive saucepan, combine the orange juice and sugar with 1 cup of water and bring to a boil over high heat, stirring from time to time to dissolve the sugar. Strain the syrup through a fine-mesh strainer into a bowl and let cool. Transfer the blood orange syrup to an airtight container and refrigerate until needed; it will keep for up to 1 week.

SPRING SANGRIA

MAKES 20 (5-OUNCE) SERVINGS

2 (750-ml) bottles Paumanok Semi-Dry
Riesling or other semi-dry Riesling

½ (750-ml) bottle Hiram Walker apricot brandy

2 cups pineapple juice, preferably fresh

2 cups mango juice, preferably fresh

5 stalks fresh lemongrass, finely chopped

½ (750-ml) bottle sparkling wine, such as prosecco

Diced mango, for garnish

Sliced kiwi, for garnish

Fresh mint leaves, for garnish

In a large pitcher, combine the Riesling, brandy, pineapple juice, mango juice, and lemongrass. Stir to combine. Allow the mixture to steep at room temperature for 6 hours. Strain through a fine-mesh strainer. For each drink, pour 5 ounces of the sangria into a highball glass filled with ice and top with a splash of sparkling wine. Garnish with mango, kiwi, and mint leaves.

SUMMER SANGRIA

MAKES 18 (5-OUNCE) SERVINGS

2 (750-ml) bottles Dow's White Port

½ (750-ml) bottle Pimm's No. 1

1 cup fresh cucumber juice

Juice of ½ medium honeydew melon

Juice of 1 mango

½ (750-ml) bottle sparkling wine, such as prosecco

Sliced cucumber, for garnish

Diced mango, for garnish

Diced honeydew melon, for garnish

In a large pitcher, combine the port, Pimm's, cucumber juice, honeydew juice, and mango juice. Stir to combine. For each drink, pour 5 ounces of the sangria into a pilsner glass filled with ice and top with a splash of the sparkling wine. Garnish with cucumber, mango, and melon and serve.

AUTUMN SANGRIA

MAKES 20 (5-OUNCE) SERVINGS

2 (750-ml) bottles young Grüner Veltliner

½ (750-ml) bottle Daron calvados or other calvados

2 cups Apple Consommé (recipe follows)

2 cups Caramel Water (recipe follows)

Salted Caramel (see page 313) or
honey, for the rim of the glass

1 cup crushed toasted hazelnuts

½ (750-ml) bottles sparkling wine, such as prosecco

Granny Smith apple wedges

In a large pitcher, combine the Grüner Veltliner, calvados, Apple Consommé, and Caramel Water. For each drink, dip half the rim of a stemless wine glass in Salted Caramel or honey and roll it in crushed hazelnuts. Fill the glass with ice, and then pour in 5 ounces of the sangria. Top with a splash of sparkling wine, garnish with a Granny Smith apple wedge, and serve.

APPLE CONSOMMÉ

MAKES 2 CUPS

2 cups fresh apple juice, or store-bought

½ rosemary sprig

2 tablespoons fresh lemon juice

Place the apple juice and rosemary in a small nonreactive saucepan and bring to a boil over high heat. Skim off any foam that rises to the top. Stir in the lemon juice and remove from the heat. Strain the consommé through a fine-mesh strainer into a bowl and let cool. Transfer the consommé to an airtight container and refrigerate until needed; it will keep for up to 1 week.

CARAMEL WATER

MAKES 1¼ CUPS

2 cups sugar

In a small saucepot, combine the sugar with 1 cup of water and bring to a boil over high heat. Cook until medium amber in color; the liquid should have a syrupy consistency. If you find that the syrup is too thick upon cooling, add a bit of water to thin it out until you reach the desired consistency. Use immediately, or transfer the caramel water to an airtight container and refrigerate until needed; it will keep for up to 1 week.

WINTER SANGRIA

MAKES 18 (5-OUNCE) SERVINGS

2 (750-ml) bottles Jam Jar Sweet
Shiraz or other sweet Shiraz

¾ cups Averna amaro or other amaro

¾ cups Sombra mezcal or other mezcal

½ cup whole espresso beans

Peel from 1 orange, plus additional for garnish

½ (750-ml) bottle sparkling rosé

Fresh rosemary sprigs, for garnish

In a large pitcher, combine the Shiraz, amaro, mezcal, espresso beans, and orange peel. Stir. Let sit at room temperature for 2 hours, then strain through a fine-mesh strainer. For each drink, pour 5 ounces of the sangria into a double rocks glass filled with ice. Add a splash of rosé and garnish with a rosemary sprig wrapped in a strip of orange peel.

SMOKY SOPHISTICATION

MAKES 1 DRINK A little while back, Ron Cooper and Steve Olson invited me to Oaxaca, Mexico, to see how Del Maguey mezcal, my favorite spirit, is made. The trip truly moved me: I was blown away by the small villages that we visited, the spirit of the people living there, and the connection of the people to the land. They showed me how to make their respective mezcals—and it was life changing.

I like to drink my mezcal straight, but here is a cool way to incorporate it into your cocktail repertoire.

2 to 3 fresh kumquats, halved

Chiffonade of fresh mint

2 ounces mezcal, preferably Del Maguey Vida

1 ounce Kumquat Simple Syrup (recipe follows)

½ to 1 ounce fresh lime juice, or to taste

Champagne or sparkling wine

In a double rocks glass, muddle together the fresh kumquats and mint. Fill the glass with ice and add the mezcal, Kumquat Simple Syrup, and lime juice. Add enough Champagne to fill the glass. Serve immediately.

KUMQUAT SIMPLE SYRUP

MAKES ABOUT 4 CUPS

12 kumquats

2 cups sugar

1 to 2 fresh mint sprigs

Slice and mash the kumquats. Combine them with the sugar and 2 cups of water in a saucepot and bring to a boil over high heat. Cook for 2 to 3 minutes. Remove from heat and transfer the syrup to a cool saucepot. Add the mint, wrap the pot in plastic wrap, and let the syrup infuse for 5 minutes. The accumulated moisture on the plastic wrap will make it look as if it is raining inside the pot—this is where the infusion of flavor takes place. Strain the syrup through a fine-mesh strainer into a bowl and let cool. Transfer the syrup to an airtight container and refrigerate until needed; it will keep for up to 1 week.

Beverage manager
Cary Goldberg

MAKES 1 (750-ML) BOTTLE WHISKEY This is us having fun with Elvis again. We just can't get enough of him—the man knew how to live! During the New York Cochon 555 competition, while people waited in line for our pork, our team passed shots of this whiskey around to keep them happy. It certainly worked—guests kept coming back just to get an extra shot.

4 (¼-inch-thick) slices Mangalitsa bacon

¼ cup rendered Mangalitsa or other pig fat

1 (750-ml) bottle Banana Jameson (recipe follows)

1. Preheat the oven to 350°F; position a rack in the middle. Place the bacon on a shallow cooking tray and bake until crispy, 12 to 15 minutes.

2. Place the rendered Mangalitsa fat in a small pot and warm it over low heat until it is liquid and warm.

3. Pour the Banana Jameson into a sterilized wide mouth jar, and while the cooked bacon and liquid fat are still warm, add them to the whiskey. Cover the jar and let sit at room temperature for 2 days. Scoop off the fat, strain the whiskey through a fine-mesh strainer into an airtight container, and refrigerate until ready to serve. Serve neat or on the rocks. The whiskey will keep for 4 weeks.

BANANA JAMESON

MAKES 1 (750-ML) BOTTLE WHISKEY

3 bananas, peeled and sliced

One (750-ml) bottle Jameson Irish Whiskey or other whiskey

Place the bananas and Jameson in a sealed, sterilized container and let stand at room temperature for 3 to 4 days. Strain the mixture through a fine-mesh strainer into a bowl and discard the banana slices. The infusion should be slightly viscous and cloudy—this is what gives the infused whiskey its body, structure, and taste. Pour the infused whiskey back into the container or the original bottle. It will keep indefinitely.

THE
BACKBONES

"In the finest cooking, there are no shortcuts. That's especially true when it comes to stocks and sauces, the baseline for so much of what we chefs do. There's a proper way to make them, and the results can't be rushed. Though it isn't always glamorous, the work we put in now pays off later in subtlety, complexity and depth of flavor. It's a lesson I pass on to every young chef at the French Laundry, where a pot of veal stock simmers on the stove each morning: the journey may take longer, but the rewards are all the greater when you arrive.

THOMAS KELLER, THE FRENCH LAUNDRY

10-MINUTE TOMATO SAUCE

MAKES 3½ CUPS

2 (28-ounce) cans peeled tomatoes, preferably San Marzano

¼ cup extra-virgin olive oil

10 garlic cloves, thinly sliced

2 teaspoons red pepper flakes

1 sprig of basil

Kosher salt (optional)

Roughly chop the tomatoes and return them to the can with their juices. Place the oil and garlic in a large, cold saucepot and turn the heat to medium. Watching carefully (this is the crucial part of the sauce—do not take your eyes off it or it will burn), cook the garlic until it is golden brown and smells roasted. Add the tomatoes and reduce the heat to low. Stir to combine. Cook the tomatoes for 10 minutes. Stir in the red pepper flakes and basil; taste for seasoning and add salt, if necessary. The tomato sauce will keep in an airtight container in the refrigerator for up to 1 week.

MAYONNAISE

MAKES 2 CUPS

1 large egg yolk, room temperature

1 teaspoon kosher salt

1 teaspoon Dijon mustard

2 cups canola or other neutral oil

1 tablespoon white wine vinegar

Juice of 1 lemon

In a food processor fitted with a blade, pulse the yolk, salt, and mustard with 1 tablespoon of water until combined. With the motor running, slowly drizzle in the oil in a thin stream until emulsified. With the motor running, drizzle in the vinegar and lemon juice until emulsified. The mayonnaise will keep in an airtight container in the refrigerator for up to 1 week.

BREAD CRUMBS

MAKES 3 TO 4 CUPS While you can easily buy bread crumbs at any grocery store, there is no comparison with those you make at home. It's an excellent way to use up stale bread and will make you feel like a resourceful cook who doesn't let anything go to waste. The yield will depend on the size of the loaf of bread you use.

1 loaf bread (not multigrain), preferably a day old

1. Preheat the oven to 300°F; position a rack in the middle. Roughly chop the bread into cubes and place them on a baking sheet. Toast the bread in the oven until completely dried out, 10 to 15 minutes, stirring halfway through the baking time.

2. Transfer the bread cubes to a food processor fitted with a blade and pulse until the crumbs are finely ground. Make sure that the crumbs are dry before transferring them to an airtight container. They will keep for up to 3 months.

BACON LARDONS

MAKES ABOUT 1 CUP Having these on hand makes just about any meal better. Lardons are versatile and can spruce up many a dish—try adding them to a salad or tossing them with some pasta. It's important to find the best-quality bacon available, as it will make a great difference in your lardons.

Canola oil, for the pan

2 cups chopped bacon

Add enough oil to a large skillet to just cover the bottom of the pan. Set the pan over high heat and warm the oil. Just before it starts to smoke, add the bacon, reduce the heat to medium, and cook the bacon until crispy and fat renders out, 5 to 7 minutes. Using a slotted spoon, transfer the cooked lardons to a paper towel–lined plate, and let cool completely. Reserve the rendered bacon fat for use anywhere you might use butter: home fries, fried eggs, etc. The lardons will keep in an airtight container in the refrigerator for up to 1 week; the rendered fat will keep for 6 months.

BACON BREAD CRUMBS

MAKES ABOUT 6 CUPS

4 cups Bread Crumbs (see page 380)

1 cup Bacon Lardons (see left)

½ cup chopped fresh curly parsley

½ cup finely grated Parmigiano-Reggiano

1 garlic clove

Kosher salt

Freshly ground black pepper

In a food processor fitted with a blade, combine the Bread Crumbs, Bacon Lardons, parsley, Parmigiano-Reggiano, garlic, and salt and pepper to taste. Pulse until everything is finely ground and well combined. The bread crumbs will keep in an airtight container in the refrigerator for up to 2 days.

CHICKEN STOCK

MAKES 10 CUPS

2 (3-pound) chickens

1 large carrot, diced

1 large celery stalk, diced

1 large onion, diced

3 sprigs fresh thyme

1 fresh or ½ dried bay leaf

1. Remove the breasts from the chickens and reserve them for later use. Remove the legs and thighs, and place the carcasses, legs, and thighs in a bowl. Rinse the chicken pieces under cold water and then place them in a stockpot large enough to hold the bones and 1 gallon of water. Bring to a boil over high heat, then reduce to maintain a simmer and cook, uncovered, for 3½ hours, skimming off any foam that rises to the surface. Add the carrot, celery, and onion, and simmer for 1½ hours more.

2. Remove from the heat, add the thyme and bay leaf, and allow the stock to infuse for 20 minutes. Strain the stock through a fine-mesh strainer into a large bowl and discard the solids. Let the stock cool slightly, then transfer to an airtight container or containers and refrigerate or freeze until needed. Before using, while the stock is still cold, remove the fat that has coagulated at the top. The stock will keep in the refrigerator for up to 3 days or in the freezer for up to 3 months.

VEAL STOCK

MAKES 8 CUPS

3 pounds veal leg bones, cut into 3-inch pieces

Canola oil

1 recipe Onion Brûlé (see page 393)

1 large carrot, diced

1 large celery stalk, diced

¼ cup whole black peppercorns

1 cup tomato paste

6 cups Chicken Stock (see left) or store-bought

3 sprigs fresh thyme

1 fresh or ½ dried bay leaf

1. Soak the veal bones in cold water for 2 hours. Preheat the oven to 400°F; position the rack in the middle. Add enough oil to a roasting pan to cover the bottom of the pan. Add the veal bones and toss them in the oil. Roast the bones for 30 to 40 minutes or until well caramelized.

2. Set the roasting pan on the stovetop over medium heat. Add the Onion Brûlé, carrot, celery, and peppercorns, and deglaze the pan, using a wooden spoon to scrape the brown bits off the bottom of the pan. Stir in the tomato paste, cook for 1 minute, then add the stock and enough cold water to just cover the bones.

STOCKS

Stocks are something people don't often make these days. We are busy, harried, and stock feels like something that takes too much time to prepare. Many of us also have limited freezer space and can't make and freeze large batches of stock. Besides, some might argue, stock is readily available in grocery stores everywhere. Even

something as exotic as lobster stock can be found at fine foods stores in the freezer section.

All that is true. But it's also true that a homemade stock will trump store-bought stock any day of the week. If you're in a pinch, store-bought stock will do, but to get the most flavor out

of a dish, I highly recommend you try a hand at making your own stocks. It will make remarkable difference in the way your food tastes. Making stock also allows you to use up scraps of this and that, so it's an excellent and resourceful way to reduce waste. If nothing else, your food will taste better and you'll feel more accomplished

3. Transfer everything to a large stockpot set over medium-low heat, and skim off any foam that rises to the surface. Simmer, uncovered, for 12 hours. Do not skim—the fat will act as a seal to preserve the stock.

4. Remove from the heat, add the thyme and bay leaf, and allow the stock to infuse for 20 minutes. Strain the stock through a fine-mesh strainer into a large bowl and discard the solids. Let cool slightly, then transfer to an airtight container or containers and refrigerate or freeze until needed. Before using, while the stock is still cold, remove the fat that has coagulated at the top. The stock will keep in the refrigerator for up to 3 days or in the freezer for up to 3 months.

SMALL GAME JUS

MAKES 5 TO 6 CUPS Use this method to make chicken, duck, squab, quail, rabbit, turkey, or other small game stocks. Some different spices could easily be added, such as cinnamon or cloves, depending on the season or the animal.

Canola oil

1 pound small game bones, chopped into large pieces, fat trimmed

4 chicken wings

1 large carrot, diced

1 large celery stalk, diced

1 large onion, diced

3 tablespoons whole black peppercorns

⅓ cup tomato paste

4 cups Chicken Stock (see page 382) or store-bought

3 sprigs fresh thyme

1 fresh or ½ dried bay leaf

1. Preheat the oven to 400°F; position the rack in the middle. Add enough oil to a roasting pan to cover the bottom of the pan. Add the bones and wings and toss to coat in the oil. Roast for about 20 minutes or until the bones are well caramelized.

2. Place the roasting pan on the stovetop over medium heat. Add the carrot, celery, onion, and peppercorns, and deglaze the pan, using a wooden spoon to scrape the brown bits off the bottom of the pan. Stir in the tomato paste, cook for 1 minute, then add the stock.

3. Transfer everything to a large stockpot set over medium heat, and skim off any foam that rises to the surface. Bring the liquid to a boil, reduce the heat to medium-low, and simmer, uncovered, for 4 hours. Do not skim—the fat will act as a seal to preserve the stock.

4. Remove from the heat, add the thyme and bay leaf, and allow the stock to infuse for 20 minutes. Strain the stock through a fine-mesh strainer into a large bowl and discard the solids. Let cool slightly, then transfer to an airtight container or containers and refrigerate or freeze until needed. Before using, while the stock is still cold, remove the fat that has coagulated at the top. The stock will keep in the refrigerator for up to 3 days or in the freezer for up to 3 months.

VENISON JUS

MAKES 3 CUPS

1 pound diced venison

Canola oil, for the pan

¾ cup chopped button mushrooms

3 shallots, sliced

1 garlic clove, chopped

2 tablespoons whole black peppercorns

1 tablespoon granulated sugar

½ cup red wine vinegar, plus more as needed

4 cups dry red wine

1 cup ruby port

1 sprig fresh thyme

1 fresh or ½ dried bay leaf

1 tablespoon dried juniper berries

4 cups Veal Stock (see page 382) or store-bought

1 cup Chicken Stock (see page 382) or store-bought

Kosher salt

1. Pat the venison dry. Add enough oil to a large sauté pan to cover the bottom of the pan and set the pan over high heat. Just before the oil starts to smoke, add the diced venison in an even layer and reduce heat to medium high. Do not touch the meat for at least 4 to 5 minutes or until the venison begins to brown on the bottom and starts to smell delicious. Stir—the venison will release some juices. Cook the juices, until the pan is dry. Keep in mind, there will be times that the meat will release a lot of juices and times when it'll barely release any. And thus, the cooking time for reducing the juices will vary accordingly.

2. Reduce the heat to medium, and add the mushrooms, shallots, and garlic. Cook until the shallots are translucent, about 4 minutes. Add the peppercorns and cook for 1 minute more. Add the sugar, stir, and cook for 1 minute more. Add the vinegar and deglaze the pan, scraping the brown bits off the bottom of the pan. Cook until the pan is dry, then add the wine, port, thyme, and bay leaf.

3. Raise the heat to medium-high and cook until the liquid is reduced by about half. Add the stocks and cook until the liquid has reduced to about 3 cups. Remove from the heat and strain the liquid through a fine-mesh strainer. Return the liquid to the stove over medium heat, and skim off any fat that rises to the surface. Taste and season with salt as necessary; you may also want to add a bit more vinegar, depending on your preference. Once again, strain the jus through a fine-mesh strainer into a bowl, add the juniper berries, and wrap tightly with plastic wrap. The accumulated moisture will look like it is raining inside. Let stand for 30 minutes or until cool. Transfer the jus to an airtight container and refrigerate or freeze until ready to use. The jus will keep in the refrigerator for up to 3 days or in the freezer for up to 3 months.

FISH FUMET

MAKES 14 CUPS *Fumet* is a fancy French term for stock.

3 pounds halibut bones, cut into 5-inch sections

¼ cup thinly sliced onions

¼ cup thinly sliced leeks

¼ cup thinly sliced celery

¼ cup thinly sliced fennel

2 tablespoons whole white peppercorns

3 sprigs fresh thyme

Peel of 1 lemon, white pith removed

1 sprig fresh tarragon

1 fresh or ½ dried bay leaf

Soak the fish bones in cold water in the refrigerator for 3 hours. Drain. Place the bones in a large stockpot with 15 cups of water. Bring to a boil over high heat, then reduce the heat to medium-low and simmer, uncovered, for 1 hour. Skim off any foam that rises to the surface. Add the onions, leeks, celery, fennel, peppercorns, thyme, lemon peel, tarragon, and bay leaf. Simmer, uncovered, for 30 minutes. Strain the stock through a fine-mesh strainer lined with cheesecloth into a bowl and let cool slightly. Transfer to an airtight container or containers and refrigerate or freeze until ready to use. The fumet will keep in the refrigerator for up to 3 days or in the freezer for up to 3 months.

LOBSTER STOCK

MAKES ABOUT 4½ CUPS This recipe will also work to make crab or shrimp stock; just substitute the respective shells for the lobster shells.

>Canola oil, for the pan
>
>1 pound lobster heads, feathers removed
>
>¼ cup chopped onions
>
>¼ cup chopped celery
>
>¼ cup chopped fennel
>
>¼ cup tomato paste
>
>1 cup dry white wine
>
>3 sprigs fresh thyme
>
>3 sprigs fresh tarragon
>
>1 fresh or ½ dried bay leaf

1. Preheat the oven to 400°F; position the rack in the middle. Add enough oil to a roasting pan to cover the bottom of the pan. Add the lobster heads and toss to coat them in the oil. Roast for about 20 minutes or until the bones are well caramelized.

2. Place the roasting pan on the stovetop over medium heat. Crush the bones with a wooden spoon. Add the onions, celery, and fennel, and deglaze the pan, using a wooden spoon to scrape the brown bits off the bottom of the pan. Stir in the tomato paste, and then add the wine and 4 cups of cold water.

3. Transfer everything to a large stockpot set over medium heat, and skim off any foam that rises to the surface. Bring to a boil, reduce the heat to medium-low, and simmer, uncovered, for 1 hour and 40 minutes.

4. Remove from the heat, add the thyme, tarragon, and bay leaf, and allow the stock to infuse for 20 minutes. Strain the stock through a fine-mesh strainer into a bowl and let cool slightly. Transfer to an airtight container or containers and refrigerate or freeze until ready to use. The stock will keep in the refrigerator for up to 3 days or in the freezer for up to 3 months.

MUSSEL STOCK

MAKES 3 QUARTS If you are a pescatarian, this is an amazing resource to have in your freezer any time you need to enhance the flavors of a dish. It's easy to make, and at the end, you have delicious mussels left over. So chill a bottle of your favorite wine, invite some friends over, and eat some mussels while you're at it.

>1 pound mussels, scrubbed and debearded
>
>2½ cups dry white wine
>
>1 large shallot, thinly sliced
>
>1 tablespoon canola oil
>
>6 sprigs fresh thyme
>
>1 medium garlic clove, thinly sliced
>
>1 fresh or ½ dried bay leaf

In a large stockpot, combine the mussels, wine, shallot, oil, thyme, garlic, and bay leaf with 1 quart of cold water and cook over medium-high heat for 20 to 25 minutes, or until the mussels open (you must bring the stock to a simmer). Immediately strain the stock through a fine-mesh strainer into a bowl. Serve the mussels as desired and reserve the stock in an airtight container or containers. The stock will keep in the refrigerator for up to 3 days or in the freezer for up to 3 months.

MAÎTRE D'HOTEL BUTTER

MAKES ABOUT 8 OUNCES

8 ounces (16 tablespoons) unsalted butter, softened

2 tablespoons finely chopped fresh curly parsley

1 shallot, finely chopped

1 tablespoon chopped fresh chives

½ garlic clove

Kosher salt

Freshly ground black pepper

In the bowl of a stand mixer fitted with a paddle attachment, combine the butter, parsley, shallot, chives, garlic, and salt and pepper to taste. Mix on medium speed until incorporated. Wrap the butter in plastic wrap and shape into a log. The butter will keep in the refrigerator for up to 3 days or in the freezer for up to 3 months.

PICKLED RED ONIONS

MAKES ABOUT 2 CUPS

1 red onion, thinly julienned

½ cup red wine vinegar

1 tablespoon freshly cracked black pepper

2 teaspoons kosher salt

1 teaspoon granulated sugar

1 fresh or ½ dried bay leaf

Place the onion in a nonreactive bowl. In a small saucepot, combine the vinegar, pepper, salt, sugar, and bay leaf with ¼ cup of water, and bring to a boil over medium heat. Pour the liquid over the onion and let sit for at least 1 hour before using. Use immediately, or store in an airtight container in the refrigerator for up to 1 month.

LEMON CONFIT

MAKES 6 CONFIT LEMONS

6 lemons, preferably organic

3½ cups plus 3 tablespoons (1 pound 10 ounces) granulated sugar

1 tablespoon toasted cumin seeds

1 teaspoon ground turmeric

1 fresh or ½ dried bay leaf

1. Preheat the oven to 300°F; position the rack in the middle. Rinse and scrub the lemons well under cold water. Place the lemons in a roasting pan and add enough water to come halfway up the sides of the lemons. Cover the pan with foil. Bake for about 30 minutes, or until the lemons are soft. Transfer the pan to a cooling rack and let cool to room temperature.

2. Meanwhile, in a medium saucepot, combine the sugar, cumin, turmeric, and bay leaf with 8 cups of water and bring to a boil. Set aside.

3. Quarter the cooled lemons and add them to the sugar-cumin liquid. Return the pot to the heat and bring the liquid back to a boil. Transfer the lemons and liquid to a large nonreactive container. Wrap the container tightly in plastic, and let it sit overnight at room temperature. The accumulated moisture on the plastic wrap will make it look as if it is raining inside the pot—this is where the infusion of flavor takes place. Transfer the lemons to a glass jar and pour the cooking liquid over them. Seal the jar and store the lemon confit in the refrigerator for up to 3 months.

BOUQUET GARNI

MAKES 1 BOUQUET

2 outer leaves of leeks or 2 celery stalks

3 sprigs fresh thyme

2 sprigs fresh flat-leaf parsley

2 fresh bay leaves, or 1 dried bay leaf

1 strip bacon

Make a "sandwich" with the leeks on the outside and the thyme, parsley, and bay leaves on the inside. Wrap the "sandwich" in bacon and tie the bouquet with kitchen twine to secure. Use immediately.

HOMEMADE BARBECUE SAUCE

MAKES ABOUT 4½ CUPS

1 head garlic, unpeeled

Kosher salt

Freshly ground black pepper

2 cups Heinz ketchup or other ketchup

½ cup packed light brown sugar

4 ounces (8 tablespoons) unsalted butter

½ cup Worcestershire sauce

½ cup apple cider vinegar

1 sweet onion, finely diced

2 celery stalks, finely diced

2 tablespoons chili powder

½ tablespoon instant espresso powder

½ teaspoon cayenne pepper

½ teaspoon crushed red pepper flakes

½ teaspoon ground cloves

½ teaspoon kosher salt

1. Preheat the oven to 400°F; position the rack in the middle. Cut the top off of the garlic and season the exposed cloves with salt and pepper. Place the garlic in a small, ovenproof pan, and add about 1 inch of water. Cover the pan and roast the garlic for 20 to 30 minutes or until the garlic is brown and soft. Set aside to cool. Squeeze the roasted garlic cloves out of their skins.

2. In a 4-quart saucepot, combine the ketchup, sugar, butter, Worcestershire, vinegar, onion, celery, chili powder, espresso powder, cayenne pepper, red pepper flakes, cloves, and salt, with 1 cup of water, and bring to a boil over medium heat. Reduce the heat to low, and cook, covered, for 1 hour, stirring frequently to prevent scorching on the bottom. Transfer the mixture to a blender and blend on high until emulsified. Strain the mixture through a fine-mesh strainer into an airtight container. Use immediately or store in the refrigerator for up to 2 weeks.

PASTA DOUGH

MAKES ABOUT 1 POUND I got to do an *Iron Chef* battle alongside Michael Symon and he made these gorgeous tortellini that I loved so much, I asked him for the recipe. We changed a couple of things, and this is now our go-to pasta recipe for all our stuffed pasta.

1¾ cups type 00 flour, plus additional for the work surface

1¼ cups semolina flour

Pinch of kosher salt

9 large egg yolks, preferably farm-fresh

1. In a large bowl, whisk both flours with salt until combined. Make a well in the center and add the egg yolks with ½ cup water.

2. Using a fork, whisk together the yolks and water and gradually start to incorporate the flour, starting from the inner rim of the well. As you expand the well, keep pushing the flour from the base of the mound up to keep the well shape. The dough will start to come together when about half of the flour is incorporated. Once this happens, knead the dough with your hands, using your palms and the heels of your hands to flatten out the dough. Once the dough has come together, dump it onto a lightly floured work surface and knead it for 5 minutes more. Wrap the dough in plastic wrap and let sit for 1 hour at room temperature. After resting, use the dough immediately to make the pasta of your choosing.

SPAGHETTI

MAKES ABOUT 24 OUNCES A bigoli press is certainly a commitment since you need to screw it into a bench and sit behind it and crank the pasta into a bowl on the floor. But if you want to take your pasta making to the next level, we found that this spaghetti and the bigoli that come out of this press are memorable.

SPECIAL EQUIPMENT

Bigoli press

½ cup whole milk

½ ounce (1 tablespoon) unsalted butter, melted

3 large eggs, preferably farm-fresh

4 cups all-purpose flour, plus more as needed

½ teaspoon kosher salt

1. In a small saucepot, warm the milk and butter over low heat until the butter is melted and the liquid is warm to the touch. Transfer the milk mixture to a large bowl and whisk in the eggs 1 at a time, fully incorporating each egg before adding the next. Add the flour and salt, and, using a fork, mix well until thoroughly combined. Transfer the dough to a lightly floured large bowl and knead for 2 to 3 minutes. Wrap the dough in plastic and refrigerate for at least 1 hour and up to 1 day.

2. Set up the bigoli press with the small die and run the dough through the press to make spaghetti. Set the finished pasta aside on a floured tray or counter as it comes out of the press. Let the pasta dry for 1 hour and use immediately.

PICKLED RAMPS

MAKES 5 (1-QUART) JARS

    3 tablespoons coriander seeds

    3 tablespoons whole white peppercorns

    3 tablespoons whole black peppercorns

    3 tablespoons cumin seeds

    8 bunches ramps (about 3 pounds)

    6 cups white wine vinegar

    6 cups red wine vinegar

    2½ cups granulated sugar

    1 cup kosher salt

    6 sprigs fresh thyme

    6 fresh or 3 dried bay leaves

    4 jalapeños, sliced

    30 garlic cloves

    2 tablespoons turmeric

1. In a small, dry skillet, toast the coriander, the white and black peppercorns, and the cumin over medium heat until fragrant, about 3 minutes. Transfer to a plate to cool (see Note). Transfer the cool spices to cheesecloth and tie the corners to make a sachet.

2. Thoroughly rinse the ramps, removing all traces of dirt. Separate the bulbs from the greens. Place the bulbs in a large nonreactive container or sterilized 1-quart jars. You can use the greens in Ramp Chimichurri (see page 155).

3. In a 4-quart saucepot, combine the red wine and white wine vinegars, sugar, salt, thyme, bay leaves, jalapeños, garlic, and turmeric with 4 cups of water and bring to a boil. Pour the liquid over the ramps. Let sit at room temperature for at least 4 hours before using. The ramps will keep in an airtight container in the refrigerator for up to 1 month.

Note *As soon as your spices are fragrant, transfer them to a cool place. Don't simply remove the pan from the heat and let the spices cool. The heat from the pan will continue to toast the spices—and you'll mostly likely wind up with spices that are burned and bitter.*

BRINE

MAKES ENOUGH FOR 4½ POUNDS OF MEAT Brining is a great way to infuse meat with more moisture and flavor. If all you have to work with are supermarket cuts, you can transform them from mediocre to delicious just by the simple step of brining. This brine works well for all meats and game.

    1 cup kosher salt

    3 tablespoons whole black peppercorns

    4 sprigs fresh thyme

    1 fresh or ½ dried bay leaf

In a large stockpot, combine the salt, peppercorns, thyme, and bay leaf with 1 gallon of water and bring to a boil. Transfer the brine to a bowl and set it over an ice bath. Whisk until the brine is still warm, but you can easily put your finger in it. Use the warm brine immediately on whatever meat you would like: pork, veal, lamb, etc.

CHLOROPHYLL

MAKES 8 OUNCES

    2 bunches curly parsley, leaves picked off the stems

    1 to 2 tablespoons canola oil, plus more as needed (optional)

1. Bring a pot of water to a boil and blanch the parsley for 10 seconds. Immediately shock the parsley in an ice bath and let cool to room temperature.

2. Squeeze out as much water from the leaves as possible. Form the leaves into a ball and wrap it tightly in plastic wrap. Transfer the parsley ball to the freezer until ready to use.

3. When ready to use, allow the parsley ball to defrost for 30 minutes. In a food processor fitted with a metal blade, puree the parsley ball with enough canola oil to obtain a smooth consistency (start with adding 1 tablespoon before adding any more); you may also use cold water instead. Transfer the emulsion immediately to a bowl set over an ice bath. Stir until cold and set aside until ready to use. The chlorophyll will keep in an airtight container in the refrigerator for up to 3 days.

SMOKED ONION

MAKES 1 CUP Making this Smoked Onion will create a lot of smoke, so if you live in an apartment and don't want to set off the smoke alarm, just make Caramelized Onions (see page 398) instead.

1 large onion, julienned

Olive oil

Kosher salt

Soak 1 cup of applewood chips in water for 20 minutes. Line the bottom of a 4-quart saucepot with foil. Place the soaked wood chips over the foil. Make a "basket" out of foil to hang over the edges of the pot so that when you place the onion in it, it will be suspended over the chips. Poke 8 to 10 holes in the basket using a paring knife, then remove it from the pot and set it nearby. Place the pot over high heat until the wood chips begin to smoke, 8 to 10 minutes. Reduce the heat to medium and gently slide the foil basket over the pot. In a bowl, toss the onion with some olive oil and salt, and gently spoon into the basket. Smoke the onion, covered, for about 10 minutes. Remove from the heat and let cool completely. Store in the refrigerator for up to 3 days.

SMOKED ONION RÉMOULADE

MAKES 4 CUPS

1 recipe Smoked Onion (see left)

4 large egg yolks

5 tablespoons white wine vinegar

4 cups Blended Oil (see page 395)

3 tablespoons Ararat spice mix (see Sources, page 403)

1 teaspoon cayenne pepper

¼ cup brunoise shallots (see page 48)

¼ cup chopped fresh chives

In a food processor fitted with a metal blade, combine the Smoked Onion, egg yolks, and vinegar and pulse until combined. With the motor running, drizzle in the Blended Oil until emulsified. Add the Ararat and cayenne. Transfer the mixture to a bowl and fold in the shallots and chives. Season to taste and use immediately, or transfer to an airtight container and store in the refrigerator for up to 3 days.

CLARIFIED BUTTER

MAKES ⅔ CUP

24 ounces (48 tablespoons) unsalted butter

In the top half of a double boiler set over simmering water, melt the butter. Transfer to a bowl and refrigerate the butter until firm, about 1 hour. Remove the solid clarified butter from the surface and place it in a small saucepan. Discard the milky liquid. Melt the clarified butter over low heat and pour it into a large bowl. Cover and keep warm so the butter remains liquid until needed. Alternatively, once you remove the solid clarified butter, you can store it in an airtight container in the refrigerator for up to 1 month.

PRESERVED MEYER LEMONS

MAKES 1 (1-QUART) JAR This works just as well with regular lemons if Meyer lemons are out of season or unavailable.

12 Meyer lemons, preferably organic, scrubbed

3 cups kosher salt

2 cups granulated sugar

1 cinnamon stick

1 jalapeño, quartered

4 fresh or 2 dried bay leaves

1. Quarter the lemons three-fourths of the way down (i.e., leaving the lemon intact). Place the lemons in a nonreactive container with a lid.

2. In a large bowl, combine the salt, sugar, cinnamon stick, jalapeño, and bay leaves. Pour the curing mixture over the lemons, making sure that they are all submerged. Cover and refrigerate. Allow the lemons to cure for 28 days before using.

3. To use, cut the white pith and flesh from the lemons to be used. Feel free to juice the lemons or reserve them for another use. Julienne the skin and soak it in cold water for at least 30 minutes, changing the water another 2 times before using. The lemons will keep in an airtight container in the refrigerator for up to 6 days.

Note *Don't put your bare hands in the jar—it's unsanitary. Use gloves or a spoon to remove the lemons.*

DUCK GLAZE

MAKES ABOUT 1½ CUPS We call this Duck Glaze but we use it for anything: It's great on chicken, pork, Brussels sprouts, and so on.

1½ cups mild honey

3 tablespoons low-sodium soy sauce

1 sprig fresh rosemary

1 cinnamon stick

1 star anise

In a small saucepot, combine the honey, soy sauce, rosemary, cinnamon stick, and star anise and bring to a boil over medium heat. Cook for 15 seconds. Whisk in the soy sauce. Remove the pan from the heat, and let sit until ready to use. If not using immediately, transfer to an airtight container and store at room temperature for up to 1 week.

THE CURE

MAKES ABOUT 2 CUPS

1 cup kosher salt

½ cup dark brown sugar

3 tablespoons whole black peppercorns

3 tablespoons red pepper flakes

Leaves from 2 sprigs fresh thyme

Leaves from 1 sprig fresh rosemary

3 fresh or 1½ dried bay leaves, crushed

In a large bowl, combine the salt, sugar, peppercorns, red pepper flakes, thyme leaves, rosemary leaves, and bay leaves. Use immediately.

PORT-WINE REDUCTION

MAKES ABOUT 2 CUPS

4 cups dry red wine

2 cups ruby port

½ cup granulated sugar

4 sprigs fresh thyme

1 fresh or ½ dried bay leaf

Pinch of freshly ground black pepper

In a medium saucepot, combine the wine, port, sugar, thyme, bay leaf, and pepper and bring to a boil over high heat. Reduce the heat to medium and simmer until the liquid has reduced to about 2 cups. Use immediately, or transfer to an airtight container and store at room temperature for up to 1 week.

RED WINE SAUCE

MAKES ABOUT 3 CUPS

3 tablespoons canola oil, plus more as needed

¾ cup chopped button mushrooms

3 shallots, sliced

1 garlic clove, chopped

2 tablespoons whole black peppercorns

1 tablespoon granulated sugar

½ cup red wine vinegar, plus more to taste

4 cups dry red wine

1 cup ruby port

1 sprig fresh thyme

1 fresh or ½ dried bay leaf

4 cups Veal Stock (see page 382) or store-bought

1 cup Chicken Stock (see page 382) or store-bought

Kosher salt

1. In a 3-quart saucepot, heat 3 tablespoons of canola oil over medium heat until shimmering. Add the mushrooms, shallots, and garlic, and cook, stirring, until the shallots are translucent, 5 to 6 minutes. Add the peppercorns and cook, stirring for 1 minute. Add the sugar and cook for 1 minute more. Add the vinegar and deglaze the pan, scraping the bottom of the pan. Cook until the pan is dry. Add the wine, port, thyme, and bay leaf. Raise the heat to medium-high and cook until the liquid has reduced by half, about 30 minutes. Add the stocks and cook until the liquid has reduced by half, about 40 minutes more. Strain the liquid through a fine-mesh strainer and return it to the pot over medium heat. Skim off any excess fat, carefully tilting the pot slightly to make it easier to skim. Taste and season with salt and more red wine vinegar, if you like.

2. Again, strain the sauce through a fine-mesh strainer into a large bowl. Use immediately, or transfer 1-cup portions to individual airtight containers and store in the freezer for up to 3 months.

BALSAMIC ONIONS

MAKES ABOUT 1 CUP ONIONS

1 cup pearl onions, soaked briefly in warm water (to aid peeling) and peeled

½ cup balsamic vinegar

¼ cup granulated sugar

2 sprigs fresh mint

Freshly ground black pepper

Place the onions, vinegar, sugar, mint, and pepper in a small nonreactive saucepan. Add ½ cup of water and bring to a simmer over medium heat. Reduce the heat to low and cook for 45 minutes to 1 hour or until the onions are soft. Remove from the heat and set aside until ready to use. Use immediately or transfer to an airtight container and store in the refrigerator for up to 3 days.

BABY FENNEL CONFIT

MAKES ABOUT 1 CUP This is a great way to have something delicious on hand in your fridge for a few weeks. If you can't find baby fennel or it's out of season, you can just use thinly shaved regular fennel.

1½ cups duck fat or olive oil

1 cup shaved baby fennel (about 4 bulbs)

4 fresh sage leaves

1 fresh or ½ dried bay leaf

Kosher salt

1. In a medium saucepot, warm the duck fat over medium heat until it registers 250°F on a deep-frying thermometer.

2. Add the fennel, sage, bay leaf, and a couple of pinches of salt. Cook for 5 minutes or until the fennel is cooked through. Remove from the heat, transfer to an airtight container, and refrigerate until needed; it will keep for up to 4 weeks.

BÉARNAISE REDUCTION

MAKES ABOUT ⅓ CUP

2½ cups white wine vinegar

1 cup diced shallots

4 sprigs fresh tarragon

2 tablespoons cracked black peppercorns

In a small nonreactive saucepan, combine the vinegar, shallots, tarragon, and pepper and bring to a simmer over medium heat. Reduce the heat to low and cook until the liquid has reduced to about ⅓ cup, about 25 minutes. Discard the tarragon. Use immediately or transfer to an airtight container and store at room temperature for up to 1 week.

ONION BRÛLÉ (BLACKENED ONION)

MAKES 1 BLACKENED ONION This is a very popular French technique designed to add a great deal of flavor to whatever you are cooking. It's dead easy, but its impact is profound.

1 yellow onion, halved and peeled

Warm a dry skillet over high heat. Add the onion halves, cut side down, and sear until blackened. Remove the onion from the heat. Use immediately.

EVERYTHING BAGEL SPICE MIX

MAKES 1¾ CUPS

2 ounces onion flakes

2 ounces garlic flakes

4 ounces sesame seeds

4 ounces poppy seeds

¼ cup flaky sea salt, such as Maldon

Place the onion and garlic flakes into a food processor fitted with a metal blade. Pulse until the mixture is the consistency of everything bagel mix. Transfer to a large bowl and combine with the sesame seeds, poppy seeds, and salt. Use immediately or transfer to an airtight container and store at room temperature for up to 2 weeks.

TOMATO CONCASSÉ

This is a classic French technique for preparing tomatoes for cooking in various dishes throughout the book. This technique works with all kinds of tomatoes, including small cherry tomatoes. The amount of tomatoes will depend entirely on what you need them for.

Tomatoes

Bring a pot of water to a boil. Core and seed the tomatoes and blanch the tomatoes in the boiling water for 1 minute. Transfer the blanched tomatoes to an ice bath and let cool. Peel the skin off and cut the flesh into medium dice. Use immediately or transfer to an airtight container and store in the refrigerator for up to 3 days.

BLANCHED LEMON ZEST

Another classic French technique. The three-times blanching-and-ice bath method removes any bitterness from the zest and makes it perfect for any dish where you want to add a bright burst of citrus essence.

Strips of lemon peel, white pith removed

Bring a pot of water to a boil. Blanch the lemon strips in the boiling water for 1 minute, and immediately transfer the strips to an ice bath. While the lemon peel is cooling, fill the pot with fresh water and bring it to a boil. Repeat the blanching-and-cooling process twice more. Use immediately.

HOMEMADE RICOTTA

MAKES 1 CUP

4 cups whole milk

½ cup fresh lemon juice

2 teaspoons kosher salt

Finely grated zest of 1 lemon

1. In a nonreactive saucepot, combine the milk, lemon juice, and salt, and bring to a boil over medium heat. Stir the mixture from time to time to prevent the milk from burning on the bottom. As soon as the liquid comes to a boil, decrease the heat to low and simmer for 5 minutes.

2. Pour the liquid through a fine-mesh strainer lined with several layers of cheesecloth set in the sink or over a bowl. Pull up on the ends of the cheesecloth, gently squeeze the curds, and transfer the curds to a bowl. Fold in the lemon zest, return the curds to the cheesecloth, and let them sit for about 1 hour or until most of the liquid has dripped out. If you prefer your ricotta drier, let it drain for a longer amount of time; for wetter ricotta, a shorter amount. Use immediately, or transfer to an airtight container and store in the refrigerator for up to 5 days.

SIMPLE SYRUP

MAKES ABOUT 1¾ CUPS This syrup is a staple at the restaurant and might just become a staple in your fridge. Use it anywhere from making lemonade to putting together sorbet (see page 310) to sweetening your iced coffee to adding it to cocktails. Easy to make and incredibly useful.

1 cup granulated sugar

In a small pot combine the sugar with 1 cup of water and bring to a boil over high heat, stirring from time to time until the sugar has dissolved. Remove from the heat, transfer to an airtight container, and store in the refrigerator for up to 2 weeks.

HERB OILS: CHIVE, MINT, AND BASIL

MAKES ABOUT ½ CUP These oils are used widely in our dishes, and I think they're a great staple to have in your pantry. You can also make a larger batch to keep in the refrigerator and use for anything from flavoring salad dressings to putting beautiful finishing touches on a dish. Do not blanch the chives if making chive oil.

1 generous bunch fresh mint, basil, or chives

½ cup canola oil

1. If using mint or basil, bring a large pot of water to a boil. While the water is heating, pick the leaves off the stems and discard the stems. Blanch the leaves in the boiling water for 10 to 15 seconds, and immediately transfer the leaves to an ice bath. Cool the leaves completely, drain, and squeeze out as much excess water as possible. Measure out a packed 1 cup of herbs. If using chives, roughly chop the chives and measure out a packed 1 cup.

2. In a blender, combine the herbs with the oil and blend for no less than 3 minutes on high speed. Set a clean bowl over an ice bath and set a fine-mesh strainer lined with a coffee filter over the bowl. Strain the herb oil through the coffee filter and transfer the oil to an airtight container. Keep the green oils in the fridge, as this will help retain their color. After 2 days, they will start to lose their brightness.

BLACK PEPPER OIL

MAKES ABOUT ½ CUP

1 cup whole black peppercorns

½ cup canola oil

In a small, dry skillet, toast the peppercorns over low heat for about 3 minutes or until fragrant. Transfer the peppercorns to a small saucepot and add the oil. Warm the oil and peppercorns over medium heat until a deep-frying thermometer registers 180°F. Remove the pot from the heat and allow the oil to infuse at room temperature for 4 hours before using. Strain the oil through a coffee filter into a container. Cover and store at room temperature for up to 2 weeks.

BLENDED OIL

MAKES 1 CUP We use Blended Oil throughout our cooking at the restaurant, and I recommend you make a large batch to keep on hand. It's great for frying and sautéing, and it also imparts a light taste of the olive oil without lowering the smoking point too much.

¾ cup canola oil

¼ cup olive oil

In a container or a bottle, combine the oils together. Use as needed. Store in a cool, dark place.

MUSHROOM DUXELLES

MAKES ABOUT 2 CUPS Mushroom duxelles is a delicious and incredibly versatile side dish to make. We make it most often for our Bone Marrow Beef Wellington (see page 295), but it can also be used just about anywhere else. It's great by itself on buttered toast, or as a topping for poached eggs and home fries. With duxelles, the possibilities are nearly endless.

1 pound sliced fresh porcini or other fresh mushrooms, cleaned

Kosher salt

Freshly ground black pepper

Canola oil

1 ounce (2 tablespoons) unsalted butter

2 garlic cloves, minced

2 sprigs fresh thyme

1 fresh or ½ dried bay leaf

2 tablespoons chopped fresh curly parsley

1 cup dry red wine

¼ cup ruby port

1 teaspoon black truffle oil (optional)

1 tablespoon black truffle scraps (optional)

Season the mushrooms with salt and pepper. Add enough oil to a large sauté pan to cover the bottom of the pan and set it over high heat. Just before it starts to smoke, add the mushrooms and reduce the heat to medium. Cook the mushrooms until they start to brown, 3 to 5 minutes. Add the butter, garlic, thyme, and bay leaf and cook, stirring, until the garlic is toasted. Add the parsley and stir for 1 minute. Add the wine and port, and deglaze the pan, scraping the brown bits off the bottom of the pan with a wooden spoon. Cook until the liquid has reduced by about half, 6 to 8 minutes. Discard the thyme and bay leaf, and transfer the mixture to a food processor fitted with a metal blade. Add the truffle oil and truffle scraps, if using, and puree for 30 seconds or until the mixture resembles a paste. Taste for seasoning and adjust if needed. Use immediately, or transfer to an airtight container and store in the refrigerator for up to 1 week.

BASIC POTATO PUREE

SERVES 4 Everyone needs a great potato puree recipe in their arsenal—and this is ours. It makes a luxurious, silky-smooth potato puree that you can adapt to whatever your heart desires. For example, you can make a Smoked Potato Puree (see page 66) or a Marrow–Potato Puree (see page 272), just to name a few. The recipe is easily doubled or tripled.

2 pounds Idaho potatoes, scrubbed

1½ pounds Yukon Gold potatoes, scrubbed

6 sprigs fresh thyme

2 fresh or 1 dried bay leaves

1 head garlic, halved crosswise

Kosher salt

2 cups heavy cream

2 cups whole milk, plus more as needed

24 ounces (48 tablespoons) unsalted butter, diced

1. Because the potatoes will be done cooking at different times, you will need to cook them separately. Place the Idaho potatoes in one pot and the Yukon Golds in another pot. Tie together 3 sprigs of thyme and 1 bay leaf and repeat to make a second bunch. Add one bunch to each pot. Divide the garlic halves between the pots. Cover the potatoes with cold water and add a pinch of salt to each pot. Bring to a boil over high heat, then reduce the heat to medium and simmer until the potatoes are fork-tender, about 25 minutes for the Idahos and 30 minutes for the Yukon Golds.

2. In a medium pot, combine the cream and milk and bring to a boil over medium-high heat. Remove from the heat and set aside; keep warm.

3. Drain the potatoes, and either wearing latex gloves or using 2 forks, carefully peel the potatoes. If peeling with forks, use one fork to hold down a potato while you peel the skin off with the other. Working quickly while the potatoes are still hot, push them through a food mill into a large bowl. Whisk in the butter piece by piece, adding some of the milk mixture between each addition to maintain a smooth consistency. Continue whisking until no more butter remains. You may have some of the milk mixture remaining.

4. Pass the potato mixture through a fine-mesh strainer directly into a pot. Season to taste with salt. Cut a piece of parchment paper to fit the pot, butter it, and place it over the potato puree to prevent it from drying out. Keep warm. Use immediately or transfer to an airtight container and store in the refrigerator for up to 1 week.

MF PICKLES

MAKES ABOUT 2 (1-QUART) JARS

1 cauliflower head, cut into florets

2 Kirby cucumbers, sliced

1 Vidalia onion, julienned

3 cups white wine vinegar

½ cup drained capers

⅓ cup granulated sugar

3 tablespoons kosher salt

3 tablespoons mustard seeds

1 tablespoon ground turmeric

In a large nonreactive bowl, toss together the cauliflower, cucumbers, and onion. Divide the vegetable mixture between 2 quart-size jars. In a medium nonreactive saucepot, combine the vinegar, capers, sugar, salt, mustard seeds, and turmeric with 1½ cups of water, and bring everything to a boil over high heat. Pour the marinade over the vegetables, and let stand at room temperature for at least 3 hours before serving. The pickles will keep in the covered jars in the refrigerator for up to 1 month.

OVEN-DRIED TOMATOES

MAKES ABOUT 1 PINT

    10 plum tomatoes

    1 tablespoon granulated sugar

    Kosher salt

    Olive oil (optional)

1. Preheat the oven to 200°F; position a rack in the middle. Line a 13 x 19-inch baking sheet with parchment paper. Core and quarter the tomatoes and toss them with the sugar and a couple of pinches of salt.

2. Lay the tomatoes in a single layer on the lined baking sheet and place them in the oven. Let sit in the oven overnight with the door slightly ajar. Use immediately or transfer to an airtight container, add oil to cover, and store in the refrigerator for up to 1 week.

MARINATED TOMATOES

MAKES 1 QUART

    1½ cups extra-virgin olive oil

    1 teaspoon red pepper flakes

    2 packed cups sun-dried tomatoes

    3 fresh basil leaves

In a small saucepan, heat the oil and red pepper flakes until the oil registers 200°F on a deep-frying thermometer. Pack the tomatoes into a clean 1-quart jar. Pour the oil over the tomatoes, add the basil leaves, and close the jar. Wait at least 2 hours before using. Store the jar in the refrigerator. The tomatoes will last indefinitely.

CARAMELIZED ONIONS

MAKES ABOUT 1 CUP

    1 sprig fresh thyme

    1 fresh or ½ dried bay leaf

    Canola oil

    1 large onion, halved and julienned as thinly as possible

    2 tablespoons sherry vinegar

    Kosher salt

    Freshly ground black pepper

    Pinch of sugar

1. Using kitchen twine, tie together the thyme and bay leaf. Add enough oil to a 2-quart pot to cover the bottom of the pot and set over high heat. Just before the oil starts to smoke, add the onion to the pot and give everything one good stir. Reduce the heat to medium-low, add the herb bundle, and cook, stirring from time to time, for about 40 minutes or until the onions are golden, wilted, and caramelized. Be sure to stir the onion every 5 minutes.

2. Add the vinegar and 2 tablespoons of water, and stir to incorporate. Season to taste with salt and pepper and add the sugar. Taste for seasoning and adjust if necessary. Remove from the heat and set aside until needed. Use immediately, or transfer to an airtight container and store in the refrigerator for up to 1 week.

THE BACKBONES

TOOLS

BLENDER

At the restaurant, we use a Vitamix and find it indispensable. While it is very expensive, its ability to make silky smooth soups and sauces cannot be matched. I think that a Vitamix blender is worth saving up for; it will last a lifetime and outperform any other blender. Plus, it's the blender *Cook's Illustrated* magazine recommends above all others.

BUTCHER'S TWINE

Indispensable for tying bouquets garnis or trussing chicken.

CAST IRON PAN

This might be the cheapest lifetime investment for your batterie de cuisine. A 10-inch cast iron skillet costs less than $20, and with proper care (i.e., not cleaning it with soap or leaving it to soak overnight), it is guaranteed to last you a lifetime.

CUTTING BOARDS

I find that this is the number one thing lacking in people's kitchens. Get a few good cutting boards and take care of them. One should be for meat—I'd recommend sticking with plastic on that one. For vegetables and other foods, a good butcher's block will last you many years. And if you don't want your fruit to have any hints of garlic taste to it, a small dedicated fruit cutting board is in order.

DIGITAL KITCHEN SCALE

In some of our recipes, precision is incredibly important, so gram weights are given. In these cases, a kitchen scale will be indispensable. Most are very affordable, and the more you use a scale, you might find that measuring by weight instead of volume is not only more precise, but a time saver as well.

DUTCH OVEN

Depending on who you're cooking for— just yourself and another person, or a crowd—you might want either a 5- or 8-quart Dutch oven. Possibly even both. Le Creuset and Staub make excellent ones, and while they are a financial investment (and heavy) they are unmatched at conducting, and retaining, heat. The oval ones are slightly more versatile than the round ones (such as for fitting awkwardly shaped chicken parts)—Julia Child thought so, too.

FINE-MESH STRAINER

Straining is an essential part to cooking, and not just in this book. When making ice creams and custards, or a reduction that requires a perfectly smooth texture, straining is something you will do over and over. A good fine-mesh strainer is going to be something you can't do without. A good-quality one is inexpensive and will last forever.

FISH SPATULA

Fish spatulas are not only essential for lifting and flipping delicate fish, but are also the best tool for lifting cookies off a baking sheet.

FOOD PROCESSOR

A food processor is one of the main workhorses in the kitchen. It can make pie dough; chop, shred, and puree vegetables; and aerate dry ingredients for baking. While it can be an investment, a quality food processor should last you for many years.

HALF-SHEET (13X18-INCH) AND QUARTER-SHEET (13X9-INCH) BAKING PANS

These are very useful pans, almost without limits. You can use them to roast vegetables, bake cookies, toast nuts, make sheet cake, and so on. Look for light-colored pans made out of sturdy, thick metal. A thick, sturdy sheet will last you a long time, whereas a cheap, flimsy one will not only buckle under intense heat, but will aid in burning your food.

HEAVY-BOTTOMED SKILLETS AND POTS

Having a basic set of pots of varied sizes will get you started on the right foot. A few quality pots will last you a lifetime and will cook your food better than cheap, lightweight pots, which you will need to replace every few years. In the long run, getting a few good pots will be cheaper than having to replace them all the time. At the restaurant, we like to use All-Clad. Amazon.com also has a great selection of pots and offers decent prices.

IMMERSION BLENDER

An immersion blender is essential for quick jobs. At the restaurant, we use an immersion blender to emulsify sauces right in the pan. For a home cook with a small kitchen, an immersion blender is a must, as it takes up little room, reduces the number of dishes dirtied when cooking, and is easily stored.

IMMERSION CIRCULATOR AND VACUUM SEALER

An immersion circulator is not a commonplace tool in most home kitchens, but it is one that is finding its way into many fine restaurants across the world. The immersion circulator allows you to cook food sous-vide (meaning "under pressure") in a vacuum-sealed bag while immersed in a temperature-controlled water bath. The result is something that cannot be replicated by any other cooking techniques—meat becomes meltingly tender as it cooks in its own juices aided by delicate, steady heat; eggs are silky smooth, almost custardlike; fish is flaky, moist, and perfect each and every time. While an immersion circulator is expensive, takes up a lot of room, and sounds unapproachable, I guarantee that if you ever treat yourself to one, you will not only not regret it, you will try to convince all your friends that they need one, too. Trust me.

JAPANESE MANDOLINE

Japanese mandolines tend to be flatter and easier to store than other types. They also tend to be easier to clean and easier to adjust (meaning you can manipulate the thickness or thinness of the cut easily). They are, however, incredibly sharp, so please be very alert and careful while using them.

KITCHEN SHEARS

Perfect for snipping herbs, cutting through chicken, and many other tasks, kitchen shears are versatile and will make your life easier.

KNIVES: CHEF'S, PARING, CLEAVER, BREAD, BONING, FILLETING

You do not need to purchase a knife block set to properly outfit your kitchen. But you *do* need a few good knives to be most efficient and effective while cooking. A good chef's knife (8 or 10 inches) will be your most used knife. Pick a knife with a good heft to it, and make sure that the handle feels comfortable in your hand. A paring knife is a must, but contrary to intuition, this is where you don't need to spend a lot of money. You can get a very good paring knife for about $5, and it will last a very long time. A cleaver is very useful, especially if you plan on separating hunks of meat and chopping through bone. A good bread knife is not only essential in getting clean slices of bread but is also very useful for slicing ripe tomatoes; the serrated edge of the knife helps catch the tomatoes' soft, delicate skin. If you're ever planning on breaking down a chicken, a boning knife is something you must have. Choose a quality knife with a long, curved blade and a comfortable handle. And finally, if you plan on filleting fish, a filleting knife will be a good addition to your arsenal. But if you just want the bare minimum, having good chef's, paring, and bread knives on hand is the way to go.

MEASURING SPOONS, DRY MEASURING CUPS, LIQUID MEASURING CUPS

Proper measuring equipment is a must for every kitchen, home or professionals, whether for cooking or baking. It's helpful to have a couple of sets of each so you don't wind up having to constantly wash your measuring cups while cooking.

MICROPLANE GRATER

A rasp grater is essential for grating cheese, citrus zest, chocolate, or spices, and the Microplane brand grater cannot be matched. It is sharper than its competition, works better and lasts longer than any other grater. It is also very affordable.

OYSTER KNIFE

Cheap and sturdy, oyster knives are essential for shucking oysters. Be careful when doing so, and be steady with your knife.

HEAT-RESISTANT RUBBER SPATULAS

Rubber spatulas are great for mixing and folding ingredients and for scraping that last bit of cake batter into the pan. I recommend having a few of various shapes and sizes on hand. They are easy to clean, inexpensive, and are much better at stirring than wooden or metal spoons. A heat-resistant rubber spatula can do everything a cold one can do, so this is the best overall investment.

SALAD SPINNER

The fastest and most effective way to dry your lettuces and herbs is a salad spinner. Aside from the fact that no one likes soggy lettuce, dry lettuce is essential if you want the dressing to coat and adhere to the greens. Water creates a barrier between the greens and the dressing, which results in your salad dressing collecting at the bottom of the bowl while your leaves sit undressed.

SILPAT

Buying a couple of Silpats, the nonstick, silicone baking mats used by professional bakers all over the world, will save you from having to buy parchment paper ever again. Silpats are easy to clean, last a very long time and, while they require a bit of an initial investment, are better for the environment—and your wallet—in the long run.

STAND MIXER

A stand mixer, such as a KitchenAid mixer, is another indispensable item. Even though it takes up a considerable amount of counter space and is heavy, it will get regular use and will last for well over a decade, maybe even well over *two* decades. Like a food processor, a stand mixer is a workhorse, whipping up egg whites, mixing batters, kneading bread doughs, and more. If you invest in any of the stand mixer attachments, such as a meat grinder (below), pasta roller, or ice cream attachment, you extend the usefulness and versatility of your stand mixer even further.

MEAT GRINDER STAND MIXER ATTACHMENT

While, generally, I do not recommend buying a kitchen item that will only do one thing, a meat-grinding attachment for your stand mixer is an exception to the rule. Once you have your own meat grinder, you will never buy pre-ground meat again. It will allow you to better control the quality of the ground meat and sausage you use in your cooking.

STOCKPOT

If you plan on making your own stocks and soups, or just want to cook some pasta, a good stockpot is essential. In a home kitchen, an 8-quart stockpot will be the perfect size.

TAMIS

Even though a tamis, or drum sieve, is not commonly present in most home cooks' kitchens, it should be. Used to create fine purees or textures in many dishes, it also sifts flour and cornstarch. Instead of awkwardly pushing purees through a cone-shaped chinois, the flat bottom of a tamis allows a cook to easily push the food through.

VEGETABLE PEELER

A good-quality vegetable peelers is affordable, so you can easily replace it when it gets dull. The ones we buy for the restaurant cost about $2.50 at restaurant supply stores. I prefer Y-shaped peelers and find them a bit more efficient and effective than straight peelers.

SOURCES

ACTIVA: Amazon, www.amazon.com

AFFILIA CRESS: Koppert Cress, www.koppertcress.com

AGAR: WillPowder, www.willpowder.net

AMBER: La Boîte à Épice, www.laboiteaepice.com

APOLLONIA: La Boîte à Épice, www.laboiteaepice.com

ARARAT: La Boîte à Épice, www.laboiteaepice.com

BABY RADISH: Chefs' Garden, www.chefsgarden.com

BABY WHITE ASPARAGUS: Sid Wainer, www.sidwainer.com

BACON: North Country Smokehouse, www.ncsmokehouse.com

BACON: The Black Pig Meat Co., www.blackpigmeatco.com

BATCH 22: www.dontcallitamary.com

BLACK GARLIC: La Boîte à Épice, www.laboiteaepice.com

BLACK VOLCANIC SALT: La Boîte à Épice, www.laboiteaepice.com

BRIOCHE: Amy's Bread, www.amysbread.com

CATULUÑA: La Boîte à Épice, www.laboiteaepice.com

CHEESE: Marcelli's Cheeses, www.marcelliformaggi.com

CHIOS: La Boîte à Épice, www.laboiteaepice.com

CHOCOLATE: Valrhona, www.valrhona-chocolate.com

CHORIZO SECCO: Salumeria Biellese, www.salumeriabiellese.com

CLAY PEPPER: Societe Orignal, www.societe-orignal.com

CORN SHOOTS: Solex Fine Foods, www.solexfinefoods.com/products/micro-greens

CURED CHORIZO: Salumeria Biellese, www.salumeriabiellese.com

EGGS: Feather Ridge Farm, www.featherridgeeggs.com

FILONE: Grandaisy Bakery, www.grandaisybakery.com

FLAKY SEA SALT: Maldon

FOIE GRAS AND FOIE GRAS TERRINE: Rougié, www.rougie.us

GLUCOSE: WillPowder, www.willpowder.net

GRITS: Anson Mills

HEIRLOOM Hominy: Anson Mills

ISOMALT: WillPowder, www.willpowder.net

KOSHER SALT: Diamond Crystal

MANGALITSA PORK: Møsefund Farms, www.mosefund.com

METHYLCELLULOSE F50: WillPowder, www.willpowder.net

MICRO ARUGULA: Solex Fine Foods, www.solexfinefoods.com/products/micro-greens

MICRO BASIL: Koppert Cress, www.koppertcress.com

MICRO CELERY: Solex Fine Foods, www.solexfinefoods.com/products/micro-greens

MICRO LIMONE: Koppert Cress, www.koppertcress.com

MICRO MITSUBA: Koppert Cress, www.koppertcress.com

MILK: Ronnybrook Farm, www.ronnybrook.com

MUSTARD OIL: Laxmi, www.indianblend.com/site/664954/product/HB-19a

PEPPUINO MELONS: Koppert Cress, www.koppertcress.com

PINK CURING SALT: The Meadow, www.atthemeadow.com/shop

PIERRE POIVRE: La Boîte à Épice, www.laboiteaepice.com

PUFF PASTRY: Dufour, www.dufourpastrykitchens.com

ROCK CHIVES: Koppert Cress, www.koppertcress.com

SZECHUAN BUTTON: Koppert Cress, www.koppertcress.com

SMOKED CINNAMON: La Boîte à Épice, www.laboiteaepice.com

SMOKED SALT: La Boîte à Épice, www.laboiteaepice.com

SODIUM ALGINATE: WillPowder, www.willpowder.net

SOPPRESSATA PICANTE: Salumeria Biellese, www.salumeriabiellese.com

SOY LECITHIN: WillPowder, www.willpowder.net

TAHOON CRESS: Koppert Cress, www.koppertcress.com

TASSO HAM: Dickson's Farmstand Meats, www.dicksonsfarmstand.com

TRUFFLES: Regalis, www.regalis.com

TRUFFLE JUICE: Regalis, www.regalis.com

TRUFFLE OIL: Regalis, www.regalis.com

UPLAND CRESS: R.L. Irwin, www.irwinmushrooms.com

VADOUVAN CURRY POWDER: La Boîte à Épice, www.laboiteaepice.com

INDEX

MARC FORGIONE

G

H

I

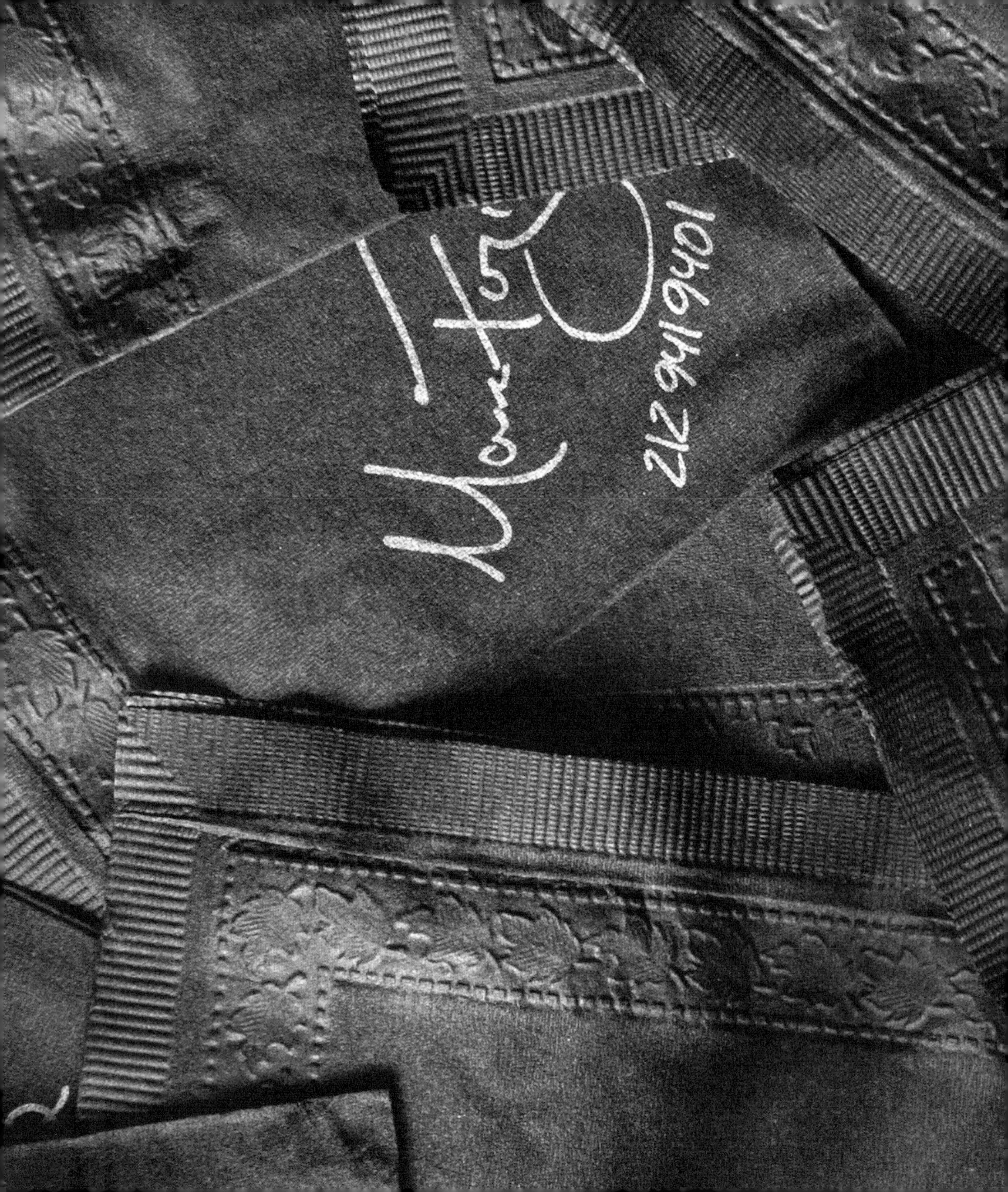
212 9419401